P9-ECL-651

FIVE CENTURIES
OF CHORAL MUSIC

Essays in Honor of Howard Swan

Howard Swan

FIVE CENTURIES OF CHORAL MUSIC

Essays in Honor of Howard Swan

Edited by Gordon Paine

FESTSCHRIFT SERIES No. 6

PENDRAGON PRESS
STUYVESANT, NY

Other titles in this series:

No. 1 *A Musical Offering: Essays in Honor of Martin Bernstein* edited by
       E. Clinkscale and C. Brook (1977) ISBN 0-918728-03-7
No. 2 *Aspects of Medieval and Renaissance Music: A Birthday Offering to
       Gustave Reese* edited by Jan LaRue (Pendragon Edition 1978)
       ISBN 0-918728-07-X
No. 5 *Music in the Classic Period: Essays in Honor of Barry S. Brook* edited
       by Allan W. Atlas (1985) ISBN 0-918728-37-1

Library of Congress Cataloging-in-Publication Data
Main entry under title:

Five centuries of choral music

  (Festschrift series; no. 6)
  Bibliography: p.
  1. Choral music. 2. Swan, Howard, 1906-
I. Paine, Gordon. II. Swan, Howard, 1906-
III. Series.
ML1500.E87 1988   784.1   87-32816
ISBN 0-918728-84-3 (lib. bdg.)

Copyright 1988 Pendragon Press

Contents

Dedication   vii

Preface   ix

A Biographical Conversation with Howard Swan   1
Gordon Paine

The "Conductor's Process"   15
Jameson Marvin

Integrity in the Teaching and Performing of Choral Music   35
Lynn Whitten

The Creative Experience: Some Implications for the
    Choral Conductor   49
Allen Lannom

The Art and Craft of Choral Arranging   67
Lloyd Pfautsch

Understanding Male Adolescent Voice Maturation—
    Some Significant Contributions by European
    and American Researchers   75
John Cooksey

The Reconstruction of the Evening Service for Seven
    Voices by Thomas Weelkes   93
Walter S. Collins

Some Puzzling Intabulations of Vocal Music for
    Keyboard, Ca. 1600, at Castell'Arquato   127
H. Colin Slim

Rhythm: the Key to Vitalizing Renaissance Music   153
John B. Haberlen

Tactus, Tempo, and Praetorius   167
Gordon Paine

The Opus ultimum: Heinrich Schütz's Artistic and
       Spiritual Testament   217
   Ray Robinson

Bach's Motets in the Twentieth Century   233
   Wesley K. Morgan

Handel's Funeral Anthem for Queen Caroline:
       a Neglected Masterpiece   255
   Harold A. Decker

Aspects of Performance Practice During the Classic Era   281
   Dennis Shrock

The Vocal Quartets of Brahms (Op. 31, 64, and 92):
       a Textual Encounter   323
   G. Roberts Kolb

The Text of Britten's War Requiem   357
   Robert Shaw

Index   385

Dedication

This volume is an attempt to say "thank you" to Howard Swan. There is not a choral musician in North America whose life and work has not been enriched by his life and work, whether he knows it or not—and most of us do.

Surely, somewhere in this thanksgiving there will be a tracing of Howard's biographical trajectory across this dwindling century. I first beheld him—shielding my eyes—at the end of the 'twenties when he appeared as an Olympian teacher of history at Eagle Rock Junior High School in Los Angeles. By the middle 'thirties he had moved a few blocks south to the campus of Occidental College, from where his glee clubs annually proceeded to give singing lessons to the rest of Southern California, including Pomona College, his alma mater (and soon to be mine), which had been foolish enough to teach him everything he—or they—knew, up to that time.

It's entirely possible that his decades of service to Occidental College witnessed the most distinguished and varied choral repertoire at the highest levels of performance in American collegiate musical history.

But Howard slumbered not. As a matter of fact, he bloom'd, lately. His *real* contribution to choral music began to emerge as his work at Occidental matured and settled in.

What Howard did was extend his *campii*—his learning campus and his teaching campus. Soon, there was scarcely a choral center in the western world he had not visited or a recording he had not studied, a musicologist he had not interviewed, or a performance style he had not analyzed.

And he passed *everything* on. North America became his classroom, his rehearsal hall. We all became his students.

What were his gifts to us?

Well—obviously, information. And information about where to go for more information. He knew repertoire, performance practices and personalities, vocal methods, and church and campus organizational structures. He knew curriculum-curriculorum ad infinitum. He knew a lot of "what," all of "where to find out," and more than anyone else about "how."

But his greatest gift of all was passion. His giving didn't stop with information. Howard Swan gave blood.

You'd sit there listening to his high half-voice, all but screaming at you. (He'd completely lost it a half-century back.) You'd think, "Holy smoke! It can't be as important as all that!" And then you'd realize that for Howard it was. And that it ought to be for you, too.

Dear Howard:
Thank you very much. (And Katherine, too.) Much love.

Robert Shaw
Atlanta, Georgia

Preface

On March 29, 1986 Howard Swan celebrated his eightieth birthday. 1986 also marked the forty-ninth year of Howard's teaching career.

All of the contributors have been touched by that career, some many times over many years. Three of us, the present writer included, were so enriched by our experiences with Howard at Occidental College that we became university choral conductors ourselves, after graduating with degrees in English, economics, and political science. Such is the strength of his inspiration and personal example.

Robert Shaw's words of dedication speak eloquently for all of us. We wish to add only the hope that this volume might permit us to return in some small measure what we have received.

This publication was made possible by subventions from three institutions with which Howard Swan has been associated: the American Choral Directors Association, Occidental College, and the School of the Fine Arts of the University of California, Irvine. The editor and contributors wish to express their appreciation for this generous support.

Gordon Paine
Fullerton, California

Gordon Paine

A Biographical Conversation
With Howard Swan

*(Conducted in Fullerton, California with the editor
on October 31, 1986)*

G.P.: Many of us have wondered about the early experiences that made
you who you are. Could you tell us about your early life and involvement with music?

H.S.: I was born in Denver on March 29, 1906. My family came out
to California in 1913 and lived in Hollywood. All of my family loved
to sing. Mother played the piano, and Dad had a nice tenor voice and
had done some conducting. Nearly all of our music was centered on
the church. I can remember singing as a soloist when I was five and
six years old. I went through the eight years of elementary school but
didn't do much singing there—we didn't have classes in music. But when
I went to Hollywood High School and as a sophomore didn't sing with
any group, somebody told the director of music, Edna Ames, that I
was enrolled and that my father was a choir director. Miss Ames had
me come into the glee club, and later I was selected as the second lead
in "The Chimes of Normandy," the school opera that year.

Edna Ames was way ahead of her time. There was a common repertoire for most glee clubs of the period. The boys sang "Old Man Noah,"
"The Green Grass Grew All Around," sailor chanties, and a few
spirituals. The girls sang pieces such as "The Green Cathedral" and
similar romantic things. Edna Ames insisted that we perform some of
the oratorio choruses for what was called the "Vesper Service" for
each graduating class. So we sang things like "The Heavens Are Telling," the "Hallelujah" chorus, and excerpts from *Elijah.* It wasn't time
as yet for the a-cappella revolution, which later was to change things
radically in the choral-music world.

I entered Pomona College in the fall of 1923. Up to that time I had

1

not done much musically except to sing with church choirs. I had worked with violin for about ten years, for my family thought it would be nice if I played the instrument. I wish now that it had been piano.

When I went to Pomona I auditioned for the Men's Glee Club, which was a very fine organization. I was selected for membership in the Club and enjoyed several tours with them under the leadership of Mr. Lyman, a man affectionately called "Prof." by his students. This was an excellent musical experience. Beginning with my sophomore year, I had the opportunity to be a paid soloist for churches in Pomona and Ontario. I became ill with rheumatoid arthritis during the first term of my junior year, dropped out of school, and was in bed for several months. When I returned to Pomona my musical experiences began in earnest. I sang as soloist with the Glee Club and the large college choir. The repertoire was not too exciting: we continued to do performances of *Elijah, Messiah,* and *The Creation.*

The following years, as a senior and then as a graduate student, I was fortunate enough to hold two very fine church positions in Los Angeles. I was a soloist for the First Methodist Church in Hollywood for a year or more and then I moved to the Immanuel Presbyterian Church. At about the same time, one of the teachers on the faculty at Hollywood High School, who also was the organist-director at Temple B'nai Brith, asked me to audition for their octet. I was successful and for several years had some great experiences with church music.

I neglected to say that when I went to Pomona I did not become a music major. My father had said, "You don't want to be a poor musician the rest of your life. I know you want to teach and you enjoy history, so why don't you become a history major?" I took his advice but enrolled in many music classes for my academic electives. I took better than the equivalent of a minor in music.

As I began my high school teaching in 1929 I was unaware of two unusual musical happenings, one national and the other local, that were to influence the development of choral music and my life as well. On the national scene appeared the a-cappella movement, encouraged by Peter Lutkin and Noble Cain in Chicago; by John Finley Williamson, who had begun his choral work in 1926 at the Westminster Church in Dayton, Ohio; by Father William J. Finn in New York; and by F. Melius Christiansen at St. Olaf College in Minnesota. A-cappella singing quickly captured the minds and hearts of performers and listeners.

At about that same time, in the late '20s, a man named John Smallman came to Los Angeles, an Englishman by way of Boston, and he set agog the choral world of southern California. After about two or three years, in addition to having a full voice studio, Smallman had organized a chorus of two hundred women teachers, the Caecilian Choir; he directed a large male chorus called the Cauldron Singers, situated primarily in Pasadena; he was the conductor of the Los Angeles Oratorio Society; and he had the choir at the First Congregational Church in the city. Mr. Smallman conducted all of these groups and then formed an a-cappella choir in about 1928, which was the first one west of Chicago. Charles Hirt, at that time in his teens, was the youngest member of that choir.

After my graduation from Pomona I stayed another year to get my high-school credential and during that time I conducted a small ensemble that sang for the chapel services. One semester, when Mr. Lyman was on sabbatical, I conducted the glee clubs just as Robert Shaw was to do ten years later. When I began to teach in my first high-school position at Eagle Rock High School in the northern part of Los Angeles, somebody found out that I had done this conducting.

G.P.: You were teaching history now?

H.S.: I was teaching history—social studies—and then I was asked to take on the Boys' Glee Club at Eagle Rock High School. But the great thing that happened to me was that I was introduced to Mr. Smallman. He made me the tenor in a quartet that specialized in wonderful music— madrigals and motets that had been composed many centuries before; names I had never known! Smallman was the baritone,—Lawrence Tibbett had been so before him—there were two women—professional soloists—and Swan. We performed for women's clubs, gave school programs, etc. Down in Pacific Palisades, there was a Chataqua modelled after the one in New York, and we became one of their official performing groups during the summer months.

After several years time somebody else became director of the Boys' Glee Club because I had gone to the principal and had asked if I could conduct an a-cappella choir. She said, "I don't know what that means, but if you want it, you can have it." So I started an a-cappella choir and we were the second such group, after that conducted by Ida Bach at Dorsey High School. Louis Curtis, who was the Supervisor of Music in Los Angeles, became very much interested and helped me a lot, and I began an a-cappella choir festival at Eagle Rock that continued until after the war. The tremendous learning experience that I was having with Dr. Smallman was wonderful. We performed everything that was new and exciting and all that was old and good.

One day the minister of Highland Park Presbyterian Church, a good-sized church of about 1,000-1,200 members, came to me and—I'll never know how—pursuaded me to leave my position at Immanuel and go to Highland Park at the same salary I had been receiving at Immanuel.

G.P.: He must have been a very persuasive man.

H.S.: He was, yes. And as a result of this change several new experiences were my good fortune. I became the first conductor of the University Glee Club of Los Angeles. This was a male group patterned after a similar organization in New York City: men who had graduated from college and had been members of college glee clubs and wanted to continue with their singing. We had a fine group of forty or fifty men. I conducted them for two or three years. I also directed several all-city high-school choirs through the instrumentality of Louis Curtis. In addition, my choirs at the Highland Park church—I had three of them—supplied me with many fine musical experiences.

The music department at Occidental College was quite new in 1929-1930 when I started my teaching at Eagle Rock High School. The chairman, Walter Hartley, had been a good friend of mine at Pomona. In 1933 he was to conduct the Glee Clubs for the Occidental graduation ceremonies, but he became quite ill with a sudden attack of appendicitis. The College President called and asked if I could bring the church choir to sing for the Commencement. I said I thought we could come. The choir performed well and the President, Dr. Remsen Bird, was very enthusiastic. He said—and of course, this was in the midst of the Depression—"I only wish we had the money to add you to our staff." Some months later, Ted Broadhead, the graduate [athletic] manager at Occidental, came to me and said: "I've got a proposition for you. How about coming to Occcidental and conducting the Men's and Women's Glee Clubs? I've got enough money to pay you $40 a month from my athletic budget." (Laughter.) So that is how I came to Occidental. From '34 to '37 I retained my position at Eagle Rock High School but I taught the two glee clubs at Occidental, and in the second year I was there, I formed the College Choir.

G.P.: Wasn't it about this time you noticed something going wrong with your voice?

H.S.: Yes, it was. In 1933, as I recall, I woke up one morning and could not make any sound on "A" below "middle C." By the middle of that week, my entire singing voice was gone. Then I couldn't speak normally. I went to a specialist and was told that I had a paralyzed vocal cord and there was nothing that could be done about it. The telephone people made me a very crude kind of wooden box containing an amplifier of sorts, so that even when I rasped like this, I could make myself heard.

G.P.: So you used this for all your classes, your rehearsals?

H.S.: Yes, I did. I picked it up and took it with me.

G.P.: This must just have been totally devastating. How did you keep going?

H.S.: Well, I don't know. I'm a rather optimistic person and I don't worry a lot, and we were just too young to realize just how devastating this thing might be over the years.

I forgot to tell you about this. While I still had my voice, for many summers I went over to the movie studios and sang in the chorus in a number of sound pictures. The studios would hire anybody who could match pitch, and reading gave me no trouble. I also sang with some radio groups. One, the Paul Taylor octet, did commercials. Usually he allowed me to come only for the final rehearsal on a Sunday—we had a Sunday-night program at Warner Brothers—because I could read better than most of the other singers. The studios were paying $50 a day, which was good money in those Depression times.

G.P.: Especially in comparison with your $40/month at Occidental! Had you met Katherine by this time?

H.S.: Oh yes. We were married in December, 1929. With my first school check I had enough to make the down-payment on a Ford, and with my second check, we were married. We had gone together for several years.

In 1937 Occidental representatives came to me and asked that I consider a full time position with the college. We thought it over, and even though I probably would have been able to advance in the L.A. City school system and quitting would cost me my pension, we decided to accept Occidental's invitation. Their principal reason for asking me to join their staff was the need for a person to manage a new auditorium, Thorne Hall. I continued conducting the singing groups at the college, kept my choirs at the Highland Park church, and taught singing to individual vocalists. It was in this same period that I met Dr. Williamson and he began to work on my throat. He also gave me many ideas, such as the importance of teaching voice to every member of my choir, which I did every week together with my other responsibilities. For a time I was teaching forty-four individual lessons a week; yet it was a great way to learn. During this particular time I started my M.A. work at Pomona, and decided upon the study of Gestalt psychology as my major concentration. I soon found out that the Thorne Hall position required my knowing something about bookkeeping and accounting, I had to talk to women's clubs, I had to organize support groups, I had to set up the lecture series and all the musical events, and many other activities that were centered in the building. Also, I moved from Highland Park to the Pasadena Presbyterian Church.

G.P.: And all of this speaking was with your telephone-company contraption?

H.S.: That's right. Eventually, of course, by about 1940 or '41, Dr. Williamson was able to give me my falsetto voice. Then I could speak like this [in a rough, forced falsetto].

I have been one of the most fortunate of men in the way that in my life one good thing led to another. Some of it was just plain good luck; witness the fact that the whole country, musically speaking, exploded with the excitement of working with finer available repertoire during the '30s and up to the first days of the war. I still remember when only six of the madrigals of Monteverdi were published. It's hard to believe! Then, in every way, the period from 1946 to about 1960-1965 was a "golden age" for choral music. Excellent choirs were heard everywhere, repertoire was without fault, and procedures were imaginative and helpful. During the '30s, because of the emphasis on a cappella singing, the *tone* that one chose and the choir used became the principal objective of every rehearsal. That's why there were so many published treatises on the subject. Williamson had one method, Christiansen had another, Fred Waring used a different approach, and all were busily engaged in sending out students with the gospel, so to speak.

G.P.: All with different gospels, of course.

H.S.: That's right, that's exactly it. During the late '30s or early '40s, a group of about a dozen or so of us organized ourselves into a group called the *Rumslumps*—"the disreputable ones."

G.P.: Oh yes—Allen Lannom wrote me about this.

H.S.: That's right. Professor Lyman was in the group, as well as Charles Hirt, Ed Qualen (who is still living), Ray Moremen (who was at UCLA), and Joseph Klein; also several others. We met at Joe Klein's studio in Glendale. Once a month on Friday we would come together at 4:00 p.m. and discuss various vocal and choral problems, talk on right through dinner at one of the restaurants in Glendale, then return and continue until late in the evening. This happened in '38, '39, '40—in those years. Then, someone suggested forming a chorus from our church and college choirs. Each man supplied a quartet of the best singers he knew. We would appoint three men to work each time—I think we moved up the sessions so that they were held every two weeks or so. Our chorus came at 7:00, and each of the three directors was given forty minutes to conduct two pieces. Of course, the singers were excellent readers, so that each conductor had the opportunity to show what he could do in rehearsal. After the third man had finished, we would dismiss the choir and start in on a "post mortem." It was a wonderful learning experience; we were all such good friends and nobody was sensitive to any criticism.

Incidentally, this group of men helped me with my Master's thesis. I worked on the subject of fatigue in rehearsal. I took three groups of twenty singers and measured with three different tests their musicianship and vocal ability, so that they were just about the same. Then I rehearsed each group using the same repertoire but with varying rehearsal conditions. One ensemble had no rest in an hour's rehearsal and they were worked to exhaustion. Another group had a five-minute rest period that was taken up with certain announcements. To the third chorus I gave a period during which they could leave the rehearsal room for about fifteen minutes—for conversation, a smoke, or simply to rest. Since there were no tapes at this time, we recorded the rehearsals on discs and later presented these to the group of eleven men for their evaluations.

G.P.: What did you find out about fatigue?

H.S.: The result one would expect: the group that had the five-minute break did the best in every respect.

G.P.: The fifteen-minute break was not more effective, or even possibly less so?

H.S.: The group lost interest and abandoned the rhythm of the rehearsal, so to speak. One had to bring them back and start all over again, build rehearsal goals anew. I think we make this mistake today in our rehearsals.

G.P.: Let's go ahead a few years to the end of World War II, when you no longer had a campus devoid of men, but rather, it was just overflowing with them. What happened then?

H.S.: The most interesting fact was that the average GI who came back to school was three or four years older than most college women. During the last couple of years of the war we had a Navy and Marine unit of about 300-400 men training on the Occidental campus. It was really an officers'-training mini-course. I saw all of these men moving about the campus and I wanted to hear them sing. (Laughter.) Although the men could join a glee club, they were not allowed to perform off campus. Also, they were forbidden to touch anything on the stage during our concerts. We used a girl stage crew; here were all these big, hefty men sitting around and looking quite self conscious. I thought that in spite of the regulations, a larger audience in the Los Angeles community should hear them sing. I talked with the president of the Ebell Club and arranged for her to write to our Commandant, saying that she had heard about the unit training on the Occidental campus and that some of the men sang in a choir. Would he like to come over to Ebell and bring this group with him—he to give a twenty-minute talk and the choir to sing? Well, it worked out in every detail.

G.P.: The psychologist at work!

H.S.: You win a few! For two years, I remember I had this marvelous group of men singing with the girls in our "Home Concert" on the campus.

G.P.: In the years that you didn't have this male group, did you have any Men's Glee Club at all, or was it just the women?

H.S.: I didn't have a male glee club. I put the few 4Fs we had together with a number of women so that we had a chorus of sorts. When the Navy men came onto the campus in great numbers, I had not only the Men's Glee Club and Women's Glee Club, but also a large chorus. There were many men and girls who wanted to sing. What did we do with them? In the outdoor theatre on campus we gave a performance of the Mozart *Requiem.* I got the Kiwanis Club in Eagle Rock to support it. You would see cars running around Eagle Rock with bumper stickers: "Mozart *Requiem* at Occidental College!" (Laughter.) We had a full house. And the orchestra! During the middle of the war years, a man by the name of Anthony Collins (he was quite a prominent English composer and conductor and looked like Sir Thomas Beecham with his goatee) stopped at my office at Thorne Hall, introduced himself, and said that he had come to this country to conduct and compose for film studios. He said, "I'm sick of conducting trash and I just love Mozart. If I pay the cost of the hall and hire the orchestra, will you give me the hall?" With the exception of Bruno Walter and one or two others, I've never heard Mozart like that man produced. He was our conductor for the *Requiem.* What a sound! But one wondered how many of the men in their white spic-and-span uniforms were singing their own Requiem.

Before the Navy came, I had a few boys who sang with my "mixed chorus." There were three tenors, so I placed one in each corner and one in the middle in the back row. Fortunately, two of the three possessed rather good voices. This was my first experience in working with a "scrambled formation!"

I gave up the management of Thorne Hall soon after the end of the war because I wanted to do more classroom teaching. I established courses in church music and did much lecturing on that subject. I became very much interested in repertoire and in both the Choral Conductors' Guild and the Southern California Vocal Association, which were formed at Occidental College. In the two years following the war there were enrolled in the Men's Glee Club thirteen tenors who sang a beautiful high "C." Several went on to work in opera and in commercial music. These powerful male voices made a great difference; you put them to singing a Russian motet and the result was magnificent. It changed my concept of balance because the girls in the chorus sang with a lighter and brighter sound. I don't think that I sat down and thought through all of this, but I realized something different was happening to my concepts of beautiful choral tone.

G.P.: What changes or developments have you seen in choral music in general in the last twenty years?

H.S.: You are now speaking of concerns that will have some consideration in my address for the national convention of ACDA. There have been some changes in the choral world that I would characterize as negative. You were saying a few minutes ago that your music-major enrollment here has dropped in numbers. This is true with nearly all campuses and it is a reflection of the secondary schools cutting down and in some places abandoning their music programs. I regret to say it, but speaking generally, this situation is worse in California than in almost any other state.

Another negative factor is the fact that in many places we perform nothing but popular music. Too many conductors have used this trend as a kind of a "cop out," and because they don't know better or don't care, they choose poor music. There is much repertoire in the "popular" field that reveals an excellent artistry and imaginative musicianship on the part of the composer or arranger. Too much of this material is not used.

G.P.: The best is often very difficult stuff.

H.S.: Of course it is. There is considerable confusion at the present time as to the nature of a choral-music program in a school or a church and what should be its end result. Unfortunately, with too many of us, there is a desire to take it easy, if I can put it that way, to emphasize the beat, to make music completely an entertainment thing. It's too easy for a choral person to say, "that's the direction I'm going in, because that's what my principal or minister wants, that's what my service clubs want," and so on. The idea that music as an art is needed, not for entainment values but as an aesthetic necessity, seems to escape people. I am absolutely certain that most people who go to church these days do not know the meaning of worship. They evaluate what they hear from the choir or the organ or the soloist basically in terms of entertainment. If it has a beat, if it has a melody, if it has a text with which they agree, it becomes a "useful" piece of music. Few in our churches understand that it is the responsibility of the worshipper to utilize music as one form of liturgy: as a form of worship or that which helps one worship. As is true of the beautiful architecture of a building and the many visible religious symbols in a church, music can used to help with worship. We seem to have lost the idea that worship in part is an offering to Almighty God. Rather, everything is "me, me, me." "That piece brought me no comfort, . . ." "I didn't understand that piece of music, . . ." etc. Some of this feeling is a reflection of our restless society—the loss of credibility and the abandonment of all save that which moves or excites. It thus becomes difficult to set standards. Some will declare that the belief in goals or standards is "old hat." Well, it isn't so!

G.P.: What would you say to a first-year choral-music teacher who is going into the type of setup that you describe and has the overwhelming feeling that if he doesn't do just pop music, he won't have any kids in his choir?

H.S.: I don't believe that everything in music including repertoire has to be only of one kind, or one activity, or directed toward one goal. There is always the possibility of a compromise. I did this at Occidental with our "second-half" programs. As I remember them I admit that some of the music possessed only "entertainment" value; pieces were selected to follow a script that provided for the staging of the second half of our concerts. This was done for two reasons. First, so I could get some students to sing who enjoyed the simpler forms of music; second, to build the college audience. When popular music was eventually not needed, the second half became the dramatization of *Les noces, Joan of Arc at the Stake, King David,* and other similar works. One can reach a goal like this but not always can it be achieved immediately. Some musicals are filled with beautiful, well-written choruses, and one can use these as a last group on a concert program. Most important is the choice of music that is superior in its composition and singability. We need to remember that it is not necessary for a piece of music to be difficult in order to possess integrity. This is particularly true with folk music. "Simple Gifts" is a good example. Even if the piece is sung in unison, one senses its honesty. Everyone loves it—even the school principal. It is not difficult to "make the search" and find other worthwhile compositions.

I would say to any first-year teacher to remember that the goal you are striving for and that people will eventually appreciate, is *excellence.* If you have only ten singers in the first year, be sure to give them a rich experience with all kinds of music and show them that you too enjoy a varied repertoire. Also, I would ask these questions: What are you going to do with your rehearsal room? How do you propose to make rehearsals interesting? Are you going to have those students hear others make music? Will you have them hear a symphony at least once during the year? Will they take some field trips? There are many opportunities for this kind of thing. In your second year will you form a few interested parents into a support group after you have become acquainted with them during your first season? Will you exchange programs with other conductors who are also in their first year of teaching? Can you go every chance you get to hear concerts conducted by others with more experience than your own?

I am quite happy to see that here in Southern California "the pendulum appears to be swinging back." It is happening primarily with the renaissance and recuscitation of the Southern California Vocal Association. It is most encouraging—that organization was practically finished four or five years ago and was being kept alive only by the efforts of a few dedicated persons. When I compare what is happening now in SCVA with its history for the last ten years, I believe that there is improvement. However, I would be hard pressed for an answer if somebody came to me and said he or she wished to talk with a teacher who had a full load of choral music in a high school; I wouldn't know where to send them. Unfortunately we have lost many fine musicians.

One other thing that makes me feel very good, even though there is some disagreement as to its virtues, is that never have we seen a time in which people in the community—not in the schools, alas, but in the community—are supporting privately what used to be financed by the government. And that seems to be true for the entire country. I hope that the new income-tax laws will not hinder this effort—I think that Americans have learned what it is to support, to give. Not only is this true of the arts; this is done for hard-of-hearing people, for handicapped children; you name the charity. Another factor is most exciting. I have no statistics on this, but I am aware that there are more civic choruses in communities, small ones and large ones, than I've ever known before. It is just startling!

G.P.: I'd like to ask you for a short answer to a hard question. What makes a great choral conductor?

H.S.: Number one is musicianship. Above everything else, a good ear and constant study to improve what you hear. I also mean by "musicianship" the ability to recognize artistic integrity, perhaps even greatness, in a piece of music, regardless of its style, newness, or age. Along with musicianship, there has to be learned—because it is learned—the best use of time, the building of organizational techniques. In the third place, I believe that a great choral person must learn how to plan for and feel like the people with whom he or she is working. Not all would agree with this premise. We both know great musicians who have not possessed this last attribute. It's not so necessary for the instrumentalist. But one must never forget that we deal with voices— voices that in one respect are related to the way in which a personality shows itself and hopefully will grow. It is very difficult for some to do this, to put themselves in the other person's place.

G.P.: As I look at different conductors at all levels, and the degree to which they are successful—applying my own standards of success—it's possible for someone who is lacking in certain areas of musicianship to still move people—and not in a manipulative way—to move people in a way that he or she is giving them something lasting and meaningful in their lives.

H.S.: I hope that I belong in your picture. I'm no great musician and have never pretended to be. I did not major in music and I never really learned to use a piano; I have had to suffer with this all my life. I had some courses—harmony, history, form and analysis—still, there wasn't very much breadth or depth in my academic experience. I have had a good ear and it has always been helpful. I can hear when things are happening. Also, I had good vocal training, enough so that even when I lost my own voice, I could still describe procedures with speech.

G.P.: That was something that struck me intuitively as I worked with you at Occidental—that this disability you had to face forced you into other means of communication.

H.S.: It is very true! When I began to teach voice one on one, what was I to do? I couldn't use my own voice to illustrate. I had to find words to describe desired results. This led to my watching responses—the students' response to what I was saying—particularly shown by their eyes. When these began to glaze, I knew I was not understood.

This approach became extended to speech—how did *others* talk? Did they speak too rapidly or too slowly? Everything they would do physically—their walk, stance, smile, frown—were these a part of their personality? Gradually I began to understand that observing in this way and then going forward with such knowledge became a great tool for my own teaching, and I could set up rehearsals to match the mood or change things for all who took part in the rehearsal. As I learned to make these observations my teaching and conducting improved greatly.

I think that particularly with choral music, with one's voice being the instrument, much of how the person *feels* shows up in the way that he or she *sounds*.

G.P.: I have one final question for you. Many, many years hence, when you're gone, for what would you like to be remembered?

H.S.: Well, not for my writing, nor for my conducting. I think that

I would like to be remembered as a teacher with all that this implies. I know that I would have a much harder job of it today than I did then, particularly at the high-school level, where so much time is taken with problems of classroom deportment. But I still think that it is a great profession. It must involve the "person who sits on the other end of the log"—teaching must be concerned with others if it is to be truly effective.

Many teachers miss that point. The emphasis today is sometimes too much on research. It can become too mannered, too dull, it isn't very exciting; it depends so much on the recital of facts. Facts are important—yes, very important—but as in the sciences, those teachers who are successful in the arts do not choose this profession because of money or prestige. Rather, they see their jobs as being centered on procedures and principles that can bring to their students the most meaningful of all goals—the opportunity for self-fulfillment. A wise teacher accepts this philosophy regardless of academic emphasis, prestige, or salary schedule. It becomes a credo that gains in importance with each passing year.

Jameson Marvin

The Conductor's Process

Some conductors have the ability to inspire greatly. Howard Swan is such a conductor. He is the personification of integrity, energy, soul-enriching purposefulness, and in more than a half century of professional choral conducting, he has inspired generations of students. Those who know him know of his breadth of humanity, his passionate support of high-quality music and music-making, his unique charisma and spirituality, his enthusiasm, and his love of music and of his fellow man.

Howard Swan has taught conductors to think seriously about their profession, to try to realize their full potential, and to be fully aware of the extraordinary challenges of their art. Today, choral conductors are expected to be knowledgeable in repertory spanning six centuries and to explore the vast diversity of styles and genres of these eras. Each of us strives to feel equally at home with a Lassus motet, a Bach cantata, and a Haydn Mass, as well as Brahms's *German Requiem*, Stravinsky's *Symphonie de Psaumes*, and Ligeti's *Lux aeterna*. We feel it is important to have a firm understanding of the voice, as well as the ex-

Jameson Marvin is Senior Lecturer on Music and Director of Choral Activities at Harvard University. His Harvard choral ensembles have appeared several times at ACDA national conventions, have recorded extensively, and have toured Europe and East Asia. He received the D.M.A. degree in choral music from the University of Illinois (1971), the M.A. in Choral Conducting/Early-Music Performance from Stanford University (1965), and the B.A. degree in Music Composition from the University of California, Santa Barbara.

A specialist in the performance of Renaissance and Baroque music, Dr. Marvin is General Editor of the Renaissance Choral Series for Men's Voices for Oxford University Press. He serves on the Fulbright-Hays Committee for selection of Fulbright Conducting Fellows and has over twenty years of experience in the conducting of major works for chorus and orchestra.

pertise to rehearse an orchestra. We should understand Baroque phrasing, Kodály's rubato, Renaissance proportionality, contemporary systems of notation, and the asymmetric macro-phrase in the music of Mozart. We work hard to achieve a conducting technique that is clear, yet expressive, serving choruses as well as orchestras, and we feel it important to have a knowledge of several languages, reasonable keyboard skills, outstanding musicianship, and the ability to rehearse effectively. We hope to inspire our singers and audiences in the process.

The challenge of the art of choral conducting today is one of breadth and depth. Elementary schools, junior high schools, high schools, colleges, universities, conservatories, churches, and communities employ choral conductors in innumerable contexts. Colleges, universities, and conservatories train conductors for multi-purpose jobs. Many offer curricula leading to the BM, BA, MM, MA, EdD, and DMA degrees in choral music. Institutional traditions, financial constraints, curricular patterns, and internal predispositions (and prejudices) play a significant role in shaping college and graduate choral curricula. Given the current multi-faceted state of the art, today's choral conductor realizes that he[1] faces a diverse and complex profession. When developing one's own approach to achieving excellence in choral conducting, priorities are difficult to sort, and important questions arise.

The purpose of this article is to provide a *conscious* perspective on the interrelationship of the multi-faceted concerns of the choral conductor. The author describes this interrelationship as the "Conductor's Process." A diagram of the process may be seen on the next page. At the center of the "Process" is *Rehearsing*. While each aspect of the "Conductor's Process" impacts on at least one other, and the composite of the aspects represents the "ideal conductor," each of the elements cannot be fully realized without the ability to rehearse.

The *Performance* (8) is the ultimate motivating goal for the rehearsal, but it is not the goal of the process. Before the performance occurs, *Rehearsing* (7) takes place; and before the rehearsal, the *Literature* (1) must be chosen, the *Score Studied* (2), and questions concerning style and *Performance Practices* (3) need to be addressed. Through stylistic and structural analysis, the conductor develops a *Mental-Aural Image* (4) that prepares him for *Rehearsing*. In the process of rehearsing, the conductor uses his *Ear* (5), *Conducting Technique* (6) and rehearsal procedures to lead the choir toward a unified musical concept of the composition.

---

[1]"He" and "his" refer equally to "she" and "her" throughout this article.

THE CONDUCTOR'S PROCESS

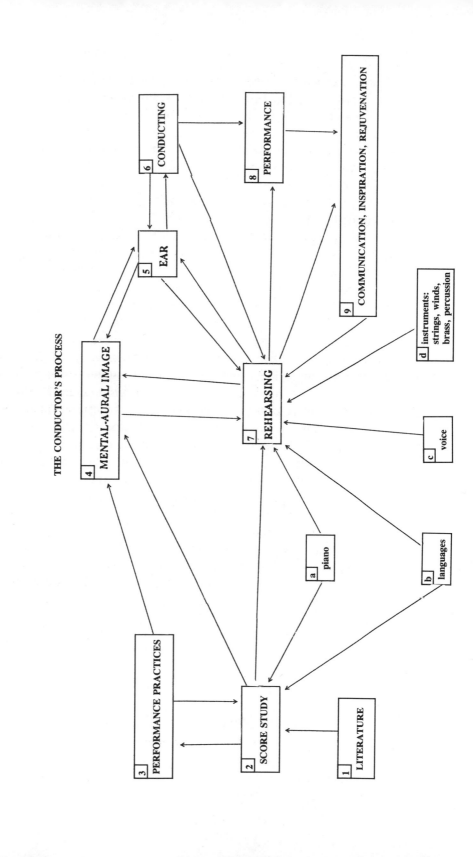

Specific skills are needed by the conductor to aid in the preparation for rehearsal, as well as the rehearsal itself: *Piano* facility (a), *Language* skills (translation and pronunciation) (b), *Voice* training (c), and for concerted works, a knowledge of orchestral *Instruments* (d). The *complete* conductor aspires to excel in all aspects—it is a life-long process.

The arrows in the diagram illustrate the interrelationship of the elements of the "Conductor's Process." The direction signifies either a one-way or a circular connection. By far the most complex is the relationship of the *Mental-Aural Image*, the *Ear*, and *Rehearsing*. It is primarily through the ear that the conductor measures his mental-aural image against what the choir is singing. Having an indelible image of the musical concept of the score acts as a powerful stimulus in directing the choir toward that image. The degree of technical, musical, and conceptual mastery of the score by the choir is therefore dependent upon the conductor's aptitude and abilities in rehearsing. The ear provides the information necessary to make the process work.

Each element of the process requires a lifetime of study and demands continuous attention. The complete process, by nature, is self-perpetuating. Its essence nourishes *Communication*, *Inspiration*, and *Rejuvenation* (9), the life-blood of the profound interaction of music and humanity.

What follows is some amplification on each aspect of the "Conductor's Process." Volumes can be (and already have been) written concerning most of these topics. In the context of this article, the principal objectives in discussing each aspect are to make explicit our common assumptions and to provide a more conscious approach to the art in which choral conductors are engaged.

The author has developed these ideas over some twenty years' experience as a college choral conductor. Inevitably, his ideas represent a composite picture of his experiences, many of which have been shaped by gifted conductors of our time, prominently among them, Robert Shaw, Helmuth Rilling, and Harold Decker.

1. LITERATURE

The choral repertoire is by far the richest and most diverse in the field of music. Today, conductors have the great fortune of being able to select from an inexhaustible treasure-trove of music from the fifteenth through the twentieth centuries. The major genres—Mass, motet, cantata, oratorio, Passion, magnificat, Requiem, chorale, anthem, chanson, Lied, madrigal, and folk song—are contained in anthologies, collections, and collected works in music libraries in most colleges and universities. Many publishers make available an enormous quantity of significant choral literature, and most offer a wide range of repertoire. Some cater to popular demand and are under financial pressure to publish music that is easily accessible, but probably will be of little enduring value.

The central thesis of this brief discussion is: *perform music of good quality.* Music of distinction, performed well, is an experience of lasting significance. In contrast, performing "trendy," easy-access, instantly effective music is, by nature, an ephemeral pleasure, a temporary titillation. The satisfaction of the experience is generally short lived. Each individual piece rarely has the capacity continuously to enrich, though the emotions it taps may be strong. Rock music, for example, appeals so greatly to so many because its principal means of communication— a pulsating, repeated beat projected at enormous volume—is primal. The sound-continuum, over time, is mesmerizing, provocative, and quasi-erotic. Appreciation of it requires little thought.

Obviously, "pop" music holds an extraordinary attraction for much of our contemporary society. If it invites an uninitiated singer into the world of choral literature, it serves a purpose in the choral art. Some pop music rises above stereotypical clichés and is of lasting value, but most of it tends only to solidify the values, traditions, and mores of the current popular culture.

One of the profound rewards of performing choral music drawn from the vast heritage of six centuries is that for the participants, the cumulative experience provides insight into the cultural and aesthetic values of past eras. Singers who are challenged and invigorated by performing great works of choral literature acquire a broad perspective upon which to base their own aesthetic values. By cultivating within them the capacity to experience the profound enrichment of "enlightened cherishing,"[2] the choral conductor satisfies one of his primary responsibilities: to educate. In the process, his singers will learn the value of the music he has chosen, and how it enriches them with its depth.

Great choral music demands participation in the process of creating and recreating, as well as listening. The reward gained in performing a Bach cantata, a Josquin motet, a Schubert Lied, a Monteverdi madrigal, Britten's *War Requiem*, or Mozart's C-Minor Mass, is directly proportional to the mental and emotional energy put into rehearsing it. The

[2]Harry Broudy, *"Enlightened Cherishing," an Essay on Aesthetic Education* (Urbana, University of Illinois Press, 1971).

greater the degree of intrinsic compositional integrity, the richer the rewards singers experience in meeting the challenge.

Much of the rich choral repertoire of the Renaissance lies dusty on library shelves, and contemporary composers of significant talent and originality languish in obscurity. This is a great shame, because this music—Schütz's motets from *Geistliche Chormusik*, Monteverdi's sacred concerted works, Handel's "other" oratorios, Haydn's Masses, Bach's motets and Passions, Purcell's anthems, Poulenc's chansons, Brahms's motets, Stravinsky's choral-orchestral works—can challenge, educate, invigorate, and impact significantly on the quality of spiritual life of students and conductors who perform them. To deny students the pleasure and life-enriching experience of rehearsing and performing the best choral literature of the master composers of western music, with its multi-leveled challenges, denigrates our principal purpose: educating and inspiring young singers.

2. SCORE STUDY

The second stage of the "Conductor's Process" is the foundation upon which choral performance is based: score study. In acquiring a thorough knowledge of the score, the conductor will be prepared for the rehearsal and will possess the perspective and security upon which to base his vision of the composer's intentions.

Notational symbols reveal an enormous amount of information. Realizing them in sound requires conceptualization of all the information that the symbols denote, and of all that they imply. Bringing this composite picture to life (in sound) requires imagination, and score study is the catalyst that fires the imagination. Score study spawns the mental-aural image of the music, which acts as a powerful energizer for conductors in motivating singers to their vision of the composer's intentions. Score study sets in motion the entire "Conductor's Process."

The core of score study is structural analysis: the study of the relationship of the total design to the details that order its architecture. Harmony, melody, rhythm, and texture (and instrumentation in concerted works) form the building blocks of structure. Duration, pitch, timbre, and intensity articulate the sound-continuum of the form and design.

In vocal music, all these elements interact with text. The degree to which text inspires or affects the elements of music will be a particularly important question to be addressed here. Throughout the history of western music, *words* have inspired the masterpieces of choral literature.

Words also impose order and prescribe limits. Furthermore, there is an inherent dialectical tension between words and music.

No other controversy in music history better illustrates this tension than the polarity of positions held by those musicians at the dawn of the Baroque who espoused the principles of the *prima prattica* and those who championed the *seconda prattica*. The two conflicting philosophies are best summarized in the preface to Claudio Monteverdi's *Scherzi musicali* of 1607, written by his brother, Giulio Cesare. The *prima prattica* is described as a style in which the technique of composition is "not commanded, but commanding, not the servant, but the mistress of the word."[3] But in the *seconda prattica*, the compositional technique is "not commanding, but commanded, and makes the words the mistress of the harmony."[4]

Discovering which of these aesthetic principles serves as the governing premise of a composer's creation deserves considerable thought. In the hands of one composer, the text may serve as a vehicle for displaying his compositional craftsmanship; in another's, the words may be the catalyst that generates each structural and expressive element of the composition. Once the kernel of inspiration is perceived, the text-music relationship understood, and the form and structure analyzed, the conductor will have come a long way toward discovering "the truth" of the composition. And that is the ultimate goal of score study.

3. PERFORMANCE PRACTICES

Over the past quarter-century there has been an enormous surge of interest in the performing practices of prior ages. Theoretical treatises, performing manuals, and modern scholarly investigation form the collective body of knowledge from which performers try to glean information about the performing practices of former eras. The principal concerns of performance-practice research are: tempo, phrasing, articulation, pitch, temperament, tuning, dynamics, instrumentation, timbre, ornamentation, improvisation, musica ficta, basso-continuo realization, balance, and the size and make-up of performing forces.

There is great value in attempting to understand the expressive nuances inherent in the ways our forebears made music. The philosophy that encourages twentieth-century performers to learn about the perform-

[3]Oliver Strunk, ed., *Source Readings in Music History III: the Baroque Era* (New York: W.W. Norton, 1965) 48.
[4]Ibid., 49.

ing practices of prior eras does so with the implicit expectation that the more we can detect about what a composer wanted and expected to hear, the closer we will come to the true meaning of the music. The closer that today's conductors can come to an understanding of the aesthetic values upon which music from past eras is based, the more likely they will be able to serve the cause of intrinsically expressive performance.

Understanding proper style and transmitting its meaning to students and listeners requires educating (and re-educating) twentieth-century ears. Furthermore, notation—the system used by composers to transmit their ideas—has changed considerably over the intervening centuries. Today's symbols convey specific meanings; often their contemporary meaning is not relevant to the performance of yesterday's music. Similarly, the significance of many symbols has changed over the centuries; the original meaning may have become lost, or at least blurred.

The process of discovering meaning in music of the past and gaining insights into the intrinsic expressive values of prior eras is invigorating. The rewards are particularly rich when one's own singers and audience begin to open their ears and minds more sensitively (and pleasurably) to the art of appreciating style in the performance of earlier music.

No one living, however, has heard Bach perform one of his cantatas, and no one knows how one of Handel's Foundling Hospital performances of *Messiah actually* sounded. We have no idea of how the singers of the Sistine Chapel *really* performed Palestrina's Masses. Nor do we know how Brahms performed tempo relationships in his multi-sectional motets. Research yields a wealth of information and insight. It offers a window into the past yet does not offer absolute confirmation.

It is sometimes possible to take the "purist approach" too far. Worse, it is possible to allow "authenticity" (even knowledgeably imagined) to be the end in itself. Furthermore, some performers lacking in imagination, with a predisposition toward scholarship alone, offer dull, lifeless performances in the name of authenticity. Insightful, imaginative performances, grounded in solid stylistic understanding, are not synonymous with perfunctory performance. Intelligent, expressive, communicative music-making that provides uplifting, enriching, and rejuvenating experiences embodies the ultimate value of music: transcendence. Without the soul of the music, answering authenticity questions in performance has little profound meaning.

Ideally, conductors today strive for a balance. But the heart of the philosophy underlying our concern with performance practices—basing modern performance upon the aesthetic values of past eras—invites conflict. The conflict centers on value systems—those of past eras and those of our own. Education, taste, and personal predisposition all play a significant role in choosing which value system will form the foundation upon which performance rests.

"If Bach had our performing forces—that is, more singers and the modern orchestra—what would he have done, or imagined?" In the context just discussed, this is an outdated question. The apt question is more sophisticated: "What priorities shall we choose from the aesthetic principles of both the past and present to make our performance meaningful?"

Serious conductors ponder this question each time they prepare a new score for rehearsal. Good answers vary greatly, if we are to judge by the highest standards of today's recorded performances of music of past eras. However, choosing to project the most pertinent essential expressive values of former eras, and combining them with our own in a fresh, new, and communicative spirit will enliven and deepen the experience of performing good music well.

4. MENTAL-AURAL IMAGE

By analyzing the form and structure of the score, and in resolving questions and making decisions concerning stylistic priorities, the conductor will have conceptualized interpretive ideas. The author calls this conceptualization the "mental-aural image." The mental-aural image is a vision of what the music "should sound like;" it is the "mind's ear." Crystallized in score study and fired by the imagination, the mental-aural image is a powerful motivating agent. It provides an ever-present standard against which to measure the choir's progress. The deeper the insights into the score, the more clear and profound the mental-aural image becomes. Clarity of insight inspires conductors to attain their vision. Inspired conductors motivate singers. Motivated singers inspire each other and the conductor; the process is self-renewing.

5. EAR

Communicating the mental-aural image to singers requires time, patience, discipline, and experience. The process is a circular one. The conductor measures the sound produced by the choir against his mental-aural image, he feeds information back to the choir, and the choir then reshapes the sound. As this process continues in rehearsal after rehearsal, inevitably the choir's sound begins more clearly to match the conductor's mental-aural image. The ear is the channel through which sound information is transferred. The ear is the yardstick—the "truth teller," the intermediary that makes possible the conductor's capacity to realize the conception.

The better the conductor's ear, the more effective he will be in attaining his mental-aural image. Every bit of information is gathered by his ear. The information received can be categorized by the four elements that comprise music: duration, pitch, timbre, and intensity. Each musical element contributes to the composite picture of the whole. The ear has the capacity to hear all four elements at the same time. The mind has the ability to focus selectively on one at a time, and also the capacity to assimilate information on all levels simultaneously.

Learning to hear simultaneously on four levels requires natural aptitude, training, and experience. Each rehearsal presents a fresh opportunity to expand the ear's capacities. Concentration is the key. Conductors who possess the capacity to concentrate will reap the rewards of increased auditory perception, and will thus be able to more quickly identify information related to duration, pitch, timbre, and intensity. As the ear improves, the conductor's ability to evaluate this information will be greatly enhanced, providing him with the knowledge necessary to implement change.

6. CONDUCTING

From the *tactus*-giver of the Renaissance, to the organist or continuo-realizer of the Baroque, to the first violinist or principal instrumentalist participating in the performance of music of the Classic period, conductors have traditionally been an integral part of the music-making ensemble—a singer or an instrumentalist who also "kept time." Until music achieved the complexity of a work like Beethoven's "Eroica" symphony, the principal function that conductors historically served was to provide pulse; they marked time and kept the ensemble together. Conducting as a "separate" profession is a comparatively recent phenomenon.

Today's conductor no longer only keeps time. He also tries to represent sound-images taking place in time. His conducting technique is expected to reveal musical meaning as well as pulse and meter. The foundation of modern conducting technique, therefore, rests principally in two areas: (1) representing information about pulse and meter, and (2) differentiating and highlighting musical events.

Historically, visual representation of metric organization is rooted in very logical and natural principles: (a) the *down* motion indicates the principal beat of the measure, which coincides with the natural downward pull of gravity; (b) the *up* motion, which is against the pull of gravity, is felt to be comparatively unstable, requiring resolution— the inevitable preparation for the *down*.

Duple meters require the down-up motion to convey pulse. Meters containing four pulses per measure are visually represented by four points, each located at the end of two lines—one vertical and the other horizontal. The secondary pulse (the third beat) lies at the (right) end-point of the horizontal line. Motion to it is perpendicular to the principal downbeat; thus, its location is clearly differentiated from the primary pulse (beat one), and clarity of the total design is therefore inherent in the entire conducting pattern.

Visual representation of triple meter involves (1) the downward motion, representing the strong beat, (2) cross-motion differentiating (in this case) the weak beat, and (3) the up motion, which requires resolution due to its degree of instability. The visual design of triple meter is that of a triangle, the points of which represent the ictus that indicates the pulse.

The visual representations of meters containing more than four beats are formed by two or more of the aforementioned patterns: down-up motion, cross motion, or triangular motion. Decisions regarding subdivisions and merging relate to tempo, musical pulse, and musical gesture.

The conductor who can command a technique that conveys clear information regarding pulse and meter satisfies the primary (and historical) purpose of conducting. The technique should be universally understood by instrumentalists as well as singers. Choral and orchestral musicians will feel compelled to respond when the conducting technique is grounded in these principles, and the control that the conductor then wields enables him to serve the music's purposes effectively.

The modern conductor, however, is expected to do more than clarify pulse and meter. He is expected to elicit expressiveness, to draw out musical gesture through physical gesture. The aim of "expressivity" is communication. Mirroring musical nuances through illustrative conducting gestures visually supports the structure of the music as it moves through time. Thus, expressive gestures are employed to visually amplify sound-images, moment by moment. Through physical gesture, expressive conducting both serves the music and allows performers more informed access to its meaning.

Expressive conducting tries to convey musical gesture through the physical representation of it. To the degree that a conductor follows this principle, he will physically maximize important gestures and minimize unimportant ones. He will differentiate, and in this way, highlight musical meaning.

At the most expressive levels of communication, however, this process may impinge upon the projection of information regarding pulse and meter. Deciding which will be the most important function—to serve expressive needs or to project pulse and meter at any given moment— is a principal concern in the art of conducting. With experience, gifted conductors instinctively achieve an appropriate balance.

Grounding one's conducting techniques in the principles of revealing pulse, meter, and the expressive elements of music in a clear, universally understood manner, arms the conductor with a repertoire of physical gestures that serve him well in the creative process of music performance. As the conducting technique becomes "second nature," his concentration also increases. In rehearsal he will be able to more effectively implement change, and in performance he will be able to respond simultaneously to technical as well as musical concerns, providing confidence and security for the performers.

How odd, though, that the act of waving one's arms has anything to do with the realization of sound! Why should physical gesture have any impact on performers?

The answer lies in the art itself: physical gestures require energy and they generate energy. The quality of the response is a mirror of the quality of the energy projected. The more meaningful the conducting gesture, the more focused the energy. The more focused the energy, the greater the power to elicit the desired response. Onward flows the circle of energy—from conductor to chorus and back to conductor. The cycle is revitalizing for both. This process is real but invisible; it is thus often felt to be spiritual, and its essence inspires and enriches the lives of the participants.

7. REHEARSING

It is in the rehearsal that each element of the "Conductor's Process" is drawn together. Through the process, the conductor has prepared himself for rehearsing. He will have begun his preparation by choosing the repertoire and studying the score. Score study and stylistic insights will have stimulated a mental-aural image. The rehearsal provides the context in which to realize that mental-aural image, while the conductor's gestures illustrate clear information regarding pulse, meter, and musical nuance. Through his ear the conductor measures the chorus's sound against his mental-aural image and implements changes. This is rehearsing.

No aspect of the "Conductor's Process" will more directly affect the results of the conductor's preparation than his ability to rehearse. Without effective rehearsing, insights into the score will not be realized. No matter how much the conductor is able to hear, no matter how visionary his interpretation, no matter how highly communicative his conducting technique may be, the principal foundation upon which the actualization of the score rests is rehearsing.

Rehearsal methods, procedures, and techniques vary greatly from one conductor to another. It is not the purpose of this discussion, however, to suggest specific rehearsal techniques. Rehearsal technique is a subject of its own, outside the scope of this essay.

It is important, however, to sort priorities when undertaking this vastly complex art—the ability to develop in choral singers a technical and musical concept of the score that matches that of the conductor's mental-aural image. The process of developing matching conceptualizations, if one stops to think about it, is quite phenomenal—perhaps fundamentally spiritual.

How does the conductor draw choral singers toward the compelling image he possesses? He achieves this through creating in them a *unanimous* vision of it: a *unity of ensemble* that reflects it.

Rehearsals are the forum in which conductor and choir come together to engage in a creative activity that is normally motivated by a concrete goal: the performance. The quality of rehearsing is inevitably measured by the quality of performance. While disagreement concerning details of interpretation and differences of opinion regarding sound ideals are as common as conductors are different, few musicians or knowledgeable listeners fail to recognize an outstanding performance when they hear one.

An outstanding performance *communicates*. It allows listeners and participants to transcend their common daily experience. Outstanding performance enriches lives and rejuvenates spirits. Good rehearsals do the same thing.

How can rehearsals best serve music's ultimate value? By focusing the energy of singers on the inherent elements of music that, when revealed, give meaning to its structure and order as it develops in time. When the meaning of a composition is revealed, communication occurs, fulfilling music's ultimate purpose.

How can we make clear the elements of music (duration, pitch, timbre, intensity) that provide the key to understanding its structure and order? Through unifying them. In the process of unifying the elements of music, the medium through which the music is being heard (the choir) absorbs and assimilates a unanimous vision: *a unity of ensemble.*

By achieving unity of ensemble, then, we simultaneously answer two questions: how does the conductor draw the choral singers toward the compelling image he possesses, and how do we make clear the elements of music?

Ensemble unity *is* unity of duration, pitch, timbre, and intensity. The expressive components of music—dynamics, phrasing, articulation, rubato, linear direction, and text nuance—are integrally connected with one or more of these basic elements. When the choir attains complete ensemble—the "ideal"—it clarifies the form, the function, and the design of the sound continuum of the music. It reveals the music's total structure, reinforcing meaning and enhancing its capacity to communicate.

Before beginning to unify any one element, one should realize that there is an interlocking relationship among all four. Each element interacts and affects at least one other. Pitch is perceived through duration, and its quality is identified by timbre. Intensity is felt through the interaction of pitch and duration. Duration provides the medium through which all three elements are given order and sound. Thus, the element of music that plays the greatest role in providing ensemble unity is duration.

Duration

Duration is articulated in music by pulse (tempo), rhythm, and meter, and makes possible the expressive components. When our primary objective in choral rehearsal is directed toward unity of duration, we provide an ordered medium through which pitch, timbre, and intensity can be more meaningfully realized.

We achieve unity of duration primarily through establishing *ensemble rhythm.* Ensemble rhythm is the interaction of pulse (tempo) on the rhythmic-metric-textural fabric of the composition. Teaching a choir to sing with good ensemble rhythm means, then, to sensitize choral singers to a unanimous group pulse. Their internal clocks must be taught to perceive sound by the same scale of measure. By sensitizing their physiological responses to it (the scale of measure), choir singers internalize pulse. As group pulse internalizes, ensemble rhythm is developed. When ensemble rhythm is established, the expressive components realized through duration—dynamics, phrasing, articulation, rubato, and linear direction—will be given a chance to project their powerful communicative potentials.

Pitch

Unifying pitch—singing with good intonation—is one of the most elusive challenges in the choral art. When a choir sings in tune, the listener is allowed to hear more clearly the music's structural components: harmony, melody, rhythm, and texture. Thus, singing in tune heightens the awareness of structure, which facilitates communication.

Good choral intonation is also beautiful. The sound of a choir singing in tune is an experience in hearing extraordinarily compelling sound-images, produced through changing patterns of timbres, textures, and sonorities. In reinforcing the overtone series, good intonation creates a rich sonority that invites the listener into the music and heightens his awareness of the beauty of the choir.

A great many factors affect the achievement of good pitch: acoustical theory and the acoustical environment, weather, health, the structural components of a composition, and most importantly, the ear/voice relationship. The voice is the medium for choral music. Healthy voices, housed in healthy bodies, full of energy, have a great capacity to sing in tune. However, a choir will not truly sing in tune until its composite vocal sound achieves a unity of timbre. Pitch and timbre together define intonation. The vowels as well as the pitch must be tuned; when vowels are matched, the pitch can be unified.

Singing in tune requires good ears (conductor's and singers'), and consistent reinforcement. The responsibility for maintaining good pitch lies ultimately with the singers. While the conductor can provide them with a pitch standard initially, acquiring good pitch perception is integrally connected to understanding the process by which it is attained. Thus, by teaching choral singers to become conscious of the process they have individually used when they attain the conductor's pitch standard, the responsibility is placed squarely on their shoulders. Once their process becomes clear to them, choir singers are invigorated by the thinking that is required to re-create good pitch each time, and are stimulated by their own abilities (with conductorial prods) to maintain it.

Timbre

There is no element in choral music with greater impact upon timbre than the sung word. The enormously colorful sound continuum of the shifting colors produced by passing mosaics of vowel sounds and vocal timbres, sustained through time, contributes significantly to the intrinsic beauty of choral sound. The individual vocal timbres of the singers color and complement the choral sonority. If the choir is to project a unanimity of sound, however, the vocal timbre of each section needs to be unified. In choral music, this means to match vowels. When the vowel sound of each section projects a unified sonority, the pitch of the choir will improve, and the sheer beauty of the vocal sound will enhance and clarify the musical meaning.

Intensity

Intensity serves primarily as an expressive element in music. It affects many agents of expression, including dynamics, articulation, phrasing, rubato, and linear direction. Intensity also serves another function—clarifying balance. Balance plays an extremely important role in projecting musical structure.

Concerning the expressive agents:

(1) *Dynamics* illuminate passing musical gestures. They highlight expressive nuances, and to a greater degree than any other expressive agent, are a powerful force in emphasizing structure.

(2) *Articulation* enhances structural clarity and it serves an expressive function as well. Words are given inherent clarity of expression through articulation. Consonants are projected, and strong-weak syllabic relationships are revealed, heightening inherent word expression. Sometimes, however, the emotion of the word (as opposed to inherent syllabic accents) is felt more powerfully by emphasizing each syllable equally, an effect that draws the listener into experiencing the meaning behind the word.

(3) *Phrasing* provides cohesion to a series of pitches, and primarily through articulation, it sets into relief specific segments of a musical line. Short phrases or note-groups heighten local expression; long phrases enhance continuity and direction. Phrasing is created by a combination of intensity and duration.

(4) *Rubato* is produced through fluctuations in duration and intensity. While duration is the primary means through which rubato is realized, shifts in intensity normally accompany it. Cadential structures are heightened when rubato momentarily draws the music behind the pulse, and dramatic gestures are energized as rubato temporarily pushes the music beyond the pulse. Ritards and accelerandos (respectively) achieve similar effects through absolute changes of pulse. Passing events are often heightened by the impact of rubato, especially in the context of musical line and harmonic color.

(5) *Linear direction*. Many styles of music are given meaningful expression through emphasizing the musical line (either the long line or shorter note-groups that form the line). Intensity of direction serves long line; dynamics, articulation, and subtle rubato highlight shorter components of the line.

When we unify each of the expressive functions related to intensity, we develop an arsenal of great communicative power to heighten, illuminate, and clarify musical meaning. Of the four elements of music, intensity most directly affects the expressive components of music-making.

In summary, the foundation upon which rehearsal rests, if it is to be effective, is ensemble unity. Ensemble unity is achieved when we unify the four basic elements of music: duration, pitch, timbre, and intensity. Each of these in turn impacts upon the expressive components of music: dynamics, phrasing, articulation, rubato, and linear direction. Thus, when the four basic elements are unified, choirs project ensemble unity, and their projection clarifies the structure, the form, and the expressive components of music. When musical meaning is revealed, communication takes place, realizing music's profound capacity to inspire.

It is important to point out that all of the principles upon which effective rehearsals are based require two essential ingredients: energy and desire. The quality of the energy that the conductor gives to the singers will be the primary force that stimulates them to implement his ideas. Singers must be motivated to accomplish conductors' goals. The conductor who is motivated by the quality of the music, by the conceptual vision he has of it, and by the joy he receives in realizing his concept, cannot help but project positive energy. Enthusiasm, encouragement, patience, humor, and positive reinforcement will serve him well as he engages the choral singers in the rehearsal process. The joy that students experience in singing with inspired conductors is transformed into a collective energy that replenishes and inspires both his and theirs.

This mutual experience is one of the deepest rewards of the pivotal element of the "Conductor's Process"—rehearsing.

8. PERFORMANCE

Performance provides the goal for rehearsals. If rehearsals have been effective and the music is progressing well, singers (and conductors) take pride in imagining a concert that demonstrates their musical achievements. As the performance draws near, the vision of it looms as a compelling image, acting as a powerful incentive to perfect the composite elements of the music. Pride in achieving musical excellence energizes the process that creates it.

In the performance the choir and conductor together engage in the creative activity of projecting their mutual conception of the score to the audience. As the concert progresses, the impact of projecting that mutual mental-aural image through ensemble unity inspires the choir, the conductor, and the audience. The multiple levels of musical expression communicate. Together, the audience, the choir, and the conductor share in the joy of an exhilarating experience. Their lives are rejuvenated through experiencing the transcendent power of music.

9. COMMUNICATION / INSPIRATION / REJUVENATION

Music can truly be experienced only through sound, and breathing life into a set of notational symbols holds the potential for enriching all those who participate in it. Thus, at each stage of the "Conductor's Process," there exists an inherent potential for inspiration and rejuvenation.

Choosing the repertoire, the experience of combing through the rich repertory of choral music to discover a profoundly crafted masterpiece, can be extremely exhilarating. Upon analyzing the structure and style of the music the conductor has chosen, a powerful image of the score fires his imagination, igniting a compelling vision that inspires him to motivate the choir to actualize his conception.

As the conductor and choir in rehearsal build an *ensemble* that is able to project a unity of conception through a unity of presentation, their spirits soar as they work together to perfect the process of the multifaceted art of recreating music. In performance, projecting their collective vision of the beauty of music inspires, rejuvenates, and enriches the lives of the participants.

A common thread runs through each component of the "Conductor's Process:" energy. Choosing good-quality music energizes a conductor. As he analyzes the structure and style of the composition, energy transforms his knowledge and insight into a vision of the sound, which in rehearsal motivates him to achieve it. Singers respond to the quality of his motivation, which is communicated by the energy of his conducting technique and by the depth of his insights. They engage in the process of realizing the conductor's vision in sound, and together are rejuvenated by a cycle of energy that emanates from the process. Thus, energy is the catalyst for making music transcendent and for breathing spirituality into the interaction of music and humanity.

The purpose of this essay has been to set forth a conscious perspective on the breadth and depth of the choral art. The "Conductor's Process" makes explicit the interrelationship of the components of choral conducting and illuminates the complexity of this multi-faceted art. It is hoped that this essay will provide an educational perspective for young conductors as they enter the field, as well as a perspective for experienced conductors that might reveal new insights into the profession in which they are already engaged.

Attaining excellence in each aspect of the "Conductor's Process" provides the foundation for achieving the ideal: becoming a complete conductor. Serious conductors devote their lives to the pursuit of this ideal, and to the extent that they achieve it, they, their singers, their audiences, and the music they perform are enriched.

Lynn Whitten

Integrity in the Teaching and
Performing of Choral Music

[Author's Note: The ideal that Howard Swan has exemplified most clearly for those of us in the choral-music profession is *integrity*. His career has spanned a time of widely expanding knowledge in our field; his teaching and conducting have reflected his staying abreast of that deepening understanding and his consistent response to it. He has been and continues to be a "preacher" both of the moral kind and for the cause of choral music. We could have no better model for teaching and performing!]

INTRODUCTION

Choral conductors with integrity strive toward impeccable musicianship, develop their analytical and critical capacities for evaluation of score and sound, inform themselves about a composition and its style,

Lynn Whitten has been supervisor of graduate degree programs in choral music and Director of Choral Activities at the University of Colorado, Boulder, since he received his Doctor of Musical Arts degree from the University of Southern California in 1966. He is additionally Associate Dean for Graduate Studies in Music at C.U.

His professional activities have included the Colorado state presidency of the American Choral Directors Association. A long-time member of the Editorial Board of the ACDA Choral Journal, *Dr. Whitten served as Editor of that magazine from 1983 to 1985. Whitten also edited* A Classified, Annotated Bibliography of Articles Related to Choral Music in Five Major Periodicals through 1980, *published by ACDA in 1981.*

and have the musical and artistic finesse to perform not only what is explicit in the score but also what is implicit. The goal of these conductors is the re-creation from the printed page of the music as the composer would have liked to hear it.

If things are not quite right in performance, the problem usually is not the conductor's goal, but his lack of information or his inability adequately to apply or sensitively to employ what he does know. When texts or musical forms are abridged, when stylistic aspects of music are not allowed to have their rightful place, when singers do not demonstrate musical growth from rehearsal to rehearsal, or when audiences are made uncomfortably restive or passively bored, something is awry with the conductor's integrity.

The choir director is most lacking in integrity when his uninformed likes and dislikes and inappropriate whims and bents improperly color the training toward performance. Too, conducting is not exempt from charlatanism and egotism. Stravinsky satirically talked of power politics through the maneuvering of money and people when one

> . . . becomes a "great" conductor . . . and as such is very nearly the worst obstacle to genuine music-making. "Great" conductors, like "great" actors, are unable to play anything but themselves; being unable to adapt themselves to the work, they adapt the work to themselves, to their "style," their mannerisms.[1]

Fortunately, most teachers of choral music are of a different ilk and are dedicated to their concepts of musical integrity. Such concepts perpetually change with conductors' increasing knowledge, experience, and understanding. The author's intent in this essay is to suggest areas of teaching and performance in which our growth enables us to have more integrity toward the music.

The conductor's *modus operandi* in the performance of choral music is directed by five sets of standards, all necessary and complementary. These clusters of guidelines must direct our training of choruses and the music-making of our ensembles. They are centered on (1) musicianship, (2) taste and artistry, (3) perspective, (4) education, and (5) communication. These criteria for performance are weighted differently according to the training and the interests of the individual conductor. Performances with integrity, though, can occur only when each of these

[1]Igor Stravinsky and Robert Craft, *Themes and Episodes* (New York: Alfred A. Knopf, Inc., 1966) 146.

groups of standards is considered. Whether in the context of a junior-high-school choir, in a church-music ministry, or at the university level, a high-principled approach in *each* of these areas to *each* composition in the repertoire is essential. Music that demands less is not substantive enough for use; conductors who demand less are not exhibiting integrity.

MUSICIANSHIP

Musicianship is the most obviously concrete of the aspects of making choral music; it must be the foundation upon which all else is based. The conductor must be a *complete musician*, under whose tutelage ensemble members are systematically developing (1) basic musicianship, (2) performing musicianship, and (3) ensemble musicianship.

One who has *basic musicianship* has an understanding of the components of music as they interact with one another to make an artistic whole; this fundamental acuity is demonstrated both in score reading and in listening. The solid *performing musician* additionally must have technical facility on his chosen instrument--in this case, the voice--as well as senses of style, finish, and communication. The *ensemble musician* must further be willing to function in proper relationship to the group and must understand and be able to respond to the conducting gestures used to facilitate music-making. (Our educational process tends to reorder the three as students are placed in ensembles to improve their musicianship and to prepare them for solo performance. This may seem to work but does not reflect a logical learning sequence.) The conductor must be masterful in these three aspects of musicianship as well as be dedicated to pedagogical transference of them to others; that is, the conductor must be both role model and tutor in a developmental process of transferring musicality to the singers in the chorus.

No one can question the necessity for impeccable musicianship in a conductor. Let us therefore consider four other areas in which conductors must strike subtle balances: taste and artistry, perspective, education, and communication. It must be realized that such adjustments do not necessarily mean compromising the music; on the contrary, it is through attaining the appropriate balances that the music keeps its integrity and, thereby, so does the conductor.

TASTE AND ARTISTRY

Judgments of excellence and appropriateness in choosing music to be programmed, teaching procedures that result in artful "finish" above and beyond "correct" execution of musical scores, and propriety and fitness in the manner of presentation in both rehearsal and concert demonstrate that the taste and artistry of the conductor are in proper focus. The transfer of aesthetic values in concert is greatly affected by musical and nonmusical matters: the listener's reception is highly colored by both the auditory and the visual signals given in music-making.

Commonly held concepts of taste usually bring to mind the subjective element, i.e., personal likes and dislikes, most often rooted in superficial assessment. Objective taste, antithetically, must be the controlling force in choosing literature and in teaching toward performance of that music. Objective taste must be based on technical training, historical knowledge, sense of style, and experience. It involves acknowledgment of the complementary and simultaneous aspects of historical, re-creative, and judicial criticisms.[2] These are related respectively to recognition of a specific work's historical character and orientation, to re-creating its unique artistic individuality, and to evaluating its artistic worth. Though objective taste must be dominant in a conductor, subjective taste is the personal love of the material to be dealt with. Ned Rorem said, "Mature artistic judgment can result only from the love of art. Any judgment in the absence of love is sterile and therefore false."[3]

If our performances are to have artistry, including fluency, polish, and finesse, as well as musicality, we must resist equating difficulty with fine quality and easiness with inferiority. As we will see under the topic *Education* below, we must allow no discomfiture of the audience. Too many of our performances are on the brink of disaster because we try to do too much too difficult literature in too little time; that is unfair both to the performers and to the listeners.

Conducting gestures are another matter that should come under scrutiny. Only techniques that are immediately communicative to performers and that are not distracting or misleading to the audience are viable. Conducting is not an end in itself; it is not for show.

Musical "good breeding" is the tasteful and artistic handling of oneself, one's performers, and the listeners. Showmanship in the good sense happens only when performers are properly prepared to communicate a work of art. "Showmanship" in a lesser sense is hoax and a sign of ulterior motives.

[2]Theodore Meyer Greene, *The Arts and the Art of Criticism* (Princeton, NJ: Princeton University Press, 1940) 372.
[3]Ned Rorem, *"Listening and Hearing,"* *Music Journal* 21 (December 1963) 66.

PERSPECTIVE

The availablility of vast bodies of choral literature from different historical periods and diverse geographical areas, as well as the ready access to an extensive and improving bibliography related to that music, is generating increased interest in authentic stylistic execution. Performance with historical perspective shows awareness of the factors that give identity to an era of music history, to a composer, or to a specific composition. Those of us involved in choral conducting seem to be in the vanguard of stylistic realization when compared to our vocal-pedagogue and orchestral-conductor colleagues, perhaps because of the longer history of our core literature compared with theirs. But we, too, have much to learn about stylistic matters. Clear-cut stylistic differentiations in the choral performances we hear are not yet the norm, though the more obvious stylistic contrasts between Romantic music and the music of earlier periods are becoming ever more apparent. There are very few times one hears a choir with wonderful stylistic separation of the various historical periods; the rewards of those performances make the illusive goal more worth the trying for.

Controversies over stylistic aspects of our performances seem to arise from two sides. On the one hand there are those who ignore stylistic integrity by remaining uninformed or preferring the existentialist approach that allows a composer's written score to become the basis of a highly subjective, personal interpretation. Conductors' prerogatives are justified in their minds. Unfortunately, some conductors still rely primarily on personal interpretation, on innate musicianship, on instinct. They ignore the information that could give them insight into such perplexing problems as the specifics of choral tone, of rhythmic, metric, and proportional relationships, and of the myriad other performance practices that separate the musical sounds of one stylistic period from those of another. It has been well proven, though, through performances and recordings of the past twenty or twenty-five years, that music fares much better when the composer's intent is followed than when it is altered, bolstered, tampered with, or changed to match one's own style. A comparison of selected recent recordings with earlier ones of works such as Bach's Mass in B Minor or Handel's *Messiah* clarifies the point.

On the other hand, controversies have grown from the seeming dichotomies between the musicologically oriented conductor and the voice-teacher conductor. Divergent opinions there should be nonexistent, for good singing has been desired throughout history; writings from our musicological past have stressed do's and don'ts for fine vocal performance, though the concepts of what constitutes "good singing" have changed from time to time. Alteration of *style* in singing does not necessarily mean abandonment of good *technique* in singing. Superior voice teachers have expanded traditional literature from the commonly used Romantic-art-song and opera-aria repertoire so that diverse materials from all periods are used in their teaching, and they are attempting to solve in satisfactory ways such vocal problems as Baroque roulades, intricate rhythmic problems of Gothic music, and "unvocal" lines in avant-garde scores. But the sounds that Machaut, Byrd, Buxtehude, and Haydn heard or idealized have yet to be approached adequately.

The vocal nature of choral performance provides us with other problems and choices. Questions certainly need to be raised about timbre, weight, and register as they relate to music of differing periods of choral-music history. An obvious example is the desired sound for a musical line that may have at times been sung by a countertenor, a castrato, an unchanged boy's voice, or a female. Vocal production, too, may need to be modified in realization of music written for certain acoustical situations and particular historic buildings, partly because of the types of singers that were used, as mentioned in the sentence above, and partly because of the drastically different acoustics of buildings, e.g., San Marco, Venice; the Thomaskirche, Leipzig; Saint Chapelle, Paris; et al. One could conceivably differentiate vocal approaches, too, for the unaccompanied *psalmi spezzati* sung from St. Mark's pulpit and the concerted works performed in the same church's opposing galleries. Other considerations, certainly, are our expectations for young voices when music demands extremes of dynamic levels, difficult tessituras, extraordinary flexibility, and extreme endurance. And there are recurrences of questioning by voice instructors regarding the solo singer in ensemble music-making. They are often concerned about things such as the inability of singers with "singer's formant" to blend in ensemble and the undesirability for young and big voices to sing at less than the forte level.

The ideal conductor will have knowledge and understanding of both the musicological and the vocal areas. Of course, the young conductor, the beginning music educator, does not start out with all these capacities in hand and must quickly grow in stylistic understanding *while* performing literature. This growth is as much a part of a choir director's maturation as are improving musicianship and gaining fluency in baton technique. Fortunately, good music is usually strong enough to survive this educational process as well as the mishandling given that music by uninformed or insensitive conductors. But for music to reach its true potential, the only uncompromising solution is for the conductor to acquire the requisite knowledge of historical perspective and to know how to apply it.

Our solid training sequences and our creative programming demand the inclusion of music with a catholicity of styles: (1) "standards" that should not be missed by choral singers, as well as new publications that have been edited or composed with insight and integrity; (2) music from plainsong and pre-Renaissance polyphony to the avant garde and the pop, all with proper perspective on performance practices whether old or new; (3) choral music that allows us to teach a logical sequence of musical concepts with a goal of improved musicianship; and (4) music that allows us understanding of our world and of ourselves. On the other hand, the resurrection of early music for history's sake is not always successful, and many compositions composed in our time are not valid for choral performance. To be viable, music must inherently have an expressiveness, an arresting nature, and an aesthetic value, regardless of its origin.

Brock McElheran has described varying degrees of historical perspective by showing steps from the "modernized-subjective extreme" (in which one would "use the printed notes as a source of material for [his] own creative ability, using full modern performance resources") to the "historical-objective extreme" (where the conductor would "re-create conditions of first performance as accurately as possible").[4] There have to be degrees of "rightness" as well as of practicality, but there are boundaries beyond which the informed and sensitive musician cannot go.

Deliberations regarding historical perspective must be controlled by understanding (the results of past training and continuing growth through study) and by objectivity (the most difficult of controls in an artistic world too often governed by the frequently stated "*I* like it that way" and too highly colored by our Romantic near past). Simply stated, we haven't the right to make changes in a work of art so that it fits our time, our process of education, or our functional need. We must have proper historical perspective as an aspect of our integrity in the teaching and performing of music.

EDUCATION

The model choral conductor is an instructor with a solid philosophical understanding of the raison d'être: growth in aesthetic understanding via performance. Both the immediate goal of superb concert-giving and

[4]Brock McElheran, *Conducting Technique for Beginners and Professionals* (New York: Oxford University Press, Inc., 1966) 102.

the long-term aim of cultivating artistic discernment demand developmental processes of training.

After a conductor-teacher has firmly in mind a philosophy of music education, decisions must be made about processes to employ for the speediest and most effective results in attaining the goals of that philosophy. Since most ensembles are comprised of members with varying degrees of capacity, training, and experience, a rigid sequence of presentation is problematic; the director must be innovative and creatively redundant in the presentation of concepts and problem-solving procedures in order to keep all members involved.

Warmups must be more than routines to get started; they must have a bearing on the day's work or on continuing vocal and musical growth. Unless the work at the beginning of the rehearsal period is directly related to material that occurs later in the session, it is likely to be of little benefit. Exercises, drills, and the like do not have to be used only at the beginning of a rehearsal: voice building, sight reading, and the solving of specific musical problems can often better be incorporated conjunctly with work on the music to be performed; certainly they must be done as complementary enterprises.

A choir in which none of the members have studied voice must be treated differently from the chorus in which members have had training by one or more vocal pedagogues. Too, the conductor must consider how vocal training en masse affects differently the inexperienced singers and the better-trained ones. Often the novice singer is unable to put into action the director's requests, while the better-trained student exaggerates to the point of affectation or even vocal distress. The conductor must constantly be aurally and visually aware of the activity of each member of the choir and must hear voices in smaller groups or individually on a frequent basis to preclude formation of problematic habits of production. Healthy and artistic singing are part of a vocalist's musicianship. The conductor must work for freedom in the breathing process, in phonation and the development of tone, in increased flexibility and agility, in dynamic contrast and control, and in other aspects of singing. In short, the choral director must be an instructor par excellence of class voice.

Students can be "forced" toward improved musical literacy and musicianship. To that end, everything the student sings should be seen--even vocalises that are learned by rote should be written out for the students after the fact. Too, self-sufficiency can be enhanced in the individual singer by the director's conducting with meaningful and well-disciplined gestures.

A choir needs to be disciplined yet loved into the making of music: too lenient a conductor has neither satisfactory rehearsals nor disciplined performances. Too dictatorial a conductor stifles the psyche of the singers and thereby the creative and re-creative spirits of the performers. But one must take into consideration that rehearsals "run" by choir members are often ineffectual.

There is a body of common-knowledge choral literature with which all students should have some contact. Introducing students to this material should be part of the responsibility of all conductors. Some conductors think that it is appropriate to start on the level of students' previous exposure and association with music. A pertinent example is the use of pop music as an entry point. Such music is not easy to do well. The musical and vocal concepts required for its best performance are often contrary to the styles and techniques we are trying to foster with our traditional choral heritage, most of the available arrangements are simply a contrivance to simulate well-known solo stylists who cannot be imitated en masse, and the athleticism involved in complex choreography hampers good singing and demands more than its share of time and energy. This writer feels that, to the contrary, immediate exposure to music that offers more inherent musical rewards, that has more aesthetic meaning, and that is accessible in terms of difficulty, ranges and tessituras, and textual meaning is more important. Hundreds of compositions in our standard choral repertoire, from simple works of Dufay to complex scores of Penderecki, have those qualities.

Another strategic decision greatly affecting the choir is the choice of performing a limited but highly polished repertoire versus the experiencing of a greater body of choral literature. Obviously students should have contact with repertory that is both musically and vocally challenging. They should be able to finish completely some compositions less imposing in nature. They should be allowed to perform some works on several occasions so that the meaningfulness of the music transcends the process of the performance itself. But they should not have to *perform* every piece to which they are introduced.

The exigencies of the performance schedules we set for our ensembles frequently negate this intended development. Because of pressure to perform, often more imagined than real, we move through performance after performance without the benefits of a process to improve students' skills and allow transference by them from one learning experience to subsequent ones. The musicianship of students should improve, from composition to composition, from rehearsal to rehearsal, from concert to concert, and from school level to school level, in a cumulative manner *for the benefit of the student.* Our regimen of too many performances too close together forces us to teach toward concerts rather than to teach toward independence and security in the making of music, to teach musicianship.

No matter what the type of choir, the conductor is always functioning as an educator. As such his functions are multifaceted. He must have the ability to teach voice, he must be a specialist in interpersonal relationships and group dynamics, and he often must serve as publicist, secretary, administrator, etc. In the educational process one must teach in ensemble rehearsal toward an understanding of music's fundamentals, toward maximum use of aptitude, and toward improved skills as one develops a choral instrument and stimulates growth in aesthetic awareness. Here, in particular, maintaining the balance between the integrity of the music and integrity to the educational process is a tremendous challenge for the conductor.

COMMUNICATION

Choral singers and conductors, like all other performing musicians, have a need and obligation to share the benefits of their labors, the aesthetic results of their training, with others. This transference of music's meaning is an awesome responsibility: the ethics of fidelity in the execution of and sympathy in the interpretation of composers' works are the public demonstration of the integrity of a conductor.[5] The art of being an intermediary between a composer, whose work has been put together with reason and plan, and an audience, whose impressions are hasty and probably uninformed, is not of little consequence.

Listeners, though, have certain rights and expectations. For communication to take place, details of the music-making must be above awkwardness and discomfort, text must be clear if it was meant by the composer to be so, and visual aspects of the performance must not distract one from listening. A member of the audience made uncomfortable because of process will not get the musical message that was intended; to excite the listener without unnerving him or to lull him without dulling him is a mark of artistry and sensitivity.

"Finishing" procedures allow the foundation of understanding music's components, the superstructure of techniques and skills, and the realization of the score to be combined into a gestalt, a work of art, an aesthetic

[5]Igor Stravinsky, *Poetics of Music,* translated by Arthur Knodel and Ingolf Dahl (Cambridge, MA; Harvard University Press, 1947) 127.

experience. There are numerous finishing details, but the art of elegant phrasing is perhaps one of the most troublesome for individuals and groups. We must instill awareness of arsis and thesis, of musical line with cognizance of proper syllabic stress of text, of control of breath for the phrase, and of styles of singing other than molto legato. The results of fine phrasing are awareness of the structure of the music and heightened communication with listeners.

Developing musical understanding and fostering attainment of polish and finesse in young singers is a slow process. There must be a growth toward sensing the effects of structure and style in delineation of the composers' intents. Awareness has to be taught re the execution of the composers' desires vs. interpretation according to the performers' *informed* likes and dislikes. And student singers have to learn the value of communication without affectation or distortion, which includes knowing proper degrees of projection inherent in the style and meaning of the music: knowing when to sing inside the ensemble and when to sing *for* or *at* an audience is a tremendously important lesson to learn.

Too often, in choirs of all levels of ability and experience, having a finely finished product is problematic because of conductors' desires to challenge themselves rather than their choir members and/or because of too frequent performances. The choir members, not the conductor or audience, should come first in deciding the amount and the difficulty of the literature to be conquered for performance.

Whether unfortunate or not, stage etiquette and the visual orientation of the performance have strong impact on the way an ensemble's singing is perceived by the audience. Entrances and exits, carriage and dress, the physical involvement of performers, and the acknowledgment of the response of the hearers have significant bearing on what is thought to be the performers' sound.

Part of this stage etiquette is the establishing of the proper frame around the music.[6] Too often the frames of silence before the beginning and at the conclusion of a composition are distorted by conductor, choir, or audience. Movement, extra preparatory gestures in the name of establishing tempo, and the conductor's lack of control of both performers and audience at the conclusion of a composition negate somewhat the artistry of performance and the aesthetic impact of the piece. Both singers and conductor must be aware of the power of music and of their influence on that power before, during, and after the music per se.

Our educational schemes, fine as they may be, often tempt us to misuse

[6]Edward T. Cone, *Musical Form and Musical Performance* (New York: W. W. Norton & Company, 1968) 16-18.

music, to make poor choices of repertoire, or to misrepresent the intent of the composer. One immediate problem is our changing of the intended function of music, such as making a noncontinuous liturgical Mass into a continuous concert piece. Another problem is our fascination with large numbers of singers; we have used this too often to justify our misuse of early music. An example is our making of Handel's *Messiah*, a fast-paced entertainment piece to the composer, into an "ungodly" Godly, but endless, marathon.

Our changing of music's functional intent, our catering to or justifying our existence to an audience, and the showmanship expected of us by an entertainment-jaded public must not deter us in the transmission of aesthetic meaning. The power of music--the strength of which is thwarted if forced, contrived, or insincere and is not communicated if aloofness, affectation, or trivialization is involved--is greatest when all performers, with the conductor simply as a facilitator, sublimate themselves to the artful experience at hand.

CLOSING

We conductors must check ourselves frequently in the five areas discussed: our musicianship, our artistic discernment, our historical perspective, our educational processes, and the communicative skills of ourselves as teachers and as conductors. The proper prioritizing of the standards related to each of the five, coupled with honesty to a composer, his music, and his time, and the making only of feasible compromises are the substances of integrity in teaching and performance. These balances of the intellectual with the aesthetic give a soundness, a wholeness, and a completeness to music-making.

Maintaining these balances is no small feat, given the dynamic, everchanging nature of our field, ourselves, and our ideals. Integrity, like all ideals, is not a quality attained and then frozen in a static state. As we know, experience, and understand more, our sense of what constitutes integrity is heightened.

A continuing program of self-assessment is in order for us choral conductors. In those areas where we have not kept up to date, where we are not on the cutting-edge of our profession, where our skills are not highly honed, or where our scholarly approach is not intact, we are obligated to make amends. Four suggestions are made as practical means for self-improvement.

(1) We conductors must have ready access to bibliographic resources

that will inform us about composers and their music and about the processes of training and the management and communication skills involved in choral work. Several hundred tax-deductible dollars invested in frequently to be used professional books and one day or so a month at one of the substantive research libraries in fairly close proximity to most of us are investments that will pay off many fold. Professional reading will greatly enhance the "correctness" of what we do as well as the inspiration on which we thrive.

(2) We conductors must hear others' choirs and/or recordings of choirs to give valid perspective on the sounds (and sights) of our own ensembles. Listening for the purpose of copying is not valid; listening for ideas, whether regarding literature, style, or technique, is a true growing process. As we analyze the sounds of choirs, and the techniques used to make them, we uncover the strengths and weaknesses of our own choral/vocal processes.

(3) We conductors must be involved in the activities of professional organizations, through perusal of periodicals and attendance at workshops and conventions, for sustained strength and growth of the organizations as well as of ourselves. These organizations act somewhat as leveling agents, making all conductors colleagues and, simultaneously, creating a forum for exchange of ideas as well as inspiration and excitement for us all. Only the most selfish of conductors can attempt to justify standing apart from professional colleagues.

(4) Conductors may wish or need short- or long-term schooling to strengthen either the academic or practical aspects of their choral musicianship and teaching skills. Most of our higher-education institutions make it easy for us to refresh our skills or acquire additional training. Courses in conducting technique, vocal pedagogy, choral literature, performance practices, learning theory, aesthetics, and a myriad of other helpful topics are offered by colleges and universities.

"Burnout," atrophy of skills, and misuses and abuses of choirs and of music are easily possible in the choral-conducting profession unless we have a continuing program for sustenance and renewal. In contrast, aesthetic experiences for audiences, singers, and self are the counterpoints for the choral conductor with integrity.

Allen Lannom

The Creative Experience:
Implications for the Choral Conductor

It is, of course, impossible to define or explain the creative experience. Its results may be examined; the journey from idea to finished creation may be described; but the genesis of artistic ideas is not really known by the artists themselves. Jung notes that "any reaction to stimulus may be causally explained; but the creative act, which is the absolute antithesis of mere reaction, will forever elude the human understanding."[1] Nevertheless, since performance is a "re-creative" art, it is incumbent on the performer to come to grips with the driving force behind the creative act. And although it is not likely that one person can project

---

[1] C.G. Jung, *Modern Man in Search of a Soul* (New York: Harcourt, Brace and Co., 1933) 177.

Allen Lannom is Director of Choral Activities at the Boston Conservatory. He retired from Boston University in 1982 after serving on the faculty of the School of Music since 1951. In 1952 he was appointed conductor of The Lexington Choral Society—now the Masterworks Chorale—and continues as that organizations's music director.

Lannom, a resident of California for over twenty years, attended Occidental College where he met Howard Swan. With Dr. Swan as his mentor, he became highly involved in the pursuit of choral music, although his major field was Speech-English. Their closest association was as members of an informal group of choral conductors—dubbed the Rumpslumps *("a mess") by a Dutch member—which met one evening a month for three years to share ideas about choral music and its performance.*

himself into another person's psyche, it is possible for the earnest performer to contact and react to the creative intent of the composer. This
is possible—but difficult—even when the composer has been dead for
several generations, for the music written will reveal much of what was
intended, if the performer is open to revelation.

Music is exceptional among the arts. Without the help of an intermediary, musical compositions would be mere markings on paper, totally
unintelligible to all but a few unusual musicians who might conjure up
some semblance of the sounds which those symbols represent. And even
the few who could make some sense of those symbols would be at the
mercy of their wild imaginings, for composers, themselves, admit to
an inability to predict precisely what the sounds will be (in concerted
music) until their works are actually performed. Though the composer
and performer may have never met, though their musical skills and ideas
may be separated by years, decades, or even centuries, the work of
the composer can only be completed by the performer. The completion may be a sympathetic reading of the composer's intent, or it may
be a violation of that intent. In any event, the performer is really more
a co-creator than a re-creator, for the work simply does not exist as
an artistic creation without his involvement. Literature and poetry may
be enhanced by oral reading (performance), but both are primarily
designed to convey meaning directly from the printed page. Drama,
on the other hand, is intended for oral and visual communication, but
it can be understood and appreciated in written form. Music alone
demands sound to give any meaning to the created work. Naturally,
the composer can also be performer—and was until about 1800—but
the roles are different. Ned Rorem reminds us that "composition and
execution, though not musically exclusive, do not go hand in hand."[2]

With this partnership as an imperative, the choral conductor should
make every possible effort to understand the creative experiences of
the composer, to let the tides of the creator invade his own shores. The
conductor who responds to the demands of such a partnership will be
less likely to establish an interpretive kingdom of self, camouflaged as
the domain of Palestrina or Haydn or Mozart. Moreover, an understanding of the nature of the creative experience could possibly challenge
the conductor to demonstrate certain of those qualities in the conducting experience.

And how does an idea take shape? What is the path from the earliest
flicker of inspiration to the final creation of a composition, a poem,
or a sculpture? There is no explanation which is generally acceptable

[2]Ned Rorem, *Music from the Inside Out* (New York: George Braziller, 1967) 89.

to artists, or, for that matter, to persons in professional fields where new ideas are sought (science, medicine, philosophy, psychology, etc.). Paul Hindemith declares, "If we cannot, in the flash of a single moment, see a composition in its absolute entirety, with every pertinent detail in its proper place, we are not genuine creators."[3] The poet Selden Rodman tells of an experience with fellow poet James Agee in which Agee wrote down a poem in a few minutes, because it was already "complete" in his mind.[4] Noam Chomsky, writer in linguistics, philosophy, and psychology, works at the typewriter; his first draft is basically the finished product.[5]

Despite these statements and the popular belief that artists receive inspirations and dash to the studio to realize these inspirations in a white heat of creativity, most creative persons subscribe to other ideas. In a book, *The Creative Experience*, interviews with creative people from many areas are transcribed. Most persons interviewed felt that the "idea" is not discovered in perfect form, but that its hazy outline is given clear shape in the working-out process. Arthur Koestler, Hungarian novelist, claims that he often does not know how his plot will develop. The development is in the writing process.[6] Merce Cunningham, dancer and choreographer, declares that the choreography evolves out of the activity itself, out of the quality of the movement.[7] Raphael Soyer, painter, says that his paintings never come out the way he had hoped they would.[8] Sidney Hook, philosopher, must sit down and write to have the ideas flow.[9] Selden Rodman finds that "the creative experience takes place with the typewriter or the pen . . . [The rest is] a process of registration."[10] Michelangelo made scores of sketches, then ignored them all so that his imagination could synthesize or invent at will.[11]

The problem here is that various creators are discussing different stages of the creative process. When Agee can produce poetry on the spot, he is transferring to paper what has been developed and recorded in his brain over a period of time, whether that period be short or long.

---

[3]Paul Hindemith, *A Composer's World* (Cambridge, MA: Harvard University Press, 1952) 61.
[4]Lawrence Abt and Stanley Rosner, eds., *The Creative Experience* (New York: Grossman Publishers, 1970) 327.
[5]Ibid., 177.
[6]Ibid., 138.
[7]Ibid., 185.
[8]Ibid., 182.
[9]Ibid., 293.
[10]Ibid., 326.
[11]Robert J. Clements, *Michelangelo's Theory of Art* (New York: Gramercy Publishing Co., 1961) 48.

While it is true that Hindemith could visualize an entire score before committing anything to manuscript, he had done a certain amount of ruminating on the material to be used in the finished composition. His own explanation of this places "vision" as imperative; behind vision he places *Einfall,* which he defines:

> Einfall, from the verb einfallen, to drop in, describes beautifully the strange spontaneity that we associate with artistic ideas in general and with musical creation in particular. Something—you know not what— drops in your mind—you know not where—and there it grows—you know not how—into some form—you know not why.[12]

Rather than proliferating the theories relative to idea germination, let us examine aspects of the creative process about which there is considerable agreement, aspects which concern, particularly, that person known to the creator as the executant. Arnold Schoenberg enumerates his thoughts about the creative experience:

> A creator has a vision of something which has not existed before this vision.

> And a creator has the power to bring his vision to life, the power to realize it. . . .

> Alas, human creators, if they be granted a vision, must travel the long path between vision and accomplishment; a hard road where, driven out of Paradise, even geniuses must reap their harvest in the sweat of their brows.

> Alas, it is one thing to envision in a creative instant of inspiration and it is another thing to materialize one's vision by painstakingly converting details until they fuse into a kind of organism.

> And alas, suppose it become an organism, a homunculus or a robot, and possesses some of the spontaneity of a vision; it remains yet another thing to organize this form so that it becomes a comprehensible message "to whom it may concern."[13]

The creative act, then, embraces several elements as it moves from conception to realization. Of greatest significance are:

*Perception   *Limitation

*Technique   *Order

---

[12]Hindemith, 57.
[13]Arnold Schoenberg, *Style and Idea* (New York: Philosophical Library, 1961) 102-3.

PERCEPTION

Artistic perception is much more than a sudden flash of inspiration. It is informed by all the disciplines of the artist's craft, and that which is seemingly intuitive may be the response of that craft to the problem at hand. Michelangelo had to be able to see the statue of David in a rejected piece of marble. The author of a play must perceive the practical elements of staging at about the same time he has a great idea for a drama. A choreographer can only create a dance out of knowledge of how the human body moves. Bach needed to know the possibilities and limitations of a fugue in order to entertain the idea of the opening "Kyrie" of the Mass in B Minor. This knowledge of form, whether intuitive or laboriously achieved through experience, is a necessary part of the germinal idea. The more clearly outlined the idea, the more complete the accompanying concept of form. The hazier the perception, the more "working out" of the form is necessary before that perception can be focused and illuminated. In both conditions there can be great creative energy.

Most creative persons experience the growth of ideas through seeming inactivity on the one hand and concentrated activity on the other. "Daydreaming" is recognized by almost all creators as a part of the process. "Daydreaming and writing are very much connected," declares Isaac Bashevis Singer, Nobel prizewinner.[14]

Sidney Lumet, film director, says that for him, daydreams provide "a real sort of working energy, a very real source of things to delve into, things to [provide] . . . emotional fuel, content fuel and form fuel."[15] Hindemith's *Einfall* represents another example of artistic ideas gathered from purposeless reverie.

There are others for whom working energy is not just the means whereby perceptions are realized, but the means for developing the perceptions themselves. One philosopher tells us, "I find I have to sit down and write in order to have my ideas flow. . . . writing seems to open the sluices of my mind." He further postulates, "It may be that the explicit motor actions stimulate adjacent areas of the brain so that one thing suggests another."[16] In similar fashion, we have seen how Merce Cunningham finds that the creative idea behind a bit of choreography comes from the physical experience of dancing.

So the creative person goes from basic idea to realization of idea,

[14]Abt and Rosner, 225.
[15]Ibid., 152.
[16]Ibid., 293.

only to find that the idea is further developed and clarified as an outgrowth of that realization. Igor Stravinsky compares this with theological reasoning about pure love. "To understand in order to love; to love in order to understand; we are here not going around in a vicious circle; we are rising spirally, providing we have made an initial effort, have even gone through a routine exercise."[17]

The problem of course, is that it is not possible to determine the precise time when perception becomes articulated in any functional way, for individual differences cannot be adequately assessed. Mozart declares in a letter that

> [the composition,] though it be long, stands almost complete and finished in my mind, so that I can survey it, like a fine picture or beautiful statue, at a glance. Nor do I hear in my imagination the parts *successively,* but I hear them, as it were, all at once [*gleich alles zusammen*]. What a delight this is I cannot tell![18]

Could it be that the young genius perceived all the elements of a given work? Did he hear the various tonalities as a single entity? Did this perception come all at once, or was it realized over a period of time? We don't know, but perhaps we can find a clue in turning to a more recent composer. It is reported that Walter Piston said to a friend that he had almost completed a work. When the friend asked if he might hear it, Piston responded, "Oh, no, I haven't yet selected the notes."[19] Perhaps a work is considered complete when the basic material is lodged in the brain in an organized way which is compatible with the driving idea but which is not yet actualized by musical symbols.

The Mozartian or Pistonian approach could not have been Charles Darwin's, for he was no instant perceiver. On the contrary, he was a recorder of fragments of ideas, of passing thoughts, of questions, even of dreams which only later might illuminate or inform a new idea.[20] But then it is possible that scientific revelation may be achieved in this fashion more easily through painstaking detail than musical revelation, where the perception and the realization of that perception are more closely linked because of the demand for a form in which to cast the idea.

Howard Gardner, the current director of Harvard University Project Zero, which since the mid-sixties has dedicated itself to the study of

[17]Igor Stravinsky, *The Poetics of Music* (New York: Vintage Books, 1947) 55.
[18]Brewster Ghiselin, *The Creative Process* (New York: Mentor, 1959) 45.
[19]Howard Gardner, *Art Mind and Brain* (New York: Basic Books, 1982) 360.
[20]Howard Gruber, *Darwin on Man*, 2nd ed. (Chicago: University of Chicago Press, 1981) 121.

creativity, sheds some light on these seeming differences in artistic perceptions. Using the simple analogy of giving a dinner party, he explains that there are many necessary elements to be considered:

> You must think about what food to eat, in what order, how to invite, how much of each dish to prepare, when to cook and serve each, whom to invite, where to seat them, during and after the meal, which individuals are likely to grate on one another, and which should get along, which decorations to display, what to wear, and much more.[21]

Gardner then explains that the host has a general schema of what a party should be. These schemata are sufficiently general and abstract to apply to all kinds of parties. Some "slots" of the schemata are relatively inflexible; other slots are quite flexible. All of the schemata have a sort of family resemblance, and the more experience he has giving parties, the more defined his schemata for future events. Yet with all the planning which is necessary, person "A" may extend the first invitation before most of the details are in place, while person "B" may wait until most, or all, of the details are under control.[22]

Gardner's analogy does help to simplify our concept of the process, but it is not specific enough to be analogous to the process for the composer. When the composer writes, he doesn't just write music; he writes a particular genre or form of music. If the host (of Gardner's analogy) is presiding at a testimonial dinner, or entertaining friends at a dinner party in a restaurant, or offering the symbolic "seder" meal to his guests, the schemata will be more precise from the outset, for the form becomes an integral part of the idea. For the composer, the revelation of idea is always accompanied by some concept of form which can transport the idea.

What does this mean for the choral conductor? It means first and foremost that he needs to make contact with the perception which motivated the composer. The psychologist Lev Vygotsky is writing about language, but gives advice applicable to performing musicians: "To understand another's speech, it is not sufficient to understand his words—we must also know his motivation."[23] But how does the performing musician make contact with the perception of the composer? Let us go to another axiom so old that it appears in some form in most civilized areas of the world. "To him who makes no attempt to com-

[21]Gardner, 353.
[22]Ibid., 355.
[23]Lev S. Vygotsky, *Thought and Language* (Cambridge, MA: M.I.T. Press, 1966) 347.

prehend the known will never be revealed the unknown." This is the very basis of what we call the scientific method. These two quotations do not represent disagreement, but rather, two aspects of comprehension.

The revelation of the "Coronation" Mass to Mozart, the complete vision of *When Lilacs Last in the Door-yard Bloom'd* to Hindemith, the heavenly inspiration of *Messiah* for Handel—these cannot be taken in by the conductor in the "twinkling of an eye." The psalmist declares, "Such knowledge is too wonderful for me: it is high, I cannot attain it," and although the psalmist is referring to the omniscience of God, his words are in some measure applicable to what many declare to be God-given inspiration. Since the performer cannot grasp the central imperative of a composition as an immediate and complete idea, he must take the route of the known to the unknown. By understanding such things as melodic units, phrases, tonalities, internal harmonies, and imitation as expressed through observable structures, he may eventually come to a better position from which to approach the perception which motivated the music. A never-ending return to the score—even after years of performing a work—is essential if we are to fulfill our obligation as co-creators. Yesterday's performance exists in memory. Tomorrow's performance exists in imagination.

Apprehending a musical work solely through its many details can be dangerous from an artistic point of view, for the "forest" may be lost in foliage awareness. We must find means to approach the central meaning beyond the details of the musical grammar. One such approach is reflection.

Even as many creators feel the necessity for periods of reflection, inaction, avoidance, or whatever, so the performer needs those times when ideas may drop in like Hindemith's *Einfall*. If a conductor is preparing a Bach "St. Matthew," he should "think" "St. Matthew," not only through organized study and rehearsal, but in unstructured ponderings. Many of us are so busy rehearsing "St. Matthew," reading what others have to say about "St. Matthew," and studying the score of "St. Matthew" that we fail to determine what we feel about "St. Matthew." If I am the person to perform the work, it can be performed by nobody but me. In reality, all the study, the reading, the listening to recordings are but means whereby I can arrive at my concept of the work. No matter how incomplete or inadequate that concept might be, I must accept it with conviction and enthusiasm. That conviction and enthusiasm can come from a more personal relationship with the work, not in any maudlin or sentimental way, but in a way which best makes me more at one with the composer's intent.

There is still another way of understanding more of the composer's perception aside from specific contact with the score. A composer reveals himself through his musical language, his particular manipulation of musical symbols. The more the exposure to that language, the better equipped the performer is to elicit meaning from that language. Listening to Bruckner symphonies may reveal the composer whose Mass in F Minor the conductor is rehearsing. Hearing Brahms's songs can alter the conductor's thinking concerning *A German Requiem.*

The choral conductor has a special problem in apprehending the idea of the composer. Instrumentalists have little choice but to seek the meaning of the music through the music itself, whereas the choral conductor can be easily seduced by text awareness. Those who work with vocal music need to remind themselves that the valid message of music is found solely in the music, and that any extra-musical meaning is assigned to it by extra-musical elements. The composer himself, in choosing a text, is utilizing an extra-musical component, but he compels that component to serve his musical needs. A text so used is no longer the property of the writer but belongs to the composer as a means whereby his expressivity is manifested. The choral conductor needs to realize that any attempt to approach the music via the written language violates the intent of the composer—to comment on the text as he perceives it, and as he perceives it at a given moment and under a given set of circumstances. If any of the factors is altered, the compositional result is altered.

TECHNIQUE

Schoenberg sets forth a second requirement for creative activity: technique. For without the ability to "materialize one's vision," the vision is of little worth. The true creator develops whatever skills are necessary to achieve his purpose. What is difficult for another is second nature to him.[24] In music, more than in any other creative endeavor, the technique must be wedded to the idea. The musical creator is not just manipulating symbols, he is manipulating a highly organized symbol system, and that system must be mastered to a certain degree before any real musical communication can be achieved. Ned Rorem writes that "what we call a 'primitive' in painting (one without formal experience) is unimaginable in musical composition."[25] The quality of the composer's intent and the quality of his talent should be at com-

[24]Gruber, 124.
[25]Rorem, 20.

parable levels for the best results, but the musical world is heavily populated by those who are deficient in one area or the other.

The technique is in itself enjoyable although it should not be an end in itself. Gardner compares the creative person to a juggler who is able to keep a number of objects under control at a particular moment and who actually derives pleasure from his ability to juggle, though the ultimate goal of creating remains regnant.[26] W.H. Auden makes a similar point but with a different analogy:

> Ask any talented surgeon why he is a surgeon, and, if he is an honest man, he will not say: "Because I want to benefit suffering humanity"; he will say: "What a silly question. Because I love operating, of course." It is perfectly possible to imagine a surgeon who hated human beings at the same time he saved their lives, because of the pleasure he took in exercising his gift.[27]

So the technique allows the creative person to "materialize his vision." But if the technique calls attention to itself, it then diverts attention from the artist's perception. Technique should not only convey the artist's intent, it should do so without seeking the spotlight and without revealing too much of the artist who wields the technique. Here we have something impossible to analyze—difficult even to discuss. A great musical work, no matter how deeply emotional, has a certain objectivity about it. Rodman calls it "nobility" and cites Beethoven as an example.[28] Schubert referred to Beethoven as having "superb coolness under the fire of creative ecstasy."[29] And the painter, Soyer, complains that his work reveals himself too much, and that he regards as a weakness. He feels that the great painters had a certain aloofness (Velasquez, Degas, Vermeer, Cezanne). One does not know how the artist felt about the people he portrayed. They are very beautiful, but very abstract in a sense. This he calls "artistic strength."[30] So the composer must utilize his compositional technique to express himself and his artistic perception. He prays that the technique will reveal the message he has in mind, but that the finished work will not be too self-revelatory. But once the composition is finished, his work as a creator is over—

[26]Gardner, 355.
[27]Rudolph Anheim, Karl Shapiro, W.H. Auden, and D.A. Stauffer, *Poets at Work* (New York: Harcourt Brace and Co., 1948) 168.
[28]Abt and Rosner, 327.
[29]Aaron Copland, *Music and Imagination* (Cambridge, MA: Harvard University Press, 1961) 46.
[30]Abt and Rosner, 282.

even if he is to perform his own composition—for his role as performer
will be distinct from his role as composer. Some composers are able
executants, but the thrust of performance differs from that of composition. Thus the composer, having finished his task, must hand over his
new creation to another person and agonizingly await the outcome.

The choral conductor should respond to the importance of technique
in several ways. First,he should comprehend, at a reasonably high level,
the technique of the composer. Second, he should make his own technique serve the creative intent of the composer. Third, he should let
his technique "illuminate" the work—not simply give it exposition.

Score study is an imperative for the conductor who is interested in
going beyond routine performance. Of course any performer can simply
try to duplicate the qualities in a recorded performance of a given work.
Tempos and dynamics can be copied and articulations can be imitated.
But the conductor who depends solely on slavish imitation of another
person's performance cannot be regarded as a co-creator in the performance process. If a conductor is to conduct Bach, he should endeavor
to apprehend Bach's melodies, counterpoint, and tonal architecture. In
this endeavor the use of recordings may have a rightful place, but the
true contact with the composer's methods can only come through the
score, for it contains the specific evidence of the composer's artistic
intent. This score reveals the artist's manipulation of the symbol system
which he is using. Not so long ago a composer of considerable repute
was present for an important rehearsal of a work which was to be
premiered within a few days. During a rehearsal intermission the composer and conductor conferred about a portion of the work just attempted. The two agreed on certain things which needed attention. As the
musicians reassembled and the conductor stood before them, he turned
to the composer and asked, "where should be we begin?" the composer replied, "start at the double fugue." The conductor hesitated for
a second, then asked, blithely, "where is that?" Is it surprising that
composers are wary of conductors?

The executant must exploit his own technique if he is to be a co-creator.
The ability to communicate by gesture and by the spoken word, the
ability to evoke the proper sounds from instrumentalists and singers,
the ability to orchestrate the proper dynamics in a given piece, the ability
to separate climax from subclimax, etc., etc.—all these are requisites
to worthy performance. The performer, only, can give life to a musical
composition, and he determines the *quality* of life in that composition
by the discipline of his talents in that work's projection.

If the conductor's technique is self serving, then he is so busy projecting himself that he cannot adequately present the true message of the composition. He is so concerned about his own responses to the music that he may misdirect the responses of his audience.

But is there no room for the conductor's particular response to a given work of music? Certainly! The composer can only communicate through symbols (notation) and words (either of interpretive instruction or of textual content). The performer must make sonorous sense of all this, usually without any direct help from the composer. Each time a conductor performs a work there will be differences from other times when he has performed the same work, even if the performances are separated only by a few hours. Each performance might represent a valid presentation of the composer's perception, though there might be variations with respect to tempi, dynamics, etc. This is true, also, when composers conduct performances of their own works. Now the conductor is no longer a student. His score study must be put aside, perhaps into his subconscious, while he projects, to the best of his ability, the many meanings in the music. To this task he must give himself totally and concentratedly; there should be no room for analysis and objectivity at the performing moment; there should be only earnest conveyance of the musical message to the sensibilities of the listeners. Study preceded the performance; it may be resumed after the performance. But it should not be an observable part of the presentation itself. Copland compares musical performance with drama and states that the performer is not just an actor—he is an actor who must play all the parts. He further tells us that ''the sensible advice one can give the performing artist is to ask that a happy balance be found to slavish adherence to inadequate signs and a too liberal straying from the clear intention of the composer.'' He concludes, ''a live performance should be just that—live to all the incidents that happen along the way, colored by the subtle nuances of momentary emotion, inspired by the sudden insights of public communication.''[31]

Our favorite recordings become dull for us after extended listening, for we have memorized all the sounds and have registered all the climaxes on our sensual Richter scale. The fun is gone; anticipation has deserted us. A live performance provides excitement, for we are dealing with first performances—even in well-known works. We are experiencing the unanticipated within the framework of that which can be predicted. In live performance there is always a risk—will the work make good sense to the listener or will it not? Rorem says of the performing situation that ''the possibility of a ceremony's getting out of hand (as at a

[31]Copland, 48-52.

bullfight) spellbinds the spectators. They may be acquainted with the ritual's climax, but only the virtuoso can lead them to it, for he knows how to get there, and he may never arrive."[32]

The conductor then, should try his best to comprehend the message which the composer communicates through his symbols. He then should develop his own musical techniques to the level where he is capable of being co-creator. Finally, he must present with conviction and skill the music as he perceives it, recognizing that he might perceive it differently with additional experience with a given composition or with music in general.

LIMITATION

Absolute freedom is no freedom at all. Fear and impotence are often the result of limitless choices. Children will repeatedly test parents in order to secure a definition of boundaries for their behavior. The creative artist, as well, must have delimitations before he can focus on the actual creation.

In poetry, rhyming patterns, meters, verse length, and stanza forms are all elements which prescribe and proscribe the poet's means of expression. "Free verse," although used well by the talented, is more often an escape for the would-be poet who is deficient in some of the poetic disciplines. Auden explains,

> The poet who writes "free" verse is like Robinson Crusoe on a desert island: he must do all his cooking, laundry, darning, etc., for himself. In a few exceptional cases this manly independence produces something original and impressive, but as a rule the result is squalor—empty bottles on the unswept floor and dirty sheets on the unmade bed.[33]

In the musical world, it is Stravinsky who makes the point clear:

> The Creator's function is to sift the elements he receives from her [imagination], for human activity must impose limits on itself. The more art is controlled, limited, worked over, the more it is free. . . . in art as in everything else one can build only upon a resisting foundation: whatever constantly gives way to pressure, constantly renders movement impossible. . . . My freedom thus consists in my moving about within the narrow frame that I assigned myself for each of my undertakings.[34]

[32]Rorem, 65.
[33]Arnheim et al., 172-73.
[34]Stravinsky, 63-65.

There are, in reality, three kinds of limitation which operate in the control—and freedom of the artist. These are (1) the boundaries imposed upon him by the nature of his material, (2) the forces outside the realm of the creative act, and (3) the boundaries which are self imposed and relate to the quality of artistic perception.

The first of these limitations the artist accepts almost automatically. A writer is bound by the limits of the language in which he writes; a sculptor cannot expect granite to yield to the same demands which can be made of marble; a western-civilization composer must content himself with the twelve notes of the chromatic scale. A composer who writes to a text must be willing to accede to some demands of word inflection and certain elements of meter. If he writes to a prescribed set of words, as in the case of a Mass, he is further bound by the form which binds these words together. Of course, a creative artist may refuse to work with a particular material, but once he has accepted his material, he has established certain general boundaries which he may shoulder around a bit by the weight and force of his genius, but which are, at best, only slightly manipulable.

Other boundaries are less definitive and less restrictive for the talented creator, for by his genius he may encircle them with his own boundaries. Since Haydn wrote for the court, he was forced to accept certain limitations for the music he offered to the court. Bach was a church musician and accepted, joyfully, this limiting factor. A composer who provides music for motion pictures may make his creative efforts more than routine satisfaction of demands, but he is still bound by limitations which deny him the right to make his music primary.

Any specific commission becomes a boundary for the artist. A composer who agrees to write a fanfare cannot expect to exploit his ability in scoring for strings. Furthermore, specific commissions usually prescribe the musical medium—string quartet, chorus, cantata for chorus and orchestra, vocal solo, and so forth. A decision must always be made as to what the specific composition will be, but in the case of a commission, the composer is relieved of this responsibility. And we must remember that the artist is not really free to create until certain of these limits are established. Once, two composers simultaneously received almost identical commissions. Both were to write cantatas for chorus and orchestra, the only difference being that in one case a text was specified, and in the other the text was left to the choice of the composer. The composer with the specified text was almost finished with his work before the other had put down a single note. The latter could do nothing until he had established his boundaries.

By far, the most important limitations are those imposed by the artist himself. It was G.K. Chesterton who said, "Art is limitation; the essence of every picture is the frame."[35] And, though the gifted painter may make a canvas include elements of a 360-degree vision, he must accept the limitations of the frame which dictates the outer edges of possibility. The creative idea, itself, suggests and even demands certain limits. A Mass written in four parts and requiring almost two and a half hours to present, most certainly is the result of a quite different musical vision from that which inspires a twenty-five-minute *Missa brevis*. In each case the composer must choose his material according to the nature of his perception. Yet a quantitative evaluation of the finished creation will not suffice to establish its artistic value, that value being more accurately ascertained by the congruence of the creative idea and its realization. Raphael's overwhelming "School of Athens," occupying an entire wall in the Vatican Museum and containing dozens of magnificently executed figures, is, assuredly, one of the finest artistic achievements of all time; but can it be said that his "Descent from the Cross," painted on a bit of canvas measuring no more than about two square feet, is less of an artistic achievement? Not at all. In each case the artist worked creatively within the limits of each dimension and within the limits of his own creative concept.

Once the creative artist has accepted whatever limitations have been imposed on him by himself or by outside forces, he must then accept the responsibility of managing his own technique so that the creative concept, in whatever limitation, is given life. For the composer this means decisions which relate to the musical character of the composition—homophonic or polyphonic, major or minor, fast or slow, few or many performers, and a host of other matters which will determine how accurately he can convey that which he has set out to convey.

For the conductor this means the comprehension of the boundaries of a particular composition and the acceptance of the responsibility for establishing certain limits of his own to insure faithful performance. The St. Matthew Passion, performed by a chorus of one thousand and accompanied by an orchestra of one hundred, can scarcely do justice to the contrapuntal writing of Bach, and a chorus of twenty and orchestra of thirty cannot be expected to give a reasonable rendition of the Beethoven Ninth Symphony. And, although duplication of original performing conditions may be undesirable as well as impossible, faithfulness to the concept and general style should be a prime imperative for all performers.

[35] G.K. Chesterton, *Orthodoxy* (New York: Dodd, Mead & Co., 1908) 71.

Both the quantity and quality of sound must be adjusted to the limits of the musical composition. Thus, the sound which is desirable for the conclusion of the sixth movement of the Brahms *German Requiem* could not adequately represent the artistic point of view of Palestrina, even in his most exalted creative moments. The conductor must direct all his skills in the field of sound toward the achievement of sound which serves particular purposes rather than toward the exploitation of sound for the sake of sound itself.

The rehearsal, also, must be limited for achievement of desired musical goals. Every choral rehearsal cannot cover all of the musical material for a given concert. Choices must be made and priorities established for each rehearsal situation. This is particularly true for choral-orchestral rehearsals where time is limited. Attempts to solve all orchestral problems within the assigned time limit will probably result in confusion and frustration. The conductor needs to decide what problems can be anticipated and dealt with by (1) careful marking of parts and (2) consultation in advance with the concertmaster or principal players. Then at the full rehearsal the conductor would be well advised to adopt the attitude expressed first by Reinhold Niebuhr in 1934 and later given universal utterance. "O God, give us serenity to accept what cannot be changed, courage to change what should be changed, and wisdom to distinguish one from the other." Without this attitude the conductor is Quixote jousting with a windmill.

ORDER

Karl Shapiro, the poet, states that "genius in art is probably only the intuitive knowledge of form."[36] There are some who might dispute this axiom, but there is none who would deny the essential quality of order in any work of art. Order is necessary for comprehensibility, as Schoenberg pointed out in the passage quoted earlier in this chapter. The creative artist must discipline his work in terms of structure, balance, continuity, and dramatic logic in order to direct the listener toward his perception. A painter blocks out his canvas to insure an internal order in the finished picture. The architecture of Bach's music has as major a share in its true artistry as does the melody. In a great work of art, form does not exist for the sake of form alone, but as a means to organize material for a more complete communication of that which is perceived in the mind of the artist. The blueprint is a necessary part of the architect's equipment. It becomes the guiding force which governs the

[36]Abt and Rosner, 120.

realization of his intent. In music, scales and harmonies are elements of order which govern the outward result while forming the inward structure. In a universe which operates in orderliness, it is only natural that man's answer to those same great forces should reflect a quality of order.

Another way of approaching this same idea is this: order is a state of health. The human body demonstrates this, for when a person is ill, he is actually "out of order," and all the forces of his being are working overtime to restore the body to orderly behavior. And when the body functions, an arm can never succeed in being a leg but must content itself with doing those things expected of arms. In musical composition, as well, each part must exercise its function, not to its own glory, but to serve the entire artistic being, and the task of the conductor is to preserve or restore that order.

A deep understanding of the internal organization of a musical creation is often difficult to come by, but is important for any performer to have and is essential for the conductor to achieve as he guides the skills of co-performers toward illumination of the musical vision of the composer.

_____

It is difficult and dangerous to draw too many or too specific conclusions in this matter. There are a few observations which seem to have justification. One is that the performer needs to "understand" the nature of the creative experience even more than does the composer; the composer's world is totally creative, whereas the performer's is re-creative, co-creative, and creative with many journeys from one area to another. The better the performer understands these areas of his world, the freer he should be to give vitality and validity to his performances.

A second justifiable observation (to me, at least) is that among performers, the job of the choral conductor is probably the most demanding, because not only is music's message multiple, but so, too, is the textual message, and the possibility of being misled is ever present. Furthermore, the choral conductor must communicate his concepts to singers who must balance their own interpretations with his. Only with strong conviction and persuasion (perhaps unspoken) can the conductor effect convincing and moving performances.

A third observation is that the conductor should enthusiastically embrace the creative possibilities inherent in each new performance (and all performances are new!), so long as he respects the integrity of the composer's message. The message transmitted by the composer's symbols may be apprehended variously, but there are always parameters which should not be trespassed, lest the message become solely that of the performer.

Composer Robert Starer admits that "often, performers have shown me things about my own music that I didn't even know. And that's a wonderful experience." But he also remarks that, "sometimes I've gone to concerts and I can almost not recognize my own music. That I don't particularly like."[37]

Intensive study can best support the composer's basic intent, but the variables of that intent become the province of the performer. W.B. Yeats warns his fellow poets against narrow interpretation of their own poems. "If a poet interprets a poem of his own he limits its suggestibility."[38] So is it also with composers.

Thus, the choral conductor needs to say to himself: "I have honestly studied this music and have tried to understand it in its historical, intellectual, and emotional contexts. I recognize that I cannot totally comprehend what the composer has expressed through his symbols of musical notation. Nevertheless, with what knowledge and sensitivity I currently possess, I will put aside analysis and intellectual concerns and will give total attention to the musical realization of the work as I perceive it. I will use all of the skills available to me through my training and will explore all valid emotional possibilities to the end that I may illuminate this message which, without me and my co-performers, would remain shrouded in darkness."

If we as choral conductors can subscribe to this, then we should have no fear of the artistic outcome, for it will be honest, at least. Beyond that, we are limited by the scope and intensity of our talent. And, in any case, we can and should return again and again to the score and to the development of the talents essential for its ever-new communication.

[37]Michael Appell, "This Way out in Case of Brahms," *Boston Today*, March 1978: 15.
[38]Allen Wade, ed., *W.B. Yeats Letters* (New York: MacMillan, 1955) 812.

Lloyd Pfautsch

The Art and Craft of
Choral Arranging

How do choral conductors select repertoire for choral ensembles to perform? Some might respond to this question by saying facetiously, "with difficulty!" When one considers the great quantity of publications available, such an answer is understandable. No one can possibly review all that has been published in the past for choral ensembles or even keep up with repertoire currently being published. The volume of publications found in files and on shelves in any one music store, or in the personal library of many choral conductors, can be overwhelming. However, the selection process is an ongoing task that all choral conductors must accept, though the extent of involvement varies greatly.

Among the publications available, the abundance of choral arrangements seems to proliferate each year. The popular appeal of an original SATB arrangement or composition leads to SA, SSA, SSAA, SAB, TB, TBB, and TTBB arrangements for obvious reasons. Some

Lloyd Pfautsch has been Professor of Sacred Music and Director of Choral Activities at the Meadows School of the Arts at Southern Methodist University in Dallas, Texas, since 1958. He is also conductor of the Dallas Civic Chorus, which he organized in 1960. Known to the American choral community in large part from his over 200 published arrangements for voices, Dr. Pfautsch has received ASCAP awards yearly since 1961.

A native of Washington, Missouri, Dr. Pfautsch holds Master of Divinity and Master of Sacred Music degrees from Union Theological Seminary. His alma mater, Elmhurst College of Elmhurst, Illinois, honored him with the honorary degree of Doctor of Music in 1959 and an Alumni Merit Award in 1971. Dr. Pfautsch was awarded the honorary degree Doctor of Humane Letters by Illinois Wesleyan University in 1978 and by West Virginia Wesleyan College in 1985.

years ago, there was a dearth of compositions for women's and men's choruses. In an attempt to provide repertoire for these ensembles, many compositions for mixed chorus were arranged for women's and men's voices. Many catalogs still retain these arrangements although, in the past thirty years, most publishers have added music written (in the past and present) for women's and men's choruses. In the same catalogs are arrangements of folksongs, folkhymns, popular songs, show tunes, spirituals, hymn tunes, opera choruses, etc.

The variety and volume of published choral arrangements result from the creative work of musicians who employ both art and craft. Dictionaries differ when defining ''art''and ''craft,''but for this monograph the terms will be used to signify the following: art involves creativeness, and to be distinctive requires creativeness at its highest level; craft involves ingenuity or a special skill and is often distinguished from art in that it involves less skill and creative thought.

Choral arranging, as an art and craft, is often considered a relatively recent contribution to choral music, but vocal works were being written in the form of arrangements as early as the fourteenth century. The early motets, parody Masses or cantus firmus Masses, while considered compositions, were based on borrowed musical material and thus also involved arranging. Adrian Willaert (c.1490-1562) and Orlando di Lasso (1532-1594) wrote chansons that were choral arrangements of a monophonic model, *Dessus le marché d'Arras*. In his chorale cantata *Christ lag in Todesbanden*, Bach arranged a hymn tune for choir with accompaniment as a hermaneutic treatment of the chorale text in the musical arrangement. Franz Schubert had to arrange his *Ständchen* for women's voices when he discovered that the friends who had asked him to set the Grillparzer poem had not expected a setting for male chorus. We are indebted to Johannes Brahms for his superb arrangements of many folksongs for mixed voices as well as other arrangements for solo voice with ingenious piano accompaniments. William Cummings, organist at England's Waltham Abbey, arranged the beloved music for *Hark, the Herald Angels Sing* from Felix Mendelssohn's *Festgesang*, a work celebrating the invention of the printing press by Gutenberg. The original *Vaterland in deinen Grauen* was for male chorus. A more recent example of arranging would be William Schuman's *Prelude for Voices*, a mixed-chorus arrangement of the original *Prelude for Women's Voices*. Kodály, Bartók, Vaughan Williams and Britten have also added sensitive arrangements of folksongs to the choral repertoire. Many other names could be added, attesting to the involvement of composers in choral arranging.

Many other musicians who would not consider themselves composers (in that composition is neither their major nor sole professional commitment) have contributed a wealth of excellent choral arrangements to the available repertoire. There is great diversity of style, facility, and purpose. Many of these arrangements might be considered works of art because of the high level of creativity manifested in them. Others might be appraised as well crafted. When choral conductors consider these published arrangements, they must make qualitative judgements in which art and craft are determining factors.

What does the art and craft of choral arranging involve beyond what has been suggested in the definitions given earlier? It is obvious that these definitions imply varying degrees of competency. Having appraised countless published arrangements in addition to many submitted in choral arranging classes, I have found it obvious that there are musicians who arrange with great ease and ingenuity, and there are musicians who arrange with great effort and patient reworking. Qualitative judgement distinguishes art from craft in both groups. Ease and ingenuity do not necessarily produce quality, just as great effort and patient reworking do not suggest mediocrity or inadequacy. Each group is capable of producing arrangements that are excellent or trite.

In making choices, a choral conductor must determine if the arranger understands the limitations and potential of choral ensembles. Does the arrangement indicate an awareness of age, vocal development, range extremes, tessitura, balance of parts, rhythmic interest, chord structure, verbal and melodic nuances, syllabic accents, and the relations of pitch to vowel production? Does the arranger show an understanding of the unique sounds produced by voices in mixed, women's, men's, children's, middle school, high school, church, university, and professional ensembles?

Some arrangements have been made for specific groups such as the Robert Shaw Chorale, the Roger Wagner Chorale, or the King's Singers. Not only are these arrangements for professional singers but they are also often intended specifically for recordings. When other choral groups prepare these arrangements for performance, they encounter problems that engineers have overcome in the recording, such as balance between a soloist and the full chorus singing forte.

Not all arrangers are equally successful when arranging for different ensembles. In the past few years, many publishers have released arrangements for middle school choirs which often involve more craft than art. In my choral arranging classes, arrangements for men's voices have been submitted that sound better when sung an octave higher. In other words, the arrangers unintentionally wrote for women's voices. The use of sixth chords in a very low range indicated that the arranger had not learned to hear or write for men's voices. The opposite often occurs when arrangements for women's voices are submitted with voicings that sound better with men's voices. Frequently men have difficulty arranging for women and women for men. They are generally more familiar with the sounds of their own voices and ensembles. Published arrangements often contain the same mistakes. Choral conductors should use their eyes and ears when selecting repertoire!

Use of the eyes should be of primary importance in appraising arrangements. The considerations listed above should be seen and, ideally, heard internally. Not every choral conductor is able to do this. Many play the parts on a piano and rely on their ears. Unfortunately, what might sound pleasing and acceptable on the piano will not necessarily be pleasing and acceptable chorally. When playing the parts on a piano, a choral conductor should be hearing choral sounds internally and not just the external keyboard sounds. This ability can and should be developed by all choral conductors *and* arrangers!

It is essential that any choral arrangement show respect for the original musical material, whether it is in public domain or copyrighted. (Publication of an arrangement of copyrighted material requires obtaining permission from the owner of the copyright.) The performers and audience should have little difficulty hearing what has been arranged, especially at the beginning of the arrangement. This is particularly essential if the original musical material is unfamiliar! The choice of key or mode should be consistent with the original, and all variations should be carefully prepared so that the sequence is subtle and not anticipated.

Many choral arrangements are self-conscious in that they call attention to the arrangement itself and its cleverness. Here craft is too obvious and art suffers. Other arrangements contain repeated and predictable key changes that negate what positive attributes the arrangements might have. One of the most challenging disciplines in choral arranging is to remain in the same tonality and rely on imaginative variety in rhythm, harmony, textures, voicing, etc.

It is expected that an arranger will develop or expand upon the original thematic material, especially in relation to the strophic sequence of the text, regardless of its origin. Each part should have an interesting line. In too many arrangements the altos and tenors have parts that are neither challenging nor satisfying. Frequently, the enjoyment of singing the part with the melodic line is contrasted with the drudgery of the other parts with limited melodic movement. However, at the other extreme are arrangements in which each part has melodic interest to the extent that the music being arranged is lost in the maze. Canons, fugues, and variations are useful, as are homophonic, polyphonic, polyrhythmic, and polychoral techniques. But discipline must temper creative imagination to raise craft to the level of art.

The use of a solo voice in a choral arrangement can present problems. Members of the choir do not appreciate merely providing background vocal accompaniment in arrangements that feature a solo voice throughout. Balanced participation is generally preferred. Many arrangements require that the soloist use a microphone because of the chord distribution and/or dynamics. It is often difficult to balance a soloist and chorus because of the location of the solo line within the choral texture. Conductors who rely only on recordings to select choral arrangements may overlook these balance problems since they do not show up on recordings. Again, such problems should be seen and heard internally when looking at the arrangement!

Arrangers should learn that what looks correct and satisfactory on the manuscript will not always be correct and satisfying when sung. Frequently arrangers use the wrong voice for a solo. For example, a tenor may be lost within the choral texture while a soprano might emerge with balance and clarity from that same texture. When using an alto or a bass as soloist, the voicing of the chords should surround the solo in a open position and in such a way that the soloist emerges distinctly. Quite often the text dictates that a solo voice be used and how it should be accompanied.

Accompaniments for choral arrangements employ the piano, organ, and a variety of other instruments depending upon style, age, ability of performers, and purpose of arrangement, e.g. festival occasions. There are three basic types of accompaniment: (1) those that are supportive and for the most part duplicate the voice parts; (2) those that are supportive but are also somewhat free in that they sound semi-independent; (3) those that are independent and have an identity of their own while still undergirding the harmonic motion and rhythm of the vocal parts.

In selecting arrangements, choral conductors must consider the ability and experience of accompanists. Choral performances are often disasters because of the technical limitations of the accompanying instrumentalists. Some arrangers expect too much from accompanists while making modest demands on the singers. In arrangements for younger voices, the demands on singers and accompanists should be compatible. When choosing arrangements for performance, the capability of musicians providing accompaniment must be considered at all stages of choral development.

The choral conductor should also ask the following questions. Is the accompaniment consistent with the style of the music being arranged? Does the accompaniment augment the choral sounds? Does the accompaniment or the choral sound have priority in the arrangement? Does the accompaniment add rhythmic, melodic, and contrapuntal interest? Does the accompaniment assist the voices in expanding the content of the text? Are there appropriate contrasts and/or supportive tonal effects in the accompaniment? How much time will be required to rehearse the accompanying instruments? How soon and how often will the non-keyboard accompanists be needed in rehearsal? Has the arranger provided proper balance between the voices and instruments? (This is especially important when brass instruments are involved.) Is the accompaniment appropriate or excessive for the particular ensemble whose repertoire is being selected?

There are three additional aspects of accompaniments that choral conductors must consider when selecting arrangements: introductions, interludes, and endings. Each must fit perfectly into the total structure of the arrangement. The purpose and duration of each must seem natural and not contrived, hackneyed, or predictable. Introductions should do more than merely establish tonality or tempo. They should lead the singers and audience to the choral sounds with stylistic integrity. Interludes should not just be necessary connections between strophes or a means of changing tonality. They should be subtle transitions in the formal sequence of the arrangement. Endings should be neither abrupt nor expansive but always harmonically, rhythmically, and dynamically climactic. Again, both art and craft are involved as arrangers achieve various levels of skillful and creative introductions, interludes, and endings.

In spite of the abundance of arrangements available in catalogs, choral conductors frequently cannot find arrangements that meet the needs or limitations of a particular choral group. Since these needs and limitations are often unusual or perhaps even unique, it is helpful for conductors to develop the ability to write arrangements that fit their choral ensembles. All choral conductors should be encouraged to develop this ability even if they have had no training in choral arranging. In this context, they should not arrange with publication as the goal but rather to serve specific demands, needs, or limitations. If, during the process of rehearsing and performing, the arrangement is refined to a level that suggests practical use by other choral ensembles, the conductor/arranger should submit the arrangement for possible publication. Perhaps another serviceable arrangement will be added to the choral repertoire.

In providing the arrangements for specific performances or choruses, a choral conductor can learn much about the art and craft of choral arranging. Personal skill will be developed and refined. An appreciation of both limitations and potential will be enlarged. Even if the arrangements produced serve only a specific group or occasion and never merit publication, the choral conductor will be able to appraise published arrangements with more sensitive awareness of the art and craft involved in choral arranging.

John M. Cooksey

Understanding Male-Adolescent Voice Maturation: Some Significant Contributions by European and American Researchers

Adolescent-male voice maturation has presented researchers and music educators with some interesting and perplexing questions over the years. In fact, the voice-change phenomenon has been studied for many years, both in Europe and America. The Greeks and Romans were fascinated with the unusual, youthful quality of the unchanged male voice and sought ways to preserve it. Weiss (1950) reports that castration was used as early as 2000 B.C., reaching its apex in Italy by the eighteenth century.[1] In the latter part of the nineteenth century, a controversy arose between Manuel Garcia, an Italian singing teacher, and Sir Morell MacKenzie, a well-known English laryngologist, on whether or not the pubescent voice should be exercised.[2] Garcia proposed that the voice

---

[1] D.A. Weiss, ''The Pubertal Change of the Human Voice,'' *Folia Phoniatrica* 2 (3) (1950) 125-59.
[2] Ibid., 126-29.

Dr. Cooksey is Professor of Music and Director of Choral Activities at the University of Utah, Salt Lake City. He is one of the nation's leading authorities on adolescent voice maturaton and has received numerous grants and published several articles on the subject.

As an active member of ACDA, Dr. Cooksey has served as National Chairman of the Committee on Children's and Boys' Choirs and as President of the Tennessee ACDA. Before coming to Utah, Cooksey was Coordinator of Choral-Music Activities at Memphis State University. Under his direction, the University Singers performed at state and regional MENC and ACDA Conventions and represented the United States at the Hellbrunn International Music Festival, Salzburg, Austria in 1984. He also taught at California State University, Fullerton and in the secondary schools of Tampa, Florida.

should be rested during its time of change, and MacKenzie took the opposite view. Garcia also initiated the traditional "voice-break" theory, which influenced many choirmasters throughout Europe. Members of such famous groups as the Vienna Boy's Choir were dropped when their voices began to change. In general, no encouragement was given for further vocal training during puberty. In the 1930s attitudes began to change in England. Dr. April Winn, H.M. Staff Inspector of Music for the Public Schools of England, began to promote a view that music publishers should write music to fit the limits of the male changing voice. In support of this position, Duncan McKenzie (1956), an English authority on youth choirs, introduced his "alto-tenor" plan—a new theory for developing and training the male adolescent voice during puberty.[3]

In America, the problems associated with the male changing voice came into focus when the junior high school came into existence during the early 1900s. The question was not whether the young adolescent should sing during puberty, but rather how the voice should be classified and trained during that time. Hollis Dan (1918), and W.L. Tomkins (1914) introduced music for the changing voice.[4] In the 1930s and 1940s Genevieve Rorke (1939) and Mae Nightingale (1939) recognized some the problems associated with the changing voice—its breaks, limited range, etc.—and attempted to write music to meet the unique vocal capabilities of the adolescent male.[5] In the 1950s and 1960s Cooper (1965) and Swanson (1959) developed integrated theories and methodologies for the changing male voice.[6] Their views were very different and, as a result, much discussion and some confusion arose among many educators about the entire phenomenon. Following a series of heated debates and further investigation on the part of voice scientists, some key issues were delineated:

(1)   Is the rate of voice change erratic and fast, or slow and gradual?

(2)   What are the ranges and tessituras of the voice as it progresses through its stages of maturation?

(3)   What are the stages of voice maturation? How can they be described?

[3]Duncan McKenzie, *Training the Boy's Changing Voice* (London: Bradford and Dickens, Drayton House, 1956).
[4]Ibid., 8.
[5]G.A. Rorke, *Choral Teaching at the Junior High School Level* (Chicago: Hall and McCreary Co., 1947). Mae Nightingale, *Troubadours: A Collection of Four-Part Choruses* (New York: Carl Fischer, Inc., 1939).
[6]I. Cooper and K. Kuersteiner, *Teaching Junior High Music* (Boston: Allyn and Bacon, 1965).

(4)   Is there a predictable pattern to the rate, scope, and sequence of voice maturation?

(5)   Does the boy's voice "break" during adolescence?

(6)   How does one classify a voice during maturation? What criteria should be used?

(7)   How does voice training affect the outcome of voice classification? Does more training, for example, in high-register singing produce more tenors? Does training help the voice to make register transitions more smoothly?

(8)   How should one use the falsetto register during maturation? Is it healthy to develop techniques for range extension using this register?

(9)   Is there a "blank" spot in the voice when it first changes?

(10)   How should one regard the quality of the sound while it is maturing? Is the quality naturally thin and ugly?

(11)   Given the fact that male voices are in various stages of change within any given grade level during the junior high years, is unison singing possible—or advisable?

(12)   Should singing be allowed at all during the most crucial period of voice change?

(13)   Is there such a thing as a mature bass or tenor during adolescence?

(14)   Can the speaking voice be used as a valid criterion in understanding voice maturation?

(15)   How does one determine the onset of voice change? What criteria should be used?

(16)   Does singing have a harmful effect on the larynx as it grows? How stressful is the activity of singing during this time?

(17)   Can vocal dysphonias be expected to appear within and across individual voice-change stages?

(18)   Is vocal abuse more likely to occur in the voice because of rapid muscular development and cartilage growth in the larynx?

Research studies by Naidr, Zboril, and Sevcik (1965), Frank and Sparber (1970a, b), and Cooksey, Beckett, and Wiseman (1981) have contributed significant information concerning the issues listed above.[7]

THE NAIDR, ZBORIL, AND SEVCIK STUDY

In the early 1960s, Czechoslovakian Drs. Naidr, Zboril, and Sevcik, conducted an important longitudinal study of male adolescent voice maturation. They investigated the onset and rate of pubertal voice changes in 100 boys, all of whom were students at a boarding school. Testing was begun when the boys were all eleven years of age, and continued at regular four-month intervals until they were sixteen. Changes in the singing and speaking voice were correlated with the development of the primary and secondary sexual characteristics, and concomitant anatomical developments in the larynx, body height, and weight were measured. The researchers found that voice maturation occurs in three easily defined stages, with the maximum number of changes occurring during the ages of thirteen, fourteen, and fifteen. On the average the maturation process in the singing and speaking voice lasted for thirteen months, beginning at age thirteen in the majority of cases, reaching a high point at fourteen, and tapering off thereafter. Age was, however, an unreliable indicator, since individuals began and progressed through the three stages at different rates. For example, while most boys began mutation (stage 1) at thirteen, many began stage 1 at fourteen, and a few at fifteen! The researchers also found that the greatest amount of vocal, sexual, and bodily growth occurs on the average seven months between the beginning of stage 1 and the high point of maturation, stage 2. Overall, the growth and development of the singing voice continues for several years after its initial stabilization at stage 3.

Figures 1 and 2 give a visual representation of the premutational and mutational singing ranges found by Naidr et. al., according to developmental phases and age groups respectively:

---

[7]J. Naidr, M. Zboril, and K. Sevcik, "Die pubertalen Veränderungen der Stimme bei Jungen im Verlauf von 5 Jahren" (Pubertal voice changes in boys over a period of 5 years). *Folia Phoniatrica* 17 (1965) 1-18. F. Frank and M. Sparber, "Stimmumfänge bei Kindern aus neuer Sicht" (Vocal ranges in children from a new perspective). *Folia Phoniatrica* 22 (1970) 397-402. J.M. Cooksey, R.L. Beckett, and R. Wiseman, "A Longitudinal Investigation of Selected Vocal, Physiological, and Acoustical Factors Associated with Voice Maturation in the Junior High School Male Adolescent." Report for the National ACDA Convention, New Orleans, Louisiana, March, 1981; update to same, Southern Division MENC Convention, Louisville, Kentucky, Feb., 1983; Kentucky state music-education reports, 1982.

Figure 1. Average Range of the Singing Voice during the Mutation Stages

Before Mutation   Beg. Mutation (I)   Highpoint (II)   End of Mutation (III)
              Most rapid, dramatic (7 mos.) Tapering pd. (6 mos.)

Figure 2. Average Range of the Singing Voice According to Age Groups

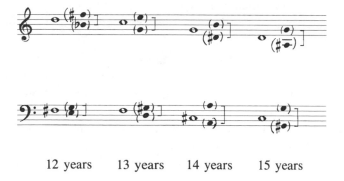

12 years   13 years   14 years   15 years

There are small differences in ranges between the two figures; however, Figure 2 (age groups) shows wider pitch deviation for extreme upper and lower range limits than Figure 1 (mutation stages). This indicates that there are wider individual disparities in range if only age is used as the criterion. The pubertal mutation stages (1-3) show less deviation in range extremes; hence, they would be a more valid indicator of stabilized, sequential growth patterns in voice development. One should also notice that the greatest range of deviation from mean tone occurs in the upper range-limit extremes in all stages (both figures). The lower range-limit deviations are much smaller, which indicates much more stability in lower range development throughout the period of voice maturation. It seems that lower range limits increase with much less individual variation during puberty. One should also note that in the latter stages the lower border of the singing range descends in ever-increasing intervals, while the upper limits descend in decreasing intervals; thus, the activity of the mutation process shifts somewhat between these areas of the singing voice during puberty. Finally, there seems to be more stability and less individual variation during the tapering period of voice change.

The investigation of the larynx was conducted both externally and with indirect laryngoscopy, and three different types of measurements were taken. The first symptom of the onset of mutational changes was growth in the overall height of the larynx. The thyroid cartilage became visible in 40% of the cases by stage 2. The vocal cords maintained a moderate length until the transition period between stages 2 and 3, when there was maximal growth and extension. All told, the most significant increases in larynx development took place between the ages of thirteen and fourteen, but growth continued well beyond this time.

Height and weight measurements were taken only according to age; however, some statistics were derived according to the voice-change stages. In general, these measures showed a growth trend throughout the period of change.

In summary, Naidr et al. established that the principal voice changes occur in the first half of the pubertal growth period, when the increase in height is the greatest, but is somewhat in advance of the increase in the size of the larynx. Voice changes first become evident by the lowering of the upper limit of the singing-voice range, then as a narrowing of the voice range, and finally as renewed extension. Maximum weight increase begins after the height spurt and corresponds most closely to stages 2 and 3. In stage 3 (fourteen-fifteen years of age), there are continued increases in weight, but height increases generally taper quite dramatically. The complete development of the voice could be described in the following way:

I.	Boy's voice, prepubescence;
II.	Begin mutation (stage 1), pubescence: twelve-thirteen years of age;
III.	High point of mutation (stage 2), pubescence: thirteen-fourteen years of age;
IV.	End of mutation (stage 3), pubescence: fourteen-fifteen years of age;
V.	Development of adult voice, Post-pubescence: sixteen years and older.

THE FRANK AND SPARBER STUDIES (1970a, 1970b)

In a period of ten years, Dr. F. Frank (Otolaryngology Clinic, University of Vienna, Austria) and Professor M. Sparber (College of Music, same institution) examined the voices of 5000 children between the ages of seven and fourteen to determine changes in the singing range. They found that the acceleration of pubertal development is paralleled by an acceleration of vocal development, and that three stages of growth in the voice can be identified:

I.   Premutation (corresponding to stages 1 and 2 in the Naidr et al. study),

II.   Mutation (stage 2 of the Naidr et al. study),

III.   Newly changed baritone voice, and

IV.   Post mutation (stage in which the timbre of the voice develops an adult quality).

Frank and Sparber say that only after several years of continued growth during Post mutation can proper voice classification be made and formal training of the singing voice begun.

In another study on voice changes (1970b), Frank and Sparber followed the vocal development of 130 male boarding-school students from about age ten through sixteen. The researchers compared body height, singing ranges, breath capacity, and voice quality (sonagraphic analysis) in the three stages of voice maturation. They found that the changing voice (premutational stage) has three registers (modal, falsetto, and whistle), and that there are distinguishing qualities of sounds for each of the three stages of voice mutation. These results seem to support in part the findings of Naidr et al. and confirm some of the principal ideas of Duncan McKenzie and Irvin Cooper.[8]

THE COOKSEY, BECKETT, AND WISEMAN STUDY (1981)

The issues mentioned at the begining of this paper formed the basis for a comprehensive longitudinal study of the adolescent-male chang-

[8]The late Irvin Cooper, as professor of music education at Florida State University, Tallahassee, Florida, proposed a new system for classifying the adolescent changing voice. He introduced the term "cambiata" to represent voices in the first stage of change. Boys designated as cambiatas could sing in the range between F^3 and C^5. Cooper also identified a second stage of voice change, the "baritone," which included the singing range B-flat^2 - F^4.

Duncan McKenzie labeled the changing voice an "alto-tenor." He designated the singing range F^3 - G^4 to represent this stage. McKenzie, like Cooper, believed that the changing voice could also be identified because of its unique quality of sound.

ing voice. The research of Naidr et al. and Frank and Sparber also provided the researchers with significant findings from which certain
methodological directions could be taken. The primary purpose of this
study was to develop an "index of voice change" (a chart showing the
stages of vocal maturation) and to determine how certain vocal,
physiological, and acoustical factors might define those different voice-
change stages in the adolescent male. The research project was begun
in October, 1977 and completed in June, 1980. With the cooperation
of the Orange Unified School District, Orange County, California,
eighty-six seventh-grade boys from two junior high schools were chosen
to participate. Forty-one of the sample were enrolled in a choir, while
forty-five of the subjects had no choral experience or vocal training.

A research team consisting of specialists in the vocal-choral area and
speech communication visited each school once each month (October-
June) to take measurements on the following variables:

Vocal Factors:	Range, tessitura, quality (breathiness and constriction ratings), register development (modal, falsetto).
Physiological Factors:	Sitting and standing height, weight, chest size, waist size, body-fat measurement, vital capacity, phonation time.
Acoustical Factors:	Speaking-voice fundamental frequency, dynamic ranges (gross and singing), lower/upper modal tones and falsetto tones: sonagraphic analysis of formant location, number of formants, F1-F2 spread, upper- and lower-level noise components.

The data gathered were used initially to provide baseline information for the development of an index of voice change. The criteria of
range and tessitura (See "Vocal Factors" above) were applied initially, but the tessitura factor, which reflected high amounts of variance,
was dropped as work proceeded. The voice-stage indices of Frank and
Sparber, Naidr and Sevcik, and Cooksey (1977b) served as primary
references in the development of the new index. Overlapping ranges
and exceptional individual cases were taken into account in this process (Figure 3).

Figure 3. Revised Index of Voice Classification in Junior High School Male Adolescents

Unchanged   Midvoice I

Midvoice II   Midvoice IIA

New Baritone   Settling Baritone

*Bracketed notes—Primary Range Boundaries
**Notes in parentheses—Case exceptions

All of the cases could be classified utilizing the new index. It is important to note that the basic six-stage sequence of voice development in the adolescent male as proposed by this author (1977b) was confirmed. Individuals seem to follow a logical pattern in their vocal development:

Stage 1: Unchanged;
Stage 2: Midvoice I (initial period of voice change);
Stage 3: Midvoice II (high mutation period);
Stage 4: Midvoice IIa (climax of mutation, and transitory in terms of time);
Stage 5: New Baritone (stabilizing period);
Stage 6: Settling Baritone (postmutation, development/expansion period).

Because of variability within each stage (with range being considered
as the sole criterion), a one-way analysis of variance by voice change
stage for LTPs ("lowest terminal pitch," the lowest tone that can be
sung in the modal register) and HTPs ("highest terminal pitch," the
highest tone that can be sung in the modal register, falsetto specifically
excluded) was completed. The multiple-comparisons test (least significant difference) showed that all groups (voice-change stages) were
significantly different.

Figure 4 shows the mean ranges and tessituras for the voice-change
stages. These statistics closely match the Cooksey model developed in
1977.

Figure 4. Mean Ranges and Tessituras for the Voice-Change Stages

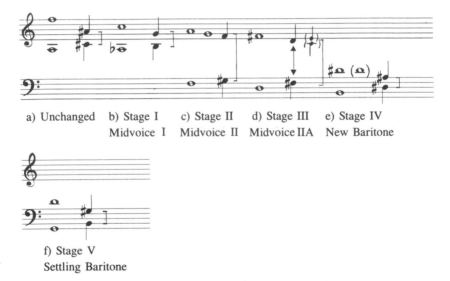

a) Unchanged   b) Stage I   c) Stage II   d) Stage III   e) Stage IV
                Midvoice I   Midvoice II   Midvoice IIA   New Baritone

f) Stage V
Settling Baritone

*Bracketed notes—tessituras

The index (Figure 3) shows that range boundaries for each of the
stages are fairly wide, but the upper and lower limits do not overlap.
When overlap occurred in the lower-range limit, compensations for the
ranges were made in the upper limit. Thus, as the voice develops its
lower range, it remains in one stage until the upper border descends.
This growth pattern, which proceeds at a somewhat uneven rate, is sequential and stabilizes during the new-baritone phase. Range extensions
(considering both LTPs and HTPs) for most voices occur during the
final stage of maturation (settling baritone). Means, standard deviations,
and medians for HTPs and LTPs of range, tessitura, and register lift

points were computed. There was much more instability and individual variation for HTPs than for LTPs. Individual variability for both limits decreased across the voice-change stages, suggesting more stability toward the end of the growth process. It should be added that the lower border of the singing range descends in ever-increasing intervals, while the lowering of the upper limit occurs more gradually. The variance for the HTPs representing tessitura (i.e., the highest tone in the comfortable region) is more substantial than for the LTPs in all the voice change stages, thus indicating the same relative instability that was found for range (in which the HTP represented the highest pitch that could be sung in the modal register). In summary, there is much instability in the upper-range limit during the most active phases of voice change; the voice is losing its higher pitches while gaining stability in the lower range. Changes in range follow a predictable pattern of stages, but in order to more fully understand this phenomenon, other facts must be mentioned.

Once the maturation process begins, the range decreases or constricts itself slightly (about four semitones), but remains stable across the various voice-change stages. This seems to contradict some of the reports issued by Weiss and others who claim that the changing voice has a very restricted range during maturation.

Considering frequency distributions across voice-change stages and grade level and voice-change velocity rates, it was found that:

(1)   Many voices begin the constriction of range associated with puberty prior to the seventh grade.

(2)   All voice classifications in this study were represented in the eighth grade.

(3)   There is more shifting between midvoice II to settling baritone during the summer months between the seventh and eighth grades, than for the same period between the eighth and ninth grades.

(4)   The midvoice II classification remains strongly represented throughout the seventh and eighth grades.

(5)   One can expect to find very few unchanged and midvoice I voices in the eighth grade.

(6)   There is a strong upsurge of new baritones and settling baritones during the spring months of the eighth grade.

(7)   Individual growth rates within and across the voice-change stages are very different, but the average time

spent in the most actives phases of mutation closely ap-
proximate the same measures reported by Naidr et al.

(8)   Individuals tend to stay in the midvoice II stage more
         than twice as long as any other stage (excluding the un-
         changed and settling-baritone categories).

(9)   Finally, because of the wide and skewed dispersions,
         a truly accurate and precise measure of the velocity
         growth rate could not be ascertained. It seems obvious
         that individual variability exists throughout the voice-
         change period, and thus far, it is not possible to predict
         how long individuals will remain in each of the voice-
         change stages.

The register and vocal-quality criteria were not utilized in the index;
however, these factors were important in defining mutation stages.
Analysis of 6,500 sonagrams, plus other rating-scale measures of these
criteria (the Likert Scale),[9] revealed that during midvoice II and IIa:

(1)   There is significant strain and breathiness in the upper
         range of the singing voice.

(2)   The lift points and transition areas between modal and
         falsetto registers change often, depending on the state
         of voice maturation.There is more variability during
         midvoice II and IIa (the latter the high point of
         maturation).

(3)   There is a low level of noise generally for the falsetto
         register, and the first and second overtones are strong.

(4)   Neither the amount nor distribution of formant energy
         above 4000 Hz was adult-like in nature.

(5)   The noise components in the vocal signal tend to in-
         crease throughout the entire voice maturation process,
         especially in the frequencies below 4000 Hz.

In summary, range was the most effective criterion for classifying
the voices into developmental stages. The other criteria of tessitura,
register development, and voice quality were useful in serving as vocal-
acoustical descriptors of those stages.

The physiological variables that were measured for each voice-change
stage included age, sitting and standing height, weight, chest size, waist

[9]R. Likert, "A Technique for the Measurement of Attitudes," *Archives of Psychology*
140 (1932).

size, total body fat, percentage of body fat, phonation time, and vital air capacity. Confirming the findings of others (Tanner, 1972; Weiss, 1950; and Smart, 1978), age does not appear to be a valid or reliable criterion for determining a specific vocal-physiological stage of maturation; however, in general terms, the most dramatic changes in vocal maturation take place between twelve-and-one-half and fourteen years of age. This correlates highly with the growth spurt described by many authorities in the field. Tanner's belief that the growth process is a continuous, steady phenomenon[10] is supported by the findings of this study. Growth spurts do occur, and the various physiological variables seem to have their own velocity growth rates, but all measures steadily increase over time (the body-fat measurement, which tends to decrease, excepted).

In summary:

(1)   Increases in sitting and standing height and in weight closely parallel normative charts when age is the criterion, and increases in these measures for the most active voice-change stages closely match statistics given by other researchers.

(2)   The physiological variables of sitting height and standing height, weight, chest size, waist size, phonation time, and vital air capacity all show a steady increase across the voice-change stages.

(3)   The subcutaneous body-fat measurements yielded inconsistent results; the overall pattern of change seems to indicate a general loss of "baby fat" and more muscular development in the chest and arm regions.

(4)   Maximum phonation time (how long the subject could sing a sustained tone in one breath) in this study was above established norms for adolescents and approached adult levels; however, there was decreased glottal efficiency in the last two stages of voice maturation.

(5)   Finally, for each of the voice-change stages, vital air capacity seemed to be the most steady and consistent measure of all the physiological variables tested.

The acoustical factors that were particularly important in this study

[10]J.M. Tanner, "Sequence, Tempo, and Individual Variation in Growth and Development of Boys and Girls Aged Twelve to Sixteen," ed. Kagan, J. and Coles, R. *Twelve to Sixteen: Early Adolescence* (New York: W.W. Norton, 1972) 3.

were speaking-voice pitch, dynamic range, and tape-recorded lower, upper, and modal tones, as well as falsetto tones. It was found that there is a very close relationship between changes in the speaking voice and the singing voice. Beginning with midvoice II, the intervallic distance between the lowest singing tone and the speaking voice remained stable across the voice-change stages. Confirming the findings of Groom (1979), Frank and Sparber, Naidr et al., Hollien (1967), and Van Oordt (1963), the speaking-voice pitch during and after the most active stages of voice change remained at about three to four semitones above the lowest terminal pitch of the singing range. Changes in the speaking voice are not so noticeable in the early stages of voice change, but overall, the upper-to-lower speaking-voice pitch parameters (the normal pitch fluctuations in the speaking voice) do stay in relative position with the upper to lower singing-voice boundaries throughout the voice-change stages.

Cooksey et al. found through spectrographic analysis that the voice loses some harmonic energy as the peak of maturation, midvoice IIa, is reached. This seems to be the time when the voice is most vulnerable and susceptible to vocal abuse. Results were inconclusive as to the effect of choral training on voice development. Also, no serious dysphonias were found at any time for the subjects participating in the study. Voice change does not appear to cause vocal trauma, jitter, etc. Hence, adolescent males can sing through the voice-change period, but care must be taken not to exceed the pitch-range limitations delineated for the various stages of vocal maturation.

CLOSING COMMENTS

The European and American research findings reported in this paper have provided music educators with important information about the vocal, physiological, and acoustical characteristics associated with adolescent-male voice maturation. These studies show that:

(1)   Singing-voice maturation proceeds at various rates of velocity through a predictable, sequential pattern of stages. Table 1 shows how the various stages developed by the three groups of voice scientists can be compared.

(2)   Range is probably the most important vocal criterion in determining a particular voice-change stage. HTPs and LTPs are variable within (depending on nervousness

and other factors) and across individuals; nevertheless, the criterion of range is very reliable in determining the stage of voice maturation.

(3)   Other important criteria for voice classification include tessitura, voice quality, register development, and speaking-voice pitch.

(4)   One can expect voices representing all stages of maturation during the seventh grade, especially at mid-year.

(5)   For the majority of boys, voice maturation begins at twelve-thirteen years of age, reaches its most active phase between thirteen and fourteen, then tapers off between fifteen and eighteen. The voice, however, continues to mature and expand its range during this time.

(6)   There tends to be more stability and less individual variation in the lower-range limits throughout the different stages of voice maturation than in the upper-range limits. There are great variations in the upper range areas, but stability comes after the high point of voice maturation is reached.

(7)   Triggered by hormone secretions, the first stage of voice maturation occurs at different times in different individuals. It is often difficult to detect at first. The upper range descends, but the timbre of the voice changes only slightly.

(8)   The pubertal stages of sexual development closely parallel the stages of voice maturation. The most dramatic changes in the singing voice occur at the climax of puberty, when the secondary sex characteristics are fully developed and reproductive powers begin.

(9)   On the average, the most active period of voice change occurs over about a thirteen-month period.

(10)   One should not expect "adult" quality from the junior-high male voice, even after the settling-baritone stage has been reached.

(11)   The width of the comfortable singing range (tessitura) of the voice remains fairly stable throughout the stages of voice change, but there is high individual variability.

(12)   The physiological variables of sitting height, standing height, weight, chest size, waist size, phonation time, and vital capacity show a steady increase across the

voice-change stages. Height seems to be very closely related to the most dramatic voice-change stages, while weight increases occur more dramatically as the voice settles.

(13)   The falsetto register first appears during the active stage of voice maturation (the author's midvoice II) and shows consistent levels of noise in succeeding stages.

(14)   The speaking-voice pitch is located close to the bottom of the singing range throughout the period of change (about three-and-one half semitones above the LTP).

(15)   Acoustical data reveal increased breathiness and constriction during the most active phases of voice change, but no serious dysphonias are apparent.

Table 1

A Comparison of Voice Change Stages

Voice-Change Stage	Naidr et al. Terminology	Frank & Sparber Terminology	Cooksey, Beckett, & Wiseman Terminology
Before Puberty	Unchanged	Unchanged	Unchanged
First Stage	Before Mutation	—	Midvoice I
Second Stage	Beginning Mutation	Premutation	Midvoice II
Third Stage	Highpoint of Mutation	—	Midvoice IIa
Fourth Stage	End of Mutation (Tapering Period)	Mutation	New Baritone
Fifth Stage	Voice development continues	Postmutation	Settling Baritone

As voice scientists continue to share their research concerning voice maturation, new methodologies can be devised, and this should have significant impact on teaching practices in many countries of the world. There appear to be many similarities in voice maturation among adolescent males, regardless of their nationality.

BIBLIOGRAPHY

Cooksey, John M. 1977a: "The Development of a Contemporary, Eclectic Theory for the Training and Cultivation of the Junior High School Male Changing Voice. Part I: Existing Theories," *The Choral Journal* 18 (October, 1977) 5-14. 1977b: ". . . Part II: Scientific and Empirical Findings; Some Tentative Solutions," *The Choral Journal* 18 (November, 1977) 5-16. 1977c: ". . . Part III: Developing an Integrated Approach to the Care and Training of the Junior High School Male Changing Voice," *The Choral Journal* 18 (December, 1977) 5-15. 1977d: " . . . Part IV: Selecting Music for the Junior High School Male Changing Voice," *The Choral Journal* 18 (January, 1978) 5-18.

Cooksey, J.M., Beckett, R.L., and Wiseman, R. "A Longitudinal Investigation of Selected Vocal, Physiological, and Acoustical Factors Associated with Voice Maturation in the Junior High School Male Adolescent," Report for the National ACDA Convention, New Orleans, Louisiana, March, 1981; update to same, Southern Division MENC Convention, Louisville, Kentucky, Feb., 1983; Kentucky state music-education reports, 1982.

Cooper, I. and Kuersteiner, K. *Teaching Junior High Music*. (Boston: Allyn and Bacon, 1965.)

Frank, F., and Sparber, M. "Stimmumfänge bei Kindern aus neuer Sicht" (Vocal ranges in children from a new perspective). *Folia Phoniatrica* 22 (1970) 397-402.

Frank, F. and Sparber, M. "Die Premutationsstimme, die Mutationsstimme und die Postmutationsstimme in Sonagramm" (The premutation voice, mutation voice, and the postmutation voice, as seen in sonagram). *Folia Phoniatrica* 22 (1970) 425-33.

Gehrkens, K.W. *Music in the Junior High School*. (Boston: C.C. Birchard and Co., 1936)

Groom, M. "A Descriptive Analysis of Development in Adolescent Male Voices during the Summer Time Period," Unpublished Ph.D. dissertation, The Florida State University, 1979.

Hollien, H. and Malcik, E. "Evaluation of Cross-Section Studies of Adolescent Voice Change in Males." *Speech Monographs* 34 (1967) 80-84.

Likert, R. "A Technique for the Measurement of Attitudes." *Archives of Psychology* 140 (1932).

McKenzie, Duncan. *Training the Boy's Changing Voice*. (London: Bradford and Dickens, Drayton House, 1956)

Naidr, J., Zboril, M., and Sevcik, K. "Die pubertalen Veränderungen der Stimme bei Jungen im Verlauf von 5 Jahren" (Pubertal voice changes in boys over a period of 5 years). *Folia Phoniatrica* 17 (1965) 1-18.

Nightingale, Mae. *Troubadours: a Collection of Four-Part Choruses.*(New York: Carl Fischer, Inc., 1939)

Rorke, G.A. *Choral Teaching at the Junior High School Level.* (Chicago: Hall and McCreary Co., 1947)

Smart, M.S., Smart, R.C., and Smart, L.S. *Adolescents: Development and Relationships.* (New York: Macmillan, 1978)

Swanson, Frederick. "Voice Mutation in the Adolescent Male: An Experiment in Guiding the Voice Development of Adolescent Boys in General Music Classes." (Unpublished Ph.D. dissertation, University of Wisconsin, 1959)

Tanner, J.M. "Sequence, Tempo, and Individual Variation in Growth and Development of Boys and Girls Aged Twelve to Sixteen." In *Twelve to Sixteen: Early Adolescence.* ed. Kagan, J. and Coles, R. (New York: W.W. Norton, 1972)

Van Oordt, H.W. and Drost, H.A. "Development of the Frequency Range in Children." *Folia Phoniatrica* 15 (1963) 289-98.

Weiss, D.A. "The Pubertal Change of the Human Voice," *Folia Phoniatrica* 2 (3) (1950) 125-59.

Walter S. Collins

The Reconstruction of the Evening Service for Seven Voices by Thomas Weelkes

THE WEELKES SERVICES

For many years the great Elizabethan composer Thomas Weelkes (c. 1576-1623) was known largely for the excellence and innovative style of his madrigals and other secular works. In the last several decades, however, increasing reasearch on his sacred music has revealed a composer equally at home in the major genres of the Anglican Church, the Service and the anthem. Authoritative editions of most of these works have appeared since 1960, and many of them have entered the repertoire of the Church with those of the other major composers of the time.

Coming at the end of a period that devoted greater energy and creative

---

A native of Connecticut, Dr. Collins received the Bachelor of Arts and Bachelor of Music degrees from Yale University and the Master of Arts and Doctor of Philosophy degrees from the University of Michigan. He is a frequent adjudicator and clinician, author of numerous articles, editor of early choral-music editions, and co-author of two books: Thomas Weelkes: Collected Anthems (Musica Britannica, *vol. 23) and* Choral Conducting: A Symposium. *He currently serves as Secretary-General of the International Federation for Choral Music and is a past president of the College Music Society and of the American Choral Directors Association.*

Professor Collins has been Professor of Choral Music and Musicology at the University of Colorado, Boulder, since 1971. At Oakland University, Rochester, Michigan, he originated the Meadow Brook Festival and School of Music with the Detroit Symphony Orchestra in 1964 and 1965.

ingenuity to the Service than did any era since, Weelkes was in an advantageous position to become the climax of a tradition. As Edmund Fellowes, the most active early-twentieth-century scholar of English music, said,

> Weelkes was the most original and perhaps the greatest of all the English Service-writers in the Golden Age with the exception of Byrd. . . .
>   The position to which he advanced this branch of music was not reached again until the latter part of the nineteenth century.[1]

Apparently no other major composer of the time wrote as many Services as did Weelkes, nor did any other show greater variety or originality in his treatment of the form. Whether Chichester Cathedral, where Weelkes served as organist and choir director, demanded new Service music more often than did other establishments—an unlikely thesis, considering the smallness of the choir at Chichester and the fact that no Weelkes Service music is mentioned in the list of the Cathedral's music in 1621[2] while Weelkes was still organist there—or whether the challenge of setting the old and well-known texts of the canticles appealed to Weelkes more than it did to other composers, we shall probably never know. Perhaps it was simply that the ten Weelkes Services that survive were more popular, or luckier, than were those of other composers and thus represented a larger percentage of his total output than do the surviving seven of Thomas Tomkins, Morley's five, Byrd's four, or the two of Gibbons. None by Weelkes, however, was popular enough to have been printed in any of the major published collections of Service music throughout the seventeenth, eighteenth, and nineteenth centuries. Indeed, not until the early twentieth century, three hundred years after his death, did a single Weelkes Service appear in print, probably because only part of one Service survives intact. Most, however, have now been reconstructed with varying degrees of success but well enough to provide an indication of their content and their worth.

The harmonic, rhythmic, and melodic styles of the Weelkes Services, even more than those of his anthems, are relatively conservative compared to his madrigals. The most striking trait of originality to be found in the Services is the use of recurrent material with which to build a sense of unity and formal structure in larger pieces. The beginnings and endings on the same chord of all major sections of a Service, in-

---

[1]Edmund Fellowes, *English Cathedral Music*, fifth edition, revised by J. A. Westrup (London: Methuen & Co. Ltd., 1969) 90-91.
[2]Diocese of Chichester Diocesan Record Office, MS Cap. I/10.

cluding Morning, Communion, and Evening canticles, is commonplace for the era, but the statement that nearly every Weelkes Service also uses repeated melodic material cannot be made about any other composer of the time.

Sometimes such examples of musical integration may consist of similar beginnings or endings to the different canticles—a carry-over from the head-motif or tail-motif techniques of earlier Latin church music that was used more obviously by Byrd in his *Great Service*. At other times it consists of the recalling of themes, motifs, or whole points of imitation later in the work, as happens frequently with tail-motifs in Weelkes's Services. Most striking, however, is the clear recapitulation of whole sections in order to give a rational plan to a large work. There are even instances of repetition from one Service to another, but most of these are brief, and they probably derive more from stylistic consistency than from intent.

Still another unifying device used by Weelkes relates to his well-known skill in text setting: texts such as "and ever shall be," "to be a light," and "He hath put down" often evoke from Weelkes similar melodic and rhythmic treatment, if not actual repetition, in a Service or between different Services. "All generations" frequently brings forth longer and more elaborate points of imitation. The words "Holy, Holy, Holy" often evoke a four-note motif descending scalewise from mediant to leading tone, which, as Denis Stevens points out, is also found in the music of a number of other composers of the time.[3]

In addition, Weelkes, as do most of his contemporaries, uses color to delineate internal sections of longer texts, but few use the device with his originality. In several cases Weelkes methodically alternates each verse of the text between chorus and solo timbres or between *decani* and *cantoris* sides of the choir. This alternation device reaches its height in the verse Services where he has available to him different kinds of solo voices as well as duets, trios, quartets, and different combinations of choral voices. In several of the Services, he exploits all such options to the limit. Indeed, this continual shifting of tone quality is one of the more attractive features of Weelkes's Service music.

An even more intriguing use of color by Weelkes appears when he relates different portions of a work to each other by means of recurring combinations of colors. We shall see below how useful such a method of musical unification can be to the reconstruction of a piece that survives incomplete.

Most interesting of all, and particularly relevant to the subject of the

[3]Denis Stevens, *Tudor Church Music* (London: Faber and Faber Limited, 1961) 56-57.

present essay, is Weelkes's habit of self-quotation among the Services and anthems, a technique so far unrecognized in other composers of the time. At least five, and perhaps more, of the Services have extended musical quotations from his own anthems (or vice versa), as if he were intentionally attempting to tie the two compositions together. One may assume in such cases that the Service and anthem were written at the same time for a certain occasion and/or were intended to be performed at the same ceremony, even though in no case do the two survive together in the partbooks. This view is supported by two cases where an offertory anthem is specifically included in the plan of a Service, and a third where an anthem is designated "for" a particular Service. All in all, eight of the ten Services are connected in one way or another to one of his anthems. One wonders how many more cases of such self-borrowing remain undetected in the works of Weelkes and of other composers.

In sum then, it can be said that although Weelkes's Services may be conservative harmonically, and many of their choruses less interesting contrapuntally than they might be, the originality in their use of recurrent forms, the complexity of their changes in color, and the subtlety of their text setting, make them works that well deserve Fellowes's praise and our attention.[4]

EVENING SERVICE FOR SEVEN VOICES

Introduction

In recent years, Weelkes's Evening Service for Seven Voices has become recognized as one of the most important liturgical works of its time. David Brown calls it

> "The most splendid of all Weelkes' Services . . . with spacious, even gigantic paragraphs, and imposing sonorities. . . . must surely have been designed for the Chapel Royal. . . . It is the one Service from the period which really rivals the achievement of the evening canticles in Byrd's Great Service as much in style and technique as in scale and . . . elaboration . . . perhaps the most lastingly impressive experience in the whole range of his [Weelkes's] music."[5]

[4]A more complete discussion of the Services may be found in: David Brown, *Thomas Weelkes* (London: Faber and Faber Limited 1969) 180-199.
[5]Brown, 198-199.

Denis Stevens says that "in richness and resource it is perhaps without parallel in the whole of the Elizabethan repertory."[6] It is indeed an overwhelming tour de force unlike anything else from the era.

The Title

Before discussing its reconstruction, we must establish an appropriate name for this work. It has variously been called "The Ninth Service," due to its position on Fellowes's and Brown's lists of all the Weelkes Services; "Evensong of Seven Voices;" "Evening Service in Seven Parts;" "Magnificat and Nunc dimittis in seven parts;" "Service for Seven Voices," etc. In the one published edition of the work it is called "Magnificat and Nunc dimittis (the Ninth Service)."[7] The latter title, which says nothing about seven voices, seems to be the least satisfactory of all, since all of the surviving original partbooks entitle the work as "Magnificat" or "Magnificat and Nunc dimittis" plus the phrases "of 7 parts" or simply "7 parts."

It is apparent that either Weelkes himself, or at least two different copyists, intended the title to include reference to the number of voices, which provides an important hint to the reconstruction of the work, as we shall see below. Therefore, because musical settings of the Evening Service of the Anglican Church traditionally consist of the two canticles *Magnificat* and *Nunc dimittis*, it seems to this author that the most appropriate modern name for this composition is "Evening Service for Seven Voices."

The Sources

The surviving sources for the work are the "former set" of the six Caroline partbooks at Peterhouse College, Cambridge:[8]

Peterhouse College MS No. 33, fol. 46 (PH. 33), a bass part
Peterhouse College MS No. 34, fol. 53 (PH. 34), a soprano part
Peterhouse College MS No. 38, fol. 54 (PH. 38), a different bass part from that in MS No. 33

[6]Stevens, 57.
[7]Thomas Weelkes, *Magnificat and Nunc dimittis (The Ninth Service)*, reconstructed and edited by David Wulstan (Oxford: Oxenford Imprint, 1979).
[8]Dom Anselm Hughes, *Catalogue of the Musical Manuscripts at Peterhouse Cambridge* (Cambridge: University Press, 1953).

Peterhouse College MS No. 39, fol. 43 and fol. 60 (PH. 39), two
    different countertenor (alto) parts
Peterhouse College unnumbered MS marked "Medius Decani,"
    fol. 52v (PH. MD), a different soprano part from that in MS
    No. 34
Peterhouse College unnumbered MS marked "Primus Contratenor
    Cantoris," fol. 51 (PH. CC), a different countertenor (alto)
    part from those in MS No. 39

and two partbooks from Durham Cathedral:

Durham Cathedral MS C. 1, the same soprano part as in Peterhouse
    MS No. 34
Durham Cathedral MS C. 18, the same bass part as in Peterhouse
    MS No. 38

Part designations given here for the unnamed partbooks and the missing parts will be derived below from internal musical evidence. It is
not positively known, however, how many partbooks originally existed
in either the Durham or Peterhouse sets.

The Need for Reconstruction

Even with these eight partbooks, the Evening Service for Seven Voices
survives incomplete, since one or more voice parts appear to be missing, not to mention a few missing measures in the extant parts. In order
to perform this masterpiece, therefore, it must be reconstructed.

Indeed, two attempts at reconstruction have been made before. The
first, by Jeremy Noble, was done in the early 1950s, when Mr. Noble
was an undergraduate at Oxford University, for several performances
by the Renaissance Singers under Michael Howard.[9] Some minor revi-
sions in the reconstruction were then made by Mr. Noble, probably
in preparation for a performance on the British Broadcasting Corporation. The scores were photo-reproduced from Noble's manuscript, and
a number of copies remain in the BBC Library, never having been
published.[10] Beginning in the early 1960s, Mr. Noble and the present
author worked together sporadically on a revised version of his

[9]*Mr. Weelkes His Evensong of Seven Voices*, edited from MSS at Peterhouse and Durham
by Jeremy Noble (in manuscript).
[10]The scores are incorrectly combined with those of Weelkes's *Service in Five Parts*
in: *BBC Music Library Choral and Opera Catalogue*, vol. 1, *Composers*, and vol.
2, *Titles* (London: British Broadcasting Corporation, 1967), 2, 495; 2, 183. The correct designation of #10511 is given in vol. 1, however.

reconstruction that combined both our opinions on the piece. That venture was abandoned in 1967, and no results were ever published.

In 1979, as cited above, a surprisingly similar reconstruction to Noble's was made by David Wulstan and published by Oxenford Imprint. At this writing it is still available from Blackwell's Music Shop (38 Holywell, Oxford, OX1 3SW, England).

In the opinion of the present author, neither the Noble nor the Wulstan reconstruction satisfies a number of the principles of reconstruction proposed below, nor do these editions appear to recognize several implications present in the structure of the piece that provide some evidence as to how it may have been written originally. There is still a need, therefore, for a reconstruction that more scientifically attempts to uncover the composer's original intent.

THE RECONSTRUCTION PROCESS

Introduction

Reconstruction of any incomplete composition is a more complex and difficult task than it appears to be at first glance. Before beginning, the reconstructor must first devote a great deal of time to, thought on, and analysis of the composition in order to understand what survives before he or she begins to augment it. Secondly, it seems to the present author that certain limitations on the reconstructor's behavior must be imposed if the reconstruction is to accomplish the goal of trying to re-establish the composer's original intent. It is one purpose of this essay, therefore, to propose a set of principles for the guidance of future reconstructors similar to those that were set forth by the present author some years ago for editors of early music.[11] Once such principles have been established, they will then be applied to the possible reconstruction of the Evening Service for Seven Voices.

The Principles of Reconstruction

The major principle of any reconstruction can be expressed in the following axiom:

[11]Walter S. Collins, "The Choral Conductor and the Musicologist," *Choral Conducting: a Symposium*, edited by Harold Decker and Julius Herford, 2d ed. (Englewood Cliffs, NJ: Prentice-Hall, 1988) 128-29.

100   WALTER S. COLLINS

The ideal reconstruction of an originally complete piece that survives incomplete is the one that reproduces precisely what the composer wrote in the first place.

While this is obviously impossible except in the rarest of cases, any other goal would violate the whole purpose of restoration, usually resulting in free composition rather than restoration. Because the task is impossible, several corollaries or related principles to this axiom are necessary:

1. A reconstruction should not ignore any evidence concerning the original state of the piece.

Such a statement may seem to be self-evident, but it is frequently ignored in practice, as it was in Wulstan's title for the piece.

2. A reconstruction should not add anything that cannot be logically deduced from what does survive in the piece or from the general style of the composer.

If a composer, for example, never uses a particular kind of non-harmonic tone, or cadence, or harmonic progression in the surviving portions of the piece, it does not behoove the reconstructor to do so. If a composer has left no piece that contains a part for the clarinet, the reconstructor should resist the temptation of writing one into his reconstruction, no matter how beautiful it might be.

A curious application of this principle is required in Weelkes's Evening Service: several cases of parallel perfect intervals appear in the surviving voices of the piece, though they are extremely rare in the rest of the composer's works. Most musicians would probably agree that the reconstructor ought not to take the liberty of adding more.

3. A reconstruction should intrude as little as possible into what survives.

In other words, the reconstructor should err on the side of understatement, adding no more than is absolutely necessary to what survives. Such a safety measure is necessary because it is too easy, either consciously or unconsciously, to impose one's own personality, or twentieth-century tastes, onto an earlier piece. In truth, a composer is the last person who should attempt a reconstruction, since he or she will always be asking whether what is added sounds beautiful, rather than whether it is correct or not. As in editing early music, a musical detective is needed, not a creator.

Two basic principles of editing that apply equally to reconstructions are self-evident:

4. A reconstruction must include everything that survives directly from the composer.

This statement is similar to the first corollary above, but in this case it requires that the reconstructor must show all evidence in the score.

5. A reconstruction must distinguish with absolute clarity between what survives from the composer and what has been added by the reconstructor.

APPLICATION OF THESE PRINCIPLES TO THE EVENING SERVICE FOR SEVEN VOICES

(The arguments that follow may be somewhat difficult to follow without a score whose sections have been marked according to the plan that follows. But since it appears unlikely that most readers will have such a score at hand, every effort will be made to keep matters as clear as possible in words and with charts and examples.)

Introduction

Keeping clearly in mind the requirements placed upon us by the principles proposed above, let us begin to investigate the evidence that exists in the surviving portions of Weelkes's Service and discuss how that evidence can be put to use in the process of reconstructing the piece. In order to assist the investigation, it is helpful to label the various sections of the piece according to changes in the combinations of voices employed:

Figure 1. Designation of Sections of the Service

MAGNIFICAT			NUNC DIMITTIS		
Sec.	*Measures*	*Text incipit*	*Sec.*	*Measures*	*Text incipit*
A	1-18	My soul doth	L	1-13	Lord, Now lettest
B	18-33	For he hath	M	13-25	For mine eyes
C	33-38	For behold	N	25-30	which Thou hast prepared

continued on next page.

Figure 1. (continued)

	MAGNIFICAT			NUNC DIMITTIS	
Sec.	Measures	Text incipit	Sec.	Measures	Text incipit
D	38-87	all generations	O	31-45	before the face of all people
E	88-105	He hath showed	P	46-89	To be a light
F	106-122	He hath put down	Q	90-98	Glory be to the Father
G	122-132	and hath exalted	R	99-143	and to the Holy Ghost
H	133-145	He hath filled			
I	146-171	He remembering			
J	172-198	Glory be to the Father			
K	199-205	Amen			

Performing Forces

The first question that must be answered by the potential reconstructor of this piece is "How many voices were in the original version, and what kinds of voices sang the undesignated surviving parts?" Let us assume at first, as have the previous reconstructors of the Service and the owners of the Peterhouse partbooks,[12] that there are three missing voice parts, making a total of ten:

Figure 2. Proposed Voice-Part Names[13]

DECANI	CANTORIS
Soprano (Peterhouse MS "Medius Decani")	Soprano (Peterhouse MS No. 34 & Durham MS C. 1)
First Alto (Peterhouse MS No. 39, fol. 60)	First Alto (Peterhouse MS "Primus Contratenor Cantoris")
Second Alto (Peterhouse MS No. 39, fol. 43)	Second Alto (not extant)
Tenor (not extant)	Tenor (not extant)
Bass (Peterhouse MS No. 38 and Durham MS C.18)	Bass (Peterhouse MS No. 33

[12]Hughes, xii.
[13]This assignment of part names to each of the manuscript sources will be derived below.

An immediate difficulty arises in that it appears from the titles given in the partbooks that Weelkes intended the piece to be for seven voices, at least most of the time, though we do not know which voices. In order to resolve this apparent conflict, we must look more closely at the sources for the music. The partbooks themselves provide some evidence, though only two of the seven in the "former set" of Caroline partbooks at Peterhouse have original voice names attached to them, and neither of the Durham books does.

Sopranos

One of the Peterhouse books (PH. MD) is designated for *"medius decani,"* or soprano *decani*. It is safe to conclude, then, that the other soprano part (PH. 34 and DC C.1) must have originally been a *medius cantoris*, as expected in the Anglican tradition of two half-choirs, each complete in itself, on the Dean's and Cantor's sides of the chancel.

Altos

The only other named book (PH. CC) is called *"Primus contratenor cantoris,"* or first alto *cantoris*. This title carries a wealth of information, since it indicates not only that there must have been a first alto *decani* (PH. 39, fol. 60) but also that there must have been a second alto *cantoris* (no partbook is known) and a second alto *decani* (PH. 39, fol. 43). Thus, four alto parts are evidently necessary at some time or another during the piece, three of which are extant.

I have designated above which of the unnamed manuscript partbooks should be assigned to which voices. However, according to the discussion presented below, another plan is possible. In their reconstructions, for example, both Noble and Wulstan name the altos with the opposite pairing so that when only two alto parts are active, the first alto *decani* sings in unison with the second alto *cantoris*, and the second alto *decani* in unison with the first alto *cantoris*.

Figure 3. Alto Pairings

Source	Collins	Noble, Wulstan
PH. MS No. 39, fol. 60	First alto *decani*	Second alto *decani*
PH. *Primus Contratenor Cantoris*	First alto *cantoris*	First alto *cantoris*
PH. MS No. 39, fol. 43	Second alto *decani*	First alto *decani*
Not extant	Second alto *cantoris*	Second alto *cantoris*

Wulstan even claims that his method is the "usual" one,[14] though others appear not to agree. The "Collins" method of supplying part names to the alto parts is the same one that was chosen by Barnard in his *First Book of Selected Church Musick*, which contains Weelkes's anthem "O Lord, Grant the King a Long Life," in which (or from which) the Evening Service for Seven Voices is quoted extensively.[15] The modern Peterhouse owners of the partbooks also chose this method when they labeled the books in recent times, basing their decision not only on the Weelkes Service but also on the internal evidence contained in the many other pieces in the set.[16] It provides a consistent format of soprano, first alto, second alto, tenor, and bass for each half-choir at all times and permits duets to take place, for example, both with pairs of first and second altos *decani* on the same side of the aisle (see Figure 5), as well as with pairs of first altos *decani* and first altos *cantoris* on opposite sides (see Figure 9). It therefore seems to the present author the most appropriate way to proceed. Any choir may, of course, choose another method by re-labeling the score, if it opts to do so.

Tenor(s)

Since no tenor partbook has been found, other evidence must be sought as to whether there had originally been a tenor part to the Service at all. The best clue for the existence of at least one tenor part derives from the sections shared by the anthem "O Lord, Grant the King a Long Life" and the Service (sections H, R, and briefly A). These portions (except A) are the only ones in the anthem containing seven voice parts: soprano *decani*, soprano *cantoris*, first altos in unison, second altos in unison, tenors in unison, bass *decani*, and bass *cantoris*. The only logical conclusion to be made from this fact is that the Service must also have had at least one tenor part as well. As for whether the tenor part contained *decani* and *cantoris* divisions, the ten Barnard partbooks provide only minimal evidence. While that set includes separate tenor *decani* and tenor *cantoris* partbooks, they are identical for the Weelkes anthem, even using the same plates for printing. This proves that the anthem contained no more than seven parts in the portions shared with the Service. It would still be possible, of course, for the Service to have contained eight voices, with two tenor parts in these passages, but that possibility seems unlikely.

[14]Wulstan, i.
[15]John Barnard, *First Book of Selected Church Musick*, (London: Edward Griffin, 1641). Tenor *decani*, fol. 118r. Tenor *cantoris*.
[16]Hughes, xii.

The antiphonal "Gloria Patri" in the *Nunc dimittis* of the Service is somewhat more helpful (see Figure 4).

All the extant voices participate fully in the *decani-cantoris* split at that point, so one is tempted to assume that the tenors split into *decani* and *cantoris* parts as well. However, it is also possible that the tenors were completely silent during the passage, thereby not requiring a split, a solution that Wulstan chose in his reconstruction. Indeed, the lack of empty fifths in that passage does not *require* the addition of the tenors at all. Furthermore, the previously stated principle of minimum intrusion by the reconstructor would dictate that the tenor be limited to one part throughout the piece, even when it is possible to create two parts.

On the other hand, the portions of the Service other than the "Gloria Patri" where *decani-cantoris* splits in the upper parts are evidently intended (sections B and C, see Figures 5 and 6; also similar sections M and N) contain an unusual number of empty fifths or octaves. (See asterisks under scores). These are not typical of Weelkes's style and seem to require filling by a missing tenor *decani* part in sections B & M and later by a tenor *cantoris* in sections C & N. In addition, the above-mentioned "Gloria Patri" (Figure 4) is the only homophonic section of any significance in the entire Service, and it is hard to believe that a composer as conscious of climax as Weelkes was would have allowed the tenors to withdraw entirely at the high point of the piece in both text and music. (One can make a similar argument for the "Gloria Patri" of the *Magnificat,* though it is less compelling.)

All told, it is not yet possible to prove without doubt that Weelkes intended both tenor *decani* and tenor *cantoris* parts for the Service; but to this observer at least, the evidence certainly leans in that direction. In any case, however, the reconstructor should probably construct no more than one tenor part except in situations where the other voices require it by *decani-cantoris* divisions.

Basses

Since two different, undesignated bass parts are extant, the conclusion is inescapable that one is a *decani* part (PH. 38 and DC. 18) and the other *cantoris* (PH. 33), and the "Gloria Patri" of the *Nunc dimittis* again identifies which should be which.

"Verse" and "Full" Markings

One last question concerning the voice parts of the Service arises from the fact that both the Noble and Wulstan reconstructions contain editorial-

Figure 4. Measures 89-93, *Nunc dimittis* (section Q)[17]

[17]All musical examples in this article are transposed up a minor third.

ly added "verse" and "full" sections, indicating solo voices versus tutti, even though no such markings appear in any of the original voice parts. Wulstan maintains that "it was not unusual to omit Verse markings in partbooks."[18] If that is true, which is debatable, the reconstructor has precious little evidence to go on as to which sections would have

[18]Wulstan, i. Wulstan also says here that "David Brown thinks that the Service should be Full (i.e., Full sides) throughout." I have been unable to find any such statement, and, indeed, on p. 198 Brown even mentions "verses."

been solo and which tutti, and any suggestions to that effect would necessarily be highly speculative. Wulstan also says that "the behaviour of the alto parts belies" a full anthem throughout,[19] though which behavior he means is not clear. Nowhere in the entire body of Weelkes's sacred works do "verse" and "full" markings exist except in verse anthems and Services, where such markings are frequent. Solos in these pieces are usually entitled as "verse" and supported by independent organ accompaniments. Most of the portions of the Evening Service for Seven Voices that are marked "verse" by Noble and Wulstan are clearly able to stand by themselves without an independent accompaniment. Therefore, such indications should probably not appear in the score.

The performer, of course, always has the option of performing whatever sections he wishes as solos (which is not quite the same thing as accompanied "verses"); in fact, such sections would add considerable variety to the color of such a long piece and would not violate the laissez-faire feelings of Weelkes's time toward such matters.

Organ

No organ part has been recovered, though one probably existed originally because such parts do survive for most of Weelkes's sacred works. Since unaccompanied performance is only one option according to the practice of the time—and an unlikely one at that—an organ part that largely doubles the voices ought to be provided with the reconstruction and should be used for most performances.

Summary of Performing Forces

It seems to me that the most plausible reconstruction of the Evening Service for Seven Voices would include somewhere during the piece soprano *decani* and *cantoris* voices, first alto *decani* and *cantoris*, second alto *decani* and *cantoris*, unison *decani* and *cantoris* tenor parts (divided only where necessary), and bass *decani* and *cantoris* parts. This makes a total of nine parts that occasionally may become ten, eight, six, or fewer (with a minimum of two or three voices, as in section F) but that reduce to seven parts by combining the four alto parts into two. That basic seven-part combination occupies approximately 40% of the piece, a higher proportion than does any other, probably accounting for the piece's original title. There should be no "verse" and "full" markings in the score, unless they are clearly indicated as editorial, and an organ part doubling the voices should be editorially supplied.

[19]Wulstan, i.

RECONSTRUCTION OF THE MISSING VOICES

When Should the Missing Voices be Active?

Once the identity of the missing voices is established, one must then decide on the amount of activity the missing voices should be given. Our original corollaries of reconstruction may be of some assistance.

Color Pairings

The first corollary, that the reconstructor should use any evidence available to him, will be helpful in the case of the Service because Weelkes established certain patterns of color in the surviving voices. For example, the first five sections of the *Magnificat* are identical in color to the first five sections of the *Nunc dimittis* (sections A & L, B & M, etc.—see Figure 7), with a major cadence and double bar after the fourth section of each canticle (sections D & O). In addition, the order of voices in the contrapuntal entries for these same sections is often the same or similar: sections C & N are identical, B & M are similar, A & L are both homophonic, etc. These patterns cannot result simply from coincidence, and indeed they reflect a well-known practice of creating unity among various movements of sacred pieces that goes back at least to the fifteenth century in English music.[20] The consequence of these observations is, of course, that the reconstructor should use the same color combinations for these pairs of sections and should keep the color consistent throughout the section because the composer does so in the extant voices.

We are led to the following color choices:

Sections A and L

Sections A and L, the homophonic sections that begin each canticle, show unison basses in the surviving voices, the only places in the Service where the basses are combined. Therefore, a logical choice of color would be six voices: sopranos *decani* and *cantoris;* first altos in unison; second altos in unison; tenors in unison; and basses in unison—similar to the basic color of seven voices but compressed into six by the unison basses. One could also argue that the openings of the canticles should be thicker—with at least three or perhaps four altos, and/or two tenors—

[20]John Aplin, ''Cyclic Techniques in the Earliest Anglican Services,'' *Journal of the American Musicological Society* XXXV/3 (Fall 1982) 409-435.

but to defend that choice, one should be prepared to answer the question of why Weelkes would combine the two bass parts into one if he wanted such thickness. It should also be pointed out that the opening of the *Magnificat* (section A) is quoted briefly in the six-part portion of the anthem "O Lord, Grant the King a Long Life."

Sections B and M, C and N

Decani and *cantoris* divisions assist in deciding the intended colors for the pairs of sections B and M and sections C and N. The surviving voices for sections B and M are only *decani* voices, including both altos *decani*, but with both bass parts:

Figure 5. Measures 24-28, *Magnificat* (Section B)

Only *cantoris* upper voices survive for sections C and N, which follow B and M, again with both bass parts, requiring the creation of the second alto *cantoris* to make these two sections parallel with sections B and M.

As discussed earlier, the frequency of chords without a third (see asterisks under the scores) in sections B and M and C and N, seems to require the addition of a divided tenor part, *decani* in the case of sections B And M, and *cantoris* in the cases of sections C and N.

Sections D, H, J, O, and R

These sections, which comprise 40% of the entire piece, also contain the same color combination in the surviving voices. We can determine the color of sections H and R because they contain the quoted seven-part portions of the anthem "O Lord, Grant the King a Long Life." Thus all five of these sections should probably be reconstructed in the basic seven-part color—soprano *decani*, soprano *cantoris*, first altos in unison (except for the first two measures in section O), second altos in unison, tenors in unison, bass *decani*, and bass *cantoris*—which both Wulstan and Noble do (except for reversing the alto pairings).

(Curiously, the quoted portions of sections H and R occupy precisely measures 136-143 of each canticle, and they are contiguous in the original anthem, the reasons for both of which remain a mystery. Nor is it apparent why the mid-point of each canticle falls within its fifth section, even though there are eleven sections in the *Magnificat* and only seven in the *Nunc dimittis*.)

Sections E, I, and P

These sections, with both sopranos, both first altos, and both basses in the surviving parts, contain no empty fifths and seem full and complete enough without any editorial additions (see Figure 9). Since the second alto *decani* contains rests throughout, there is no reason to create a second alto *cantoris* part.

One might argue that the addition of a tenor voice would create a seven-voice sonority, but it would not be the standard one because of the presence of two first altos rather than first and second altos. Therefore, under the corollary of minimum intrusion, these sections should be left as is.

Sections F and G

There seems to be no obvious relationship between the colors of sections F and Q, or between G and R, though they occupy corresponding positions in the color plan. Therefore, one must look for other evidence of what was originally intended for them. With only two extant voices active in section F (see Figure 7) and three in section G, there is so little to go on that no logical answer as to how many voices to reconstruct has yet presented itself. At least one voice (or an independent organ part) must be added to both sections, because there are so many accented intervals of the fourth (not acting as suspensions) and accented

Figure 6. Measures 33-37, *Magnificat* (Section C)

second-inversion triads that are not normal in Weelkes's style. Even with all three non-surviving parts reconstructed, however, these two sections would still possess only five and six voices respectively, sonorities thinner than, or as thin as, any in the entire work.

Noble chose to add two voices throughout both sections, second alto *cantoris* and one tenor; Wulstan added the same two but split the tenors into *decani* and *cantoris*, for a total of three added voices. Since Weelkes obviously intended these sections to be thinner than the rest of the piece, a more likely solution under the principle of minimum intrusion would be to add no more than one voice, the second alto *cantoris* or perhaps a tenor, to both sections. The second alto *cantoris* is probably the better choice because of the activity of the second alto *decani* in the previous section. Any of these different solutions can be defended, however, and we shall never know what the composer originally chose unless an additional missing part or parts are discovered.

Section K

With active parts for all three extant altos, section K is unlike any other except the antiphonal section Q. One can reasonably argue that if the first altos split, the seconds should do so as well, which would require that the missing second alto *cantoris* should also be re-created, making a total of four alto parts. Since this section is the finale to the *Magnificat,* it seems likely that at least one tenor part should be active, a solution Noble chooses, or perhaps two, as Wulstan decides. The latter solution is appealing because it provides the only ten-part color for the entire first canticle, a stunning Amen finale to the whole movement.

Section Q

Section Q (Figures 4 and 8) must be dealt with in *cori spezzati*—antiphonal—style, either in eight or ten parts. As has been discussed previously, the ten-part solution—with two tenor parts—is equally as appealing here as it is in section K, even though no tenor part is actually required for completeness in either section.

Summary of Activity of Voices

The following figure summarizes by section the suggested colors for the entire piece, with the reconstructed parts in boldface type. Note that the most frequently occuring color is the basic color of seven parts that gives the piece its name. (*Decani* and *cantoris* parts on the same line horizontally are in unison for that section.):

Figure 7. Recommended Colors by Sections

Sections	Color
A & L	Soprano *decani*
	Soprano *cantoris*
	First altos *decani* and *cantoris*
	Second altos *decani* and **cantoris**
	Tenors *decani* and *cantoris*
	Basses *decani* and *cantoris*
B & M	Soprano *decani*
	First alto *decani*

	Second alto *decani*
	Tenor *decani*
	Bass *decani*
	Bass *cantoris*
C & N	Soprano *cantoris*
	First alto *cantoris*
	Second alto *cantoris*
	Tenor *cantoris*
	Bass *decani*
	Bass *cantoris*
D & O; H, J, R, ("basic seven-part color")	Soprano *decani*
	Soprano *cantoris*
	First altos *decani* and *cantoris*
	Second altos *decani* and **cantoris**
	Tenors *decani* and *cantoris*
	Bass *decani*
	Bass *cantoris*
E & P; I	Soprano *decani*
	Soprano *cantoris*
	First alto *decani*
	First alto *cantoris*
	Bass *decani*
	Bass *cantoris*
F	Soprano *cantoris*
	Second alto *decani*
	Second alto *cantoris*
G	Soprano *decani*
	Soprano *cantoris*
	Second alto *decani*
	Second alto *cantoris*
K & Q	Soprano *decani*
	Soprano *cantoris*
	First alto *decani*
	First alto *cantoris*
	Second alto *decani*
	Second alto *cantoris*
K & Q	**Tenor *decani***
	Tenor *cantoris*
	Bass *decani*
	Bass *cantoris*

What Should the Reconstructed Voices Do?

Having decided what voices should be reconstructed and when they ought to be active, one must now confront the final but most difficult problem of what they should do.

The reconstructor must balance the sometimes conflicting guidance given to him by the several corollaries discussed earlier. He must add whatever is required by the evidence he uncovers, but he should add no more than what can be logically deduced from that evidence and from the style of the piece and of the composer. Furthermore, he must avoid stylistic practices that do not exist in the style, while at the same time trying to make the portion he composes as beautiful as the original. That is no mean task, all told. It goes without saying that the portions added must be identified as such, both in an editorial note and on the score itself.

Other than the title's emphasis on "seven parts," the only external evidence for the activity of the voices in the Evening Service for Seven Voices again comes from the quoted sections in the anthem "O Lord Grant the King a Long Life" (parts of sections H and R, the first three chords of section A, and the first chord of section L, which is identical to the first chord of A). Since the anthem survives complete, the reconstruction in the Service for these portions should copy the anthem precisely, there being no indication that one ought to do otherwise.

For further help one must turn to internal musical evidence, which sometimes can be quite concrete as well. It is apparent, for example, that the imitating *cantoris* voices in the antiphonal section of the second "Gloria Patri" must precisely copy what the *decani* voices have already done (see Figure 4).

Such concrete evidence provides a reasonably secure solution to approximately 7% of the total Service.

Other kinds of internal evidence are more ephemeral. Several aspects of Weelkes's style, both overall and in this particular piece, have already been mentioned. For example, if a passage has a number of empty fifths, a voice should be added that fills them with thirds most of the time, because this is Weelkes's practice in most of his music. Or if a number of empty fourths or second-inversion triads appear on strong beats but do not act as suspensions, it is likely that a missing voice below them ought to create first-inversion or root-position triads. Sections F and G in the Service contain a number of such examples.

Homophonic texture and polyphonic imitation are other typical keystones of the style. In section A, for example, an added tenor voice should no doubt join in the general homophonic texture of the opening. In more imitative passages, such as sections F and G, the added voice should clearly participate in the contrapuntal interplay.

Canons comprise a special case of the latter kind of contrapuntal passages. Surely a second voice must exactly imitate the first one in a canon. But one has to be very careful about creating canonic imitation where it may not have existed originally. Noble has discovered an ingenious seven-measure canon in section F between a created second alto *cantoris* part and the extant second alto *decani*. Wulstan uses this same canon but also adds a brief second one between two reconstructed tenor voices. However, the *Magnificat* evidently contains no other canons by Weelkes himself, in contrast to the *Nunc dimittis* where they are more abundant and complex than anywhere else in Weelkes's music. Therefore, it is questionable whether, on principle, one should add these.

A similar instance at section N in the *Nunc dimittis* leads to the opposite conclusion. In this case, the color plan calls for the reconstruction of two *cantoris* voices to go with the four voices already extant. These four extant voices, it happens, are canonic in pairs. Both Noble and Wulstan have again found an identical solution for the two reconstructed voices: adding a third canonic voice of about seven measures to each of Weelkes's two-part canons. In this case, not only because this passage is surrounded by other canons in the *Nunc dimittis* but also because of the very complexity of creating two simultaneous three-voice canons, it seems probable that Weelkes must have used the same or a very similar one originally.

TEXT UNDERLAY

Text underlay brings a separate problem to the reconstruction of the Service. The underlay in the extant parts is, typically for the era, quite inconsistent. Even in cases of exact canonic imitation and of two partbooks containing the same voice, the text underlay of the two voices is frequently in disagreement. One can only conclude that composers, copyists, and singers of the time were not particularly concerned with precisely which syllable went with which note, a situation almost incomprehensible to us today.

The reconstructor, therefore, is compelled to use his or her own judgement in assigning syllables to notes more than would be allowable in other aspects of reconstruction. Using what actually survives in the partbooks, combined with a knowledge of the practices of the composer and the time, he or she should probably introduce, without the usual editorial identification, some consistency into the underlay for the purposes of modern performance.

THE MODERN SCORE

While not directly involved with the reconstruction itself, the question of how to present the completed Evening Service for Seven Voices in score is a potentially difficult one for the reconstructor and the publisher, who may have conflicting goals. The reconstructor wishes to provide a score to the purchaser that is an accurate rendition of the composer's original intent in a manner that would make it the most understandable and performable; the publisher, on the other hand, is justifiably concerned that the cost of the final product be as low as possible so that sales of the piece will be at maximum.

The continuously changing number of voices in the Service brings the conflict into focus. In order to keep the total number of pages required at a minimum, thus reducing engraving and printing costs, the publisher would no doubt advocate that as many measures of music as possible appear on each page. Thus, when the number of voices active is fewer, as many as two or three systems could appear on each page; but when all the voices are active, there would be room for only one system per page, unless the publisher further insists that they be squeezed onto a smaller number of staves. The method of changing the number of systems per page was chosen by both Noble and Wulstan in their reconstructions.

Any singer or conductor will immediately recognize the problem with this plan. In a piece constantly changing from four to ten parts, the location on the page of any one voice will also change frequently. The difficulties to the singers of keeping track of where they are each time the eye jumps from one system to the next are serious.

Furthermore, such changing formats are difficult for the analyst as well, as anyone who has tried to follow the arguments above while using Wulstan's score can testify. Relationships among voices and between sections, such as the antiphonal section Q (Figure 4), are much more difficult to perceive when printed in varying or compressed format.

Finally, the scholar will be unsatisfied as well, because one of his other interests in studying the score is to see how the reconstructor has re-created the missing voices, and if they are on a different location on each page, the task becomes much more difficult.

The singer, conductor, analyst, and scholar, then, will argue strongly for an unchanging, uncompressed format throughout, even though many pages will have large numbers of rests when the sonority has thinned, and much more page turning will be necessary.

Even if one decides that every voice should show on every page, regardless of whether it is active at that moment or not, several decisions still remain about the format of the score. An American, for example, would probably say that the ten voices should be shown in double-chorus format, with a five-voice *decani* choir occupying the top five staves and a five-voice *cantoris* choir below (as in Figure 4). This format provides maximum exposure to antiphonal portions of the piece but obscures unison relationships between two voices. The Englishman, who has lived with *decani* and *cantoris* divisions for centuries, would maintain that such divisions are simply splits of a single choir that sings sometimes as two half-choirs. He would advocate, therefore, a single-choir format starting at the top with the soprano *decani* voice, followed by the soprano *cantoris*, first alto *decani*, first alto *cantoris*, and so forth. Here is the same passage as that in Figure 4 shown in the "English" format:

Figure 8. Measures 89-93, *Nunc dimittis* (section Q)

Such an arrangement makes it more difficult to see divisions between *decani* and *cantoris* but clearly shows whether adjacent voices are in unison with each other or not. It also makes clear the different pairings of the four alto voices, which are sometimes paired as first and second altos on the same side of the aisle (see Figure 5), and sometimes as *decani* and *cantoris*:

Figure 9. Measures 88-92, *Magnificat* (section E)

In either case, of course, even with a consistent format, each voice should be identified on each page, and the reconstructed voices should be separately identified on each page as well.

After considerable thought, and after experimenting with a number of different formats, I would argue for a consistent nine-voice "English" format, with a single line for the tenor, since I have already proposed that the tenor be split into *decani* and *cantoris* divisions only where absolutely necessary. The only place where using *decani* and *cantoris* markings on a single tenor staff causes any difficulty is in section Q, where the antiphony requires the two tenor parts to occupy the same staff at the same time briefly (see Figure 8); but a good engraver ought to be able to cope with any resultant problem without too much difficulty, perhaps with stem direction.

CONCLUSION

The obvious next step for the present author is to try his hand at a new reconstruction based on the conclusions reached in this essay. No doubt, a number of these proposals will have to change when tested by the fires of practicality. At least, however, one hopes that the conductor, singer, analyst, or historian will be pleased with the attempt to bring Weelkes's greatest work to life again in a form as close as possible to the composer's original intentions for it.

H. Colin Slim

Some Puzzling Intabulations of Vocal Music for Keyboard, C. 1600, at Castell'Arquato

In preparing an edition of fascicles IV, VI, VIII, and IX of the keyboard manuscripts held by the Chiesa Collegiata at Castell'Arquato (near Piacenza) for a second volume in the series, *Keyboard Music at Castell'Arquato*,[1] I have been intrigued by some intabulations of vocal music, all copied in the same hand, found chiefly in fascicles IV and VI. There are several types of keyboard arrangements of vocal compositions at Castell'Arquato: almost direct transcriptions of favorite

---

[1] *Corpus of Early Keyboard Music* (Rome: American Institute of Musicology) 37, vol. 1: *Dances and Dance Songs*, ed. H. Colin Slim (1975), includes fascicles III and VII. The ten fascicles are described in my dissertation, "The Keyboard Ricercar and Fantasia in Italy c. 1500-1550 with Reference to Parallel Forms in European Lute Music of the Same Period" (unpublished Ph.D. diss., Harvard University, 1960), vol. I, 78-107. See also Knud Jeppesen, "Eine frühe Orgelmesse aus Castell'Arquato," *Archiv für Musikwissenschaft* 12 (1955) 187-205 and Slim, "Keyboard Music at Castell'Arquato by an Early Madrigalist," *Journal of the American Musicological Society* 15 (1962) 35-47.

Dr. Slim, a native of British Columbia, received his B.A. from the University of British Columbia and his Ph.D. in musicology from Harvard University (1961). He taught at the University of Chicago from 1959 to 1965 and subsequently at the University of California, Irvine.

His numerous outstanding contributions to the musicological literature focus primarily on the vocal, keyboard, and lute music of sixteenth-century Italy. Central among his publications are critical editions of Musica nova *(University of Chicago Press, 1964) and* A Gift of Madrigals and Motets *(University of Chicago Press, 1972). Dr. Slim was elected President of the American Musicological Society in 1987 and has served on the Editorial Board of* JAMS.

pieces, such as Arcadelt's "Occhi miei lassi"[2] (fascicle I); slightly decorated arrangements—perhaps best characterized as "graced"[3]—for example, Ferabosco's madrigal, "Io mi son giovenetta"[4] (fascicle III); and highly decorated arrangements, such as Reulx's "S'io credesse"[5] (fascicle IVb). The majority of the arrangements of vocal compositions, sacred or secular, for keyboard at Castell'Arquato belong to the first or second categories. Several arrangements of sacred works in fascicles IV and VI, many of them including the complete text copied between the keyboard staves, are exceptional. These I shall discuss later in this essay.

Most of the transcriptions of vocal works in fascicles IV and VI— and one in fascicle II—are copied in a single, messy, late-sixteenth-century or early-seventeenth-century hand. They pose difficult problems not only in identifying their models, but also in explaining their purpose in the fascicle.

This hand first appears on the final folio of fascicle II; then on much of the first fragment (a) of fascicle IV and entirely throughout its second fragment (b). (Both these fragments have suffered some losses of an undetermined number of folios.) The same hand again runs throughout all of fascicles VI and X (except for the first four folios of the latter, on which an earlier hand copied lute intabulations).

There follows a list (in some cases only summary) of the contents of fascicles II, IV, VI, and X. An asterisk preceding a composition indicates the above-described copyist's hand. Only the earliest-known dates of the sources of vocal models are given. Texts, where present, are given in full, but without word or phrase repetition.

Fascicle II
    ff. 1-3   [two] Recercare [by] Jacobo Fogliano[6]

[2]First published in 1539; modern edition in Jacob Arcadelt, *Opera Omnia*, ed. Albert Seay, vol. 2 (Rome: American Institute of Musicology, 1970) 79-81, no. 36.
[3]This felicitous expression appears in Howard Mayer Brown, *Embellishing Sixteenth-Century Music* (London: Oxford University Press, 1976) 1ff.
[4]First published in 1542; modern edition in Don Harrán (ed.), *The Anthologies of Black-Note Madrigals* (Rome: American Institute of Musicology, 1978), vol. 1, part 2, 109-112, no. 28. The keyboard arrangement appears in Slim, *Dances and Dance Songs*, pp. 20-21 and in Giacomo Benvenuti (ed.), *Marco Antonio Cavazzoni: ricercari, mottetti, canzoni; Jacobo Fogliano, Julio Segni ed anonimi: ricercari e ricercate* (Milan: I Classici Musicali Italiani, 1941) 83-85.
[5]First published (anonymously) in 1542; modern edition in Harrán, *Black-Note Madrigals*, vol. 1, part 1, 57-60, no. 15.
[6]Modern editions in Benvenuti, *Cavazzoni*, 65-69 and in Knud Jeppesen, *Die Italienische Orgelmusik am Anfang des Cinquencento*, 2nd ed. (Copenhagen: Wilhelm Hansen Musik-Forlag, 1960), vol. 2, 77-81.

ff. 3-13   Missa de la dominica [by] Jaches [Brumel?],
              Patrem[7]
f. 13[v]   *[final twenty-two breves, lacking text, of
              Domenico Ferabosco's madrigal, "Io mi son
              giovenetta," transposed a fourth lower than its
              model, 1542][8]

Fascicle IV, fragment a
ff. 1-10   Missa dell'Apostoli (Kyrie, Gloria primo verso
              [verses *2-*8], Amen, *Recercare, *Credo
              [verses 1-4])
ff. 10[v]-11 *[final twenty breves of unidentified high-voiced
              work lacking text, a4, presumably a madrigal]
ff. 11[v]-14 [four dances on a) passamezzo antico, b)
              romanesca, c) bergamesca, and d) passamezzo
              antico basses]
f. 14[v]   *[first fifteen breves, lacking text, of Cipriano de
              Rore's madrigal, "Anchor' che col partire," 1547][9]

Fascicle IV, fragment b
ff. 1-5   *Canti donque qui meco ogni persona
              I dolci e lieti accenti
              Mentre di geme si coron' et oro
              Il re del nostro coro
              Che per pietà del cielo alto diventa
              Puoi che sol' la virtù fama ci dona
              Deggna di reggio honore e reggn' anchora
              Viva la virtù donque e il vitio mora.
              [unidentified setting of a secular or spiritual
              madrigal, a5]
ff. 5-7[v]   *S'io credesse [per morte essere scarco,
              Anselmo Reulx's madrigal, 1542][10]
ff. 8-11   *O gloriosa domina [excelsa supra sidera, etc., a

[7]Modern edition in Jeppesen, *Italienische Orgelmusik*, vol. 2, 82-99, omitting the
"Patrem."
[8]See above, note 4.
[9]Modern editions in Cipriano Rore, *Opera Omnia*, ed. Bernhard Meier (Rome: American
Institute of Musicology, 1969), vol. 4, 31-32 and in Alfred Einstein, *The Italian
Madrigal*, 3 vols. (Princeton: Princeton University Press, 1949), vol. 2, 112-14.
[10]See above, note 5.

version of Adrian Willaert's hymn, in
manuscript c. 1530, and printed in 1542][11]

ff. 11-13[v]   *Assumpta est Maria in celum gaudent angeli
laudates benedicunt dominum [unidentified setting of a short responsory, a4]

Fascicle VI

ff. 1-8   *["Magnificat" setting of 12 verses, a4, as
follows:]

f. 1   *Anima mea dominum [in left margin:] cum quatuor
vocibus [unidentified setting of verse 1, a4]

f. 1[v]   *Et exultavit spiritus meus in deo salutari meo
[transposed a fourth lower from Orlando di
Lasso's "Magnificat primi toni," 1567][12]

ff. 2-2[v]   Quia respexit humiltatem ancille sue ecce enim
ex hoc beatam me dicent omnes generationes
[unidentified setting of verse 3, a4]

f. 3   *Quia fecit mihi magna qui potens est et sanctum
nomen eius [from Lasso, ibid.]

ff. 3[v]-4   *Et misericordia eius a progenie in progenies
timentibus eum [unidentified setting of verse 5, a4]

ff. 4-4[v]   *Fecit potentiam in brachio suo dispersit super-
bos mente cordis sui [from Lasso, ibid.]

ff. 5-5[v]   *Deposuit potentes de sede et exaltavit humiles
[unidentified setting of verse 7, a4]

ff. 5[v]-6   *Esurientes implevit bonis et divites dimissit in-
anes [from Lasso, ibid.]

ff. 6[v]-7   *Suscepit Israel puerum suum recordatus miseri-
cordie sue [unidentified setting of verse 9, a4]

f. 7   *Sicut locutus est ad patres nostros Abraham et
semini eius in secula [from Lasso, ibid.]

f. 7[v]   *Gloria patri et filio et spiritui sancto [uniden-
tified setting of verse 11, a4]

f. 8   *Sicut erat in principio et nunc et semper et in
secula seculorum. Amen. [from Lasso, ibid.]

[11]Modern edition in Adrian Willaert, *Opera Omnia*, ed. Hermann Zenck, (Rome:
American Institute of Musicology, 1951) vol. 4, 59-65.
[12]Modern edition in Orlando di Lasso, *Sämtliche Werke*, vol. 13: *Magnificat 1-24*,
ed. James Erb (Kassel: Bärenreiter, 1980) 245-50, no. 17.

ff. 8ᵛ-10   *Christe redemptor omnium [Girolamo Cavaz-
              zoni's hymn setting, 1543][13]

ff. 10ᵛ-11   *Fit porta christi pervia, fulget dies Referta
              plena gratia, ful[get] dies ista Diei solennia [sic]
              celebrat ecclesia [1561; also = four lower voices
              of Lasso's or Jacob Regnart's hymn a5, in
              manuscript c. 1565[14], printed in 1592][15]

f. 11   *[two fragments, the second a recopy of part of
              folio 10v]

ff. 11ᵛ-13ᵛ   *Ego dormio et cor meum vigilat vox dilecti mei
              pulsantis aperi mihi soror mea columba mea im-
              maculata mea. Quia caput meum plenum est
              voce [unidentified setting of an antiphon for
              Vespers and Lauds, a5]

ff. 14-18ᵛ   *Scopriro del nanino [Giovanni Maria Nanino's
              madrigai, "Scopriró l'ardor mio," 1576][16]

ff. 18ᵛ-20ᵛ   *Adoramus te Christe et benedicimus tibi. Quia
              per sanctam crucem tuam redemisti mundum
              domine miserere nobis. [unidentified setting of a
              short responsory, a5]

ff. 20ᵛ-22   *[Pavana della] battaglia [anonymous pavan, a4,
              c. 1544;[17] same pavan (with saltarello) copied in
              different hand in fascicle VIII, f. 6ᵛ]

---

[13]Modern editions in Girolamo Cavazzoni, *Orgelwerke*, ed. Oscar Mischiati, (Mainz:
B. Schotts Söhne, 1959), vol. 1, pp. 20-21 and in Cavazzoni, *Musica sacra, ricercari
e canzoni*, ed. Giacomo Benvenuti, quaderno 25 (Milan: Instituto Editoriale Italiano,
1919) 9-11, under the incorrect title "Jesu redemptor omnium."
[14]Modern edition in Lasso, *Sämtliche Werke*, vol. 18: *Das Hymnarium*, ed. Marie Louise
Göllner (Kassel: Bärenreiter, 1980) 151-52 and 180-81.
[15]Modern edition from the *Novum pratum musicum* in Godelieve Spiessens, *Leven en
Werk van de Antwerpse Luitcomponist Emanuel Adriaenssen* (Brussels: Koninkliijke
Academie voor Wetenschappen, 1974), vol. 2, 201-04, no. 46. See also, note 29.
[16]*Musica di XIII. autori illustri a cinque voci* (Venice, 1576); also in the facsimile edi-
tion of *Musica divina di XIX autori* (Antwerp, 1583), folio IIᵛ ("Corpus of Early
Music in Facsimile," ed. Bernard Huys, vol. 19 [Brussels: Éditions Culture et Civilisa-
tion, 1971]).
[17]*Musicque de Joye* (Lyons, n.d.), "Pavane. La Bataille," edited in Franz J. Giesbert,
Fröhliche Musik (Kassel: Bärenreiter, 1934) 22-23. The print is dated c. 1544 by Samuel
F. Pogue, *Jacques Moderne: Lyons Music Printer of the Sixteenth Century* (Geneva:
Librairie Droz, 1969) 182-85, no. 41. Further, see Brown, *Instrumental Music Printed
Before 1600: a Bibliography* (Cambridge, Mass.: Harvard University Press, 1969),
154?-6, no. 33 and Dietrich Kämper, *La musica strumentale nel rinascimento* (Turin:
Edizioni Rai Radiotelevisione Italiana, 1976) 187-90.

Fascicle X
    ff. 1-4ᵛ   Recercar, Pavana, [two] Saltarelli [and two
                    dance songs in Italian lute tablature]
    ff. 4ᵛ-50ᵛ   *[fifteen] canzone [nos. 5, 4, 5 (sic), 6-11, and
                    13-18, by Florentio Maschera, 1582][18]

Aside from Ferabosco's partially preserved madrigal in fascicle II—no other source presently available renders it in this transposition—and the unknown fragment in fascicle IVa of what is likely—to judge from its closing phrase repetition—a madrigal for high voices, four of the madrigals in fascicles II, IV, and VI represent relatively straightforward copying of their voice parts onto two-stave keyboard scores. Only Reulx's "S'io credesse" (fascicle IVb) is extensively decorated, not just with "gracing" cadential formulas, but with wide-ranging scale figures. As we shall see, this style of decoration also characterizes the other three arrangements of vocal works in this fascicle.

Even assuming that our copyist had a printed book or books at hand, the immense popularity of Ferabosco's "Io mi son giovenetta," Rore's "Anchor' che col partire," and Nanino's "Scopriro" makes it virtually impossible to determine what source or sources he might have employed. Ferabosco's madrigal appears in print at least twenty-five times between 1542 and 1645;[19] Rore's madrigal at least seventy-five times between 1547 and 1645;[20] and Nanino's madrigal at least nine times between 1576 and 1634.[21]

Since the six Castell'Arquato madrigals are all copied in the same hand, presumably they were entered into their respective fascicles some time after 1576, the date of the first known printing of "Scopriro"[22] (fascicle VI), and probably after 1582, the date of the first printing (now

[18]See Brown, *Instrumental Music*, 1582-4 and 1584-10, the latter the first surviving edition. Incipits of Maschera's canzone appear in Giacomo Benvenuti, *Andrea e Giovanni Gabrieli e la Musica strumentale in San Marco II*, "Istituzioni e monumenti dell'arte musicale Italiana" [Milan, 1932]), vol. 2, lv-lx; the canzone are edited in W. McKee, "The Music of Florentio Maschera (1540-1584)," (unpublished Ph.D. dissertation, North Texas State University, 1958).
[19]These editions are found in Einstein's *Bibliography of Italian Secular Vocal Music Printed between the Years 1500-1700*, appended to the reprint of Emil Vogel, *Bibliothek der gedruckten weltlichen Vocalmusik Italiens* (Hildesheim: Olms, 1962), vol. 2.
[20]See Ernest T. Ferand, "Anchor che col partire. Die Schicksale eines berühmten Madrigals," *Festschrift Karl Gustav Fellerer*, ed. Heinrich Hüschen (Regensburg: Gustav Bosse Verlag, 1962) 138.
[21]See Einstein, *Bibliography* in Vogel, *Bibliothek*, vol. 2.
[22]Born in 1543 or 1544, Nanino could have composed it as much as a decade earlier, for a lost first book of madrigals had apparently already appeared by 1571-72; see *The New Grove Dictionary of Music and Musicians* (London, 1980), s.v. "Nanino, Giovanni Maria," by Anthony Newcomb.

lost) of Maschera's canzone copied into fascicle X. Nanino's madrigal appears again in prints of 1583 and 1589. The former source,[23] which also includes Ferabosco's and Rore's madrigals (fascicles II and IVa), was reprinted many times up to 1634 and is thus a possible source for three of the six madrigals. No printed anthology includes these madrigals together with Reulx's "S'io credesse" (fascicle IVb). However, it and Ferabosco's madrigal (fascicle II) appear together in printed sources from 1542 to 1563,[24] after which date "S'io credesse" drops from the printed repertoire.

It thus seems that if printed sources do form the basis of the secular music represented here, they would not likely date from before the last two decades of the sixteenth century. There is, of course, no certainty that our copyist used printed materials, for it is just at the turn of the seventeenth century that huge retrospective manuscript anthologies of madrigals are preserved.[25] Doubtless many more of these have not survived. Whatever his source, his idiosyncratic placement of the various voice parts on the two staves of keyboard score seems to indicate that the scribe was copying from part books and not from another keyboard manuscript or print. The only exception is his copy (fascicle VI) from Cavazzoni's *Intavolatura* of 1543, which it resembles in virtually every detail.

Examination of the setting of the anonymous "Canti donque" in fascicle IVb confirms the impression that they were copied in the late sixteenth century or even the early seventeenth century. Even though the source of "Canti donque" remains unidentified, and even though the keyboard version is considerably overlaid with figuration, it is possible to show that the original vocal source was almost certainly for five voices and had a texture typical of the late madrigal. The poem entered between the staves receives a good deal of line repetition and even of phrases—only the first four words of line one are not affected—much more than is common earlier in the sixteenth century. The musical treatment of these, consisting both of sequential repetitions and of simple repetition with fuller textures, exactly resembles effects achieved by writing for three and four contrasting voice groups from among the five or six voices normal to the late madrigal. Example 1 demonstrates this procedure.

[23]*Musica divina*; see above, note 16.
[24]See Einstein, *Bibliography* (1542-2) in Vogel, *Bibliothek,* vol. 2.
[25]See for example, the entries under "London BLE 3665," "MilC s.s.," "NYorkP 4302" in Herbert Kellman and Charles Hamm, *Census-Catalogue of Manuscript Sources of Polyphonic Music 1400-1550,* (Rome: American Institute of Musicology, 1982), vol. 2 and "Paris BNC 851," in idem, vol. 3 (1984).

Example 1

Line two, repeated sequentially a fifth higher, is followed by another repetition at the same pitch but with fuller texture. The vocal model was presumably five-voiced; three lower (or middle) voices are used, followed by three upper and then by all five. Similar techniques appear throughout this work. Line six, for example, receives three statements: the second and third ones at the lower fifth and upper second, respectively, from the initial statement. Briefer sequential repetitions at the lower fifth appear for the last two words of line seven, and many more examples could be cited.

Whether the poem salutes a divine or a secular ruler is uncertain. Professor Nino Pirrotta kindly cautions me that the text does not necessarily refer to the Deity; it could well be rendering homage to some secular ruler.

Whatever the intention of the poet of ''Canti donque,'' the liturgical nature of the remaining compositions with text in fascicles IVb and VI cannot be questioned. The scribe's placement (between the staves, as usual) of the words of ''Assumpta est Maria'' (fascicle IVb) probably derives from the text of the cantus of its vocal source. His source's vocality is evident not only from the presence of text, but also from the point-of-imitation technique that allows us at certain places to glimpse the unidentified original. Example 2 shows my addition of text to what were probably tenor and bass parts (following his texted cantus), and example 3 shows my addition of text to what were probably tenor and alto parts (preceding his texted cantus).

Example 2

Example 3

The scribe's use of the repetition sign ( ) probably also follows his source's cantus. However, without any words for the lower voices, this sign is not now sufficient to allow us to supply text in many places with any certainty, and thus we cannot gain any really coherent notion of the original vocal composition. This difficulty is compounded by the scribe's omission of syllables at two page turns. And at another point it seems evident from tied notes in the uppermost line in his manuscript that he forgot to include the cantus part, because the words he supplies will not fit the voice parts he copied, as example 4 demonstrates.

Example 4

Though he sometimes dissolves the partwriting into rapid scale figures and occasionally adds a fifth voice and at the final chord even a sixth voice, it appears that the unidentified vocal model was for four voices. Its style seems close to that of the mid sixteenth century.

An opening rapid scale figure for the right hand at the first syllable ("E-") of the setting of the antiphon "Ego dormio" (fascicle VI), is clearly written over a vocal model of five voices. I use "over" rather than "on" because the first bar in the manuscript shows an erasure, difficult as it is now to read. The copyist first wrote three notes for the right-hand part and subsequently replaced them with the scale figure. Despite this brief opening chord originally of six notes for both hands, evidence that the unknown vocal model was for five voices occurs at the first statement of "pulsantis vox dilecti mei," Example 5. Here the scribe added a breve rest for the cantus (at "dilecti") and, exceptionally for him, copied the text from the altus into his manuscript. Like "Canti donque," "Ego dormio" belongs to the late Renaissance, as demonstrated by its frequent repetition of text. With the textual repetitions, either the same basic musical materials are reiterated with fuller resources, as in Example 6 at "cor meum vigilat," or a predilection for dividing the voices into opposing groups—high, low, and all together—is revealed, as in Example 7 (at "aperi"). This latter technique frequently appears in turn-of-the-century music in order to set verbs. Another extended group of repetitions at "plenum est voce" near the close demonstrates a fondness for imitative sequences.

Example 5

Example 6

et   cor me um vi - gi - lat, et   cor me- um vi - gi - lat

Example 7

a - pe - ri,   a - pe - ri, a - pe - ri mi -   hi

The last of the arrangements in fascicle VI of sacred vocal music so
far unidentified is the short responsory, ''Adoramus te, Christe.''
''Tonic'' and ''dominant'' statements in the lowest keyboard voice at
''Adoramus te'' suggest that the opening bottom keyboard line (mm.
1-3) represents a baritone voice part of the original, and that the responding lowest keyboard voice (mm. 4-6) was a bass part. This impression is strengthened by the five voices employed in mm. 4-6, which
contrast with the opening four-voiced texture. A second, briefer point
of imitation at ''Quia per sanctam crucem'' is still discernible between
the bass and (probably) an altus voice (the latter subjected to considerable
keyboard decoration), this four-voiced texture again closing in five
voices. Staggered statements of ''domine'' a5 precede a final reduction to four voices during three settings of ''miserere nobis,'' placed
in middle, low, and high voices. The brief and unpretentious nature

of the original is in keeping with similar settings by Lassus,[26] Ruffo,[27] and Palestrina[28] from the second half of the sixteenth century.

Vocal models and composers have been located for the three remaining sacred compositions—"O gloriosa domina" in fascicle IVb, and the "Magnificat" and "Fit porta Christi" in fascicle VI. I shall discuss the three works in reverse order of their appearance in the fascicles. Comparison of them to their keyboard versions reveals various facets of the intabulator's craft: as simple transcriber, as interpolator, and as radical surgeon.

For "Fit porta Christi" the source situation is complex. A setting for four voices of this hymn first appears anonymously in print in 1561. This setting next appears in 1592, but its print has only the cantus and bassus (which are also set in lute tablature).[29] However, in between these two printed editions Jacob Regnart (c. 1540/45-1599) composed a five-voiced parody Mass, dated 1587 in a German manuscript,[30] which he modelled on the same hymn setting but which had an additional, fifth voice part. The Mass was not printed until 1602, Regnart having signed its preface the last year of his life. The hymn itself appears under Regnart's name as a later addition to a German keyboard manuscript begun in 1598 and finished by 1610[31], but is not ascribed to Regnart in print until 1627.[32] Lastly, two German manuscript sources of the sixteenth century, one devoted chiefly to Lasso's hymns and the other to his Magnificats, present "Fit porta Christi" in three different ver-

[26]Modern editions of Lasso's four settings are listed in *The New Grove Dictionary*, s.v. "Lassus, Orlande de," by James Haar.

[27]Printed in Venice in 1586; see Lewis Lockwood, *The Counter-Reformation and the Masses of Vincenzo Ruffo* (Venice: Universal Edition, 1970) 258.

[28]Modern editions of Palestrina's setting are listed in Lockwood (ibid.) and *The New Grove Dictionary*, s.v. "Palestrina," by Jessie Ann Owens.

[29]*Veteres ac piae cantiones . . . Omnia quatuor vocibus composita* (Nuremberg, 1561), no. 4, listed in *Répertoire International des Sources Musicales,* vol. 1 (Munich, 1960), *Récueils imprimés XVI-XVII siècles,* ed. François Lesure, 1561-1. Further on this print and the 1592 print cited above in note 15, see Rudolf Rasch, *De cantiones natalitiae en het kerkelijke muziekleven in de zuidelijke nederlanden gedurende de zeventiende eeuw* (Utrecht, 1985), vol. I, 40-42, 215; and vol. II, 410-413, and 458, ex. 4.2.1.

[30]See Walter Pass, *Thematischer Katalog sämtlicher Werke Jacob Regnarts* (ca. 1540-99) (Vienna: Im Kommission bei Hermann Böhlaus Nachf., 1969) 98, no. 11 and pp. 137-138, no. 134. Marburg, Staatsbibliothek, Mus. Ms. 40 020 (olim Berlin, Preussische Staatsbibliothek, Ms. Z 20) is dated 1587; see Johannes Wolf, *Handbuch der Notationskunde* (Leipzig, 1913; reprint ed. Hildesheim: Olms, 1963), vol. 1, 446.

[31]See Göllner, *Bayerische Staatsbibliothek, Kataog der Musikhandschriften 2: Tabulaturen und Stimmbücher bis zur Mitte des 17. Jahrhunderts* (Munich: G. Henle Verlag, 1979) 141, Ms. 1640, no. 118.

[32]*Promptuarii musici concentus ecclesiasticos . . . pars tertia* (Strasbourg, 1627), no. 38, listed in *Répertoire International des Sources Musicales,* vol. 1 [Munich, 1960]), *Récueils imprimés XVI-XVII siècles.* ed. François Lésure, 1627-1.

sions. One anonymous version a5 of "Fit porta Christi" may have
preceded the main hand that copied Lasso's hymns, which were entered
by 1581.[33] A second anonymous version a5 was added late in the sixteenth century after the copying, c. 1565, of Lasso's Magnificats;[34]
another setting, a8, entered in the same late hand and bearing Lasso's
name, immediately precedes it.[35] Only the two anonymous versions a5
are yet available in the new edition of Lasso's hymns.[36]

Whether "Fit porta Christi" is by Lasso or by Regnart is far from
easy to decide. The two Lasso sources containing the hymn setting a5
are the oldest, suggesting Lasso composed it late in the 1560s or during the 1570s, though Lasso's name itself is not joined to "Fit porta
Christi" except for the eight-voiced version from near the end of the
sixteenth century, perhaps even after Lasso's death. Sources that ascribe
"Fit porta Christi" to Regnart are from early in the seventeenth century.

Probably the anonymous four-voiced hymn-setting from 1561 is the
original and presumably also the source of the five-voiced setting.
Publication in 1561 seems a little early for Regnart to have composed
it, though not impossible for Lasso. Whether by Lasso or by Regnart,
one of the five-voiced hymn settings is surely the source for Regnart's
parody Mass a5, for he would not likely have composed his Mass on
an eight-voiced source.

The problem of identification may be further complicated by a working
relationship between the two composers. Lasso extended a helping hand
in 1580 to his slightly younger colleague by recommending Regnart
for a court position,[37] which seems to argue for a personal connection
between the two composers. There is no barrier to Regnart having composed "Fit porta Christi" by the late 1560s or in the 1570s, for by 1564
he was already having his music published.[38] Nor is there any reason
that he could not have used his own hymn setting for his parody Mass
on it. Of Regnart's thirty-six parody Masses, thirty-three parody other
compositions. At least five of these (excluding Regnart's "Missa super

---

[33]Munich, Bayerische Staatsbibliothek, Mus. Ms. 55; see Göllner (ed.), *Lasso, Das Hymnarium*, xlv.

[34]Munich, Bayerische Staatsbibliothek, Mus. Ms. 22; see Göllner, *Lasso, Das Hymnarium*, xlv and Erb (ed.), *Lasso, Magnificat 1-24*, xxiv-xxv.

[35]See note 34.

[36]In Göllner (ed.), *Lasso, Das Hymnarium*, 151-52 and 180-81.

[37]*The New Grove Dictionary*, s.v. "Regnart, Jacob," by Walter Pass.

[38]Ibid., 693.

Fit porta Christi'') are on his own works.[39] However, because Regnart chose almost as many of Lasso's works for parody as he did works by himself—other composers represented are Josquin (1); Regnart's teacher, Monte (2); and Wert (2)—this fails to help us to assign one or the other composer to the hymn.

Four stages are discernible during the approximately seventy-year transmission of ''Fit porta Christi,'' the first being its anonymous appearance a4 in 1561. The two anonymous versions a5 in the Lasso manuscripts, which agree in most essentials save for an occasional interchange of voice parts, represent a second stage. A third stage occurs in the 1592 lute print and in Castell'Arquato's keyboard version, both modelled on the 1561 hymn. The former includes the 1561 ''cantus'' and ''bassus'' in mensural notation. This bassus agrees exactly with the lowest line of the Castell'Arquato intabulation, except for the latter's omission of B flats near the close, probably resulting from an F sharp signed in its top line. 1561, 1592, and Castell'Arquato share a variant in the bass line of their penultimate bars that does not occur in the five-voiced settings. Although the ''cantus'' of the 1561 and the 1592 prints is virtually the same as the uppermost line of the Castell'Arquato version, it is not the cantus of the five-voiced hymn, but its altus. Possibly then, the lutenist of the 1592 print and the Castell'Arquato keyboard player were expected to sing the absent cantus as they performed the hymn's lower voices on their respective instruments. The transcription below of the Castell'Arquato version adds the absent cantus part (from Munich, Mus. Ms. 55) in smaller type.

[39]Of the Masses listed by Pass, *Thematischer Katalog*, pp. 95-107, but not identified, nos. 1 and 29 are on Josquin's motet; no. 5 is on Regnart's canzona (see no. 347); no. 6 on Lasso's lied; no. 7 on Monte's chanson; nos. 10 and 15 on madrigals by Wert; nos. 16-18 on motets by Lasso; nos. 20 and 23 on Regnart's motets (see nos. 206 and 195); no. 26 on Monte's madrigal; no. 28 on a motet ascribed to Lasso (see Mus. Ms 4480, no. 15, in Göllner, *Bayerische Staatsbibliothek*, pp. 173 and 175); no. 30 on Lasso's lied; no. 31 on Regnart's motet (see no. 211); no. 34 on Lasso's motet; and no. 36 on Regnart's motet (see no. 206).

1. Third lower in M̂S, and in 1561.
2. "celebrat" begins here, obviously to accomodate its top line, the altus.

A final stage in the evolution of "Fit porta Christi" occurs in the
five-voiced version with organ continuo, first published in 1627 under
Regnart's name. This version not only supplies a continuo that is figured
in several places, but features the organ itself as a kind of concerted
instrument. The organ plays an introduction and interludes fashioned
from the ensuing voice parts as found in the earliest manuscript versions, the bass following the bass of the earliest manuscripts and not
the one common to the 1561 and 1592 prints and the Castell'Arquato
versions. Dynamic signs of "P[iano]" and "F[orte]" added to the con-

tinuo, the former sign applied at solo organ passages and the latter applied at the entry of the voices, emphasize the new composition's concerted nature. Thus the transmission of "Fit porta Christi" furnishes us with almost seventy years of stylistic change from an independent vocal piece, to a work for accompanied solo voice, to a concerted composition for organ and voices.

In the margin at the left of the first stave of "Anima mea dominum" (fascicle VI) appears "cum quatuor vocibus," an inscription that demonstrates the vocal origin of this keyboard Magnificat. Unsuspected, however, is that not one, but two *different* compositions underly it. Only the second of these, Lasso's "Magnificat primi toni" which sets the even-numbered verses of the canticle (beginning with "Et exultavit"), has so far been identified.

During the sixteenth century, polyphonic setting of the canticle's odd-numbered verses was far less usual. Lasso's own practice represents the tradition, for of his 102 Magnificat settings, only four set odd-numbered verses.[40] Continuous polyphonic settings of all twelve verses are also relatively rare. Even such settings by Costanzo Festa and Morales appear in some sources set out *alternatim* between choir and plainsong.[41]

Considerable textural disparity exists between Lasso's even-numbered verses and the unknown composer's odd-numbered verses. The latter, even when decorated, open unmistakably with points of imitation (see especially verses 1, 3, 5, 9, and 11), at least up to their medial cadences (and sometimes beyond them; see verses 5 and 7). Lasso's verse settings are by and large chordal. (There are brief duets in verses 2 and 8.) The unknown composer frequently repeats words. Verses 1, 3, 5, 7, and 11 (and perhaps 9) each have at least one set of three-fold repetitions, whereas such repetitions appear only in Lasso's settings of verses 8 and 12.

Reconstructing the original vocal model of the odd-numbered verses is relatively simple. The intabulator only rarely adds a fifth voice (verse 1, m. 6) and his "graces" are minimal, largely confined to the uppermost voice. Most of these, corresponding to his treatment of Lasso's cadences, are cadential flourishes; only in verses 1, 3, and 7 does he dissolve melodic progressions of the original into scale figures. Example 8 shows the probable vocal model for the opening of verse 3.

[40]See Erb (ed.), *Lasso, Magnificat 1-24*, viii, note 11.
[41]*The New Grove Dictionary*, s.v. "Magnificat," by Winfried Kirsch.

Example 8

Two aspects of the intabulator's treatment of Lasso's even-numbered verses deserve attention. First, all extant sources of Lasso's ''Magnificat''—eleven prints from 1567 to 1619 (and perhaps also six other prints, now lost) and ten manuscripts from about 1567 to 1630—give it a fourth higher, in G Dorian.[42] Perhaps, then, our intabulator transposed it himself so that it might be at the same pitch as

[42]See Erb (ed.), *Lasso, Magnificat 1-24*, lxxv-lxxvii.

the vocal work he chose for the odd-numbered verses. Second, no extant source of Lasso's "Magnificat" presents the same usage of accidentals found in the Castell'Arquato version, which suggests that the intabulator may have worked from a printed or manuscript source of the "Magnificat" no longer extant.

It might be argued that the curious intermingling of two different composers' works does not necessarily mean that the intabulator intended them to be played as he copied them, but rather that he wanted each set of verses to be used separately at different occasions in *alternatim* practice with a solo singer or chorus. However, had such been his intent, surely he would have copied the verses successively, rather than intermingling them.

Few keyboard intabulations modelled on polyphonic settings of the Magnificat survive, or at least few where the model has been identified.[43] For example, the Swiss organist Fridolin Sicher (1490-1546) arranged the even-numbered verses of Josquin's "Magnificat quarti toni" in German keyboard tablature, c. 1517-30, and his tablature also contains the even-numbered verses of an as yet unidentified composer's "Magnificat quinti toni."[44] However, only the last of Pierre Attaingnant's keyboard settings, the "Magnificat octavi toni," published in 1531, approaches the Castell'Arquato practice. Attaignant's "secundus versus" appropriates the "Et exultavit" from Jean Richafort's "Magnificat octavi toni" (first published in 1534).[45] Attaingnant's other three verses, though not based on Richafort, are presumably also founded on presently unidentified polyphonic verses. Thus, however eccentric the Castell'Arquato "Magnificat," it stands unique in the sixteenth century for its complete presentation of text, for its full complement of odd- and even-numbered verses, and for its total dependence on polyphonic vocal models.

The most peculiar and puzzling keyboard arrangement of a vocal work in these manuscripts at Castell'Arquato is undoubtedly the one in fascicle IVb, headed "O gloriosa domina," no further text being supplied. Peculiar, because it selects from its vocal model, Willaert's setting a6 of "O gloriosa domina—Maria, mater gratie,"[46] in an extraordinary and apparently random manner.

---

[43]See Brown, *Instrumental Music*, 1598-4.

[44]See Walter Nef, "Der St. Galler Organist Fridolin Sicher und seine Orgeltabulatur," *Schweizerisches Jahrbuch für Musikwissenschaft* 7 (1938): 173-75, nos. 43 and 42, respectively.

[45]As noted by Yvonne Rokseth (ed.), *Deux livres d'orgue parus chez Pierre Attaingnant en 1531* (Paris: E. Droz, 1925) xi.

[46]See above, note 11.

Willaert's hymn setting, which includes two slower canonic inner
voices—tenor and quintus at the upper fifth—could have supplied the
intabulator with much material, but he chose to use almost nothing but
the cantus. The keyboard voices found below this cantus—mostly three
voices, rarely four, and only at the final cadence five—are almost without
exception unrelated to anything in Willaert's altus, quintus, tenor, sextus, or bassus parts. The only clear exception is Willaert's altus, which
is selected only twice and then but briefly. The intabulator takes four
notes from its measure 60, transposing them an octave higher, and four
notes at pitch from its antepenultimate measure, 70. A longer paraphrase,
during the opening four measures of the keyboard version, may be a
quote of the sextus at pitch from its mm. 9-13, although the keyboard
could also simply be anticipating (an octave lower) the same melody
heard in the cantus during its mm. 3-7. At mm. 50-51 the keyboard
possibly selects Willaert's bassus, mm. 58-59 ("Vitam datam," though
two octaves higher and decorated), and during its final mm. 62-64, the
keyboard probably quotes the bassus's closing mm. 68-71, "plaudite."

Example 9

The method of quoting Willaert's cantus seems both willful and arbitrary. After the cantus's initial two-bar rest (equals two breves), during which the keyboard parahrase begins, Willaert's cantus appears at pitch in the top line of the keyboard, selected more or less intact from its mm. 3-22 of its original form in the motet, although its mm. 10-17 undergo considerable decoration. Since the original cantus loses a semibreve each during its mm. 12 and 13 and then gains one minim each during its mm. 21 and 22, its rhythmic shape becomes distorted in the keyboard version. Absent from mm. 22-26 of the keyboard setting, the cantus next appears during mm. 27-30 with an expanded version of mm. 29-31 of the original version and again at mm. 31-32 of the keyboard version with a few notes taken from mm. 34-35 of the cantus. Willaert's cantus fails to appear during the keyboard's mm. 33-46. Mm. 47-49 hear the original cantus's mm. 51-54. However, mm. 50-52 seem to favor mm. 58-59 of Willaert's bassus, and mm. 52-53 prefer m. 60 of his altus. No clear quotation of any voice from Willaert's motet is heard again until m. 70 of the motet's cantus and altus and m. 69 of the motet's bassus appear simultaneously in the keyboard's penultimate measure, 63. Example 9 seeks to clarify the above description of the process taking place in the intabulation. Barring above the measures corresponds to barlines drawn by the scribe in his keyboard arrangement. The text set in italics and the measure numbers in parentheses below are mostly from the cantus of Zenck's edition of Willaert's motet; parenthetical mm. 58-61 and 69-71 are drawn from the motet's bassus and altus. Except for his penultimate measure's simultaneous quotation of Willaert's cantus, altus, and bassus, the intabulator's work does not utilize the favorite compositional technique of the second half of the sixteenth century: parody. In his classic formulation, John Ward notes that "an essential feature of parody technique is the quotation—often literal—of vertical slices of the thematic complex."[47] It is difficult to fathom any reason for the treatment here of Willaert's motet, unless one supposes that the intabulator had at hand some exceedingly corrupt version of Willaert's cantus and altus parts (and only these) from which he fashioned his work. With the exception of a few different ligature placements, manuscript sources of Willaert's motet—two from

---

[47]"Parody Technique in 16th-Century Instrumental Music," in Gustave Reese and Rose Brandel (eds.), *The Commonwealth of Music: Writings on Music in History, Art, and Culture in Honor of Curt Sachs* (New York: The Free Press, 1965) 208-9.

c. 1530 and two from c. 1560 (one of the latter destroyed in World War II)—present it much as does its only printing, in 1542.[48]

Another suggestion, kindly offered to me by Dr. Bonnie Blackburn, is that the keyboard intabulation of "O gloriosa domina" might represent a written-out attempt to fulfill the terms of, or to practice for, the first part of the famous test administered at St. Mark's in Venice for prospective organists:

> The choirbook opened, the beginning of a Kyrie or of a motet is found at random. And this is written down, giving it to the competing organist who is to play this subject correctly on the organ with fantasy, not confusing the voices, as if four singers were singing.[49]

If Dr. Blackburn's suggestion is correct, then surely our organist would have failed the examination, especially had Willaert himself or any of his students been present!

Three problems remain to be discussed: transposition, the addition of text between the staves, and the instrument intended. Two reasons suggest themselves for the transpositions downwards in the keyboard arrangements of Ferabosco's "Io mi son giovenetta" (fascicle II) and of Lasso's "Magnificat" (fascicle VI). So many sources of sixteenth-century music have been lost in the course of time that both works may well once have appeared at these lower pitches. However, the transposition downwards of Lasso's even-numbered verses suggests that it was to accomodate the pitch of its unidentified companion work, which set the odd-numbered verses.

The presence of the text between the keyboard staves for "Canti donque" and "Assumpta est Maria" (fascicle IVb), and for the "Magnificat," "Fit porta Christi," "Ego dormio," and "Adoramus te, Christe" (fascicle VI) is perhaps utilitarian. I have hypothesized above that the keyboard musician sang the missing cantus part to "Fit porta Christi" himself. If so, he may have copied in the other texts, selected

[48]Listed by Edward E. Lowinsky, "A Newly Discovered Sixteenth-Century Motet Manuscript at the Biblioteca Vallicelliana in Rome," *Journal of the American Musicological Society* 3 (1950) 214 and 223.

[49]Italian in Francesco Caffi, *Storia della musica sacra nella gia cappella ducale di San Marco in Venezia dal 1318 al 1797* (Venice, 1854-55), vol. I, 28 and more accurately in Benvenuti, *Andrea e Giovanni Gabrieli I* (Milan, 1931) xlv. Although the examination is undated, Ferand, *Die Musik in Geschichte und Gegenwart* 6 (Kassel: Bärenreiter, 1957), s.v. "Improvisation," cols. 1107-8 believes it was already in use at St. Mark's by 1540. A similar examination is recorded at the duomo at Treviso in 1531; see Giovanni d'Alessi, *La cappella musicale del duomo di Treviso (1300-1633)* (Vedelago [Treviso]: Tipografia 'Ars et Religio', 1954) 98.

chiefly from their cantus partbooks, for a similar reason. His arrangement of Willaert's "O gloriosa domina" would thus be a special case— lacking text because of a possible autodidactic purpose. Since texts are lacking in his repertoire of popular madrigals—Ferabosco's "Io mi son giovenetta" (fascicle II), Rore's "Anchor che col partire" (fascicle IVa), Reulx's "S'io credesse" (fascicle IVb), and Nanino's "Scoprirò" (fascicle VI)—we may suppose that he knew these works well enough so as not to require the crutch of text underlay.

His choice of repertoire—which he copied into an already present and largely sacred group of pieces in fascicles II and IV—is chiefly sacred, though sprinkled with madrigals. And in fascicle X it embraces the purely instrumental canzone. His choices suggest by and large that he was creating a commonplace book. However, his choice of a repertoire entirely copied in his hand in fascicles IVb and VI which comprises hymns, short responsories, an Office antiphon and a Magnificat, implies that they were to be used to celebrate the Office of Vespers.

If this were so, then one would expect that the instrument used was the organ. Indeed, the printing privilege granted October 31, 1542 by the Venetian Senate for Cavazzoni's first book—which contains the hymn "Christe redemptor omnium" (fascicle VI)—describes it as "libro primo de intabolatura di organo,"[50] even though the actual book when printed in 1543 was entitled simply *Intavolatura,* without specification of the instrument. This was probably an oversight in light of the printing privilege, and since Cavazzoni's second book published shortly thereafter was entitled *Intabulatura d'organo.* Both Cavazzoni prints contain *alternatim* settings of the Magnificat (unrelated to those in fascicle VI) which were, of course, also to be performed on the organ. Even though the organ is surely intended for Cavazzoni's hymn setting in fascicle VI (and by extension perhaps for the other works in these fascicles), it would be well to remember Attaingnant's title page to his 1531 edition of Magnificats: "mys en la tabulature des Orgues Espinettes et Manicordions."[51]

Probably the greatest puzzle of all about these keyboard fascicles concerns the reason for them being at Castell'Arquato. They are totally unrelated to the considerable cache of sixteenth- and seventeenth-century printed and manuscript vocal music still preserved there, which does not provide a single source for any of the arrangements for keyboard.[52]

---

[50]See Mischiati (ed.), *Cavazzoni, Orgelwerke* (Mainz: B. Schotts Söhne, 1961), vol. 2, 5.

[51]See Rokseth (ed.), *Deux livres d'orgue,* vii.

[52]A small portion of this music is cited by Jeppesen, "Eine frühe Orgelmesse," 187-88 and by Lockwood, *Counter-Reformation,* 243, 247, and 249.

A preponderance of composers from Piacenza responsible for this vocal music as well as connections with Piacenza for two composers named in fascicles V and VII (not discussed here)[53] may suggest that some or all of this music originated in that nearby city.

Be this as it may, the extraordinary variety of arrangements for keyboard at Castell'Arquato of vocal music attests to what Otto Gombosi—writing more than thirty years ago to honor another greatly influential choral conductor and teacher—described as "the richness and freedom . . . of liturgical music-making in the Renaissance."[54]

---

[53]See Slim, "Keyboard Music at Castell'Arquato," p. 37, note 11 and p. 41; idem, *Dances and Dance Songs*, p. 44, no. 28; and Francesco Bussi, "Il compositore farnesiano Gabriele Villani e le sue Toscanelle," *Studi musicali* 13 (1984), especially 107-109.

[54]"About Organ Playing in the Divine Service, circa 1500," in *Essays on Music in Honor of Archibald Thompson Davison by his Associates*, ed. Randall Thompson (Cambridge, Mass.: Harvard University Press, 1957) 66.

John B. Haberlen

Rhythm: The Key to Vitalizing Renaissance Music

When preparing a Renaissance composition for performance, most choral conductors begin by studying the flowing melodies, the formal structure, and the modal harmonies and ensuing dissonances. They also consider the text and its relationship to the music in addition to the establishment of a proper tempo. These are desirable and necessary steps to be taken in the first stages of preparation, but there are sophisticated levels of additional study that demand attention: problems of *musica ficta*, ornamentation, proportional tempo relationships, and the various levels of rhythmic stresses within the flow of the melodic line, for example. It is the last of these problems upon which this discussion is centered.

Choral conductors can generally be counted on to highlight the harmonic suspensions of Renaissance music by effectively "rubbing" two vocal parts against one another, but insufficient attention is usually given to the possibility of generating tension by emphasizing the interplay of rhythmic counterpoint between two or more parts. Although these hid-

Dr. Haberlen earned the B.S. and M.M.E. degrees from Pennsylvania State University. He subsequently taught choral music in the public schools and performed in the San Bernardino Orchestra and the Florida Symphony Orchestra as principal timpanist. After attending summer classes with Howard Swan in 1967, Haberlen gave up a career as a professional timpanist and devoted his studies to the choral art. In 1974 he received the D.M.A. in Choral Conducting from the University of Illinois and was thereafter appointed Director of Choral Activities at Georgia State University in Atlanta, Georgia.

Dr. Haberlen is currently President of the Southern Division of ACDA and a member of the Editorial Board of the Choral Journal. *He has published two books, seven articles, and over thirty editions of choral music.*

den rhythms contain potential life for each individual line and complete rhythmic excitement when the composition is heard as a whole, the lack of rhythmic clarity in most performances of Renaissance music suggests either conductors are not acquainted with the principles of rhythmic groupings, or that they are unwilling to spend the time and effort required to teach those principles to their choirs.

The identification and subsequent phrasing of note groupings can provide the key to rhythmic vitality in Renaissance music. The following paragraphs therefore explore the rhythmic structure of Renaissance melody and its particular importance in sixteenth-century compositions,[1] and provide some suggestions for defining these irregular rhythmic patterns as we re-create early music in the choral rehearsal and performance.

THE ORIGIN OF RENAISSANCE RHYTHMIC PATTERNS

The excellent and extensive article entitled "Rhythm" by Walther Dürr and Walter Gerstenberg in *The New Grove Dictionary Of Music and Musicians* defines rhythm as

> The subdivision of a span of time into sections perceivable by the senses; the grouping of musical sounds, principally by means of duration and stress. Together with melody and harmony, rhythm is one of the three basic elements of music; but since melody and harmony both contribute to the rhythmic organization of a work, and since neither melody nor harmony can be activated without rhythm, the three must be regarded as inseparably linked processes. . . .
> The relationship between rhythm and the human organism is essential to an understanding of rhythm. . . . Heartbeat, breathing and walking order the passage of time in regular units, and have been used time and again to illustrate this relationship despite their variability and complexity.[2]

[1]Although this article concentrates on choral music of the sixteenth century, the importance of the rhythmic principles expounded, relates to all early music preceding 1500, both vocal and instrumental. Choral conductors will also discover many instances in early Baroque choral music where textural stress helps to define the free rhythmic motifs not yet confined by the application of barlines. This article is an expansion and revision of an article entitled "Microrhythms: The Key to Vitalizing Renaissiance Music," published in *Choral Journal*, November, 1972. The author and editor are indebted to that publication for consent to publish this reworked version.

[2]*The New Grove Dictionary of Music and Musicians*, edited by Stanley Sadie (London: MacMillan, 1980), s.v. "Rhythm," by Walther Dürr and Walter Gerstenberg, 804-05.

Thus the system of musical tempos already had its origins in functions of the human body and mind. Early theorists often suggested that the duration of the Renaissance *tactus* be in accordance with or related to a physical activity or involuntary function of the human organism such as breathing or the heartbeat. One must keep in mind, however, that much early music does not contain regular, recurring stresses. Irregular rhythmic patterns are the norm. The period 1450–1600 contains a prevalence of measure-free polyphony as opposed to "measure-music." One must notice that although the mensural music that prevailed throughout this period embodies the principle of regular groups of beats (*tempus perfectum, imperfectum*, etc.), the groups frequently lack the most important characteristic of "measure-music," i.e., the normal accent on the first beat of such a group.[3] The interpretation and systems of speech and music became interwoven in early times. Greek antiquity knew no independent system of musical rhythm, but instead derived it from speech. Chanting the liturgy of the church in speech rhythm led to the singing of the same in plainsong. "Much earlier music is basically vocal in character, with texts that are often in prose form or proceed in a free rhythm."[4] One must study the rhythm in this music in relation to the text and its accentuation, since the musical rhythm is closely allied to the doctrines of poetic rhythm.

Plainsong (*organum purum*), with its free succession of binary and ternary groupings, provides the historical basis for the melodic rhythms of sacred Renaissance music.

> There is no time or measure in the modern sense, and there is no "strong beat" or "accent" occurring at regular intervals. Plainsong is an entirely different idiom. Its time like its rhythm is free—a free interlacing of binary and ternary groups (of course at the discretion not of the singers but of the composer) which like the prose text which they clothe, glide along freely, in order and variety, forming periods with sections and phrases of unequal length and importance.[5]

Composers of sixteenth-century polyphony, most of whom were trained and employed in the musical establishments of the church, possessed an intimate knowledge of plainsong. It was natural that they should perpetuate the rhythmic traditions of plainsong by composing

[3]Willi Apel, *Harvard Dictionary of Music*, 2nd ed. (Cambridge, Mass., Belknap Press of Harvard University Press, 1969) 513.
[4]Dürr and Gerstenberg, "Rhythm," 807
[5]Benedictines of Solesmes, *Liber usualis* (Introduction and Rubrics in English) (New York: Desclée and Co., 1956) xix.

melodies in which binary and ternary note groupings were freely interlaced.

Noting the free succession of two and three equal-note groupings which is characteristic of Renaissance polyphony, Charles Kennedy Scott wrote:

> Plainsong was the ultimate basis of polyphonic music, and this feature of free rhythm is perhaps a survival; but, whether or not, it is evident that polyphonic composers were (1) not bound down to regular metre, and (2) did not trouble when this irregularity was at variance with the time-signature.[6]

Curt Sachs, in *Rhythm and Tempo*, does not draw a connection between plainsong and sixteenth-century polyphony, but it is clear he recognizes the existence of rhythmic patterns that differ from our present-day conception of bar-line rhythms. "In vocal polyphony," he writes,

> "norms" and "regularly recurrent accents of the first beats" were almost non-existent, and hence any "abnormal" syncopation as well. The truth is that Renaissance polyphony, very far from our normal and recurrent accents, relies on an unrestrained polyrhythmic writing, on a continual, almost erratic change from binary to ternary groupings, with or against the other parts, with or against the time signature. Often it appears only in the cadences, but oftener throughout a piece.[7]

This changing flow of binary and ternary rhythms uninfluenced by the placement of regularly recurring bar lines is easily found in the opening phrase of the cantus I part of Palestrina's motet "Alma redemptoris mater" in example 1a.[8]

---

[6]Charles Kennedy Scott, *Madrigal Singing—A Few Remarks on the Study of Madrigal Music with an Explanation of the Modes and a Note on Their Relation to Polyphony* (London: Oxford University Press, 1931) 18.

[7]Curt Sachs, *Rhythm and Tempo: A Study in Music History* (New York: W. W. Norton, 1953) 250.

[8]In this and subsequent examples, a ternary grouping of quarter notes is indicated by a square bracket and a binary grouping of the same by a curved bracket. E.g., a curved sign sets off duple groupings until contradicted by a square bracket.

Example 1a.

Alma Redemptoris Mater   Palestrina

Example 1b.

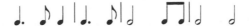

In example 1b the rhythm of the third phrase, without textual or intervallic melodic implications, is exposed, allowing one to delineate the notes into irregular note groupings or units according to the inherent agogic stresses within the rhythmic line.

Knud Jeppesen, a Danish musicologist, spoke of two dimensions of rhythmic activity in Renaissance compositions:

> The musical works themselves afford unmistakable evidence that in the 16th century, or perhaps even earlier, there was introduced a collective rhythm with regularly recurring accents, between which and the individual rhythm of the single parts there arose mutual strife and contradiction . . . . Just as melody and harmony are inclined to combat each other—the great prominence of harmonic elements tending to absorb and efface the peculiar melodic features of the single part,—so does the "Micro" (partial) rhythm contradict and combat the "Macro" (total) rhythm.[9]

Jeppesen's statement has a degree of validity, for one who is cognizant of the existence of microrhythms knows that they will not be heard unless they are stressed strongly enough to prevent their obliteration by the total or macrorhythm.

[9]Knud Jeppesen, *The Style of Palestrina and the Dissonance* (London: Oxford University Press, 1946) 26-28.

Similar to Jeppesen's theory, but more succinctly stated, is that of H.K. Andrews, who defines a double system of accentuation in sixteenth-century polyphony. He refers to "(a) the metrical (quantity) rhythm which applies to the composition as a whole and particularly to its vertical organization and (b) the stress rhythm which belongs to the individual strand." Andrews calls the metrical rhythm "a touchstone against which stress rhythms [Jeppesen's "microrhythms"] of the individual strands may be measured" and made coherent.[10]

Scott, Sachs, Jeppesen, and Andrews, though there are small differences in their views, all acknowledge the existence of rhythms that may be separate and distinctly different from the prevailing meter as indicated by the mensuration signs. This basic level of rhythmic organization may be found in the two- and three-note patterns that make up the varying rhythms at different notational levels, and that oppose the total rhythm designated by the metrical marking. Thus, the ternary rhythms in example 2, in both "b" and "c," might be labeled microrhythms, although, of course, "c" at the eighth-note level of notation is more "micro" than the quarter-note level "b."

Example 2.

(a) [$\frac{3}{2}$] 𝅝   𝅗𝅥

(b) [$\frac{3}{2}$] 𝅗𝅥   𝅗𝅥 𝅗𝅥   𝅗𝅥

(c) [$\frac{3}{2}$] 𝅗𝅥 𝅘𝅥𝅗𝅥 𝅘𝅥𝅗𝅥 𝅘𝅥𝅗𝅥 𝅘𝅥

Irregular rhythmic patterns may also occur at the level of the *tactus*, as in example 3:

Example 3.

---

[10]H. K. Andrews, *The Technique of Byrd's Vocal Polyphony* (London: Oxford University Press, 1966) 55.

It may be argued that the rhythmic irregularity seen in example 3 does not involve microrhythmic activity. While that is so according to the concept of "microrhythm" established above, such irregular groupings at the level of the *tactus* (two or three half notes) are still a very real part of the rhythmic style of Renaissance music and cannot be ignored.

HOMOPHONIC MUSIC

Although a number of different levels of rhythmic activity is particularly characteristic of polyphonic music, irregular rhythmic constructions on a single level of notation are often found in homophonic Renaissance compositions. In many cadences of sixteenth-century chorales and homophonic part-songs, a single voice line often contains microrhythmic patterns. This compositional technique has been described as "animated homophony" by Alfred Einstein. Heinrich Finck's "O quam sanctus panis iste," example 4, exhibits a cadential formula that was a musical cliché used by many composers throughout the century:

Example 4. *O quam santus panis iste*   Heinrich Finck

In many instances homophonic music contains rhythmic stress shifts simultaneously in all voice parts. This declamatory style is more characteristic of secular vocal genres than sacred; e.g. chansons, ballets, etc. In such a piece as "Fa una canzone" by Orazio Vecchi, for example, the free alternation of binary and ternary groupings must be delivered with vitality, but also with a free rhythmic flow that is the antithesis of the angularity resulting from thinking in terms of syncopation. Locating such rhythmic shifts is easy if one is aware of the concepts of rhythmic note groupings. (See Recognizing Microrhythmic Patterns.)

Example 5. *Fa una canzone*   Orazio Vecchi

PERFORMERS, THEN AND NOW

It is clear that rhythmic note groupings, determined in part by agogic stress, are a prominent feature of Renaissance music, whether polyphonic or homophonic. Some facts about the performing conventions of that epoch should help us consider how to incorporate appropriate rhythmic groups and stresses into our rehearsals and performances of early music.[11] Renaissance performers were, first of all, totally immersed in the singing of plainsong. Most of them spent their musical lives in the church, singing daily at the various liturgical functions. Many of the musicians went so far as to take religious orders. Their constant association with plainsong gave them an awareness of the "free interlacing of binary and ternary groupings," and their experience with the Latin liturgy made it easy for them to relate the textual syllabic stresses with the flow and forward movement of the melodic rhythm.

In order to reproduce these circumstances as closely as possible, we must acquaint our students with the proper accentuation of liturgical

[11]It is interesting to note that, to my knowledge, no contemporary writings by theorists exist that discuss the rhythmic structure of Renaissance melody. Obviously theorists of the time felt no need to expound on rhythmic principles that were apparently ingrained in and performed subconsciously by Renaissance performers.

Latin through chanting the basic Mass texts as warm-up exercises, for example. The singers must be exposed to recorded performances of plainsong. The Benedictine monks of Solesmes, France have produced excellent recordings which exhibit the art of singing Gregorian chant. The best guide to the proper style of chant performance is found in the preface to the *Liber usualis*, and every chant text within the *Liber usualis* is accompanied by accentual markings that identify the proper stress of the Latin texts.[12] We must constantly promote the text and its delivery as a top rehearsal priority.

Another important point concerning Renaissance performance conditions is that the singers read from a choirbook or partbooks; thus, they had only their own part before them, and *bar-lines were not included*. Reading from a single line unobstructed by bar-lines, they could easily apply the rhythmic concepts derived from their knowledge of plainsong. They could therefore, group the notes according to the actual rhythmic structure rather than according to a previous metrical scheme enforced arbitrarily by regularly recurring bar-lines.

In this connection, today's conductor will have the problem of teaching the singers to disregard the bar-lines that appear in most modern editions and distort the rhythmic flow of early music. After having had musical training that probably has never excluded barred music, today's singers will have to be taught to have a flexible and open mind in order to read or imagine barless music. In some instances, contemporary editors of music have attempted to help the conductor with this problem.

EDITION

With respect to microrhythms, a good modern edition of a piece of Renaissance music will be one in which the rhythmic patterns are readily exposed to the singers, or one in which the rhythmic patterns are not obscured by relentless barring in accordance with a modern time signature. In most cases editors append modern time signatures to their editions of early compositions that originally had mensural signs, that often did not necessarily denote meter in the modern sense. This practice has distorted the performers' view of the modern meter, and they

---

[12]It is important to recognize that our knowledge of the performance practices of plainsong in the Middle Ages and Renaissance is extremely limited. The Solesmes method of interpretation, represented both in the liturgical books and in their recordings, is based on comprehensive manuscript study. It is thoroughly musical and beautiful, but that does not change the fact that it is an attempt at modern reconstruction of a lost art. (Ed.)

are influenced by the $\frac{4}{4}$ or the $\frac{3}{4}$ meters with their prevailing strong and weak pulses.

In homophonic music, some editors have used a movable bar-line. This principle was employed by Denis Stevens in his *Penguin Book of English Madrigals*. [13] For early music, the *Mensurstrich*—a line drawn between, not through, the staves—is a widely used device that frees the music from the "tryanny of the bar-line." Invented by Heinrich Besseler and used in his *Das Chorwerk* editions (see also examples 4 and 5 above), the *Mensurstrich* is now employed by many German publishing houses in all of their Renaissance editions. A more recent innovation is the "varia-bar system," created by Dr. James McKelvy of Mark Foster Music Co. It involves placing bar-lines at various points in the individual voice lines, seldom concurrently in all the voices. McKelvy also has published several experimental editions with staves that continue horizontally across two pages in order to highlight the horizontal flow of the melodies. Neither the *mensurstrich* nor the "varia-bar system" attempts to dictate specific rhythmic interpretations; they simply avoid the metrical implications of regular barring.

The techniques cited above are exemplary; they are not the only methods that have been employed by editors intent on exposing the rhythmic potential of Renaissance music. Some editors, knowledgeable of the Renaissance principles of rhythmic groupings, define them with modern dynamic-accent marks (>) and/or stress marks (–) that point out an agogically stressed note. This editorial method tends to clutter the score with markings, which, if interpreted literally, would distort the smooth flow of the melodic line. Also, the articulation marks tend to dissuade the performer from creating his or her own interpretation of the rhythmic groups. The conductor's teaching task will be simplified if editions can be found in which rhythmic groupings are not obscured by regular barring or overly influenced by articulation marks. But often, of course, one is forced by circumstances to use editions that are less satisfactory.

RECOGNIZING MICRORHYTHMIC PATTERNS

Regardless of the quality of the edition to be used, the prime difficulty remains to be solved: how to recognize macro- or microrhythmic patterns in a particular passage of music?

[13]Denis Stevens, ed., *The Penguin Book of English Madrigals for Four Voices* (Baltimore, Maryland: Penguin Books, Inc., 1967) 45, 51.

Rhythmic groupings are determined by those notes that contain natural agogic accents. The following factors, in order of their importance, influence the location of agogic accents:

1. *Notes of longer duration indicate stress, short notes do not.* That is, the rhythm flows from long to long, through the shorter values. This is supported by the natural rhythmic flow of Medieval European languages, which flow from long to long, not stressing short syllables. Since music is so closely aligned with text, this principle has been assumed for music in the absence of any direct theoretical commentary either supporting or contesting it.[14]

2. *Ascending intervallic skips or leaps within a melodic line should be regarded as having more dramatic accents.* Each change of pitch brings with it a self-contained accent. "The more arresting the interval, the more the note is stressed."[15] Notes of higher pitch obviously require more tension in their production and are therefore more prominent.

3. *The syllabic stress of the text normally coincides with the musical stress of the rhythm.* A check of the textual stress may confirm and clarify an otherwise-ambiguous rhythmic pattern. The detection of rhythmic groupings is closely allied to the doctrines of poetic rhythm.[16]

4. *Harmonic tension within the prevailing mode or within a specific vertical chord may result in agogic stress.*

The guidelines listed above are instructive for locating agogically stressed notes and using these points as the basic determinant for grouping notes in binary (strong, weak) or ternary (strong, weak, weak) groups. One must further consider how short-value rests—those shorter in value than a semibreve—are included in and related to the rhythmic group. First, one must decide to either relate the rest(s) to those notes that precede the rest(s) or to those that follow it. The quarter rest in example 1a is related to the two quarter notes that follow it. Thus the two quarters are treated as upbeats to the binary group. The syllabic stress of "redemptoris" coincides with the rhythmic stress. "If the new phrase

[14]Timothy J. McGee, *Medieval and Renaissance Music: A Performer's Guide* (Toronto: University of Toronto Press, 1985) 21-22.
[15]Andrews, 55.
[16]Although we know that in many cases the textual underlay is not clear in the original musical source, modern editors often base their decisions of text underlay on the rhythmic groupings of the musical lines as determined largely by locating agogic stresses in accordance with numbers 1 and 2 above.

begins with an accented text syllable, the first note is considered to be the beginning of a group. [In these instances, the rest is related to the notes preceding it.] It will be found, however, that in the majority of cases the new syllable will be unaccented."[17]

Example 6. *Illumina Ocules Meos*   Orlando di Lasso

In example 6, quarter rest "a" relates to the three quarter notes of "ne quando." The rest is active with the feel of a downbeat, setting the first quarter note ("ne") into action as an upbeat. The quarter rest "b" relates in the opposite direction to the two half notes of "dicat." Rest "b" plays a less-active role than "a" and gives a third pulse to the ternary group of the second half note ("-cat"). Rest "b" also provides a convenient spot for the placement of the final consonant "t" of "dicat."

Guided by the factors above, it is usually possible to uncover the macro- and microrhythmic patterns in any given musical phrase. Occasionally, however, a definite interpretation will not emerge, usually because two or more of the above factors are in conflict with one another. In these exceptional cases, the conductor will have to weigh the alternatives and organize the notes into what seem the most satisfactory groupings. One should remember that the perception of rhythmic groupings is a mental phenomenon, not a physical one; one sensitive musician may well differ from another regarding the interpretation of an inexplicit pattern.

THE ROLE OF THE CONDUCTOR

For the conductor who elects to teach Renaissance rhythmic principles to the choir, rehearsal responsibilities will be increased. Long and tedious introductory discussions should be avoided: the principles

[17]McGee, 23.

should simply be taught as the music is rehearsed. A polyphonic work might be broken down into a single line and sung in unison by the entire choir; as other lines are added, the rhythmic complexities will become apparent to the singers. As the choir subtly stresses the melodic note groupings, the singers must be taught to establish an overall feeling of arsis and thesis within each phrase—a feeling of a floating rise and a gentle fall in the music's motion.[18]

The conductor should take every opportunity to employ materials that will reinforce the teaching of microrhythmic principles. Warm-up exercises rich in irregular rhythmic note groupings should be used: the bicinia motets of Lassus are ideal for this purpose.[19] When Baroque music is performed, it should be pointed out that frequent hemiola cadences involve a shift of melodic stress in $\frac{3}{4}$ or $\frac{3}{2}$ meter (in most modern editions) from a regularly occurring strong, weak, weak pattern to a strong, weak, strong, / weak, strong, weak pattern. Twentieth-century music containing frequent meter changes and/or free rhythms that are analogous to Renaissance rhythms can also be used profitably. Stravinsky's sacred music abounds with free rhythms—not surprising in view of his background and interest in Russian chant. The "Gloria" and "Credo" from his Mass and motets such as "Pater noster" are particularly useful materials for reinforcing the teaching of the rhythmic principles of Renaissance style.

The conductor will save valuable rehearsal time if singers are trained to respond to rhythmic phrasing marks that are inserted (perhaps in collaboration with section leaders) into the choral scores in advance of the rehearsal. For this purpose, the author has experimented with the simple system of square and curved brackets used in the musical examples here. In early rehearsals the conductor should have the singers count the note values of the melodic lines in accordance with the identifying square and curved brackets. This helps to develop a choral sense of rhythmic unity on the proper rhythmic stresses. Notice how choristers would "count" the song in example 5 according to the numbers given beneath the bass clef.

Thus, the major tasks of the conductor are to help the choir members develop an awareness of the inherent rhythmic structure of the vocal line and to give them the opportunity to create the rhythmic phrasing in their own manner. The conductor must also be sensitive to the text

[18]The names "thesis" (or "basis") and "arsis" were derived from orchestics, where they represented the rhythmic elements of dance steps. In "thesis" the foot touched the ground, in "arsis" it was lifted off the ground. Dürr and Gerstenberg, 811.
[19]Orlando di Lasso, *Cantiones duarum vocum*, edited by Paul Beopple. Dessoff Choir Series, No. 11 (New York: Music Press, 1941).

along with the individual melodic line as rhythmic patterns are sorted out and phrased accordingly. Choir members often look for individual responsibility; Renaissance music presents a vast creative opportunity for a "thinking" choir.

At performances, however, the conductor who wants to make the most of rhythmic phrasing in Renaissance music will have to play a lesser role. The conductor will be required to set and maintain good tempos, to give sectional dynamics, and to offer subtle phrasing cues; but as for rhythm, the main responsibility will be to conduct a *tactus*, leaving the singers free to take the responsibility for the rhythmic patterns of their individual lines. In short, the conductor must get out of the way of the music, conducting with small gestures that will not confuse the choir or cause the rhythmic patterns to be overly conspicuous and thus interrupt the flow of the music.

CONCLUSION

The proper rhythmic grouping of notes is among the chief elements in the interpretation of sixteenth-century vocal and instrumental literature. These rhythmic groupings energize the ebb and flow of each phrase. Unfortunately, the possibilities for articulating rhythmic groupings are often ignored, or the music is sung without any sense of structural logic within the phrase. This haphazard approach creates a disparity of group-ings within each vocal line, resulting in a chaotic lack of rhythmic clarity. Choral conductors owe it to their audiences and singers to sharpen their awareness of the important role that the interpretation of macro- and microrhythms plays in vitalizing Renaissance music. The result of such study will be more comprehensive and accurate performances of Renaissance compositions, and the spirit of the "Golden Age of Polyphony" will thus be better communicated to our present-day singers and audiences.

Gordon Paine

Tactus, Tempo, and Praetorius

When I examine the compositions of contemporary Italians, which within very few years have come to be set in an entirely new manner, I find great variety and discrepancies in their use of time signatures in both duple and triple time. . . . Many composers use the two signatures C and $\mathₓ{C}$ indiscriminately and one cannot tell any difference from the notes themselves or the entire composition. . . . But I see that most [writers] do not observe their own rules [regarding signatures] and use one indiscriminately in place of the other. Therefore it is my opinion that [the various signatures used to denote triple meter] . . . should be eliminated without hesitation (the more so since they prove not only unnecessary, useless, and extremely involved), even though very famous musicians have used them until now.[1]

---

[1]Michael Praetorius, *Syntagmatis musici / Michaelis Praetorii C. / tomus tertius* (Wolfenbüttel: author), 1619, 51, 53. Hans Lampl, "A Translation of Syntagma musicum III by Michael Praetorius," unpublished DMA dissertation, USC, 1957, 105–06, 110. Translations from the *Syntagma musicum,* part III, are quoted from Lampl with occasional minor tacit alterations or corrections. All other translations are by the present author.

Gordon Paine majored in Economics at Occidental College, where he sang with Howard Swan from 1966 to 1970. After two years as a manager for Pacific Telephone Company, he began his study in music, culminating in the M.M. and D.M.A. degrees from the University of Colorado at Boulder. He is currently Professor of Choral Music and Coordinator of Graduate Studies at California State University, Fullerton.

Dr. Paine is active in the translation of German-language literature on choral music. Among his publications are a translation of Helmuth Rilling's J. S. Bach's B-Minor Mass and the musicological essays accompanying Rilling's recording of the complete Bach cantatas. He has served on the Editorial Board of the Choral Journal, *as well as on numerous other ACDA national committees.*

167

Michael Praetorius, who published these words in 1619, was fully justified in his frustration. The decades surrounding the turn of the seventeenth century were a time of transition in musical notation. Composers were conceiving new styles of music that strained or exceeded the capabilities of the by-then antiquated system of notation they had inherited from the Middle Ages. Old symbols took on new meanings for some composers while they retained their traditional meanings for others, and trying to decipher who meant what when was a challenge. Praetorius and his contemporaries lived in that period, however, and were a part of the shaping of the new music and notation of the day. They had some understanding—albeit not always perfect—of how to interpret what their contemporaries committed to paper.

If Praetorius had reason to be frustrated with the notation of his time, our justification is all the greater. We do not live in his world, and what was everyday music-making to him is distant, fragmentarily preserved and understood history to us. Today's performer often lacks the specialized knowledge to translate into modern symbols what the composer meant. Enter the musicologist/editor, who despite study of the subject may not be certain himself, or may be faced with numerous alternative possibilities. The editions that result sometimes obfuscate more than elucidate.

Take, for example, Johann Hermann Schein's continuo duet "Nun lob mein Seel," the beginning of which (cantus 1) is shown in facsimile 1. The piece begins with groupings of three semibreves under the sign ϕ_2^3, moves to duple meter under the sign $\math0$, and then proceeds to groupings of three minims under the sign 3. In theory, the old "time signatures" (actually signs of mensuration and proportion) and the note values that went with them told the performer how fast each section should go relative to the others. In modern parlance, this is known as "proportional tempo change:" the tempos of the various sections are related to each other in a specific mathematical ratio. Let us see how the piece has fared in three published editions.[2]

Figure 1a shows Arthur Prüfer's transcription from the Schein *Sämtliche Werke,* published in the early years of this century. Here, despite the differences in the original notation, the two triple-meter sections go at the same tempo relative to the intervening duple-meter section,

[2]From *Opella nova* . . . (Leipzig: author), 1618. J. H. Schein *Sämtliche Werke,* ed. Arthur Prüfer (Leipzig: Breitkopf and Härtel), 1901-23, vol. 4, 198. J. H. Schein, *Eight Chorale Settings from Opella nova Part 1,* ed. L. Lenel (St. Louis: Concordia), no. 97-4713. J. H. Schein, *Neue Ausgabe sämtlicher Werke,* ed. Adam Adrio (Kassel: Bärenreiter), 1963-, vol. 4, 93.

with the duple-meter quarter-note pulse providing the constant. Ludwig Lenel's Concordia edition (figure 1b) also has the two triple-meter sections equivalent to each other, but in fast triplet relationship to the duple-meter section. In the *Neue Ausgabe,* Adam Adrio offers a third interpretation (figure 1c), in which the first triple-meter/duple-meter relationship is as given by Lenel, but the second triple-meter section is one-half the speed of the first.

Figure 1

Facsimile 1

Someone must be wrong. If all three transcriptions were valid, then both notations for triple meter would have to indicate a generic triple time that may be taken at any tempo desired. But if that were so, why would Schein have gone to the trouble of using *two different notations* in the first place? To confuse and confound the performer? Not likely. A more probable explanation is that they denoted two different tempos relative to the duple meter. In this regard, Adrio's transcription is philosophically on the right track, but as we shall see, he probably has the triple-meter/duple-meter tempo relationships reversed. According to Praetorius, the second triple-meter passage should be about twice as fast as the first and not vice versa.

The relationship between notation and tempo in the period of mensural notation is a topic that eludes simple answers. There were probably different ways of interpreting one and the same notation, depending on time and place, and one would search in vain for a single, universal solution. This is especially true of the early seventeenth century, when the mensural system was breaking down rapidly.

The north-German composer Michael Praetorius provides us with a unique opportunity to explore the tempo implications of mensural notation at this time, because he combined in equal measure the roles of composer and "theorist." His compositional output was staggering, including about thirty-five collections of church music (only eighteen of which have survived), and his three-volume *Syntagma musicum* is the most encyclopaedic source of the period on performance practices and numerous other subjects.

> If one looks only cursorily on those of his works preserved for posterity, they appear like tatters arbitrarily torn from a vast abundance of potentialities, seemingly thrown together helter-skelter. But one [can] only do justice to the endeavor of his genius and can only appreciate his extant work when one sees [in] it what it really is: the torso of a gigantic scheme which intended nothing less than to encompass the entire realm of music in all its facets and through its own creations to master it in one comprehensive system.[3]

In his church music, Praetorius aimed at creating this system in several ways. Most of his collections are organized according to the liturgical year and obviously were intended to provide a self-contained resource for the Lutheran church musician of the day. The surviving collections

---

[3]Friedrich Blume, "Das Werk des Michael Praetorius," *Zeitschrift für Musikwissenschaft* 17 (1935) 322. Quoted in Lampl, v.

focus strongly on the Lutheran chorale and present it in numerous styles ranging from simple, hymnbook settings to massive, polychoral concertos in the then-new Italian styles. Praetorius was intensely interested in the innovations of the Italians and in educating German musicians on the subject. To this end, in 1619 he published the third volume of his *Syntagma musicum* (henceforth *Syntagma III*), which dealt with myriad aspects of performance practices in his music and that of his contemporaries, including *tactus* and tempo. His music, particularly the last several collections, gives us the chance to compare what he said with what he actually did—especially since he peppered his later works with explanations and recommendations that complement *Syntagma III*.

Several writers—Antoine Auda, Johannes Bank, Harald Heckmann, Hans Otto Hiekel, Paul Brainard, and most importantly, Carl Dahlhaus and Franz-Jochen Machatius—have explored Praetorius's ideas on the subjects of *tactus,* tempo, and proportion and have offered some diametrically opposed interpretations of key points.[4] Of the works cited, only the least illuminating, that of Bank, is available in English. While several of the authors have carefully explored Praetorius's writings, none has systematically correlated his verbal teachings with what he did in his own music. That then, will be the purpose of this article. We will explore what Praetorius had to say on the relationship between notation and tempo and will compare his music to his writings. We will see that he expounds a logical, internally consistent system of notation that uses many of the symbols of classical mensural notation but redefines them to create a graded spectrum of not-necessarily proportional tempos that could not be expressed in the classical system. While it is beyond the scope of this article to delve into the possible application of his principles to the music of other composers, it will be shown that the Praetorius *tactus*-tempo system does provide an explanation for what seem otherwise to be notational anomalies in the works of many early-seventeenth-century composers.

The section entitled "Basic Principles of Mensural Notation" explains the background from which the Praetorius *tactus*-tempo system developed. While an understanding of this section helps to place Praetorius's system in context, it is not necessary to an understanding of the system itself.

This study is based on an examination of copies of all surviving printed works by Praetorius, as listed in *RISM* (P5348 – P5373). I am indebted to the directors of the Herzog-August Bibliothek of Wolfenbüttel (facsimiles nos. 3 and 6) and the British Library of London (facsimiles 1,

[4]See the works by these authors cited in the bibliography.

4, and 5) for their gracious permission to publish facsimilies from their collections. Sincere thanks are also due to Dr. Otto Biba, director of the Archive of the Gesellschaft der Musikfreunde in Vienna, for allowing me to examine the society's partbooks to the *Motectae et psalmi Latini* of 1607 (complete) and the *Puericinium* of 1621 (partial). Lastly, I owe a special debt of gratitude to Dr. Jürgen Kindermann of the Deutsches Musikgeschichtliches Archiv of Kassel for permitting me to study the Praetorius films in the Archive's collection, for providing photographic prints of facsimiles and obtaining permission for their publication, and for verifying details during the final stages of manuscript preparation.

BASIC PRINCIPLES OF MENSURAL NOTATION

The mensural system made use of note forms similar to those in use today:

⊏⊐ = Maxim		= Minim (♩)	
= Long		= Semiminim (♩)	
= Breve (⋈)		= Fusa (♪)	
◇ = Semibreve (○)		= Semifusa (♪)	

In modern notation, notes are divisible only by two; triplets are necessary to create a ternary division. In mensural notation, though, note values from the maxim through the semibreve were divisible by either two or three. Divisibility on any level by three was said to be "perfect," while divisibility by two was termed "imperfect." The smaller note values were divisible only by two. The division of the long into breves was called *modus,* the division of the breve into semibreves was called *tempus,* and the division of the semibreve into minims was called *prolatio.*

The combination of these variables in a given piece was its "mensuration." Symbols called "mensuration signs" were prefixed to the music in the manner of the modern time signature to indicate what mensuration was intended. A lone circle (**O**) indicated perfect *tempus,* while

imperfect *tempus* was shown by a semicircle ($\mathbb{C}$). The presence of
a dot within the circle or semicircle denoted perfect *prolatio;* its absence,
imperfect *prolatio.* More complex signs were used to show various combinations of *modus, tempus,* and *prolatio,* but these were long obsolete
by the time of Praetorius.

Tactus

The mensurations shown above ($\mathbb{C}$ and $\mathbf{O}$) were called *integer-valor*
("standard" or "unity value") mensurations, meaning that they were
the standard means of notation on which the system was based. Under
these mensurations the semibreve was generally considered to be the
standard unit of measure, one *tactus.* The idea of a standard unit of
measure is foreign to our notational system. In mensural notation,
however, the system needed a constant against which to measure the
various mensurations and proportions were measured. This was the function of the *tactus.*

The *tactus* was a both a measure of absolute time and a standardized
method of time beating. Many Renaissance theorists relate the tempo
of the *tactus* to the heartbeat, the speed of walking, or some other universal but imprecise measure of time. In his *Practica musicae* of 1496,
for example, Franchinus Gafurius says, "modern musicians have correctly ascribed a measure of one unit of time to the semibreve, com-
prehending within the sound of each semibreve diastole and systole."[5]
In other words, the semibreve—one *integer-valor tactus*—was to be about
as long as the time between heartbeats.

Tactus and Absolute Tempo

It has been suggested that there was one universal *tactus* speed throughout most of the mensural period. This idea is subject to challenge on
at least two counts. First, it presumes a means to measure and reproduce
the "master" tempo at will—something that did not exist until the
discovery of the constant period of the pendulum in the late sixteenth
century. Second, it assumes an international agreement among composers and performers lasting fifteen decades, more or less. Even if
such an agreement had been technologically possible—which it was

[5]Franchinus Gafurius, *Practica musicae* (1496), ed. and trans. Irwin Young (Madison:
University of Wisconsin Press), 1969, 74–75. Curt Sachs lists the primary sources
that equate the speed of the *tactus* with the heartbeat. *Rhythm and Tempo* (New York:
W. W. Norton), 1953, 203.

not—it is not credible that it could have existed. Several modern authors have suggested rather narrow limits—or even specific figures—for *tactus* speed in the mensural period. In two different works, for example, Willi Apel places the speed of the *tactus* at mm. 48 and mm. 60−80. Curt Sachs gives the range of mm. 60-80, and Antonius Bank says that there were two specific *tactus* tempos, at ca. mm. 60 and 72.[6]

While the tempos given by the writers cited here all lie within the range of possible *tactus* speeds, they all suffer from over-specificity, since it is axiomatic that one cannot draw a conclusion more specific than the data on which it is based. The contemporary descriptions of *tactus* speed passed down to us by Gafurius and others are clearly not the results of scientific measurement. They are attempts of a non-technological age to suggest a universal way by which a musician could find a moderate tempo appropriate to contemporary notational and performance practices. Too, performers of the Renaissance must have given consideration to acoustics, the competence of the ensemble, and the affect of the music—any of which might dicate a slower or faster tempo in specific circumstances. In sum, the *tactus* was a measure of absolute time, but one that must have varied within limits. While these limits are impossible to delineate precisely, the range of ca. mm. 50−80 is cautiously offered as a figure that will be found theoretically and practically sound.

Tactus and Time Beating

The standard, *integer-valor tactus* provided the constant for the mensural system, to which all mensurations and proportions were relative. Martin Agricola described the *tactus* as follows in his *Musica figuralis deudsch* of 1532:

> The *tactus*, or *Schlag* as it is called here, is a constant and measured movement of the singer's hand—a ruler, so to speak, that properly leads and measures the unity of the parts and the notes according to the indication of the signs [of mensuration and proportion:] for all parts must be arranged in accord so that the music might proceed well.[7]

[6]Willi Apel, *The Notation of Polyphonic Music 900−1600,* 5th ed. (Cambridge, MA: Medieval Academy of America), 1953, 191; Willi Apel, ed., *Harvard Dictionary of Music,* 2d ed. (Cambridge, MA: The Belknap Press of Harvard University Press), 1969, 832. Sachs, 219; Johannes A. Bank, *Tactus, Tempo, and Notation in Mensural Music from the 13th to the 17th Century* (Amsterdam: Annie Bank), 1972, 259.
[7]Martin Agricola, *Musica figuralis deudsch* (Wittenburg), 1532. Facsimile ed. (Hildesheim: Georg Olms), 1969, chapter 6.

The *tactus* was thus a form of time beating, intended to coordinate the ensemble. It was universally agreed that it consisted of two beats—one down, one up. It was not universally agreed, however, which of these two motions came first, though most sources, Praetorius included, advocate down-up. In duple meter the downbeat and upbeat were equal in duration—hence the name *tactus aequalis*. In triple meter (more properly, "under ternary proportions"), the first beat was twice as long as the second: the hand descended on beat one, remained motionless through beat two, and rose on beat three. The unequal duration of the two beats led to the name *tactus inaequalis*.

Proportions: Notated Tempo Changes

At the peak of its development in the fifteenth century, mensural notation had reached a degree of refinement that made it capable of notating exceedingly complex rhythmic textures. Conversely, it was also capable of notating simple rhythmic textures in complicated ways.[8] The principal tool for this type of notational game-playing was the use of "proportions."

Proportions permitted the composer to write the same music in several different ways by varying the combination of sign and note values he used. He might double the note values in one part, for example, but precede it with a "sign of proportion" that instructed the singer to sing the notes twice as fast as he would under *integer valor*. Of course, to the listener, the net result of this machination was nil. Proportions could be used to make the music move more quickly ("diminution") or more slowly ("augmentation").

The most common duple proportion of diminution was the one just described, called *dupla,* in which the tempo doubled in speed. This was indicated either by appending the numeral 2 to the mensuration sign (C2), reversing ("retorting") it (Ɔ), or by putting a slash—the "stroke of diminution" through it (¢).

Another, more-flexible method of showing proportions was to use a fractional arrangement of two digits that indicated the relationship of the new tempo (numerator) to the old (denominator). For example,

---

[8] As an appendix to his explanation of proportion in *Syntagma III,* Praetorius includes two compositions that illustrate such extreme use of proportions, one by Jakob Handl ("Subsannatores, subsannabit Deus" a 4) and one by Benedetti Palavicini ("Misero te" a 5). In order better to show the interaction of the proportions, Praetorius prints both pieces in score form rather than in the usual parts. (*Syntagma III,* 57−72; Lampl, 115−23.)

dupla could be represented by the fraction $\frac{2}{1}$: two semibreves under the sign $\frac{2}{1}$ would equal one *integer-valor* semibreve. Such fraction-like signs were also used to show augmentation, the opposite of diminution, in which the tempo slowed down relative to *integer valor*. The sign $\frac{1}{2}$ thus meant that one semibreve under that sign was the equivalent of two *integer-valor* semibreves. The proportions of augmentation were named after their corresponding diminutions, but with the prefix "sub" attached. Thus, while the sign $\frac{2}{1}$ represented *dupla* diminution, its reciprocal, $\frac{1}{2}$, denoted *subdupla* augmentation.

When used successively within a given composition, these signs of proportion were considered cumulative. A *subdupla* following a *dupla*, for example, would cancel the *dupla* and return the music to *integer valor*. Conversely, a $\frac{2}{1}$, $\mathbb{C}$, $C2$, or $\backsim$ following a passage in *dupla* proportion would create *quadrupla* proportion ($\frac{2}{1} \times \frac{2}{1} = \frac{4}{1} = quadrupla$). By the mid sixteenth century, the cumulative effect of the signatures was no longer observed. Instead, the introduction of a new sign automatically cancelled the previous one.

In *Syntagma III* Praetorius gives an example of the use of *dupla, subdupla, quadrupla*, and *subquadrupla* (facsimile 2). The upper two voices represent *integer valor*, and the lower four illustrate the proportions indicated.

Praetorius's example embodies one of the problems of understanding the mensural system in its late stages of development—more properly, during its decay: although the upper two voices are supposed to represent *integer valor*, they are signed with the slashed semicircle, which theoretically denoted dupla proportion. For reasons not entirely clear, the sign $\mathbb{C}$ became the de facto sign for *integer valor* in most sixteenth-century sacred music and much of the secular music of the same period. In the last half of the century, composers of secular music increased their use of shorter note values, and C began to reappear as the standard sign in that context. When this short-note notation started finding its way into new-style sacred music around the turn on the seventeenth century, C made its way back into the music of the church. Due to printer error, composer carelessness, and various other reasons, however, C sometimes appeared in long-note music and $\mathbb{C}$ was found ever more fequently in short-note music. By the time of Praetorius, the theoretical differentiation between C and $\mathbb{C}$ had become essentially meaningless. It was this ambiguity that Praetorius protested when he wrote:

Facsimile 2

Quod

When I examine the compositions of contemporary Italians, which within very few years have come to be set in an entirely new manner, I find great variety and discrepancies in their use of time signatures in both duple and triple time. . . . Many composers use the two signatures 𝄵 and 𝄵 indiscriminately and one cannot tell any difference from the notes themselves or the entire composition. . . .[9]

As we shall see, Praetorius attempted (with limited success) to restore distinctly different meanings to these signs, though his interpretations differed from those taught by traditional theory.

Mensural theorists discuss numerous proportions much more involved than *dupla* and *subdupla*. Johannes Tinctoris, for example, goes so far as to demonstrate the possibility of the ratio of 17:5,[10] and discussions of less-complicated but just as impractical proportions are common. But elaborate proportions rarely found their way into real music after the turn of the sixteenth century except in pedagogical demonstrations. Instead, the proportions were consigned to the comparatively mundane task of notating what we would term "triple meter."

The theory of the ternary proportions was the same as that of the binary proportions: a change of sign dictated a corresponding, mathematically proportional change in tempo. The most explicit way of notating the ternary proportions was via fractional signs. Acceleration in the ratio of 3:1, known as *tripla* proportion, could be indicated by the sign $\frac{3}{1}$, and a 3:2 acceleration, known as *sesquialtera,* could be notated by the symbol $\frac{3}{2}$.

While the theory was clear, practice was not. Until the early seventeenth century, these signs seldom appeared in actual music. Instead, one finds primarily the ambiguous signs 𝄵3, 𝄴3, 𝄴$\frac{3}{1}$, 𝄵 $\frac{3}{2}$, 𝄴$\frac{3}{2}$, and 3, and it is difficult to determine at all what the composer intended a given sign to mean. We will consider these problems together, as they are intimately intertwined.

Seay describes the basic change in notational style that occurred in the early sixteenth century:

[9]See note 1.

[10]Albert Seay, "The Setting of Tempo by Proportion in the Sixteenth Century," *The Consort* 37 (July, 1981) 395. Seay does a fine job of condensing this difficult topic and making it accessible to the performer. Two, related mistakes confuse the section on tempo, however (396). Seay seems to take the ubiquitous sixteenth-century duple signature of 𝄵 to mean a real diminution of *integer valor* and thus ascribes the *tactus* to the breve rather than the semibreve. He then attributes to the breve the tempo that should go with the semibreve (ca. mm. 60−72), and thus suggests a tempo for most sixteenth-century sacred music that is about twice what it should be.

Like the end of the fourteenth century, the end of the fifteenth found itself mired in useless notational complexity and again, like its predecessor, went back to a notational and rhythmic simplicity that was in high contrast to the immediate past. A glance at the sources of sixteenth-century music, after an inspection of some of those from the fifteenth, gives the viewer the impression that music has gone back to the equivalent of basic English, with little left to intrigue in terms of rhythmic variety.[11]

Part of the complexity to which Seay refers was the simultaneous use of different mensurations and proportions illustrated in facsimile 2. Because the voice parts *will only fit together in one way,* such simultaneous use of different signs defines their theoretical relationship to each other. Even if the composer were to use the signs in a nonstandard way, such simultaneity would permit us to learn what *that composer* intended that sign to mean—at least in the case at hand. Unfortunately, there was enough idiosyncratic use of the various signs that one often cannot generalize from a single case to the composer's complete works—much less generalize to other composers.

The most common form of mensural simultaneity in actual music was the mensuration canon—a popular intellectual pursuit of fifteenth-century composers that occasionally captured the fancy of sixteenth-century composers as well. In a mensuration canon, the composer wrote a single line of music that generated the remaining voices of the composition in canonic fashion. The twist was that each voice was usually preceded by a different sign of mensuration or proportion and thus moved at a different speed. Figure 2 shows the beginning of the "Agnus Dei" to the *Missa l'homme armé super voces musicales* of Josquin, a three-voice mensuration canon, in facsimile and transcription.[12] The middle voice is in *integer valor* ($\mathbb{C}$), while the lowest voice is in *dupla* proportion ($\mathbb{C}$), and the upper voice is in *tripla* ($\mathbb{C}3$). ($\mathbb{C}$ was frequently used in sixteenth-century mensuration canons to represent *integer valor* even though $\mathbb{C}$ was used for that purpose elsewhere.) There is no doubt as to what the temporal relationship is between the voices. Indeed, there would be no doubt even if the signs were completely incorrect, because there is only one solution that works.

As the sixteenth century progressed, the simultaneous use of different signs declined to nearly nil, and proportional writing was used almost exclusively in all voices simultaneously. This apparent simplification of notation actually led to ambiguity, since there was no objective way

---

[11]Ibid.
[12]Reproduced from Apel, *Notation,* 181.

to determine what a given composer intended a certain sign to mean in a given instance. Thus we encounter different modern editors who transcribe the same music in very different ways, as we saw in figure 1.

Figure 2

When composer X began a composition in $\mathbb{C}$ and changed all voices simultaneously to $\mathbb{C}$ 3 (or any other sign), did he intend the latter sign to denote a 3:1 acceleration (*tripla* proportion) or a 3:2 acceleration (*sesquialtera*)? To answer this question, we must know if the composer was thinking of $\mathbb{C}$ as *integer valor* or as a diminution. We must also know if the sign was being used according to its theoretical meaning or not.

The answers to these questions would at least permit us to understand the meaning of the notation. But that is only half of the equation.
*We must know if the composer truly intended the proportional relation-
ship that existed on paper to be heard in sound.* Did Renaissance and
early-Baroque performers *really* perform "proportional tempo changes"
proportionally, or was there some flexibility in terms of *tactus* speed?
What were the differences from time to time, from place to place, and
from composer to composer in the handling of proportions in
performance?

We have raised several several tempo-related questions that modern
performers face in dealing with music written in mensural notation. By
way of summary:

(1) Was the *tactus* of a single, immutable tempo (a) in general and
(b) in a given composition, or could it vary in speed from composition
to composition and section to section within a given piece?

(2) What did the signs C and ₵ mean to a given composer? Did
₵ truly denote a *dupla* diminution of *integer valor*? Did it simply
mean "faster," but not necessarily "twice as fast," or were the two
signs essentially synonymous (or meaningless)?

(3) What was the meaning of the various signs of ternary proportion? When used in all parts at once, did they denote "generic triple
meter," the speed of which was completely up to the performer; did
they in fact indicate strictly proportional relative tempos; or did they
perhaps signify non-proportional degrees of fast or slow?

For the music of most Renaissance and early-Baroque composers,
these are questions that can never be answered with much certainty.
Praetorius, however, is a happy exception.

THE PRAETORIUS *TACTUS* SYSTEM

Praetorius devotes the entirety of *Syntagma III,* part 2, chapter 7, to the subject of "*Tactus (Battuta* in Italian), Note Values, and Time Signatures; The Meaning of *Sextupla.*" Further observations that complement this but provide little new information are scattered throughout other chapters in *Syntagma III* and the prefaces and "notes to the reader" in his published collections of music dating from 1607 to 1621.[13]

At the end of chapter 7, Praetorius provides a table that summarizes his ideas:

[13]These references from *Syntagma III* (aside from chapter 7), and the Praetorius *Gesamtausgabe (GA)* (ed. Friedrich Blume *et al.,* Wolfenbüttel: Georg Kallmeyer and Möseler Verlag, 1925-40) are listed below. Some of the passages cited deal with more than one topic but are listed only under the main one.

    (a) Fast vs. slow duple meter and the meaning of C vs. ₵ : *GA* 2: x, item v; *GA* 5: xi, item iv; *GA* 14: xv, no. 14 ("Magnificat super Ut re mi fa sol la"), cantus, preceding the "Suscepit Israel"); *GA* 15: xi, item vi, and xv, item xi; *GA* 17/1: 154, introduction to no. 18; *GA* 19: vii, item iii.

    (b) Combining two *tactus* into one in order to beat fast tempo more comfortably (including *sextupla*): *GA* 14: x, item 5; *GA* 14: xiii; *GA* 15: xi, item vi and xiii, item vii; *GA* 17/2: 644, no. 37, item iv; *GA* 19: 30, item iv; *GA* 19: 94, no. 10, item ii.

    (c) Dividing one tactus into two (in essence, "subdividing" the beat) in order to help the singers stay together when there are many short notes: *GA* 5: xi, item iv.

    (d) The approximate duration of individual pieces of music, based on *tempora* counts: *Syntagma III,* pp. 87-88 (Lampl, pp. 149-50); *GA* 17/1: 86, no. 14, item x; *GA* 17/1: 141, no. 17, item iii; *GA* 17/1: 159, at end of no. 19; *GA* 17/2: 292; *GA* 17/2: 293, no. 25, item i; *GA* 17/2: 317, no. 25; *GA* 17/2: 433, no. 30, item ii; *GA* 17/2: 476, top; *GA* 17/2: 720, no. 40, item ii.

    (e) The use of a faster tempo for ritornellos and tutti sections in polychoral concertos: *Syntagma III,* 131 (Lampl, 190); *GA* 17/1: 154, introduction to no. 18; *GA* 17/1: 268, no. 24, item i; *GA* 19: vii, item iii.

    (f) The use of vertical strokes under the staff to separate *tactus* in the manner of the modern bar line: *Syntagma III,* part 2, chapter 5; *GA* 15: 14, item x.

    (g) Italian and German "tempo words:" *Syntagma III,* 132 (Lampl, pp. 191-93); GA 19: vii, item III.

    (h) "About Changes of Tempo and Dynamics" (*Syntagma III,* part 2, chapter 8) is a fascinating essay that encourages variability of tempo and dynamics for aesthetic reasons. This is a condensed version of portions of a 1598 treatise by Georg Quitscheiber entitled *De canendi elegentia, octodecim praecepta, studosis necessaria* (Eighteen rules regarding tasteful singing, necessary for students of music). Praetorius added a few of his own ideas but did not distinguish in any way between his work and what he borrowed. As given in Lampl, paragraph 1 consists of Quitscheiber's rules 14 and 15, and paragraph 5 contains rules 17 and 18.

In order to avoid all confusion and painful effort in the use of the signatures one could telescope the entire discussion of the signatures and the *tactus* succinctly and correctly in the following table (subject to correction by others), discarding entirely all other signatures.[14]

There are two kinds of *tactus*:

Equal:
- Slow / fast — under the sign
  - **C** Used in madrigals and concertos
  - **¢** Used in motets
- moderate: under the sign / signs of *sextupla*
  - $\frac{6}{1}$ / $\frac{6}{2}$ The notes being

Unequal:
- Slow & Fast — Under the sign
  - 3+ or $\frac{3}{1}$ / $\frac{3}{2}$ in
    - *Tripla* / *Sesqui- altera* The notes being

It is immediately clear that Praetorius has simplified and radically redefined classical mensural theory: (1) Nowhere is there a hint of a proportional relationship between the various *tactus* types.
(2) **C** denotes a slow *tactus*, and **¢** indicates a fast one. (Although the table does not say so explicitly, Praetorius considers the *tactus* under both signs to be the semibreve. This will be shown later.)

---

[14]*Syntagma III*, 79; Lampl, 134. At first glance, it appears as if the vertical strokes in the *sextupla* examples indicate *tactus* groupings of three minims, just as they do in the illustration of *sesquialtera*. Note, however, the height of the strokes. In the *tripla* and *sesquialtera* examples, the slash is centered on the note heads, but in the *sextupla* example, it is positioned lower. In most of his music written in *sextupla*, Praetorius uses a short or low incise to indicate the middle of the *tactus* and a high or long incise to show its beginning/end.

(3) There are three ways of notating triple meter, each of which denotes a different tempo:

(a) *Tripla,* a *tactus* consisting of three semibreves (as shown by the vertical line dividing the two *tactus*) and signed most clearly by the signature 3 or $\frac{3}{1}$, is beaten slowly in *tactus inaequalis.*

(b) *Sesquialtera,* a *tactus* of three minims, is best signed by $\frac{3}{2}$ and is beaten quickly in *tactus inaequalis.*

(c) The *sextupla tactus* consists of six colored minims under the sign $\frac{6}{1}$ or six white minims under the sign $\frac{6}{2}$. It is beaten at a moderate tempo in *tactus aequalis* (three minims on the downbeat and three on the upbeat). The tempo the listener perceives, however, is as fast as *sesquialtera* or even faster, since there are six beats rather than three in each *tactus.*

Let us look in more detail at Praetorius's ideas on *tactus,* tempo, and proportion.

The Signs $\overset{..}{C}$ and $\cancel{C}$ in Theory and Practice

Praetorius begins chapter 7 with an explanation of both the old and new meanings of C and $\cancel{C}$.

> The time value of notes is determined from the signatures. . . .
>
> Duple time is slower or faster, depending on the signature. . . .
>
> The signature indicating a slower beat is C , used in madrigals; that indicating a faster beat $\cancel{C}$, used in motets. . . .
>
> Earlier musicians called the signature C *tempus perfectum minus* or *signum minoris tactus* ["the signature of the smaller *tactus*"]. They counted one semibreve ◇ or two minims ↓ ↓ to one *tactus,* calling it, in Italian, *alla semibreve.* But the signature $\cancel{C}$ they called *tempus perfectum maius* or *signum maioris vel totalis tactus* ["the signature of the larger or whole tactus."][15] Thus they counted in compositions with

---

[15]Praetorius uses non-traditional Latin terminology for the signs C and $\cancel{C}$. He refers to both signs as denoting *tempus perfectum,* although in classical mensural terminology, *tempus perfectum* indicated the division of the breve into three semibreves, which was impossible by definition under both C and $\cancel{C}$. This incongruity is explained convincingly by Carl Dahlhaus in his article "Zur Taktlehre des Michael Praetorius," *Die Musikforschung* 17 (1964) 163−4. Dahlhaus points to the use of the word "perfect" at this time to denote non-diminished as opposed to diminished ("imperfect") mensurations. Since Praetorius did not consider $\cancel{C}$ to denote diminution, but rather, a faster tempo for the semibreve *tactus,* both C and $\cancel{C}$ could be considered *tempus perfectum* in the "new" parlance.

the signature ₵ two semibreves, in other words, two *tactus minores* to a rather slow *tactus*—called *alla breve* in Italian—one semibreve ◇ or two minims ⏐⏐ occurring on the downbeat, the other semibreve or two minims with the upbeat. This was the usual procedure in Orlando's [Orlando di Lasso's] time and is still customary in various outstanding chapels and schools. As an example, here is a composition by Orlando:

. . . At the present time these two signatures are usually distinguished in such a way that the ₵ is mostly used in madrigals, the ₵ in motets. Madrigals and other compositions, which have the signature ₵ and have an abundance of semiminims and fusas, move along at a faster pace; motets, however, with the signature ₵ and a prevalence of breves and semibreves, at a slower pace. Therefore in the latter case a faster beat, in the former case a slower beat, is necessary in order to achieve a mean between the two extremes. . . . For this reason I believe one would do well to use the signature ₵ for those motets and other sacred compositions which have many black notes, in order to show that the beat then is to be taken more slowly.[16]

This passage contains a wealth of information. In the old days, at least according to Praetorius, the Lassus example would have been conducted at about the same speed whether it was written in long notes under ₵ or in short notes under ₵ , but under ₵ the *tactus* would

---

[16]*Syntagma III*, 48–9; Lampl, 99–104.

consist of a semibreve and under ¢ a breve. In other words, the old practice considered ¢ a diminution of C .[17]

The practice advocated by Praetorius is quite different: ¢ means to beat faster than C . Although it is not stated directly in chapter 7 (but is clear from his music), this must mean that the *tactus* for both signs is the semibreve, and that ¢ is *not* thought of as a diminution of C . Praetorius would have the choice of signs be a matter of practicality and aesthetics rather than mensural theory: if the beat should be fast to compensate for long notes or just to make the music more lively, ¢ should be used; if the note values are short, or if the passage should be taken slowly for best musical effect, C is appropriate.

The distinction Praetorius makes between the notation of madrigals and concertos on one hand and motets on the other hand, is significant. As mentioned previously, in the early sixteenth century it had been usual to notate both sacred and secular music in long notes under the sign ¢ . By the end of the century, the notation of sacred music had changed little, but composers had generally adopted a short-note notation for secular music, often under the sign C . As the influence of Italian secular music was felt ever more strongly in music for the church around the turn of the seventeenth century, both in Italy and abroad, short-note "madrigal" notation became more and more common in sacred music.

---

[17]The distinction between "old" and "new" *tactus*-beating practices under the sign ¢ was likely not as clear-cut as one might infer from the quotation. Slow beating of a breve *tactus* and fast beating of a semibreve *tactus* under the sign ¢ had likely been coexistent for a hundred years or more. Praetorius apparently believed that in the time of the "earlier musicians"—probably the sixteenth century—the slow, alla-breve *tactus* had been more common than the fast, alla-semibreve *tactus,* whereas in his day, the opposite was true. Later in the chapter, however, he says that "modern Italians" advocate slow, alla-breve beating of music under ¢ (*Syntagma III,* 54-55; Lampl 108-109). It thus appears that the "old" practice and the "modern Italian" practice are identical. Unfortunately, nothing else in his writings sheds further light on this apparent incongruity.

Although Praetorius himself usually advocated a fast, semibreve *tactus* under the sign ¢ , on several occasions in both *Syntagma III* and various collections of his music, he recommends an alla-breve *tactus* when the note values are very long and fast beating of the semibreve *tactus* still would not yield a fast-enough tempo. In such cases in his own music, he usually signed the piece with C2, ¢2, ¢, or ¢2 to make explicit the need for an exceptionally fast tempo.

The idea that there was more than one relative speed of *tactus* beating has long been a source of contention among musicologists. Curt Sachs and Antoine Auda maintained that there was no fast, semibreve *tactus* beating of C in the Renaissance, and that the whole concept was the result of misunderstandings and mistranslations of the primary sources. Sachs was so committed to the idea that he offered his own strained mistranslation of a key passage in the Agricola *Musica figuralis deudsch* (1532) that fit his own preconception but made nonsense out of the rest of the treatise. See Sachs, 220-21.

But typesetters and composers were often careless or thought the sign unimportant, and the two signs often appeared in the "wrong" contexts. This led Praetorius to complain that "Many composers use the two signatures C and ₵ indiscriminately and one cannot tell any difference from the notes themselves or the entire composition." Praetorius's own works reflect this confusion, and while the long note values of a particular piece may suggest that ₵ would be the appropriate sign, just as often as not, the sign provided is C . The opposite is true as well: pieces with short note values are often signed with the sign of the fast *tactus,* ₵ .

Table 1, a summary of the mensural signs and proportions used in the eighteen collections of Praetorius's vocal music, illustrates another side to the problem: the choice between C and ₵ often seems to have made to achieve consistency within a given collection, regardless of its musical content. For example, there is no significant difference between the note values used in book 1 of the *Musae sioniae* as opposed to books 2−4, but book 1 is signed exclusively with ₵ , while the others are signed only with C . The *Motectae et psalmi Latini* of 1607 contains several pieces by Palestrina, Handl, Aichinger, and others, all of which are written in sixteenth-century, long-note notation, yet each piece bears the signature C .

Praetorius was concerned about the ambiguity of the signs C and ₵ —particularly in polychoral concertos in which he intended slow and fast sections to alternate—and he proposed a solution: the use of "tempo words:"

> It is most necessary to sustain quite a slow, stately pace in *concerti* involving several choirs. But since in such *concerti* madrigal and motet styles are found in frequent alternation [that is, passages written in short notes alternate with those in longer notes], one has to modify the beat accordingly. Therefore it is sometimes quite necessary to indicate in the parts the Italian words *adagio* and *presto,* i.e., "slow" and "fast." Mere frequent changes of the signatures C and ₵ would only create more confusion.[18]

---

[18]*Syntagma III,* 51; Lampl, 105. At the end of part 2, chapter 9 of *Syntagma III,* Praetorius gives us an idea of what he meant by a "slow, stately pace" for his polychoral concertos. He says that 640 *tempora* (two *tactus* under all signs but *sextupla,* under which it constitutes one *tactus*) can be sung in one hour using a "quite moderate *tactus.*" This works out to $\downarrow = 5$ 42, a very slow tempo by today's standards. Of course, the figure must be rough, encompassing as it does all *tactus* types. But even so, it raises the possibility that our modern concept of this music is entirely too fast.

Unfortunately, Praetorius did not do what he said he would. In the *Polyhymnia caduceatrix* of 1619, a collection of elaborate polychoral concertos, he did include many verbal tempo indications, but these were usually accompanied by a change of sign that is often contradictory: many sections that bear Italian tempos words for "fast" are signed with $\mathbf{C}$, and many of the "slow" indications are accompanied by a $\mathbf{\mathfrak{C}}$. In his *Puericinium,* which appeared just two years after *Syntagma III,* Praetorius completely abandoned his own good advice on the substitution of unambiguous tempo words for ambiguous signs:

> In order that the boys in the *Coro puerorum* might always proceed gracefully with a slow *tactus,* I have set the sign of the slow *tactus,* .
> But when the *ripieni* of the full choir enter, one must lead with a graceful, brisk *tactus,* notated with the sign of diminution or the sign of the fast *tactus,* and do this everywhere, in all verses. For these signs mean the same as if I had used the Italian words:

$$\mathbf{C} \text{ , i.e., } \textit{lento, tarde: } \text{SLOW.}$$
$$\mathbf{\mathfrak{C}} \text{ , i.e., } \textit{presto, velociter: } \text{FAST.}^{[19]}$$

When Praetorius used very long note values in homophonic hymn settings, as he did on several occasions in books 5, 6, and 7 of the *Musae sioniae* and in the *Hymnodia,* he usually made the need for a very fast *tactus* explicit by the use of the signs of diminution $\mathbf{C}2$ or even $\mathbf{\mathfrak{C}}2$ in all parts. Maddeningly, however, a number of these long-note pieces also appear under the signature $\mathbf{C}$. Facsimile 3, the cantus part to no. 20 from *Musae sioniae,* book 6, illustrates this diminished notation under the sign $\mathbf{C}2$.

On a very few occasions Praetorius wrote the cantus part of a hymn in genuine diminution under the sign $\mathbf{C}2$, while the other voices, signed with $\mathbf{C}$ or $\mathbf{\mathfrak{C}}$, were written in *integer-valor* note values.[20] This is clear evidence that Praetorius considered both $\mathbf{C}$ and $\mathbf{\mathfrak{C}}$ to be signs of *integer valor:* when $\mathbf{\mathfrak{C}}$ and $\mathbf{C}2$—two signs that are theoretically

---

[19]*GA,* vol. 19, vii.
[20]Praetorius explains this rare use of actual diminution in part 2, chapter 7 of *Syntagma III,* 56; (Lampl, p. 124):

> In addition one ought to remember that in several places in my first German compositions as well as in the hymns I have notated the chorale [melody] in the cantus with ligatures (in order to facilitate the application of the text) and indicated there the sign of diminution $\mathbf{C}2$. It must be understood then, that all the following notes lose one half of their value, as can easily be gathered by comparison with the other voices.

Facsimile 3

synonymous—occur simultaneously, $\mathbb{C}$ 2 is treated as a diminution against $\mathbb{C}$.

Two final examples of actual proportion in Praetorius's music are particularly interesting. Toward the end of *Musae sioniae,* book 5, the printer apparently realized that he was running out of eighth notes. His solution was to rewrite some voice parts that had a large number of eighths into *dupla* proportion so that quarter notes, which he had in abundance, could be substituted. For this reason, the cantus and altus parts to no. 156 are diminished (the former under the sign $\frac{4}{2}$ and the latter under $\frac{8}{4}$), while the tenor is written in *integer valor* under $\mathbb{C}$. For the same reason, the cantus to no. 158 is written in dinimution under the sign $\mathbb{C}$2 .

Can one rely at all on Praetorius's use of $\mathbb{C}$ and $\mathbb{C}$ in making decisions regarding tempo? In order to do so, three conditions would have to be met. (1) One would have to know what *the composer* originally wrote in terms of note values and signs, and these are often changed without notice by modern editors. Critical editions and their ''critical reports'' are often helpful in reconstructing the original notation, but even these can deceive. (2) One would have to have reason to believe that the composer truly meant $\mathbb{C}$ and $\mathbb{C}$ to have different meanings. (3) Finally, one would have to be reasonably certain that the composer intended the sign that appears on the page to be there, and not another.

The author's survey of the original sources of the Praetorius works and those of several other major composers of the period has led to the unhappy conclusion that the last two of these preconditions for consistently distinguishing between C and $¢$ likely cannot be met, even for Praetorius, who left us much more to go on than his contemporaries. Unless one has access to films of the original Praetorius sources, it is not possible to be certain that the signs contained in the *Gesamtausgabe* are what Praetorius actually wrote. Although the great majority of the pieces printed in the complete works bear the sign the composer assigned, many have been changed without notice.

A second problem is that in the original sources it is sometimes difficult to tell which sign the printer meant to set, since there are many signs that look like hybrids. This is explainable by the previously described transition from long-note notation under $¢$ to short-note notation under C. Printers found themselves with bushels of $¢$ s and not many C s at a time when the music they were printing demanded the opposite. They evidently found it cheaper to carve away the slashs from $¢$ s than to melt them down and recast them into C s. Pieces of type with incompletely removed slashes thus became "hybrid" signs.

The third and most troublesome problem is that many of the Praetorius collections are so full of printing errors that even if the sign is recognizable, one cannot be sure that it is the one the composer intended. The *Polyhymnia caduceatrix* provides the most extreme example. These pieces, the most diverse and complex that Praetorius wrote, contain a great variety of performing forces, musical styles, written-in dynamics, and changes of sign that would seem to indicate changes of tempo. Several pieces contain both C and $¢$, and many others have passages in both *tripla* and *sesquialtera*. In the complete works edition, the difference between the C and $¢$ sections is very clear because of the unanimity of the signs in all parts from the top to the bottom of the page.

This unanimity, however, is often a creation of the editors. There are so many simultaneous conflicts of sign in different parts that one can have little confidence that any sign is what the composer intended it to be. A comparison of two of the partbooks will suffice to make the point. The primus and basso continuo partbooks share all but a couple of the pieces in the collection. These pieces contain a total of seventy-four sections (*Teile,* as the composer labelled them) in which C, $¢$, or both are present. In twenty-four of these sections—*32%*—there is at least one occasion where the two parts have different signs simultaneously.[21] Considering that there are only two signs from which to choose, and that random chance would dictate about 50% disagreement, there is not much basis for confidence when the signs *do* agree, much less when they do not. Praetorius recognized the problem himself—apparently after it was too late to make changes—when he wrote in item 27 of the preface, "let no one be misled by the fact that the signs of *tactus aequalis,* C and ₵ , are mixed up through no fault of my own: in particular, let each conduct the *tactus* as he feels best."

The performer is thus left with Praetorius's own suggestion of what to do when all else fails: "Anyone, however, may reflect on such matters himself and decide, on the basis of text and music, where the beat has to be slow, where fast," using the printed signs as a starting point.[22]

The Interpretation of *Tripla, Sesquialtera,* and *Sextupla*

The section of part 2, chapter 7 of *Syntagma III* that deals with the duple signs is followed by a discussion of "Proportional Signatures in Triple Time:"

> There are two kinds of triple or trochaic *tactus: major* ["large"] and *minor* ["small"]. The large is commonly called *proportio tripla,* the small [*proportio*] *sesquialtera.* In *tripla* three semibreves or their equivalents make up one *tactus.* The signatures used by Orlando, Marenzio, Fel[ice] Anerio, and others are as follows:

$$3 + \tfrac{3}{1} \cdot \quad \textbf{C}\; 3 \cdot \quad \textbf{(}\!\textbf{)}\, 3 \cdot \textbf{N} \tfrac{3}{1} \cdot \quad \textbf{(}\!\textbf{)}\, \tfrac{3}{1} +$$

> In *sesquialtera* three minims ♪ ♪ ♪ or their equivalents make up one *tactus.* . . . It is appropriately marked by the signature $\tfrac{3}{2}$. Just as in *proportio tripla* $\tfrac{3}{1}$ indicates that three semibreves are equal to one *tactus,* so in *sesquialtera* $\tfrac{3}{2}$ indicates that three semibreves ◇ ◇ ◇ equal two *tactus.* One may also find other signatures such as:[23]

---

[21]The carelessness, ambivalence, or spite of the printer is most obvious in those places in the primus where the chorale melody and an alternate, ornamented version of it are printed in score form, one above the other. In nos. 1 and 2, one of these parts is signed C while the other has a ₵ ! *GA* 19, p. xi shows the same phenomenon in a facsimile from the continuo part to no. 1 in the *Puericinium.*

[22]*Syntagma III,* 51; Lampl, 105.

[23]*Syntagma III,* 52; Lampl, 107−08. What appear to be plus signs are actually periods, meant to separate one sign from another. They appear in the text as well, alternating freely with regular periods.

$$\mathbf{C}\,_{3.}\;\mathbf{O}\,_{3.}\;\mathbf{O}\,_{3.}\;\mathbf{\Phi}\;_{3+}\;\mathbf{C}\;_{2+}^{3}\;\mathbf{O}\;_{2+}^{3}\;\mathbf{\odot}.\;\mathbf{C}_{+}\mathbf{C}._{3+}\mathbf{C}_{+2+}^{3}$$

. . . *Tripla* should be retained in motets and *concerti;* but *sesquialtera* in madrigals, and particularly in galliards, courantes, voltas, and other compositions of this nature, in which a faster *tactus* is necessary.[24]

This discussion raises one of the problems a performer faces when confronted with ternary proportions in Renaissance and early-Baroque music, and suggests a solution to another. First is the uselessness of the signatures in determining what proportion was intended. The sign 3, for example, perhaps the most frequent ternary sign in the music of the day, appears in Praetorius's charts under both *tripla* and *sesquialtera*. The charts themselves look suspicious, with both the sign O3 and the sign **C** (!) listed *twice* under *tripla*. If Praetorius was trying to clarify things, he failed miserably.

The second problem is that *tripla* and *sesquialtera* appear to be two different ways of writing the same thing:

One *tactus*   =   **C** ◊   = ◊◊◊ =   ♩♩♩

                     integer valor   *tripla*   *sesquialtera*

If three beats of *tripla* and three beats of *sesquialtera* each comprise one *tactus,* why would a composer choose one notation over the other? And why would a composer include *both* proportions in a single piece, as Schein did in the piece illustrated at the beginning of this article or as Praetorius himself did on nine occasions?[25] Praetorius's explanation is simple and makes sense: they are to be taken at different speeds. But he was not content with just two degrees of tempo differentiation in triple meter. The previous quotation continues as follows:

[24]*Syntagma III,* 53; Lampl, 110. In *Terpsichore* Praetorius actually uses *sextupla* for most of these fast dances. The introduction to *Terpsichore* contains much discussion of the appropriate *tactus* for the various dance types. One example using the signature ¢3 with *tripla* note values is labelled *geschwind* ("fast"). This is the only indication in the Praetorius works that ¢3 might imply a faster tempo than   C3.
[25]*Tripla* and *sesquialtera* in the same piece: *Megalynodia* nos. 1, 2; *Polyhymnia caduceatrix* nos. 7, 11, 12, 14, 17, 40; *Musae sioniae* 6 no. 144. *Tripla* and *sextupla: Polyhymnia caduceatrix* no. 37; *Puericinium* nos. 4, 10. *Sesquialtera* and *sextupla: Hymnodia* no. 145.

Furthermore, since most of these compositions require such a fast *tactus* I felt—in view of the newness of the subject—I ought to devise new terms not previously employed in this way, and therefore I have tried to express the matter by the term *sextupla,* or *tactus trochaicus diminutus.* . . .

I should like to use the term *sextupla* where six semiminims make up one *tactus.* In this case the figure "3" is written either below or above three or six semiminims, in this fashion:

Moreover I find that there are three additional methods used by the Italians and the English to notate such *sextupla* groups: (1) Just as in *hemiola minor,* black notes are used . . . so that three colored minims ♩♩♩ or a colored semibreve and a minim ♦♩ fall on the downbeat, the following three on the upbeat. The signature ₵ means that six semiminims or black minims make up one full *tactus.* . . . Thus one *tactus aequalis* is formed.

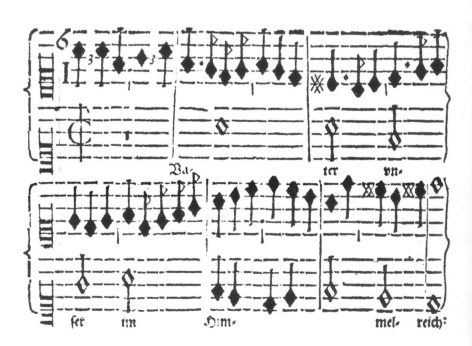

In this way one can easily change all *tripla* and *sesquialtera* proportions
in the German *Choralpsalmen* and all other works from *tactus inaequalis*
to *tactus aequalis,* as illustrated in the following examples:[26]

---

[26]*Syntagma III*, 53, 73−5; Lampl, 110, 124−5, 129−30. The "triplet" notation shown
in the first staff of the first facsimile appears in none of Praetorius's own *sextupla* pieces.
Claudio Monteverdi uses it, however (without the ¢ signature), in the "Sonata sopra
Sancta Maria" of the 1610 "Vespers." There it directly follows a section in *sesquialtera.*
This suggests very strongly that Monteverdi desired two degrees of fast triple meter,
the *sextupla* likely being the faster of the two.

The latter part of the quotation raises an intriguing question. If "one can easily change
all *tripla* and *sesquialtera* proportions in the German *Choralpsalmen* and all other works
from *tactus inaequalis* to *tactus aequalis*" by rewriting them in *sextupla,* does this
mean that *tripla* was used by other composers to denote a *fast* tempo? Or did they possibly
use *tripla* as a "generic" notation for triple meter that could be interpreted as either
slow or fast? Unfortunately, Praetorius says nothing more on the subject.

Praetorius gives two reasons for using this "unorthodox" notation: it is an unequivocal method of notating fast triple meter and it avoids the frantic-looking movements required to beat a *sesquialtera* of comparable tempo in *tactus inaequalis:*

> It could well be that here [in *sextupla* notation] one could employ the *tactus inaequalis* exclusively, at a fast pace. . . . This would be more correct and would help to prevent errors. . . . But I prefer by far the *tactus aequalis* of the kind containing two *tactus inaequales,* lest we make the spectators laugh and offend the listeners with incessant hand and arm movements and give the crowd an opportunity for raillery and mockery.[27]

It is difficult to imagine how beating fast triple meter in compound time could be so revolutionary and difficult to understand, but in Praetorius's day it apparently was. Although there are only six instances of *sextupla* in the entire Praetorius vocal works, three of the four collections in which these appear either contain explanations similar to that above or refer the reader to the as-yet unpublished *Syntagma III.*

Aids in Recognizing the Type of *Tactus*

Before turning to an examination of how Praetorius uses the ternary proportions in his music, it would be helpful to consider first the various notational devices he uses to help the performer determine what type of *tactus* is intended in any given piece. The music of Praetorius himself contains few ambiguities in this regard, but the situation is not as clear with other composers.

In *sextupla* especially, but in the other proportions as well, Praetorius was concerned that the performer be able to recognize the appropriate *tactus,* lest someone get lost. To this end, in part 2, chapter 2 of *Syntagma III,* he introduced a fail-safe means of identifying the intended *tactus,* a precursor of the modern bar line:

> In various compositions, especially in *sinfonie* without text, one can find many fusas in succession. This may easily lead to errors concerning the *tactus,* particularly in sight reading proportions. Therefore I believe it is useful to put at the bottom and top of the staff little strokes between the measures (as found in my *Terpsichore*), so that at a fast tempo one may more easily follow the *tactus* and find one's place if lost. But it is especially necessary in *tripla* and *sesquialtera* proportion to mark

[27]*Syntagma III,* 74; Lampl, 129–30.

the first and second *tactus* at the beginning with a little stroke, so that one can see from the outset which kind of *tactus* is involved, whether a large triple *tactus*, in semibreves, or a small triple *tactus*, in minims (particularly since until now—as shown in the preceding third chapter [*sic:* read "fourth"]—most musicians used the signs for *tripla* and *sesquialtera* without distinction so that one cannot tell one from the other).[28]

The first *tactus*-division strokes appear in *Musae sionae*, book 7 (1609) and then in the *Hymnodia* (1611) and the *Polyhymnia caduceatrix* (1619). Praetorius's collection of French dances, the *Terpsichore* of 1615, is filled with them in pieces representing all types of *tactus*.

A second device for identifying the *tactus* is the first found in the *Polyhymnia caduceatrix*, which consists of very long and elaborate polychoral pieces involving independent instruments and frequent alternation of soloists and choirs. The notation of the day had not been devised for such pieces, nor was Praetorius's printer accustomed to such complexity. The resulting parts were often confusing—even chaotic—in appearance. Praetorius was worried that the singers would not count their rests accurately, so instead of simply writing rests when a performer did not sing, he usually appended a numeral that indicated the number of *tactus* occupied by the rests. He explains this practice as follows:

> In *concerti* involving several choirs a great many rests often occur in the various choirs. Thus a musician not paying the utmost attention is inclined to lose himself at times because of the frequency and change of such rests, also, because he may be enjoying himself listening to the other voices. Therefore I have decided, as a most necessary expedient, to put the number of rests above or below the notes, especially when the signatures of duple $\mathbb{C}$ $\mathbf{C}$ and triple time 3 $\frac{3}{2}$ are used in frequent alternation. For one and the same rest in duple time may amount to four *tactus*, in *tripla*, however, only to two *tactus*. All this can easily cause confusion, as anyone will discover, and as I was taught by experience, not without some embarrassment.[29]

Praetorius's *tactus*-division strokes and *tactus* numbers are of no use in a modern edition with bar lines. They were intended to help singers who were reading from unbarred parts, not scores. But they do permit us to test his statements on what note value comprises the *tactus* under each binary and ternary sign. *Without a single exception,* both *tactus*

[28]*Syntagma III*, 34; Lampl, 86−87.
[29]*Syntagma III*, 33−34; Lampl, 84. The $\mathbb{C}$ in the original erroneously has a horizontal stroke of diminution.

Facsimile 4

numbers and division strokes confirm what Praetorius says in *Syntagma III* and elsewhere:

(1) the *tactus* under C and ₵ is the semibreve.

(2) Rhythmic movement in units of three semibreves constitutes one *tripla tactus* under all signs (C3,   ₵3, 3).

(3) Rhythmic movement in three-minim units denotes a sesquialtera *tactus*.

Facsimile 4, the beginning of the tenor part to no. 12 from the *Polyhymnia caduceatrix*, "Puer natus in Bethlehem," illustrates both *tactus* numbers and *tactus*-division strokes. Praetorius provides *tactus* numbers for rests under duple meter (C) and *sesquialtera* ($\frac{3}{2}$), and there are also *tactus*-division strokes under both signs. Both indicators show the *tactus* to be a semibreve—imperfect under C and perfect under $\frac{3}{2}$.

Facsimile 5

On only a handful of occasions in Praetorius's music is there a simultaneous overlap between duple and triple mensurations. Since the parts will only fit together in one way, the simultaneity of the two mensurations defines their proportional relationship to each other. In the first forty-five *tactus* of this piece we encounter two such overlaps. As can be seen from the rests at the beginning of the tenor part, the first two sections of the piece—an instrumental sinfonia and a section for soloists—consist of twenty-six and nineteen ₵ semibreve *tactus,* respectively. The beginning of the basso continuo part to the same piece, facsimile 5, shows what happens in the parts that are not tacet for these forty-five measures. In graphic form:

Overlap 1
   Basso continuo: C ◊ x 13   +   3 ◊◊◊ x 6   +   C ◊ x 7

                                                    = 26 *tactus*

   Tenor: C ➖ x 26

Overlap 2
   Basso continuo: C ◊ x 6   + $\frac{3}{2}$ ♩♩♩ x 8   +   C ◊ x 5

                                                      = 19 *tactus*

   Tenor: C ➖ x 19

           1 *tactus*   =   C ◊   =   3 ◊◊◊   = $\frac{3}{2}$ ♩♩♩

The resulting *tactus* values are entirely consistent with Praetorius's teachings. The *tactus* type and speed would have changed several times while the tenor was counting his ₵ rests, but if he had been counting downbeats accurately, he would have come in at the right time. Without knowing the differentiation Praetorius makes between *tripla* and *sesquialtera,* there would seem to be no reason to use both *tripla* and *sesquialtera* writing in this piece, since, as shown previously, they are notationally equivalent. The presence of both forms of notation in a single piece makes sense only if they denote different *tactus* speeds, and that is precisely what Praetorius teaches.

Facsimile 4 illustrates three other indicators that can help the performer determine the type of *tactus* intended by the composer: coloration, the use of perfect notes and rests, and special notation of rests preceding an anacrusis. In modern notation, a time signature indicates a repeated metric pattern of downbeat stress. This was not one of the functions of the mensuration sign or sign of proportion, at least in theory. In practice, however, the signs for *tripla* and *sesquialtera* invariably

denoted clearly recognizable triple meter. But composers often introduced syncopation into their triple-meter sections, most often in the form
of hemiola rhythm. In order to help the singer recognize the syncopation, it was common to blacken or "color" the syncopated notes.[30] Colored breves or semibreve-breve pairs are typical of *tripla,* while colored semibreves or semibreve-minim pairs characterize *sesquialtera.*
We see four black semibreves on staff six of facsimile 4, each of which
falls on the second minim of the *tactus.* Since the usual, "metrical"
rhythm under triple meter was long-short, the written rhythm constituted
a syncopation to be emphasized visually by coloration.

Under *sesquialtera* (as the term is defined by Praetorius), the
semibreve was treated as perfect, as was the breve under *tripla.*[31] The
presence of perfection on these levels is thus an indicator of the proportion the composer intended. Looking again at staff six of the tenor
part, we see that Praetorius did not dot the perfect semibreve rests that
follow the first two colored semibreves. He *could have* dotted them
for clarity—as he did the two white semibreves at the end of the staff—but
under the rules of mensural notation, he *did not have to.*

When other composers of the period wanted to write an imperfect
semibreve rest, they wrote two, individual, minim rests, as did Praetorius
twice on staff 6. Rests written in this form are yet another indicator
of the value of the *tactus.*

The Ternary Proportions in the Music of Praetorius

As can be seen in table 1, *tripla* is by far the most common ternary
proportion, appearing in no fewer than 309 compositions as opposed
to only 58 instances of *sesquialtera.* The signs used for *tripla* at the
beginnings of individual pieces or their major sections are ₵ 3 and
₵ 3. When a *tripla* passage occurs following a section in duple meter,
the sign ("medial sign" in table 1) is almost invariably a simple 3. Most
of Praetorius's *sesquialteras* bear the sign ₵ 3 when they occur at the
beginning of a composition, and the sign 3 when they occur medially.
With one exception in the *Hymnodia* of 1611, $\frac{3}{2}$ (and its synonym ₵$\frac{3}{2}$),
the sign advocated by Praetorius in *Syntagma III,* does not appear at

---

[30]Praetorius explains this in *Syntagma III,* 29–30 (Lampl, 76–77) and in the introduction to *Musae sioniae,* book 2 (*GA,* vol. 2, x).

[31]The *Gesamtausgabe* ignores semibreve perfection in one *sesquialtera* piece, no. 145
from *Musae sioniae,* book 8, and correspondingly distorts the transcription (*GA,* vol.
8, p. 111). The penultimate note in all parts preceding the repeat sign and the penultimate
note at the end of the piece should be *dotted* semibreves.

all until the *Polyhymnia caduceatrix* of 1619, published the same year
as *Syntagma III.*

In the notation of the time, one could also indicate *sesquialtera* by
the sign Ȼ , but that sign could have two meanings, depending on context. Praetorius says:

> It must be noted that the signature of major prolation Ꙩ or Ȼ marks
> *sesquialtera* when it is put into all parts simultaneously. But when it is
> found in one voice only, it signifies augmentation, or *subdupla.*[32]

Praetorius used this notation for *sesquialtera* only three times in all his
works: twice in *Musae sioniae,* book 8 of 1610 and once in the *Eulogodia
sionia* of the following year.

On occasion Praetorius used a type of notation for *tripla* and *sesquialtera* that we have not yet encountered. When the text dealt with
strongly affective words like "death," "darkness," "night," "Satan,"
"woe," etc., he blackened the normally white notes of his *tripla* or
sesquialtera as a form of "eye music." Twelve of his twenty-one uses
of this notation can be explained in this way, as can be seen in table
2. Of the nine "non-affective" examples, four are short Easter hymns
that are colored in their entirety. Perhaps the coloration here can be
explained as a symbolic way of connecting the Passion with the Resurrection. Facsimile 6, no. 144 from *Musae sioniae,* book 6, is the most
unusual of these, with the first half in colored *tripla* (*hemiola maior*
in mensural terminology) and the second half in colored *sesquialtera*
(*hemiola minor*). The remaining five pieces are all settings of positive—
even joyful—texts that contain episodes of colored notation lasting from
two to nine *tactus.* Some composers used *hemiola maior* and *hemiola
minor* when the triple-meter section was very short, probably in order
to save inserting a new sign of proportion and then another sign to cancel
it. Perhaps this is what Praetorius had in mind.

Given the extraordinary amount of effort Praetorius expended to explain his concept of the compound triple-meter *sextupla tactus* in *Syntagma III* and elsewhere, it is amazing to find that it only appears six
times in his vocal works (see table 1). *Sextupla* is first found in the
two 1611 collections, *Megalynodia sionia* (no. 14)[33] and *Hymnodia
sionia* (no. 145). In the latter, it directly follows a section in *sesquialtera,*
implying a slightly faster tempo.

---

[32]*Syntagma III,* 52; Lampl, 108.
[33]The preface to the *Megalonodia* says that the music dates from 1602 in Regensburg.
The presence of *sextupla*—totally absent from Praetorius's works until the publications
of 1611—suggests that at least no. 14 was revised shortly before publication.

Facsimile 6

Praetorius never did settle on a method of notating *sextupla*. He was so concerned that his reader grasp the concept that he vascillated in his notation, always trying to be clearer. All of the ca. sixty examples in *Terpsichore* are notated in colored *sesquialtera* under the sign ₵, as are the two examples cited above. Praetorius must have found this to be confusing to others, so in the *Polyhymnia caduceatrix* he used white *sesquialtera* notation with the signs ₵$\frac{3}{2}$ (no. 37) and ₵$\frac{3}{2}$ (no. 9). In the latter case, *tactus* numbers show that he was thinking of a three-minim, *sesquialtera tactus* rather than his beloved, six-minim, *tactus aequalis sextuplae*. In the *Puericinium,* which contains the last two examples of *sextupla* (no. 4, in white notes under ₵$\frac{3}{2}$ and no. 10, in colored *sesquialtera* with no sign at all), he explains the strange signature ₵$\frac{3}{2}$:

. . . Where the full ensemble enters for the first time, a double *tactus* of the *sextupla* variety in *tactus aequalis* must be maintained (as in *Syntagma musicum*, vol. 3, fol. 73−4). But if one wishes to to beat a *sesquialtera tactus*, [note that] two *tactus* are always combined and distinguished one from another by a slash. Such a *sesquialtera tactus* [must be beaten] quite quickly, for which reason I have set the sign of diminished diminution $\frac{3}{2}$.[34]

---

[34]*GA*, vol. 19, p. 30, item iv.

Table I

Mensural Signs and Proportions in the Vocal Collections of Michael Praetorius[a]

Source (Date of Publication)	Number of Compositions	Duple Sign(s)	Number of Triplas (Parentheses = Medial Sign) Sign / Quantity	Number of Sesquialteras (Parentheses = Medial Sign) Sign / Quantity	Number of Sextuplas Sign / Quantity	Number of Colored Triplas Sign / Quantity	Number of Colored Sesquialteras Sign / Quantity
Motectae et Psalmi Latini (1607)	52	C	(3)/26 C3/5	—	—	1[b]	—
Megalynodia sionia (1611)	14	C., ₵	₵3,C3/2' (3)/2 C3/1 ₵3/1	C.3	6/1 (colored)[d]	—	—
Musae sioniae 1 (1605)	21	₵	(3)/4 ₵3/7	—	—	—	—
Musae sioniae 2 (1607)	30	C	(3)/5	—	—	—	—
Musae sioniae 3 (1607)	31	C	(3)/6 C3/1	—	—	—	—
Musae sioniae 4 (1607)	34	C	(3)/9	—	—	1[e]	—

[a] The collections are grouped by solid horizontal lines into the four compositional periods established by Friedrich Blume. Within each compositional periods... collections are listed chronologically by date of publication. All compositions in the collections are included, even if attributed by Praetorius to other composers. Pieces containing two different ternary proportions (tripla and sesquialtera, sesquialtera and sextupla, for example) are counted in both categories. Works beginning with a proportion and containing medial incidents of the same proportion (usually signed with a 3) are counted under the initial sign only. Counts under medial signs indicate the number of pieces in which the proportion occurs only medially.

[b] No. 43, a piece not by Praetorius.

[c] C, ₵, and ₵3 occur successively in two pieces (nos. 1 & 2).

[d] Sextupla in the upper voices is simultaneous with C mensuration in the bass (no. 14).

[e] No. 4, not by Praetorius, contains both white and colored tripla.

Continued on next page.

Table I (continued)

Source (Date of Publication)	Number of Compositions	Duple Sign(s)	Number of *Triplas* (Parentheses = Medial Sign) Sign / Quantity	Number of *Sesquialteras* (Parentheses = Medial Sign) Sign / Quantity	Number of *Sextuplas* Sign / Quantity	Number of Colored *Triplas* Sign / Quantity	Number of Colored *Sesquialteras* Sign / Quantity
Musae sioniae 5 (1608)	166	₵, ₵; ₵2	₵3 / 33 (3) / 5 ₵3 / 3 ₵3 / 1	—	—	2	—
Musae sioniae 6 (1609)	200	₵, ₵; ₵2, ₵2	₵3 / 34 ₵3 / 8 (3) / 3 (₵3) / 1	₵3 / 8 (3) / 2	—	5	2[f]
Musae sioniae 7 (1609)	244	₵, ₵; ₵2	₵3 / 12 ₵3 / 1	₵3 / 9 ₵ / 2	—	2	1[g]
Musae sioniae 8 (1610)	302	₵, ₵	₵3 / 15 ₵3 / 15	₵ 3 / 7	—	6	1
Musae sioniae 9 (1610)	216	₵, ₵	(3) / 11 ₵3 / 6 (3) / 10	(3) / 11 ₵3 / 3	—	1	—
Missodia sionia (1611)	104	₵, ₵	(3) / 13 ₵3 / 2 ₵3 / 7 (3) / 3	—	—	—	—
Hymnodia sionia (1611)	145	₵, ₵; ₵2		$\frac{3}{2}$ / 1[h]	₵$^6_1$ / 1 (colored)[h]	—	—

[f] No. 239, a piece not by Praetorius.

[g] No. 144. The first half is colored *tripla*, the second half, colored *sesquialtera*.

[h] *Sesquialtera* and *sextupla* occur adjacently in the same piece (no. 145).

Source (Date of Publication)	Number of Compositions	Duple Sign(s)	Number of *Triplas* (Parentheses = Medial Sign) Sign / Quantity	Number of *Sesquialteras* (Parentheses = Medial Sign) Sign / Quantity	Number of *Sextuplas* Sign / Quantity	Number of Colored *Triplas* Sign / Quantity	Number of Colored *Sesquialteras* Sign / Quantity
Eulogodia sionia (1611)	60	¢	¢3/14 ¢(3)/3	(3)/2 ¢/1	—	—	—
Urania (1613)	28	¢, ¢	3/8	—	—	—	—
Polyhymnia caduceatrix (1619)	40	¢, ¢	(3)/30 ¢3/3 ¢3/1	(3)/8[i] C3/1	¢3/1(white) ¢3/1(white)[j]	—	—
Polyhymnia exerciatrix (1619)	14	¢, ¢	¢(3)/2	(3)/1	—	—	—
Puericinium (1621)	14	¢, ¢	¢3/10 ¢3/3	—	¢3/1(white) ¢/1 (colored)	—	—

[i] Six works contain both *tripla* and *sesquialtera* (nos. 7, 11, 12, 14, 17, and 40).

[j] *Tripla* and *sextupla* occur in the same piece (no. 37).

[k] All are contained in pieces also containing sections under ¢ 3 (nos. 3, 7, and 8).

Table 2

Colored *Tripla* and *Sesquialtera* in the Vocal Works of Praetorius

A. Affectively Used Coloration

Source	Piece Number	Sign/Proportion/Duration of Coloration	Likely Textual Reason for Coloration (Text of colored passage itself = italic. Textual context = Roman.)	Comment (*GA* retains original note values unless otherwise stated.
Motectae 1607	43	**3** / *Tripla* / 16 *tactus*	*"In the night...."*	Piece is by G. Lebon.
M.s. 6 1609	120	₵ / *Tripla* / 5 *tactus*	Lenten text. "O innocent Lamb of God ... *have mercy upon us, o Jesus."*	GA retains original note values, but critical report says they are halved.
M.s. 6	121	₵ / *Tripla* / entire piece	Lenten text. " '*Show who you are, sinful man,' says our Lord, Jesus Christ....*"	
M.s. 7 1609	220	₵ / *Tripla* / 6 *tactus*	Christmas text pleads "make me calm in the face of Satan's wrath; in the face of sin and the pain of death.... *Eya, eya, Christ, abandon me not."*	

A. Affectively Used Coloration

Source	Piece Number	Sign/Proportion/Duration of Coloration	Likely Textual Reason for Coloration (Text of colored passage itself = italic, Textual context = Roman.)	Comment (GA retains original note values unless otherwise stated.)
M.s. 7	223	₵ / Tripla / 4 tactus	"Which he hath, with His own *death, sealed and shown.*"	
M.s. 7	239	[₵] / Sesquialtera / 3x: 5, 3, & 5 tactus	"Then God shall redeem us *com-pletely from all woe, from the devil, from all evil, from anguish, fear, and mockery....*"	GA halves the note values without notice. Not by Praetorius; author-ship uncertain.
M.s. 8 1610	101	₵ / Tripla / 3 tactus	(Text from *Ein feste Burg*, speaking of Satan:) "Of great power and *cunning is his cruel armament....*"	
M.s. 8	126	₵ / Tripla / 2 x 9 tactus	"O Lord God, Thy divine word has *long remained in darkness....*"	
M.s. 8	246	₵ / Tripla / 3 tactus	"In this dangerous night in which I lay so hard, surrounded by darkness, *for that reason in great anguish....*"	

Continued on next page.

Table 2 (continued)

Colored *Tripla* and *Sesquialtera* in the Vocal Works of Praetorius

A. Affectively Used Coloration

Source	Piece Number	Sign/Proportion/Duration of Coloration	Likely Textual Reason for Coloration (Text of colored passage itself = italic, Textual context = Roman.)	Comment (*GA* retains original note values unless otherwise stated.
M.s. 8	255	₵ / *Tripla* / entire piece	"*Day drives away the gloomy night.…*"	The original sign is retained, with no indication that the piece is in triple meter.
M.s. 8	294	₵ / *Tripla* / 6 *tactus*	"In this good night we wish much good to one and all … *God will let us come into grace.*"	
M.s. 9 1610	190	₵ / *Tripla* / 2x: 8 & 7 *tactus*	"*In this dangerous night in which I lay so hard* [duple meter.…] *for that reason in great anguish.*"	Text in part identical to *M.s.* 8, no. 246, above.

B. Non-Affectively Used Coloration

Source	Piece Number	Sign/Proportion/Duration of Coloration	Comment (*GA* retains original note values unless otherwise stated.)
M.s. 4 1607	4	**C** / *Tripla* / 5 *tactus*	*GA* halves the note values. This is the only piece of the 21 here in which *GA* transcribes coloration as triplets. Also contains uncolored tripla.
M.s. 5 1608	133	**C3** / *Tripla* / entire piece	
M.s. 5	140	**C3** / *Tripla* / entire piece	
M.s. 6 1609	90	**C** / *Sesquialtera* / 9 *tactus*	By Joachim à Burck. *GA* provides sign ([3]) not in the original.
M.s. 6	144	**3** / *Tripla* & *Sesquialtera*	Entire piece colored: first half *tripla*, second half *sesquialtera*.
M.s. 6	146	**3** / *Tripla* / entire piece	

Continued on next page.

Table 2 (continued)

B. Non-Affectively Used Coloration

Source	Piece Number	Sign/Proportion/Duration of Coloration	Comment (GA retains original note values unless otherwise stated.)
M.s. 6	152	ℂ / Tripla / 2 tactus	
M.s. 8 1610	63	₵ / Sesquialtera / 4 tactus	GA halves the note values without notice. Classified M.s. 8, under hymns of "the cross, persecution, and temptation."
M.s. 8	139	₵ / Tripla / 7 tactus	

SUMMARY

The Praetorius *tactus* system simplifies, redefines, and augments the symbols of the classical mensural system to provide gradations of tempo that were required by the new music of his time but that could not be notated subtly enough in the old notation. He teaches that there are different speeds of *tactus* in both duple and triple meter. The sign $\mathbb{C}$ denotes slow duple meter, and the sign $\mathbb{C}$, fast duple meter. There are many problems with these signs in both his works and those of others, however. Reliance solely on the sign used in a given piece would thus seem not to be the best approach to setting an appropriate tempo. Praetorius himself offers a better one: consider in addition the affect of the music and its text and the note values in which the piece is written.

The confusion regarding the meaning of the duple signs is yet greater in the case of the ternary signs because there are so many of them and because they were so carelessly and inconsistently used. The three common ternary *tactus* types are best recognized not by sign, but by their characteristic rhythmic movement: *tripla* (slow) in groups of three semibreves, *sesquialtera* (fast) in groups of three minims, and *sextupla* (beaten at a moderate tempo but sounding as fast or faster than *sesquialtera*) in groups of six colored or white minims under one of the unique *sextupla* signs.

The music itself contains additional indicators unique to *tripla* and *sesquialtera*. In the case of *tripla:*

(1) the presence of rhythmic groups of three semibreves,

(2) the perfection of the breve (except in some late works that use the dot of perfection instead),

(3) coloration of semibreves and breves to show syncopation,

(4) the use of two semibreve rests (instead of a single breve rest) preceding a semibreve when the *tactus* begins with an anacrusis ▀ ▀ ◔ . *Sesquialtera* can be recognized by the same characteristics, but on the next lower notational level (read "minim" for "semibreve," etc.).

Praetorius always recommends conducting *tripla* in *tactus inaequalis,* *sextupla* in *tactus aequalis,* and *sesquialtera* in one or the other, depending on how fast the piece is to go. This suggests some rules of thumb for deciding how fast or slow each type of *tactus* should be taken.

(1) *Sextupla* must be at least fast enough to be conducted comfortably in compound meter and may go faster yet.

(2) *Sesquialtera* may range in tempo from the equivalent of a *sextupla* to just slow enough that it is more comfortable conducted "in three" rather than "in one."

(3) *Tripla*—by far the most common notation in the music of Praetorius and his contemporaries—must on no account be taken so fast that three beats could be conducted "in one." If Praetorius had intended such a fast tempo, he could have used *sesquialtera* or *sextupla* notation.

Praetorius provides us with much information, but not all that we would like, and he is confusing, contradictory, or silent on many points that we, nearly four hundred years later, yearn to have clarified. His own practice evolved and became more sophisticated as his career progressed, and his writings focus more on the style of the later works than the earlier ones. We can thus have more confidence in applying his ideas on *tactus* and tempo to the latter than to the former. The *triplas* of *Musae sioniae*, books 1-5, are a case in point. Since Praetorius did not use *sesquialtera* and *sextupla* until after these collections were published, there is a (slim) possibility that these early *triplas* could have been a generic notation for triple meter of any tempo.

It seems significant to the author that Praetorius used *sesquialtera* and *sextupla* so sparingly and that he made such a fuss over the novelty of the fast triple meter denoted by the latter. Perhaps the fast, compound-time triple meter of which we choral directors are so fond in Renaissance music was much rarer than we suspect and only began to gain ground with the growing influence of secular music, dance music, and dramatic music in the years surrounding the turn of the seventeenth century. (Compare the great frequency of fast triple meter in *Terpsichore* with the rather rare occurances of same in the sacred music.)

It is impossible to say how widely Praetorius's views were held in his day and therefore how applicable they are to the music of other composers. He had a habit of intermixing what he claims to be descriptions of "general" practice with his own personal ideas, and much of the time it is impossible to determine which is which. Nonetheless, it makes sense for this era of widening musical horizons that the *tactus* could vary in speed according to the demands of the music and the words. Chapter 8 of *Syntagma III* is devoted to this subject. (See note 13h.) Praetorius's *tactus* system is an attempt to make it possible to notate these gradations of tempo. Although it is not without its ambiguities, his system is logical and internally consistent, and it seems likely that others might have taken a similar path. When another composer of the period used similar notation of similar variety—especially some combination of *tripla, sesquialtera,* and/or *sextupla* in a single piece—it is likely that he was trying to notate tempo gradations. The Praetorius *tactus* system might well help to understanding what he intended.

BIBLIOGRAPHY

Books

Apel, Willi. *The Notation of Polyphonic Music 900—1600*. 5th ed., revised.
    Cambridge, MA: The Mediaeval Academy of America, 1953.
Auda, Antoine. *Theorie et pratique du tactus*. Brussels: (privately printed),
    1965.
Bank, Johannes A. *Tactus, Tempo, and Notation in Mensural Music from the
    13th to the 17th Century*. Amsterdam: Annie Bank, 1972.
Gafurius, Franchinus. *Practica musicae* (1496). Ed. and trans. Irwin Young.
    Madison: University of Wisconsin Press, 1969.
Lampl, Hans. "A Translation of *Syntagma musicum III*." Unpublished Ph.D.
    dissertation. University of Southern California, 1957.
Machatius, Franz-Jochen. *Die Tempi in der Musik um 1600. Fortwirken u.
    Auflösung einer Tradition*. Laaber bei Bernau: Laaber, 1977.
Mendel, Arthur. "Some Ambiguities in the Mensural System." *Studies in
    Music History: Essays in Honor of Oliver Strunk*. Ed. Harold Powers.
    Princeton: Princeton University Press, 1968.
Praetorius, Michael. *Syntagmatis musici tomus tertius*. Wolfenbüttel: author,
    1619. Facsimile ed. Kassel: Bärenreiter, 1958.
Sachs, Curt. *Rhythm and Tempo: A Study in Music History*. New York: W.
    W. Norton, 1953.
Schünemann, Georg. *Geschichte des Dirigierens*. Reprint. Hildesheim: Georg
    Olms, 1965.

Periodicals

Brainard, Paul. "Zur Deutung der Diminution in der Tactuslehre des Michael
    Praetorius." *Die Musikforschung* 17 (1964) 169—74.
Collins, Michael B. "The Performance of Sesquialtera and Hemiola in the
    Sixteenth Century." *JAMS* 17 (1964) 5—28.
Collins, Michael B. Reply to the review by Arthur Hills of "The Performance
    of Coloration, Sesquialtera, and Hemiola (1450-1750)," by Michael B.
    Collins. *Current Musicology* 5 (1967) 128—30.
Dahlhaus, Carl. "Über den Motettenbegriff des Michael Praetorius." *Beiträge
    zur Musikgeschichte Nordeuropas: Kurt Gudewill zum 65. Geburtstag*.
    Ed. Uwe Haensel. Wolfenbüttel: Möseler, 1978.
——"Zur Taktlehre des Michael Praetorius." *Die Musikforschung* 17 (1964):
    162—69.
——"Studien zur Geschichte der Rhythmustheorie." *Jahrbuch des Staatlichen
    Instituts für Musikforschung preussischer Kulturbesitz* 1979-80 (1981):
    133—53.

Heckmann, Harald. "Der Takt in der Musiklehre des siebzehnten Jahrhunderts." *Archiv für Musikwissenschaft* 10 (1953) 116−39.

Hiekel, Hans Otto. "Der Madrigal- und Motettentypus in der Mensurallehre des Michael Praetorius." *Archiv für Musikwissenschaft* 19−20 (1962−63) 40−55.

Machatius, Franz-Jochen. "Über mensurale und spielmännische Reduktion." *Die Musikforschung* 7 (1955) 139−51.

Martin, Josef. "Tempo-Probleme um den Tactus." *Österreichische Musikzeitung* 28/12 (December, 1973) 564−74.

Powell, Newman. "The Function of the *Tactus* in the Performance of Renaissance Music." *Musical Heritage of the Church* 6 (1963) 64−84.

Seay, Albert. "The Setting of Tempo by Proportion in the Sixteenth Century." *The Consort* 37 (July, 1981) 394−98.

von Dadelson, Georg. "Zu den Vorreden des Michael Praetorius." *Kongressbericht: Wien Mozartjahr 1956*, p. 107.

Music

Praetorius, Michael. *Gesamtausgabe der musikalischen Werke*. Ed. Friedrich Blume et. al. 21 vols. Wolfenbüttel, Möseler, 1928−40, 1960.

This study was supported in part by research grants from the President of California State University, Fullerton.

Ray Robinson

The Opus Ultimum:
Heinrich Schütz's Artistic and
Spiritual Testament

One of the more interesting musicological events of the twentieth century has been the discovery, the reconstruction, the performance, and finally the publication of a well-known seventeenth-century work that was long considered lost: the *Opus ultimum* of Heinrich Schütz (1585-1672). Consisting of the eleven-part *Psalm 119* (SWV 482-492), "Psalm 100" (SWV 493), and the "German Magnificat" (SWV 494), this imposing cycle of thirteen motet-settings from the Lutheran Bible, written during the last years of the composer's life, was reconstructed and premiered in May 1981 by the Dresden scholar Wolfram Steude (b. 1931). The first complete performance outside East Germany took place on September 21, 1985 in Stuttgart, West Germany as part of the celebration surrounding the 400th anniversary of the composer's birth. Heinz Hennig led the Knabenchor Hannover, the Hilliard Ensem-

Ray Robinson, a native Californian, served as President of Westminster Choir College, Princeton, New Jersey, from 1969 to 1987. Trained as a violist and conductor at San Jose State University and Indiana University, Dr. Robinson served as Dean of the Peabody Conservatory of Music from 1963 to 1969. Prior to the Peabody position he held appointments on the faculty of his alma mater, the Indiana University School of Music (1958-1959), and Cascade College, Portland, Oregon (1959-1963). He is the author of four books: The Choral Experience *(New York: Harper and Row, 1976),* Choral Music: A Norton Historical Anthology *(New York: W. W. Norton, 1978),* Krzysztof Penderecki: A Guide to His Works *(Princeton: Prestige Publications, 1983), and* A Study of the Penderecki St. Luke Passion *(Celle: Moeck Verlag, 1983).*

ble, and the London Baroque Ensemble in this performance in the Stiftskirche.

While a complete reading of this work has not yet been given on American soil, selected movements were programmed at the two most recent American Schütz Festivals. The first performance of "Psalm 100" occurred on March 6, 1983 in Princeton as part of the Twenty-Eighth International Heinrich Schütz Festival. The choir of Trinity Church was conducted by John Bertalot. Two years later, at the Thirtieth International Heinrich Schütz Festival in Urbana, Heinz Hennig led a group of German students on October 19 and 20, 1985, in "Psalm 100" and the "German Magnificat."

CIRCUMSTANCES SURROUNDING ITS COMPOSITION

Little is actually known about the circumstances that led to the composition of this epic work. In fact, there exists little information at all concerning the external events of the composer's last years. Most of the knowledge about Schütz's later life is gleaned from the sermon Martin Geier (1614-80), the senior minister of the Court of Dresden, preached on November 17, 1672 at Schütz's funeral service.

We do know that the twelve years immediately preceding the composer's death had seen the completion of four of his most important works: *The Christmas Story* (SWV 435) in 1660 and the three Passions— St.Matthew (SWV 479), St. Luke (SWV 480) and St. John (SWV 481)—in 1665-66. As the decade of the 1660s ended, Schütz was living in Dresden and enjoying a peaceful and creative semi-retirement in which "he devoted much of his time to the reading of Holy Scripture and the books of distinguished theologians. He also continued to compose with great diligence outstanding musical works on a number of psalms, especially Psalm 119."[1]

It is fairly certain that the earliest of the three parts of the *Opus ultimum* to reach completion was "Psalm 100" (SWV 493), which was composed for the consecration of the renovated Dresden Court Church on September 28, 1662. This motet was performed at least two other times during the composer's lifetime.[2] As far as the other two parts are con-

[1]Martin Geier's funeral sermon for Heinrich Schütz. Quoted by Robin A. Leaver in his article "The Funeral Sermon for Heinrich Schütz," Part III, *Bach* 3 (July 1974) 18-19.
[2]Wolfram Steude, foreword to Heinrich Schütz, *Schwanengesang*, edited and reconstructed by Wolfram Steude. *Heinrich Schütz: Neue Ausgabe sämtlicher Werke*, vol. 39 (Kassel: Bärenreiter Verlag, 1984) xvi-xvii.

cerned, there is no record of a completion date—only the notation "FINIS" written in large letters in Schütz's own hand beneath the final line of the bass part of chorus II. Perhaps it is not inaccurate to speculate that the composer was fully aware that the "German Magnificat" fell not only at the end of a cycle of thirteen motets but at the end of his life's work as well.

An orthodox Lutheran, the aged Schütz was not caught off-guard by the thought of death. By 1670 he had made the arrangements for his own funeral service. A poem written by Constantin Christian Dedekind (1628-1715), a Dresden poet and composer, marked the completion of his tomb at the Dresden Frauenkirche. Johann Mattheson (1681-1764), the composer, singer, writer, and friend of Handel, reported some years later (1740)[3] that about this time Schütz also wrote to his student Christoph Bernhard (1627-92) in Hamburg requesting a five-voice setting "in the Palestrina style of counterpoint" of Psalm 119:54, the text he had chosen for his funeral sermon. Receipt of this work, which does not survive, was acknowledged by the composer in 1670. It is clear from these events that Schütz viewed death "not as the unwelcome stranger but rather as the culmination of his life, work, and faith which would lead him on to an entirely new existence with Christ."[4]

It was in this spirit of faith and assurance that the Dresden master put the finishing touches on this his final work (commonly called his "swan song"), supervised the copying of the manuscript, and presented it to his patron, Elector Johann Georg II (1613-80). Its extended and complete title reads:

The King and Prophet David his one hundred and nineteenth Psalm in eleven sections together with an appended Psalm 100: O be joyful in the Lord, and a German Magnificat: My soul doth magnify the Lord. Set to music for eight voices in two choirs to the usual church tones for the Chapel Royal of Saxony to the glory of God by Heinrich Schütz, Senior Director of Music to the Electoral Saxon Court, Cantus I [designation of partbook]. Dresden, printed by Seyffert, 1671.[5]

Only the title page and the table of contents (*Catalogus*) were actually

[3]Johann Mattheson, *Grundlage einer Ehren-Pforte* (Hamburg, 1740). Edited by M. Schneider (Berlin, 1910); revised ed. (Kassel: Bärenreiter Verlag, 1969).

[4]Geier funeral sermon, quoted by Leaver in "The Funeral Sermon for Heinrich Schütz," Part I, *Bach* 4 (October, 1973) 5.

[5]Quoted from the English "Introductory notes to the score," Heinrich Schütz, *Wohl denen, die ohne Tadel leben: Des Königs und Propheten Davids 119. Psalm in 11 Stücken 1671. Opus ultimum* Nr. 1 (SWV 482, HE 20.482) (Neuhausen-Stuttgart: Hänssler-Verlag, 1969) iii.

printed; the notes themselves were carefully hand copied.

On November 6, 1672, Heinrich Schütz died at the age of eighty-seven years and twenty-nine days, after having served as Kapellmeister in the Saxon Court for fifty-seven years. His elaborate funeral took place eleven days later in the Frauenkirche, but there is no evidence that any part of the *Opus ultimum* was included in the service. In fact, the diaries of Johann Georg's court, usually quite detailed about musical performances there, are mute concerning a performance of any part of Schütz's final work. The court's entire Protestant musical establishment, which Joshua Rifkin has called "the largest and most important one in Protestant Germany,"[6] was disbanded in 1697 when Elector August "The Strong" converted to Catholicism.

Thus the master's *Opus ultimum*, which may never have been performed in its entirety prior to the twentieth century, fell into immediate oblivion. When the Electoral palace, along with its musical archives, was destroyed by fire in the Prussian bombardment of Dresden in 1760, it was assumed that the great *Schwanengesang* was lost forever. Therefore, in a period that spanned 228 years, the only evidence that this work had ever existed was confined to the reference quoted above from Martin Geier's funeral sermon in 1672.

THE ODYSSEY

In 1900 it was announced that six of the dedicatory manuscript's original nine partbooks had been discovered during the renovation of the parish church in Guben (near Poland) by its rector, a Pastor Werner. The six partbooks found by the rector, identified by the theologian Friedrich Spitta (1852-1924) and catalogued by his brother, the musicologist Philipp Spitta (1841-94), were:

> Cantus I Chori
> Altus I Chori   Altus II Chori
> Tenor I Chori
> Bassus I Chori   Bassus II Chori

Missing were:

> Cantus II Chori
> Tenor II Chori
> Organum

[6]Joshua Rifkin and Kurt Gudewill, S.v. "Heinrich Schütz," *The New Grove Dictionary of Music and Musicians*, ed. Stanley Sadie (London: Macmillan Publishers Ltd, 1980) vol. 17, p. 6.

A seventh partbook (the organ part) was traced in 1930 by the second-hand bookstore of Kaspar-Buhlmann to M. Lengfeld in Cologne, where it was ultimately acquired by Stefan Zweig (1881-1942),[7] in whose London estate it still resides. How the organ book got to Cologne is a mystery. (How it may have gotten to Guben will be touched upon later.) The most fortunate aspect of this discovery was that this organ book (the so-called "London manuscript") was precisely the one that bore the dedicatory inscription to the Elector in Schütz's own hand:

> Wherewith my most humble petition is forwarded to your Serene Highness, my most gracious Lord, that you may show your most gracious favor to this, to be sure, humble little work, to have it tried and sung, at your most gracious opportunity, in Your Highness' Court Chapel by eight good voices, with two organs, by the two beautiful musical choirs placed opposite each other above the altar.
>
> Author.[8]

For the performer of seventeenth-century music, this autograph dedication holds a significant practical value because it contains the composer's own specifications for two equal choirs set off antiphonally. This information also indicates a return, at the end of his life, to the *chori spezzati* of his beloved early mentor, Giovanni Gabrieli (1557-1612), in Venice.

A photocopy of the six Guben partbook manuscript was made about 1934 for Max Seiffert of the Staatliches Institut für deutsche Musikforschung (who became the photocopy's owner); this is the copy Hans Joachim Moser (1889-1967) examined while writing his Schütz biography in the early 1930s. As a part of his study, Moser reconstructed the two missing voice parts. (Heinrich Spitta had made copies of the first and a portion of the eleventh motet [SWV 482 and 492] with his own version of the missing voices; this copy was the basis for the Hänssler edition published in 1969). The Guben partbooks were last examined in September, 1944 before their alleged destruction by fire in January, 1945.

During the forty-five years the Guben manuscript was available for examination, only the "German Magnificat" (SWV 494), which had survived fully intact in an earlier version (the so-called "Grimma" manuscript, SWV 494a), was published. This was due in all probability to the fact that the two missing voice parts of such a long work proved

[7]Hans Joachim Moser, *Heinrich Schütz: His Life and Work*. Trans. from the 2nd revised edition by Carl F. Pfatteicher (St. Louis: Concordia Publishing House, 1959) 686.
[8]Ibid.

to be an insurmountable obstacle to the would-be editors of the time. The fact that the Guben partbooks had proved so elusive prompted Werner Breig to write as recently as 1971 that "with the exception of a few sections, this opus must now be regarded as finally lost."[9]

Despair, however, was premature, for the six Guben partbooks, thirty years given up as permanently lost, were rediscovered in 1975 at the Saxon State Library in Dresden by Wolfram Steude, who rightly called the amazing find a "cause for joy."[10] Steude subsequently reconstructed the two missing voices and prepared the work for publication. In May 1981, the complete thirteen-part work, the long-lost "swan song" of Heinrich Schütz, was given its first modern-day reading—in all likelihood its first performance ever—in the course of two highly acclaimed concert evenings that opened the Dresden Musikfestspiele. The performers were the Berliner Solisten directed by Dietrich Knothe, the Dresdener Kruezchor led by Martin Fläming, and the Cappella Sagittariana under Steude himself, who also provided an idiomatic instrumental accompaniment in the spirit of the optional instrumentation of the seventeenth century.[11] The first complete printed edition was published in 1984 by Deutscher Verlag für Musik (Leipzig) in cooperation with Bärenreiter Verlag (Kassel).

THE TEXT

When considering the text of this work it is necessary to understand that Schütz possessed a deep, personal Christian faith. He knew and loved the Bible, growing closer to it the older he became, as is evidenced by the musical compositions of his later years, nearly all of which were based solely on Biblical texts. He was also a man of keen intellect who finally settled on a musical career only after having acquired a thorough general and legal education that equipped him with a splendid erudition, perhaps unique among the composers of the time. Especially adept at languages, Schütz was familiar not only with German, French, and Latin, but was also comfortable with Greek (the language of the New Testament), and at some stage of his life, he became accomplished in Hebrew as well, probably because of his interest in setting texts from the Old Testament.

[9]Werner Breig, "Preface" to *Heinrich Schütz: Neue Ausgabe sämtlicher Werke*, vol. 28 (Kassel: Bärenreiter, 1971) xi.
[10]Wolfram Steude, "Das wiedergefundene Opus Ultimum von Heinrich Schütz: Bermerkungen zur Quelle und zum Werk." *Schütz-Jahrbuch* 4-5 (Jahrgang 1982-83) 10.
[11]Siegfried Köhler, "Schütz-Uraufführung nach drei Jahrhunderten," *Musik und Gesellschaft* Jahrgang 31 (August 1981) 482-83.

As a composer whose compositional output was almost exclusively sacred, the major exception being the Italian Madrigals (SWV 1-19, 1611), he clearly preferred the Bible as his source of texts. Among his approximately 500 works, the religious literature of the period—such as devotional poetry, Protestant hymnody, liturgical texts, and even the Lutheran chorale itself—is almost entirely absent. It is clear that inspiration for Schütz came from the Bible, and that his main preoccupation, like Luther's, was with the Old Testament and particularly the Book of Psalms (the Psalter). Not only did he use the Psalter more than any other book of the Bible, he used it "more than twice as often" as J.S. Bach, for whom it was also a primary text source. It is therefore not surprising that he would turn to the Psalter as the text of this epic work.

In the seventeenth century (the formative period of Lutheran theology, with its emphasis on the primacy of scripture as the ultimate spiritual authority), the Bible was regarded in Lutheran circles literally as "the voice of God." With the same care and integrity with which theologians expounded the Word, Schütz composed musical works, thus giving the Biblical message another dimension, that of musical sound. Moreover, the Psalter was seen by Luther (and almost surely by Schütz as well) as nothing less than the distilled essence of the entire Bible (*eine kleine Biblia*, complete with prophetic New Testament implications). Luther's collaborator Philipp Melanchton called it "the summa and whole content of godliness;" Johann Bugenhagen, in his commentary on Psalm 119, saw this one Psalm as the distillation of the whole Psalter; and Luther as well regarded Psalm 119 as a short Bible (*eine kurtze* [*sic*] *Bibel*). Summing up the importance of this passage to the Dresden master, Schütz, Steude writes: "When Heinrich Schütz set the entire 119th Psalm at the end of his long life, he did it with the consciousness of setting the whole Bible in a nutshell ⋮ [*die ganze Bibel in nuce*] to music."[12]

It is thus appropriate that Schütz would choose the fifty-fourth verse ("Thy statutes have been my song in the house of my pilgrimage") as the text for his funeral sermon. If this were not enough evidence of the importance of this passage to the aging composer, he also asked his favorite pupil, Christoph Bernhard, to set this verse as a motet for his funeral; a request which led Steude to declare, "Schütz had, with the setting of such a significance-fraught text, quite consciously and purposely created his 'swan song' (*Schwanengesang*),"[13] a designation

---

[12]Steude, *"Das wiedergefundene Opus Ultimum,"* 14.
[13]Ibid., 15.

224   RAY ROBINSON

that undoubtedly originated with the composer himself. Thus the *Opus ultimum*, in which Schütz lovingly and painstakingly set his favorite passage of all Holy Scripture to a musical structure of epic proportions, is in fact a great statement of personal faith. Could we not think of it as his artistic and spiritual testament?

Psalm 119 as a scriptural passage is unique in all the Psalter for both its length and its structure. Called "The Christian's ABC" (*Der Christen güldnes ABC*) since the time of Luther, this longest single chapter in the Bible is an acrostic in which each eight-verse subdivision (called an *octonaria*) begins with the corresponding letter of the Hebrew alphabet. Since the Hebrew alphabet contains twenty-two letters, this acrostic-Psalm (there are others—for example, Psalm 111—but the 119th is the most extensive) consists of twenty-two *octonariae*, yielding the 176 verses of the entire Psalm. Otto Brodde describes the Psalm's theme as the "praise, love, power and application of the word of God," with each *octonaria* treated as an individual "song." [14] When conceived in this way, Psalm 119 is more a cycle of relatively self-sufficient parts than a closed whole. Liturgical usage takes this structural autonomy into account; the *Antiphonale Romanum* divides the Psalm so that of the twenty-two subdivisions, two are always sung together. Schütz followed this precise format, composing eleven motets in his setting of *Psalm 119,* to which he added "Psalm 100" and the "German Magnificat" as the twelfth and thirteenth motets respectively. In this manner he viewed the thirteen motets together as a significant symmetrical unity. An outline of this text structure with text incipit, text source, modal basis and appropriate liturgical use, is shown in the Appendix.

THE FORMAL STRUCTURE

The evidence that Schütz did indeed conceive of *Psalm 119* as a single unit, followed by an appendix of two smaller motets is found first of all in the nature of these three passages of scripture and the manner in which they are related. In his introductory notes to the collected-works edition, Steude identifies a three-part structure where the sequence of the motets forms "an ascending line of theological thought:"

Psalm 119 praises God's law, "Psalm 100" praises the lawgiver Himself—the "Deus absconditus" (unrevealed God) of the Old Testa-

[14]Otto Brodde, *Heinrich Schütz: Weg und Werk* (Kassel: Bärenreiter Verlag, 1972) 269.

ment, whose revelation and incarnation are celebrated in Mary's *Magnificat* at the end of the cycle. So too the poetic form of the New Testament canticle is like that of the Psalms and is thus related to the Old Testament Psalter.[15]

Table I

Opus ultimum—the Macro Form[16]

SWVNo.		Text Incipit	No. and Mode of Psalm Tone	Key of Motet
482	1	Wohl denen, die ohne Wandel [Tadel] leben	3. Phrygian	A minor
483	2	Tue wohl deinem Knechte	3. Phrygian	A minor
484	3	Zeige mir, Herr, den Weg deiner Rechte	2. Hypodorian	G minor
485	4	Gedenke deinem Knechte	8. Hypomixolydian	G Major
486	5	Du tust Guts deinem Knechte	4. Hypophrygian	E minor
487	6	Meine Seele verlanget nach deinem Heil	1. Dorian	D minor
488	7	Wie habe ich dein Gesetze so lieb	2. Hypodorian (Central motet)	G minor
489	8	Ich hasse die Flatter-geister	6. Hypolydian	F Major
490	9	Deine Zeugnisse sind wunderbarlich	4. Hypophrygian	E minor
491	10	Ich rufe von ganzem Herzen	5. Lydian	C Major
492	11	Die Fürsten verfolgen mich ohne Ursach	9. Aeolian	D minor
493	12	"Psalm 100:" Jauchzet dem Herrn alle Welt	3. Phrygian	A minor
494	13	"Deutsches Magnificat:" Meine Seele erhebt den Herren	10. Hypoaeolian	A minor

[15]Steude, *Schwanengesang*, xvii.
[16]Adapted from Moser, 687-88.

While *Psalm 119* by itself encapsulates the entire Bible in the Lutheran view of theology, it seems as though Schütz, in adding "Psalm 100" and the "German Magnificat," wished to make his testimony unmistakably clear.

Another type of formal unity is found in the liturgical elements that the composer incorporates into the work. The intonations from the altar before each of the thirteen motets and the lesser doxology (the *Gloria patri*) added to the ending confirm the relation of each to a specific psalm tone. Added to the theological and poetic consistencies, the tonalities of the individual movements, presented in Table I (page 225) , convincingly demonstrate the macro-formal method Schütz uses to unify the composition.

When one views the overall structure of the thirteen motets, one observes not merely a concise tonal symmetry, but also a compelling dramatic plan as well. The two outer "dyptichs" in A minor (motets 1 & 2, plus 12 & 13) enclose the three internal modulating "tryptichs" (motets 3-5, 6-8, and 9-11), thus creating a musical frame for the inner motets. In each of the three tryptichs, the center of expression lies in the middle piece: no. 4 ("Gedenke deinem Knechte"), based on the fifty-fourth verse of the 119th Psalm, the composer's funeral text; no. 7 ("Wie habe ich dein Gesetze so lieb"), the central motet of the entire cycle; and no. 10 ("Ich rufe von ganzem Herzen"), the most expressive of the motets. The seventh motet, with its especially poetic and euphonious text (shown below), is literally the central piece of the entire work. Not only is it the longest and most developed of the thirteen motets, but it was conceived by Schütz as representing the unity of Law and Gospel, the classical opposites brought together by the unity of the Old and New Testaments. One might thus think of this motet alone as the master's own testament in a nutshell of the reconciliation of these opposites in Christ. As a text for meditation, Psalm 119:97-112 is without peer:

> Oh, how I love thy law! It is my meditation all the day.
> Thou, through thy commandments, hast made me wiser than
>   mine enemies; for they are ever with me.
> I have more understanding than all my teachers; for thy
>   testimonies are my meditation.
> I understand more than the ancients, because I keep thy
>   precepts.

I have refrained my feet from every evil way, that I might
   keep thy word.
I have not departed from thine ordinances; for thou hast
   taught me.
How sweet are thy words unto my taste! Yea, sweeter than
   honey to my mouth.
Through thy precepts I get understanding; therefore, I
   hate every false way.

Thy word is a lamp unto my feet, and a light unto my path.
I have sworn, and I will perform it, that I will keep thy
   righteous ordinances.
I am afflicted very much; quicken me, O Lord, according
   to thy word.
Accept, I beseech thee, the freewill offerings of my
   mouth, O Lord, and teach me thine ordinances.
My soul is continually in my hand; yet do I not forget
   thy law.
The wicked have laid a snare for me; yet I erred not
   from thy precepts.
Thy testimonies have I taken as an heritage forever; for
   they are the rejoicing of my heart.
I have inclined mine heart to perform thy statutes always,
   even unto the end.[17]

Other aspects of the tonal scheme of the cycle that bear emphasizing
are: (1) the identical tonalities that occur between motets 3 & 7 (G minor),
5 & 9 (E minor), 6 & 11 (D minor) and the outer dyptichs (A minor);
and (2) the "sectionalizing" aural clarity to the form that ensues when
each tryptich (featuring mostly "close" harmonic relationships of a third
or fourth or the parallel key) is set off from the preceding group by
a tonal retrogression to a second (either major or minor).

THE MUSICAL STYLE CHARACTERISTICS

While it is not within the scope of this article to attempt an in-depth
musical analysis, the musical style characteristics of the *Schwanengesang*
can be considered a continuation and summation of everything that the
composer had done before (up to and including the great Biblical works

[17]Psalm 119: 97-112, King James Version.

of the 1660s, (*The Christmas Story* and the three Passions). By any standard, the *Opus ultimum* is representative of the personal warmth and creative invention of these other late works and reveals a composer whose powers are undiminished by the years. Siegfried Köhler, in reviewing the 1981 Dresden "premiere," calls this valedictory cycle a "work of great maturity;" he writes glowingly of the work's emotional intensity and clarity of declamation and its cumulative effect of "not only peace and sublimity, but, at the same time, freshness and assurance."[18]

Steude sees in this work not so much a distinctive "late style" as simply the final consummation of the full maturity of a master's craft;[19] while Kurt Gudewill states that the "youthful fire . . . still blazes" in the settings of *Psalm 119* and "Psalm 100," but "has gone out" in the "German Magnificat," in which expressive devices (such as word painting) are reduced to a minimum.[20] Writing in the 1930s, Moser observed in this work a deeply felt (*seelenvolle*) emotion in the noblest sense of the word:

> It is no icily rigid old man who is speaking here; to the very end Schütz remained receptive and kindly to everything human. We feel this especially in the new fondness for warm chords of the seventh and all kinds of liberties which have given Schütz's tonal language that peculiar "romantic" late turn . . . .[21]

All in all, these views evoke the same sense of "fire and ice" freshness and vitality we associate with Haydn in his old age.

As far as specific style characteristics are concerned, one immediately recognizes a marked difference in musical texture among the three text settings. *Psalm 119* and "Psalm 100" conform to the motet style of the seventeenth century in that the imitative choral writing and double-choir technique involving the musical interaction of both choirs dominate. They also differ in their use of motivic interaction within the polyphonic setting. *Psalm 119* is a work in which the chordal homophony serves a structural function, while "Psalm 100" is much tighter in its construction. There is hardly a passage in this motet where a pervading linear imitation is not present among the individual voices. The texture of the "German Magnificat," on the other hand, seems to point to an earlier era in which there is an almost seamless blending of homophonic and polyphonic elements.

---

[18]Köhler, 482.
[19]Steude, *"Das wiedergefundene Opus Ultimum"*, 16
[20]Rifkin and Gudewill, 17, 23.
[21]Moser, 696.

This reference to the past is also seen in the treatment of the psalm tones that begin each of the movements except the "Magnificat." Each motet employs a different tone (thereby emphasizing its musical self-sufficiency), and each concluding doxology treats the psalm tone (intonation) as a chorale-like cantus firmus in augmentation in the soprano (cantus) voice of both choirs. This deliberate use of the old church modes as a model to his own time and posterity of the best of a dying art (which is precisely what Bach accomplished in his time with *The Art of the Fugue*) might be considered a kind of musical confession to his successors of the faith that supported his creative endeavors.

Finally, all of the "fire and ice," the "old and new" are bound together and sealed by that uniquely pithy musical declamation of which Schütz is commonly considered the unquestioned master. It is here that he always achieves the most rare and perfect balance between the word—textual rhythm correctly accented and meaning faithfully expressed—and ultimately singable melodic "figures" of grace and self-sufficiency that combine in an indissoluble union to raise the Word—the Word of God, the very "voice of God"—to a level of definitive expression. Thus Heinrich Schütz, in this his final musical statement, has returned full circle to his first published psalm settings, the *Psalmen Davids* (1619), likewise written for the same "Venetian" combination of two equal choirs with organ continuo. Now, more than a half century later, in his *Opus ultimum* he has left an "artistic and spiritual testament" that bears out the truth which came from the pen of none other than Martin Luther a century earlier: "The new is in the old concealed, the old is in the new revealed."

CONCLUSION

In spite of the originality of his compositional legacy, and the genius displayed in the works of his final years, Schütz (like Bach) was almost immediately forgotten after his death. Even the Becker Psalter (first published in 1628), which had kept the composer's memory alive throughout Germany and was called by Moser "that last remnant of Schütz music," was replaced for Protestant congregational use by the Schemelli *Musicalisches Gesangbuch* (1736). Schütz remained virtually unknown until the early nineteenth century when his music was rediscovered by the musicologist Carl von Winterfeld (1784-1852) in the course of compiling material for a book on Giovanni Gabrieli (1834). While Winterfeld's work sparked the Schütz revival, other nineteenth-century composers and scholars contributed along the way; Brahms performed individual works in Vienna, and Liszt campaigned for new editions of so daring a ''modern'' master. In 1885 (the 300th anniversary of the composer's birth), the Chrysander and Spitta edition of the complete works of Schütz appeared. The *Singbewegung* (''Singing Movement'') in Germany during the early twentieth century and the establishment of the Internationale Heinrich-Schütz-Gesellschaft in 1930 added fuel to a fire that continues to grow brighter to this day.

A similar phoenix-like trajectory has marked the odyssey of the *Opus ultimum*. The manuscript, as it turns out three centuries later, was removed at an early point from Dresden to Guben either by a cantor from Guben (perhaps Schütz's one-time Vice-Kapellmeister Johann Georg Hofkunz) or more likely by Duke Christian von Sachsen-Merseburg, a younger brother of Elector Johann Georg II who had been, as Inspector of the Dresdener Hofkapelle from 1649 to 1653, Schütz's immediate supervisor. Steude speculates that Duke Christian (whose domain included Guben) might have taken the manuscript as a personal souvenir, thus preventing its contemporary performance at the Hofkapelle, but saving it from being destroyed along with the Electoral palace and its musical archives in the 1760 bombardment of Dresden. A second time, in our own century, the manuscript was rescued from wartime destruction by fire when it was obviously removed sometime before January, 1945 from Guben (or perhaps even from Berlin) to the Sächsische Landesbibliothek in Dresden, where for some unexplained reason it was never incorporated into the library's inventory of manuscripts. Consequently, no one knew it was there until it was rediscovered in 1975 by Wolfram Steude.

Doubtless the great Kapellmeister would see the hand of Providence in all of this: in the two miraculous escapes of his *Opus ultimum* and in his own resurrection as one of western music's most significant musical figures. This composer of the Bible and true lover of the Word of God would surely view the ultimate endurance of this artistic and spiritual testament across the centuries and against tremendous odds as a confirmation of a prophecy from Isaiah: ''So shall my word be that goeth forth out of my mouth; it shall not return unto me void, but it shall accomplish that which I please, and it shall prosper in the thing whereunto I sent it.''[22]

---

[22]Isaiah 55:11.

APPENDIX

Text Structure, Modal Basis, and Liturgical Use

SWVNo.		Text Incipit	Text Source	Mode No.	Liturgical Use
482	1	Wohl denen, die ohne Wandel [Tadel] leben (Blessed are the undefiled in the way)	Ps. 119, Aleph: vv. 1-8 Beth: vv. 9-16	Third tone	Introit psalm, 17th Sunday after Trinity; Ordination.
483	2	Tue wohl deinem Knechte (Deal bountifully with thy servant)	Ps. 119, Gimel: vv. 17-24 Daleth: vv. 25-32	Third tone	Communion
484	3	Zeige mir, Herr, den Weg deiner Rechte (Lord, show me the way of thy laws)	Ps. 119, He: vv. 33-40 Vav: vv. 41-48	Second tone	Gradual, Rogation service for propagation of the Gospel.
485	4	Gedenke deinem Knecht an dein Wort (Remember thy word unto thy servant)	Ps. 119, Dsäin: vv. 49-56 Chet: vv. 57-64	Eighth tone	Introit psalm, 21st Sunday after Trinity
486	5	Du tust Guts deinem Knecht (Thou hast dealt well with thy servant)	Ps. 119, Thet: vv. 65-72 Jod: vv. 73-80	Fourth tone	Communion
487	6	Meine Seele verlanget nach deinem Heil (My soul fainteth for thy salvation)	Ps. 119, Kaph: vv. 81-88 Lamed: vv. 89-96	First tone	Introit psalm, day of Arch-martyr Stephen; day of a martyr
488	7	Wie habe ich dein Gesetze so lieb (O how I love thy law)	Ps. 119, Mem: vv. 97-104 Nun: vv. 105-12	Second tone	Introit or gradual, Rogation service for propagation of the Gospel
489	8	Ich hasse die Flattergeister (I hate vain thoughts)	Ps. 119, Samech: vv. 113-20 Aïn: vv. 121-28	Sixth tone	Same as SWV 488 also on penitential days.
490	9	Deine Zeugnisse sind wunderbarlich (Thy testimonies are wonderful)	Ps. 119, Pe: vv. 129-136 Zade: vv. 37-144	Fourth tone	Same as SWV 488
491	10	Ich rufe von ganzen Herzen (I cried with my whole heart)	Ps. 119, Koph: vv. 145-52 Resch: vv. 153-60	Fifth tone	Introit or Gradual, penetential days

Continued on next page

APPENDIX

Text Structure, Modal Basis, and Liturgical Use

SWVNo.		Text Incipit	Text Source	Mode No.	Liturgical Use
492	11	Die Fürsten verfolgen mich ohne Ursach (The princes persecute me without reason)	Ps. 119, Schin: vv. 161-68 Tau: vv. 169-76	Ninth tone	Same as SWV 491
493	12	Jauchzet dem Herrn alle Welt (Make a joyful noise unto the Lord, all ye lands)	Ps. 100, vv. 1-5	Third tone	Introit Psalm, 1st Sunday after Epiphany; Psalm of Thanksgiving
494	13	"Deutsches Magnificat:" Meine Seele erhebt den Herren (My soul doth magnify the Lord)	(Doxo- logy) Luke 1:46-49, 51-55	Tenth tone	Vesper canticle

Wesley Morgan

J.S. Bach's Motets
in the Twentieth Century

Bach had been in his new Leipzig position at the Thomaskirche scarcely two months before he had written and performed five new cantatas, plus four he revised from earlier Weimar days, a new "Sanctus" in C, and one new motet of eleven movements. This one new motet is of unusual interest: it was written in the old, true motet style, a cappella in nature, with no accompaniment, either of instruments or a continuo indicated in the score—a genre long since fallen into disuse. Before coming to Leipzig in May, 1723, Bach had written, among other things, only three-dozen or so vocal works and they were concerted pieces, cantatas for soli and/or four-part chorus with obbligato instrumental parts and continuo. But he had written no motets in the old style. Now, in the eighth week of his new cantorate, a motet—and one of a very special sort—was suddenly required of him: a piece for which no doubling nor obbligato instruments would be permitted. For the first time in his life he was confronted with a form into which he had had neither occasion nor inclination to venture, insofar as we know. The result was the chorale motet for five voices, *Jesu, meine Freude.*

Wesley Morgan received his B.A. degree from Occidental College in 1944, an M.S.M. from Union Theological Seminary (1946), and the Ph.D. in musicology from U.S.C. (1956). He has taught at the University of the Pacific, Southern Illinois University, and the University of Kentucky. He is author of numerous articles, and has edited music for such publications as Das Chorwerk. *He has been guest lecturer at numerous universities and symposia in the United States and England.*

In collaboration with Professor Howard Mayer Brown of the University of Chicago, Dr. Morgan recorded the entire first volume of the Harvard Historical Anthology of Music, *using the* collegia musica *of both universities. He retired in 1983 and has continued writing and lecturing, particularly on the vocal music of J.S. Bach.*

This must have been a strange turn of events for Bach; to compose choral music for unaccompanied voices could have been nothing less than foreign to the instrumental character of his own compositional style. Furthermore, the unaccompanied motet as a singular genre unquestionably remained foreign to him, for in the next seven years, records indicate that he wrote only four more, and after 1730, he wrote no more at all.[1] Bach thus composed five unaccompanied motets in all incorporating the Lutheran chorale: the five-voice *Jesu, meine Freude*, and four for double-chorus: *Singet dem Herrn ein neues Lied; Der Geist hilft unser Schwachheit auf; Komm, Jesu, komm;* and *Fürchte dich nicht*—superb, brilliant works, all of them. Friedrich Richter categorically claimed they were the highest manfestation of Bach's genius among his church music.[2]

Toward the end of the seventeenth century in Protestant Germany, the motet was thrust more and more to the periphery of musical thought and practice. It became a special piece for special occasions such as a funeral, a grave-side ceremony, a memorial service, or the relatively unimportant introit to the morning church service. In the Lutheran churches the motet was displaced by the far more exciting concerted church cantata, or *Kirchenstück*. It was so when Bach reached Leipzig. But Leipzig had one curious regulation with which Bach had not yet had to cope: in times of official mourning, or in memorial services for deceased persons held in the city churches, instruments had generally been forbidden by civic law. For these services, the music sung had to be without instrumental accompaniment. Thus, the five magnificent unaccompanied chorale motets by Bach that have come down to us may likely be attributed to the unfortunate demise of five individuals of the Leipzig community whose importance and, one suspects, munificent legacies were substantial enough to insure that a special piece be written for their memorial services.[3]

Performances of Bach's unaccompanied motets, both live and recorded, have proliferated in the twentieth century. There have been well

[1]Works that Bach composed and himself called "Motette," but are concerted pieces with obbligato instruments, will not be considered in this discussion, e.g. BWV 118, BWV 230, and BWV 231 (the last a borrowing from Telemann). For the sake of simplicity, the motets incorporating a chorale in any form will henceforth be referred to as "chorale motets."

[2]Friedrich Richter Bernhard, "Über die Motetten Seb. Bachs," *Bach-Jahrbuch* (1912) 1.

[3]Ibid., 9-10. The funeral sermon for the wife of Oberpostmeister Käse was given in St. Thomas's on July 18, 1723. In her will, Frau Käse had provided for *Jesu, meine Freude* to be sung at her funeral. The text used in the sermon was Romans 8:11, which Bach incorporated into the motet of the same name, undoubtedly sung on this occasion.

over one hundred fifty recordings of individual motets since the advent of long-playing records shortly before 1950. This is splendid, even if some of the performances are not. However, the great variety of performance styles and curious discrepancies raise questions, one might gather, that are beyond the resources of those who write jacket notes to answer at best, or agree upon, at least. And it is quite likely that the cause for these discrepancies lies in part with those equally curious descrepancies between different performing editions issued by publishing firms of considerable stature. The discrepancies, incidentally, are not always those of wrong notes that slip in; they are also found in the forewords to many editions that invariably have the ring of musicological authority. For example, a few editions date the motets with alarming confidence. But the question of dates, the answer for which even the *New Grove* could not supply with confidence, unfortuantely still lingers; the dates for four of the motets the *New Grove* precedes by the ubiquitous question mark. In the 1957 *Bach-Jahrbuch,* Alfred Dürr published the first results of his brilliant research on the new Bach chronology in which convincing proof dated *Singet dem Herrn* toward the end of 1726, or possibly early in 1727.[4] Yet two years later, in 1959, an edition of this motet was published by C.F. Peters Company, edited by Werner Neumann. The foreword, written by Walter Buszin, quite flatly states that "Werner Newmann joins Arnold Schering in assuming the *Singet dem Herrn* was written as a song of praise for a New Year's service conducted on January 1, 1746. . . ." In addition to Dürr's established chronology, other considerations suggest this date and this occasion are not possible.

Though its chronology has been established, *Singet dem Herrn,* indeed, is the only one of the chorale motets about which confusion persists as to the purpose or occasion for which it was written. It has been attributed to New Year's Day, the birthday of the Elector of Saxony, and Reformation Sunday. Logic, as well as facts, cannot support any of these: for such festive occasions Bach was required to provide a cantata, concerted music with brilliant instrumentation, which he did.[5] Without exception, these cantatas pointedly refer to the special event: "das Neue Jahr," "der Geburtstag," or the appropriate Gospel for Reformation Day. None appears in *Singet dem Herrn*; had it been com-

---

[4]Alfred Dürr, "Zur Chronologie der Leipziger Vokalwerke J.S. Bachs," *Bach-Jahrbuch* (1957) 49. (Expanded and published under the same title by Bärenreiter-Verlag, Kassel, 1976. See pp. 92-93 and pp. 133ff.)

[5]Charles Sanford Terry, *Bach: A Biography.* Rev. ed. (London: Oxford University Press, 1933) 161.

posed for one of these three occasions, a pointed reference to the occasion would surely be found in the text. By the eighteenth century, unaccompanied motets were for funeral, burial, or memorial services; to present such a piece for a festive celebration would have suggested contradictory connotations wholly unacceptable. Also, the frequent preemptive dismissal that *Singet dem Herrn* cannot be a funeral piece on the grounds of its jubilant text regrettably ignores the impact of the second movement.[6] The poetry of its chorale is undeniably funeral:

> Wie sich ein Vater erbarmet über seine junge Kinderlein,
>   so tut der Herr uns allen, so wir ihn kindlich fürchten rein.
> Er kennt das arm Gemächte, Gott weiß, wir sind nur Staub,
>   gleichwie das Gras vom Rechen, ein Blum und fallend Laub.
> Der Wind nur drüber wehet, so ist es nicht mehr da
>   also der Mensch vergehet, sein End das ist ihm nah.

> As a father is merciful to his little children,
>   so is the Lord to us all as long as we are obedient and pure.
> He knows our frailty, God knows we are but dust,
>   as grass, flower, and foliage falling under the rake.
> Let but the wind blow over it and it is gone;
>   thus man passes away, his end is near.

(Translation by William Bartholomew)

The joyous character of text and music in the third and fourth movements in no way negates the funeral idea.[7] Gebhardt, in his *Thüringische Kirchengeschichte*, tells us that after the funeral sermon (*Leichenpredigt*) at the memorial service, a cheerful, happy, and indeed festive atmosphere prevailed. The orthodox Lutheran saw death as a joyful event for the true believer.[8]

Another area in which confusion still abounds is that of who, and how many sang the motets. Most Bach scholars—and record jackets—insist that the motets were sung by the number of voices Bach describes

---

[6]The booklet inserted in the record box of J.S. Bach motets (L'Oiseau-Lyre, SOL 340-41, 1972), performed by the Louis Halsey Singers, for example, makes this statement on p. 5: "A glance at the text will show the *Singet dem Herrn* cannot be a funeral motet, and to interpret it as such has defeated even the most ingenious of commentators."
[7]For a lengthier discussion of this motet, see W. Morgan, "Bach's *Singet dem Herrn ein neues Lied*: An Old Problem," in *Bach: The Quarterly Journal of the Riemenschneider Bach Institute* XI (4) (Oct., 1980) and XII (1) (January, 1981).
[8]H. Gebhardt, *Thüringische Kirchengeschichte*. (Gotha, 1879-82) 90-91.

in his famous memorandum to the Town Council of Leipzig dated August 3, 1730, where he says, "Every musical choir should contain at least 3 sopranos, 3 altos, 3 tenors, and as many basses, so that even if one happens to fall ill . . . at least a double-chorus motet may be sung."[9] To assume this disposition of voices for Bach's own performances of his double-choir motets may be questioned. Those relying on this quotation stop too soon in Bach's memorandum, for in his next paragraph we find,

> Thus far only the Sunday music has been touched upon. But if I should mention the music of the Holy Days (on which days I must supply both the principal Churches with music), the deficiency of indispensable players will show even more clearly, particularly since I must give up to the other choir all those pupils who play one instrument or another and must get along altogether without their help.[10]

Thus it is apparent that two full choirs would have been available for memorial services, since the motets required no instrumentalists; indeed, instrumentalists frequently had to sing rather than play. However, an anomoly surfaces here, for Terry claims, in regard to performances of the St. Matthew Passion, "To provide the two choirs the work demands, he employed his *chorus primus* and *chorus secundus*; hence the directions *Coro primo* and *Coro secondo* in his score bear a particular and local meaning."[11] However, Terry's claim can be true only if Bach had a full complement of singers in each of the two best choirs. If he did not, the Thomasschule instrumentalists had to be drawn in as singers, in which case Bach had to call upon instrumentalists from the university or alumni of the Thomasschule.[12] Thus, for the double-choir motets, the two best of the four choirs under his supervision would be available; no conflict with regular church services would interfere with using instrumentalists as singers if necessary.

For one year, at least, the number of singers in these choirs can be determined. A petition dated May 18, 1729, drawn up by Bach, was forwarded to the City Council; in it Bach presents the results of audi-

---

[9]H.T. David and A. Mendel, *The Bach Reader* (New York: W.W. Norton, 1945) 121; Werner Neumann and Hans-Joachim Schulze, eds., *Bach-Dokumente*, 4 vols. (Kassel: Bärenreiter, 1963), vol. 1, 60.

[10]*Bach Reader*, 122; *Bach-Dokumente*, vol. 1, 62.

[11]Terry, *Bach*, 196. See also *Bach-Dokumente*, vol. 1, 250 and Phillipp Spitta, *J.S. Bach*, trans. C. Bell and J.A. Fuller Maitland (reprint ed; New York: Dover, 1951), vol. 2, 240-41.

[12]*Bach Reader*, 121-22.

tions of singers for all four choirs for which he was responsible (though he personally directed only the first two). A supplement to this petition listed the number of singers supplying the music at the four civic churches. In that year, at both the Thomaskirche and the Nicolaikirche, there were three singers on each part in the first choir, and three on each part in the second.[13] (In truth, Bach would have preferred four on a part, "giving sixteen voices to each choir.")[14] It is thus certain that in 1729 two choirs of twelve voices each were available to perform double-choir works sung at events other than regular morning church services. These included not only the Good Friday performances of the St. Matthew Passion, but memorial services held at Vespers on Sundays "to commemorate the passing of prominent citizens."[15] It may be assumed, with tolerable certainty, that the above numbers approximated those with which Bach had had to work since his arrival in Leipzig, and represented the resources for performances of the motets which, as has been noted, were written between the years of 1723 and 1730. That he wanted more on each part implies that he must have been dissatisfied with those very numbers with which he had worked for several years.

In the last few decades, Bach scholars have taken, quite literally, an intensely emotional, parental attitude toward the motets and have insisted that a chaperon is necessary: the motets must not venture out alone, they must be accompanied at least by a continuo, but preferably with the added protection of instruments doubling the vocal lines as well. The strongest argument in favor of such performance is the fact that Bach himself left doubling instrumental parts and a figured bass for *Der Geist hilft unser Schwachheit auf* in his own hand,[16] which is a pretty good argument. But this may be explained away. This motet was written specifically upon the death of Johann Heinrich Ernesti, Rector of the Thomasschule and Professor at the University. The original score provided for neither instruments nor continuo. Instrumental parts may have been copied out after it was decided that the memorial service for Rector Ernesti would be held in St. Paul's, the University church, which was not subject to the civic rules that forbade instruments at such ser-

[13]*Bach-Dokumente*, vol. 1, 250.
[14]Ibid., 60.
[15]Terry, *Bach*, 161.
[16]See the *Nachwort* by Konrad Ameln to the facsimile of the autograph (Kassel: Brenreiter Verlag, 1964).

vices in the civic churches.[17] Terry's speculation that the motet was first performed a cappella at the Thomaskirche has little evidence for support. Bach may have assumed the memorial service would be held at the Thomaskirche and thus omitted instrumental parts, knowing they would not be permitted; when the change of churches was announced, the doubling instrumental parts were hurriedly copied out. In any event, the existence of these parts for *Der Geist hilft* proves nothing as far as performance practices in the civic churches were concerned. That the existence of instrumental parts indicates a latent intent on the part of Bach may very well be, but let us go further.

Though civic law may have prompted Bach to write these motets with no doubling instruments, inherent characteristics within them strengthen the argument for a cappella performances. From the earliest of his choral music in 1707 (cantata BWV 4?), Bach did not compose for more than four vocal lines, SATB (cantata BWV 31 notwithstanding)[18]; four-part vocal writing was his norm. It was not until his arrival at the Thomaskirche in 1723 that this norm was altered, not by design, but by the custom that precluded accompaniment or obbligato instruments at memorial services. The problem was then, how to compensate for the musical interest, richness, and fullness of sound that instruments heretofore had provided in his cantatas. His first solution was simply to add one vocal line to his customary four-part vocal texture: his first motet, *Jesu, meine Freude*, he set for five voices. His second solution was to compose motets for double choir, of four voices each. Though this may have been a

---

[17]Ibid., *Nachwort*:

> "In der Bach-Literatur ist wiederholt davon die Rede, daß für die Stadtkirchen in Leipzig ein Verbot bestanden hätte, bei Trauerfeiern Instrumente zu verwenden. Ein solches Verbot ist jedoch für die Fastenzeit, an Buß tagen, während der Karwoche und zur Zeit der Landestraucr bclcgt.

> It is said repeatedly in the Bach literature that for the civic churches in Leipzig there existed a prohibition against the use of instruments at funeral rites. Such a prohibition is reserved only for Lent, days of penitence, Holy Week, and times of state mourning, however. (Trans. ed.)

He fails, however, to authenticate this contradiction in the research of Richter, Spitta, *et al.* That instruments were used at grave-side services there can be no question, and perhaps it is this that Ameln had in mind. The evidence of the ban on instruments at memorial services held in the civic churches of Leipzig appears to be overwhelming. See also the *Kritischer Bericht* to the *Neue Bach-Ausgabe*, series III, vol. 1, 23.

[18]Cantata BWV 31, *Der Himmel lacht, die Erde jubilieret*, was written in 1715; apparently the opening chorus was originally for four voices, but it was revised in 1931 and a fifth vocal part added. (See Spitta, *Bach*, vol.1, 541.) Dürr suggests that Bach performed this cantata in Leipzig on Easter Day, 1724 (Dürr, *Bach-Jahrbuch*, 68); records indicate for certain that he performed it again on Easter Day, 1731.

new dimension for Bach's compositional procedures, it was hardly a new idea. The Thomasschule library was filled with vocal music set up for as many as twenty voices,[19] and there can be no doubt that Bach was quite familiar with such choral potential long before he came to Leipzig. He embraced the idea with extraordinary results. There followed not only the unaccompanied double-choir motets, but the *Magnificat* for five voices the same year as *Jesu, meine Freude*; cantata BWV 50, *Nun ist das Heil und die Kraft*, for double choir;[20] further on, the St. Matthew Passion using two choirs, and of course, the B-Minor Mass demanding four, five, and six voices, plus the *Osanna* for double choir. Though, apart from the motets, all were concerted pieces using orchestral colors and obbligato instruments, it is possible Bach took the five-voice *Jesu, meine Freude* as his point of departure for increasing the number of vocal lines in subsequent concerted music. Nonetheless, the main point persists: a five-voice motet and those for double chorus could omit doubling or obbligato instruments and support of the continuo and the resulting a cappella music could still effectively compensate for their absence. There are several supportive facts.

First, the autograph score and parts of *Singet dem Herrn ein neues Lied* survive intact, complete. This is well known; no instrumental parts nor figured bass exist. The logical conclusion is that Bach wrote this motet knowing the performance would have to be without instruments.

Second, the practice of accompanying these motets today may not have been as rigid a tradition in those days as thought. Only a few years after Bach's death the well-known Gerber report states that "the Thomasschule boys were wont to sing these compositions by Bach without any accompaniment."[21] Did Bach's successor all of a sudden start performing the motets a cappella when only a few years earlier they had not been performed at the Thomaskirche in such a manner by the composer himself? When Mozart visited Leipzig in 1789, the Thomaskirche Cantor, Johann Friedrich Doles, surprised him with a

---

[19]See Arnold Schering, "Die alte Chorbibliothek der Thomasschule in Leipzig," in *Archiv für Musikwissenschaft* I (1918-1919) 275-88.

[20]See Gerhard Herz, "The New Chronology of Bach's Vocal Music," in *Cantata No. 140* (New York: W.W. Norton & Co., 1972) 18. Recent research, however, indicates the original scoring for cantata BWV 50, *Nun ist das Heil und die Kraft*, was likely for five voices—SAATB—and was later revised by someone other than Bach for double choir. Since cantata BWV 50 followed the five-voice *Jesu, Meine Freude* rather closely, the evidence is convincing and reinforces the observation of Bach's departure from four-voice choral writing. See William H. Scheide, "'Nun ist das Heil und die Kraft' BWV 50: Doppelchörigkeit, Datierung und Bestimmung," *Bach-Jahrbuch* (1982) 81-96.

[21]Spitta, *Bach*, vol. 2, 609-10.

performance of *Singet dem Herrn*, and Mozart, who knew little of Bach and nothing of the motets, was astonished and captured by the music and requested a copy. His astonishment was the greater because it must have been sung a cappella, a style of performance identified with the sixteenth century, Palestrina, and Lassus, not the instrumentally oriented Bach of the eighteenth century.[22] Undoubtedly it was this that prompted him later to write on the copy given him, ''NB müsste ein ganzes Orchestre *dazu* gesezt werden.'' If that performance had included doubling instruments, it would not have occured to Mozart to comment that ''an entire orchestra must be set *in addition*.'' (Emphases mine.)

Furthermore, there exists a piece from Bach's Leipzig period, *Sei Lob und Preis* (BWV 231), which is actually a motet-style chorale movement from his cantata BWV 28 in which the doubling strings and winds are omitted and the independent basso continuo blended in with the bass vocal line, making four parts out of an original five, and omitting the continuo entirely. Why was this done? It must have been for a strictly a cappella performance. Franz Wüllner one of the *Bach-Gesellschaft* editors, felt that the recomposition was so skillful as to suggest it stems from Bach himself.[23] If this is so, it is certain that Bach was inclined to no accompaniment of any sort, at least in this four-part motet.

Third, the need for the 16' pitch supplied by the continuo to correct so-called bad harmonies or inversions resulting in $^6_4$ chords when the tenor line drops below the bass line may not have been as important to Bach as we have been led to believe. If it were, why did he permit the tenor line to go below the bass line in several places of the *Art of the Fugue*?[24] This sort of thing occasionally happens in *Jesu, meine Freude*, but it occurs so seldom and so fleetingly in the double-choir motets as to be inconsequential.

Fourth, funeral and memorial services called for motets in the old style known as *Sterbemotetten*. For the performances of these pieces at Vesper services, Bach and the singers were paid extra, The many receipts that exist which Bach signed for providing music at these services specify payment only to the singers of the Thomasschule and to Bach; there is no record of payments to instrumentalists for memorial services.

Fifth, why, in four of the funeral motets, did Bach write for two choirs

---

[22]Alfred Einstein, *Mozart, His Character, His Work*, trans. A. Mendel and N. Broder (New York: Oxford University Press, 1965) 319.

[23]J. S. Bach: *Werke*. (Leipzig: Breitkopf and Härtel, 1851-99), vol. 39 (1892).

[24]See, for example, the following: *Contrapunctus* V, m. 70; VIII, m. 37; XIX, mm. 137 and 169; and in *Contrapunctus* XII, m. 30 of the Inversus, a $^6_4$ chord occurs on the first beat.

of four (SATB) voices in the first place? We have already proposed one reason—that is, to compensate for the absence of obbligato instruments. But there is another that is best explained by a preliminary speculation, if one may be permitted the luxury. In writing his first *Sterbemotette* in Leipzig for five voices to compensate for omitting doubling instruments, suppose Bach, who had been there only a few weeks, was not aware of the civic rules forbidding instruments at memorial services, or at least pretended he was not. Assuming then that *always* a thorough bass of one sort or another was used (which was a safe assumption), he went right ahead and used a cello, bass viol, and/or organ continuo, perhaps using only his *coro primo*. After such a performance he could well have been criticized for using even that sparse an instrumental accompaniment in a time of mourning; it is certain the town fathers were not known for their generous attitudes toward infractions of civic law. The next time Bach was commissioned to write a *Sterbemotette*, he was struck with the idea that both his best choirs would be available for the service, and he wrote a piece for two equal choirs where one serves as continuo for the other; the presence of both insures a fullness of sound, and with two vocal bass lines available, the tenors of either choir need never go below the bass lines of one or the other of them.

The principle of the basso continuo, or figured bass, was one with which Bach was completely comfortable, it was second nature to him; he and that period of German baroque music were saturated with it through and through. But if circumstances required alternatives, which it did for funeral or memorial-service music in Leipzig civic churches, Bach's imagination would hardly have been found wanting. The vocal orchestration of the funeral motets was his response to the limitations imposed by the ban on instruments which, by definition, included a basso continuo instrument, or any other for that matter.[25]

Today's confusion surrounding the unaccompanied motets can in part be set right by recognizing that all were pieces written for the memorial services of important deceased citizens of Leipzig. Abundant evidence exists to support unaccompanied performances by a choir of modest proportions, and it becomes self evident that these conclusions should

[25]See Wilhelm Ehmann, "Performance Practice of Bach's Motets," *American Choral Review* XV, no. 2, for an undocumented discussion of this matter. On pp. 11-13 he speaks of the ban on instruments "during funeral rites at St. Thomas," but insists this need have no bearing on performance practices today.

bear substantially on the question of twentieth-century performance practices. One cannot be blind to Bach's intent, his mental process, for it
was this that determined how he should compose a particular piece of
music in a particular way.

As mentioned earlier, the confusions of Bach's intent can be seen
as well as heard. The tyrannical eradicability of the printed word and
note perpetuates and recapitulates discrepancies that the soundest scholarship cannot prevent. The subject in the first exposition of the fugue in
the center of *Jesu, meine Freude*, for example, appears in two different
forms in the *Bach Gesellschaft* edition. The tenor and alto have the correct contour, shown in Example 1a, while the soprano and bass have
the incorrect pattern shown in Example 1b. Note the difference in the
last four sixteenth notes.

Example 1. *Bach Gesallschaft* **Edition, Vol. 39, p. 71.**

The discrepancy is readily apparent: changing the contour within a fugue subject, however slightly, Bach was not likely to do. Curiously enough, the notes are corrected in both soprano and bass in their next entrances. The editor of the *Neue Bach-Ausgabe* set straight the errors in Example 1b in the volume of the motets published in 1965.

Now it is significant to note that Breitkopf & Härtel—the original publishers of the *Bach-Gesellschaft* edition—were the first to publish a performing edition of the motets in 1802/1803. Here the exposition of the fugue in *Jesu meine Freude* was printed correctly:

Example 2. *Jesu, meine Freude* (Facsimile courtesy of Riemenscheider Bach Institute) Breitkopf und Härtel, 1802-1803.

Ihr a-ber seyd nicht fleisch - lich, sondern geist

But they returned to the incorrect version of the *Bach-Gesellschaft* edition in their performing edition of 1972 (!). Strangely enough, an editor by the name of Frank Damrosch had corrected the inconsistency in both the soprano I and bass lines in his G. Schirmer edition as early as 1899, as had the Ewer (London) edition forty-nine years before. Of particular interest is an edition by C.F. Peters in 1958, edited by Werner Neumann and Walter Buszin. Prof. Neumann had become a co-editor of the *Neue Bach-Ausgabe* in 1953, yet five years later, his edition of *Jesu, meine Freude* returned to the wrong notes of the old *Bach-Gesellschaft* edition.

Example 3.

— but   in   the   Spir -   -   -   -
— lich, son-dern geist -   -   -   -

Singet dem Herrn ein neues Lied is another of the motets that has suffered at the hands of editors. For just one example, the last note of measure 26 in the first movement appears this way in the *Bach-Gesellschaft* edition:

Example 4.

ein   neu -   es   Lied

It was corrected in the *Neue Bach-Ausgabe* to read as follows:

Example 5.

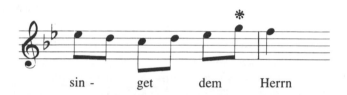

sin -   get   dem   Herrn

Lest the reader think that the wrong measures were extracted for Examples 4 and 5, the wrong text also was underlaid in the original, as a close look at Example 6 from the 1958 Bärenreiter facsimile edition will reveal:

Example 6. (mm. 24-27 from *Singet dem Herrn* autograph)

Bach's autograph is admittedly a little unclear at this point, but careful observation reveals the note should be "G," but under no circumstances the "C" below, which most editions up until 1975 had erroneously printed (the C.F. Peters edition of 1959 edited by Werner Neumann, for one; the H.W. Gray edition of 1927 edited by John E. West, for another, the latter being the most widely used in the United States). Only recently have performing editions become available such as those of Hänssler-Verlag (1975), edited by Günter Graulich, with the notes corrected.

These are but a few examples of a much longer list of discrepancies and corrections appearing in editions since the early years of the nineteenth century. Of equal interest is the variety of ways with which these various editions have been translated into performances recorded since the advent of long-playing records. To this end, the author has listened to over one hundred fifty such recordings with great care, often more than once. Many of these were made by college and university groups who were most cooperative in sending tapes or recordings made purely for their immediate community. It seems wisest, however, to select a few from the many recordings made by professional groups for commercial distribution; in the final analysis they carry the greater responsibility for faithful performance practices in the arena of public criticism. For the sake of expediency the field will be narrowed to the same two representative motets, the five-voice *Jesu, meine Freude*, and *Singet dem Herrn ein neues Lied* for double chorus.

Shortly before 1950, the RCA Victor Chorale and Orchestra, under the direction of Robert Shaw, recorded *Jesu, meine Freude* in English ("Jesus, Dearest Master") which was transferred to long-playing records in 1953 (RCA Victor, LM 11). The edition used for this recording was one prepared by Henry S. Drinker, who simply took an existing Novello and Co. edition in the public domain and underlaid his new English translation in the score. This was then reissued by the Association of American Choruses, whose holdings were later absorbed by the Drinker Library of Choral Music in Philadelphia.[26] Shaw recorded the same motet once more in 1959 with the Robert Shaw Chorale (RCA LSC-2273), this time in German. Instruments are used in both recordings, though in the second they are omitted from time to time, being reserved for the four-part chorale settings and the five-voice choruses generally. The original Novello edition printed the correct notes which,

---

[26]This information and a score were kindly furnished me by Mr. Frederick Kent of the Drinker Library of Choral Music, Philadelphia.

of course, are reflected in these performances, which are surpassing and tasteful.

In 1951, the Thomanerchor of Leipzig recorded all the motets for Archiv (ARC 3040/1) under Günther Ramin; here however, the wrong notes of that group of sixteenths in the fugue exposition of *Jesu, meine Freude* surface, as they did in another Thomanerchor recording of 1958-59 under the direction of Kurt Thomas (Archiv 3347 009-10). Also in 1958, the Westfälische Kantorei under the direction of Wilhelm Ehmann recorded the motet using scores that again went back to the incorrect notes (Cantate 12 06 LP). Twenty years later Ehmann recorded the same work with The Westminster Choir with corrected notes under the label of Peters International (PLE 124/5).

One of the most stunning recordings of *Jesu, meine Freude* comes from the Gächinger Kantorei and Bach Collegium of Stuttgart, Helmuth Rilling, conductor (Bärenreiter-Musicaphon, BM 30 SK 1327/28, 1967 -?). Not only are the correct notes sung, but the entire motet is performed with style and conviction. However, the Norddeutscher Singkreis, accompanied by basso continuo, used a faulty edition with the wrong notes in its recording two years earlier in 1965 (Nonesuch H1060), which was recapitulated in a reissue two years later on the Camerata label (CMS 30009 LPT). A sensitive performance with the right notes and *entirely* a cappella was recorded by the Birnauer Kantorei, Klaus Reiners, director, in 1976, issued by MPS (BB 229 408).

As for the new "G" in the soprano line in m. 26 of *Singet dem Herrn ein neues Lied*, quite a few professional performances recorded since the *Neue Bach-Ausgabe* volume of motets appeared remain blithely oblivious to the correction. Though Rilling correctly performed *Jesu, meine Freude,* no correction was made in *Singet dem Herrn* on the same recording mentioned in the preceding paragraph. Nor did Sebastian Forbes's Aeolian Singers in 1971 (London, STS 15186). It is difficult to believe that Nikolaus Harnoncourt and the Concentus musicus would ignore such a correction, but they did in a thoroughly romanticized recording of 1980, no less! (Telefunken, 6.35470 EK). However, others delight the ear by lifting the soprano line correctly to the "G": the Regensburger Domspatzen (Archiv 2708 031, 1974), the Heinrich Schütz Choir (MHS 1164-65, 1972), the Westminster Choir (Peters, PLE 124/5, 1978), the Louis Halsey Singers (L'Oiseau-Lyre, SOL 340/1, 1972), and the Cantata Singers (Sine Qua Non, C2001, 1978), to name a few.

These are small details in the overall grandeur of the motets, and perhaps they are relatively unimportant, but I don't think so. In the first place, there is no reason to perform a piece of music incorrectly if well-known, authentic sources are available with which to check correctness. In the second place, not to do so implies a rush to performance that ignores musical substance and scholarship, thereby sacrificing the composer's intent, however small the infraction.

A most controversial question is that of how the motets should be performed: with or without instruments and/or continuo, and whether or not the solo-versus-tutti principle should be involved.

Of these problems, the matter of accompaniment is the thorniest. We are now experiencing an extreme reaction to the nineteenth-century concept of the "a cappella ideal" that encouraged performance of baroque choral music with no instrumental accompaniment where, ostensibly, no instrumental parts were provided. Many feel an a cappella performance is a violation not only of baroque practices, but in the case of Bach's motets, his intent as well.[27] We have seen that this is not necessarily so (supra, pp. 6ff.). Yet there is enormous resistance to singing the motets today without doubling instruments and/or the basso continuo. The recordings of the Regensburger Domspatzen, Concentus musicus, and others, are backed by orchestras somewhat larger than Bach may have had at his disposal, especially when his instrumentalists had to sing rather than play. The choirs are much larger: the Thomanerchor numbers between sixty and sixty-five boys and men; the Regensburg choir of boys and men totals sixty-three and an orchestra of twenty; Harnoncourt's recording gives no clue other than that of a substantial chorus of mature voices of women and men plus ample instrumental support. The Westminster Choir recording lists a total of forty-four mature voices of well-trained women and men.

The jacket notes of all the above, nonetheless, assure the reader of every attempt at "authenticity." Can these practices possibly be Bach's intent? Alfred Dürr suggests that "modern performance practice should be guided by the intentions of the composer—as far as these can be ascertained—not by the imperfections with which he [Bach] had to reckon."[28] If there were no question that Bach's intent stemmed from those circumstances in Leipzig of which we spoke earlier, the matter would then be settled.

Bach's intent as far as vocal forces are concerned was determined by the small choir of boys and men for whom he wrote the motets. We know that—it was all he had. But "the imperfections with which he had to reckon" were found in that particular choir, the Thomasschule

---

[27]Ehmann, "Performance Practice," 19-21.
[28]Alfred Dürr, "Performance Practice of Bach's Cantatas," in the *American Choral Review* XVI, no. 2 (April, 1974) 13.

singers, not boys' choirs as an ideal. This does not preclude the use today of mature women's and men's voices discreetly trained, but this discretion is too often absent. The Westminster Choir recording with forty-four mature voices of women and men with pronounced vibratos obscures the slender vocal lines, especially when all eight parts are singing together; the doubling strings and woodwinds do not help. The director, Wilhelm Ehmann, states on the record jacket, "in this recording we have followed Baroque procedures. The number of singers is small. In his Leipzig choir, Bach probably had three singers on a part. . . ." Ehmann's recording uses thirty-two more voices than he suggests Bach did, so it is not at all clear what he meant by "baroque procedures." In contrast, those recordings that use twenty-four voices or less with no accompaniment other than a continuo, such as the Louis Halsey Singers, are patently much clearer; vocal lines, even in thick contrapuntal textures, can be identified and followed. Satisfyingly clear is the performance by the Birnauer Kantorei even without the support of doubling instruments. The concerto-grosso idea—that is, using solo voices in selected passages, particularly in the exposition of a fugue, to contrast with the full choir—has infected many recordings. This principle is not at all likely to have been Bach's intent in the chorale motets, and in two of them it can be proven by his own autograph copies. For the final four-voice fugue in Singet dem Herrn, Bach notates the bass and tenor entrances of both choirs before reducing the score to four staves. This is clearly seen in the following example:

Example 7. (Choral fugue of *Singet dem Herrn*, from the autograph)

Unquestionably his instructions are for basses and tenors of both choirs to enter on the words, *Alles was Odem hat, lobet den Herrn*. Yet more than one recording resorts to the affectation of one, single solo voice introducing the fugue. (It perhaps is unnecessary to add that the text does say "*all* that has breath praise the Lord!") It is the same in the autograph of *Der Geist hilft unser Schwachheit auf*; all voices of both choirs are notated in the final fugue, *Der aber die Herzen forschet*. . . . If soloists or concertists of each choir were to introduce the fugue, there still would be two on a part, which is hardly a solo.

Example 8. (Final fugue of *Der Geist hilft*, from the autograph.)

To assign solo voices to Coro I and the chorus to Coro II in the second movement of *Singet dem Herrn* equally may be invalid; here Bach surely intended two equal choirs. First, at the end of that movement is a note in Bach's own hand:

Example 9.

Der 2. Versus—ist wie der erste, nur da die Chöre ümwechseln, nur das erste Chor den Choral, das andre die Aria singe.[29]

The 2nd verse is like the first, except that the choirs change around; the first choir sings the chorale, and the second the aria.

That he abandoned the idea of the second verse, or merely failed to include the text, is irrelevant; the intent was for two equal choirs which could exchange with each other. Second, for *Singet dem Herrn* there exists the score and eight parts. These eight parts had to be shared among a minimum of eight voices—a number far from likely, since no baroque chorister was afforded the luxury of a single, hand-copied part all to himself—or a maximum of twenty-four (twelve in each choir) with the concertist holds the part with two ripienists looking on.[30] Third, the autographs bear no directions for a soloist at the fugue entrances, nor, further along in the score, the word "tutti" instructing the rest of the chorus to join.

There is no question that this *concerto* principle was applied occasionally in concerted choral music. Gerhard Herz tells us that "in Bach's time, *soli-tutti* alternation was a natural part of the style. It was so commonly understood that Bach indicated it only in a few exceptional cases—in cantatas BWV 71, 21, 76, and 24. . . ." Herz goes on to say "that Bach himself added the word 'tutti' at the beginning of bar 88 in the 1724 score of the Sanctus, thus implying solo treatment certainly before, or perhaps even up to this point."[31] In all cases, the orchestration is invariably reduced at the fugal entrances for voices, a

[29]Facsimile of the autograph, Bärenreiter Verlag, Kassel, 1958, 32.
[30]Arnold Schering, *Johann Sebastian Bachs Leipziger Kirchenmusik*, (Leipzig: Breitkopf and Härtel, 1936) 30.
[31]Gerhard Herz, "Bach's B-Minor Mass in History," guest lecture at the University of North Carolina, Chapel Hill, 1978. Alfred Dürr ("Performance Practice," 8), on the other hand, has this to say:

> " . . . a systematic division of choral portions into passages intended for solo ensemble and those intended for full chorus, such as has been suggested by Wilhelm Ehmann for the B minor Mass, can be documented only in special instances; it could *not* have been the rule." (Italics his.)

reduction that lasts through the initial exposition of the fugue. But the motets do not present an analogous situation; they involve no orchestral colors nor obbligato instrumental parts; there is every indication that voices alone are the resources upon which performance depends.

Ehmann carries the solo-versus-tutti principle much further. He says, "in our recording of *Jesu, meine Freude*, we have assigned the forte passages to the tutti, and the piano passages to the solo ensemble, by which a concerto grosso-like effect is achieved."[32] It is difficult to understand the reasoning that insists a chorale motet for a funeral service must "achieve a concerto-grosso-like effect." The motets simply are not concerto-grosso pieces; to try to make them so is to make them something they are not. Solo instruments are never heard to take those brief places marked "piano" in the first movement of the third Brandenburg concerto, where Bach effectively writes for three "choirs" of strings.[33]

Example 10. (Concerto III [BWV 1048], first movement.)

[32]Wilhelm Ehmann, from the notes to *Singet dem Herrn ein neues Lied* and *Jesu, meine Freude* (Cantate CAN 12 06 LP) 6.
[33]Johann Sebastian Bach. *Neue Ausgabe sämtlicher Werke*, series VII, vol. 2: *Sechs brandenburgische Konzerte*, ed. Heinrich Besseler, 75.

With Bach the matter of intent does not stop with musical substance. Always in the back of his mind were liturgical responsibilities as well as a sensitive reflection of the poetry in the musical lines. In several recordings the singers' attempt for cleanly articulated contrapuntal lines is so pronounced that vocal athletics appear to take over as though competing in the Motet Olympics. Or, in another instance, Harnoncourt converts the $\frac{3}{8}$ rhythm of the opening chorus of *Der Geist hilft* into a charming Viennese waltz with exaggerated, strong accents on the first beat of each measure. Ehmann and the Westmister Choir unmistakably capture nineteenth-century romanticism in *Komm, Jesu, komm* with their exaggerated crescendos on each *komm*.

For clarity and purity, it is difficult to match a well-trained choir of boys and men for performances of the motets. Not only do the Thomasschule recordings corroborate this, but others—the King's College Choir, for example. The recording of the latter, incidentally, lists a cello, double bass, and organ continuo used in the performance, but these are not heard in the two motets for double choir: *Der Geist hilft* and *Fürchte dich nicht*; these are sung most winsomely with no accompaniment. Not until the four-voice motet *Lobet den Herrn, alle Heiden* are instruments used, which, of course, Bach himself provided for in the score. Compare their recording (Angel, S-36804, 1972) of *Der Geist hilft* with that of Harnoncourt. King's College Choir beautifully demonstrates that restraint, not excess, better serves not only the case for authenticity, but the composer's intent as well.

The attempt throughout this discussion has been to understand the chorale motets on Bach's terms, and to recognize, where possible, his intentions. Twentieth-century performance practices indicate a few make this effort, but that far more do not. Those who decry the infiltration of nineteenth-century romanticism seen in a cappella performances are often the first to be seduced by its charms in other ways, such as Ehmann in his recordings. Others, like Harnoncourt, who boast authority of authenticity of original instruments and historic guidelines, appear either naively or arrogantly unaware of Bach's own intent.

As to the question of accompaniment, it can be demonstrated that the motets fare as well without it as with it. Musically, the double-choir motets do not demand instrumental support—doubling instruments add nothing to what is already there. If accompaniment in the way of a continuo must be introduced for the pragmatic reason of keeping singers on pitch, then let it not interfere with the vocal lines, but discreetly lend a hand only with the problem of staying on pitch. The principle of the concerto grosso—soli versus tutti—applied to purely vocal music intended for funeral services, superimposes a self-conscious stamp of dogged and misguided attempts at authenticity that are at once unnecessary and incongruous. The philosophy implied earlier bears repeating: do not try to make anything more of the motets than what they simply are. What they are is magnificent enough.

In spite of minor inaccuracies in the printed notes of various editions, and in spite of curious and sometimes bizarre interpretations in performance, the incredible beauty, sonorities, and impact of spirit of Bach's motets survives the gamut of good and bad performances. Such is, altogether, the mystery, credibility, and ineradicability of genius.

Harold Decker

G.F. Handel's Funeral Anthem for Queen Caroline: A Neglected Masterpiece

HISTORICAL BACKGROUND

Handel's association with King George II and Queen Caroline began with his appointment as Kapellmeister to the Court of Hannover (1710), before the King's ascension to the throne of England and prior to Handel's becoming established as an impresario and composer of Italian opera in London. Because of this earlier relationship, the new King requested that Handel compose the music for his coronation ceremonies. The Coronation Anthems met with unanimous approval and served to foster a renewed friendship between the composer and the King's family. Handel was appointed Music Master to the royal family, and among his duties was the responsibility of giving harpsichord lessons to the children. For this service an annual stipend was established for him.

The Queen was a trained musician and an excellent singer for whom Handel, while still in Hannover, had composed a group of twelve

---

Prior to his retirement in 1981, Harold Decker was Chairman of the Choral Division, School of Music, University of Illinois. He holds a graduate degree from Oberlin Conservatory of Music and an undergraduate degree from Morningside College, which in 1957 conferred on him the Doctor of Music degree "for outstanding service to music and education."

A charter member of the American Choral Directors Association and national president from 1966-68, Decker was awarded the organization's Distinguished Service Award for his leadership in organizing the 1976 Bicentennial Celebration. His writings include the co-authorship of Choral Conducting Symposium *with Julius Herford and a textbook,* Choral Conducting: Focus on Communication, *with Dr. Colleen Kirk.*

chamber duets in the then-popular Italian style. While Handel was in
Germany, and throughout Caroline's reign in England, he had received
her friendship, encouragement, and loyal support. After the Queen's
death it was not surprising that George II turned to Handel for music
to honor her at the funeral ceremonies in Westminster Abbey. The King's
appreciation and the high esteem in which Handel's Funeral Anthem
for Queen Caroline was held by his contemporaries is apparent in
documents of the period.

> . . . The King, being willing [that] this should be executed in the best
> manner, an Invitation was given to Mr. Handel that he should compose
> it, and this he immediately set to work upon, and in 8 days [actually,
> it was only 6 days, December 7-12] finished that Inimitable Piece of
> Harmony. The King was so well satisfied with his work, that He honored
> him with a gracious message expressing His Satisfaction.[1]

Charles Burney's comment reflects the same high regard in which
this music was held: "The Queen's death [was] an event that produced
a funeral anthem which in expression, harmony, and pleasing effects,
appears to me at the head of all his works."[2]

The Bishop of Chichester attended the funeral rites at Westminster
Abbey and wrote to his son: "After the service there was a long anthem, the words of the Sub-Dean and the music by Mr. Handel, and
it reckoned to be as good a piece as he ever made."[3] Newman Flower,
an early-twentieth-century biographer of Handel, enthusiastically
characterized this music by Handel as "the greatest Anthem that was
ever put to paper for the passing of a human soul."[4] More recently,
Paul Henry Lang states: "if there were any misgivings about the after-
math of Handel's illness, [after he had taken the "cures" at the baths
in Aachen] the Funeral Anthem should have dispelled them, for it showed
Handel's creative faculties not only unimpaired but rising to the sum-
mit."[5]

The Funeral Anthem for Queen Caroline is unique in Handel's writing

[1]Otto Deutsch, *Handel, a Documentary Biography* (New York: W. W. Norton, 1955)
842, quoting *The Gentleman's Magazine*, May, 1760.
[2]Charles Burney, *A General History of Music from Earliest Ages to the Present Period*,
4 vols. (London, 1776-79; reprint editions, 1935 & 1957), footnote p. 818.
[3]Deutsch, 443.
[4]Newman Flower, *George Frideric Handel, His Personality and His Time* (New York:
Cassell, 1923) 240.
[5]Paul Henry Lang, *George Frideric Handel* (New York: W. W. Norton, 1966) 297.
Bracketed addendum by this author.

of music for chorus. His opera choruses are notably lackluster and perfunctory, his Chandos Anthems display an amazing command of compositional techniques, his oratorio choruses and Coronation Anthems
are dramatic and even at times sensational, but the choruses within the
Funeral Anthem are his warmest and most expressive, possessing dignity
as well as charm. Stanley Sadie evaluates the work as follows: "It was
no mere formal attribute but a work of dignity and restraint, closer to
the English traditions of church music than was usual for Handel."[6]
Lang is of the opinion that "This anthem is not pure ceremonial music,
it is ceremonial music with a profound personal involvement, which
gives it an altogether unique cast."[7]

Part of its special character is due to Handel's avoidance of solo arias
and recitatives within the work. In spite of this, contrasts in texture
are plentiful, and rhythmic diversity, melodic invention, and harmonic
richness are present throughout. Handel was not primarily seeking individual expression, but rather, an expression of all loyal subjects who
loved their queen. To substantiate this idea, one may turn to records
of the first performance.[8] For this funeral service Handel assembled
80 singers and 100 instrumentalists. The choir was composed of men
from St. Paul's Cathedral, St. George's Chapel at Windsor Castle, the
Chapel Royal, and Westminster Abbey, plus "several musical Gentlemen
of distinction."[9] In addition,there were boys from the Chapel Royal
and Abbey choirs and instrumentalists drawn from His Majesty's Band
(as the King's strings were known during the time of Charles II) and
from Handel's opera orchestra. The orchestration is unelaborate, with
only two oboes, strings, and continuo parts. A special organ was con-
structed in Westminster Abbey for the occasion.

Jens Peter Larsen clarifies the employment of chorus in the Funeral
Anthem as follows:

> The use of the chorus in the Funeral Anthem was determined by the
> special character of the work. Here, as in *Alexander's Feast,* the choir
> does not have to act as a collective body, in contrast to the soloist's ex-
> pressions of the emotions of an individual. But whereas in *Alexander's
> Feast* the chorus was, from the point of view of expression, on a par
> with the aria, the situation in the Funeral Anthem is that the chorus alone

[6]Stanley Sadie, *Handel* (London: John Calder, 1962) 97.
[7]Lang, 226.
[8]*Grub Street Journal*, December 22, 1737.
[9]Ibid.

has to create the variety which would normally be achieved by recitative, aria, and chorus."[10]

Handel was well aware that he had composed a work of the highest quality and, almost immediately after the ceremony, he conceived the idea of including it, with appropriate text alterations, in his forthcoming oratorio, *Saul*. In the end he decided to replace it there with Saul's "Dead March." Soon after, however, he changed the title to "The Lamentations of the Israelites Over the Death of Joseph" and, with other alterations in the text, he performed it in its entirety as Part I of *Israel in Egypt*. H. C. Robbins Landon comments on Handel's utilization of this music: "Handel later attached it to *Saul*, then changed his mind and used it as a preface to *Israel in Egypt*, being loathe to see such exceptional music disappear along with the bones of the Queen."[11] Subsequently he extracted two movements and placed them in his Foundling Hospital Anthem, with yet another text.

After the composer's death, Samuel Arnold published in 1786 an edition of the work in which he assigned certain sections to solo voices, applying the Baroque solo-tutti principle. Later, in the nineteenth century, Chrysander divided this extended anthem into two separate parts and, following Samuel Arnold's example, also assigned parts to solo voices. "They shall receive a Glorious Kingdom" (VIII) specifies solo voices throughout; "When the Ear Heard Her" (III) and "The Righteous Shall Be Had in Everlasting Remembrance" (Vb) are assigned to both soloists and chorus. Historically there is no justification for this rearrangement; it does not conform with Handel's conception of the work. Although his personal devotion to the Queen is in evidence in numerous passages, he was quite obviously composing this memorial as a musical eulogy from all her subjects.

The Sub-Dean of Westminster Abbey, Edward Willes, provided Handel with texts selected from the Old and New Testaments and the Apocrypha. The following outline indicates the Biblical sources with Willes's adaptations that relate them specifically to the deceased Queen. The division into movements, as shown in the Structural Outline (Table 1), follows the composer's architectural design.

---

[10]Jens Peter Larsen, *Handel's Messiah: Origin, Composition, Sources* (London: Adam and Charles Black, 1957) 70, 71.

[11]H. C. Robbins Landon, *Handel and His World* (Boston: Little and Brown, 1984) 156.

Table 1

Biblical Sources and Anthem Texts
of The Funeral Anthem for Queen Caroline

Biblical Sources	*Anthem Texts*
IIa	IIa
The ways of Zion do mourn, because none come to the solemn feasts: all her gates are desolate; her priests sigh, her virgins are afflicted, and she is in bitterness. Lamentations 1:4	The ways of Zion do mourn, and she is in bitterness; all her people sigh
. . . the virgins of Jerusalem hang down their heads to the ground. Lamentations 2:10	and hang down their heads to the ground.
The beauty of Israel is slain upon thy high places: how are the mighty fallen! II Samuel 1:19.	How are the mighty fall'n!
. . . she that was great among the nations, princess of the provinces, how is she become tributary! Lamentations 1:1	She that was great among the nations and princess of the provinces.
IIb	IIb
I put on righteousness and it clothed me: my judgment was as a robe and a diadem. Job 29:14.	She put on righteousness and it clothed her; her judgment was a robe and a diadem.
III	III
When the ear heard me, then it blessed me; and when the eye saw me, it gave witness to me. Job 29:11.	When the ear heard her, then it blessed her; and when the eye saw her, it gave witness of her.

Continued on next page

Table I, continued

Biblical Sources	*Anthem Texts*
IVa	IVa
The beauty of Israel is slain upon the high places: how are the mighty fallen! II Samuel 1:19.	How are the mighty fall'n!
. . . she that was great among the nations, princess among the provinces, how is she become tributary! Lamentations 1:1	She that was great among the nations and princess of the provinces.
IVb	IVb
because I delivered the poor that cried, and the fatherless, and him that hath none to help him. Job 29:12	She deliver'd the poor that cried, the fatherless, and him that hath none to help him.
. . . if there be any virtue, and if there was any praise, think on these things. Philippians 4:8	Kindness, meekness and comfort were in her tongue. If there was any virtue and if there was any praise, she thought on those things.
Va	Va
The beauty of Israel is slain upon the high places: how are the mighty fallen! II Samuel 1:19.	How are the mighty fall'n!
. . . she that was great among the nations, princess among the provinces, how is she become tributary! Lamentations 1:1	She that was great among the nations and princess of the provinces.
Vb	Vb
Surely he shall not be moved forever: the righteous shall be in everlasting remembrance. Psalm 112:6	The righteous shall be had in everlasting remembrance,

Biblical Sources	*Anthem Texts*
And they that be wise shall shine as the brightness of the firmament; and they that turn many to righteousness as the stars forever and ever. Daniel 12:3	and the wise will shine as the brightness of the firmament.

VI

VI	VI
Their bodies are buried in peace, but their name liveth forevermore. Ecclesiasticus 44:14 (Apocrypha)	Their bodies are buried in peace, but their name liveth evermore.

VII

VII	VII
The people will tell of their wisdom, and the congregation will shew forth their praise; Ecclesiasticus 44:15	The people will tell of their wisdom, and the congregation will shew forth their praise,
But the righteous shall live forevermore; their reward is also with the Lord, and the care of them is with the Most High. Wisdom of Solomon 5:15 (Apochrypha)	their reward also is with the Lord, and the care of them is with the Most High.

VIII

VIII	VIII
Therefore they shall receive a glorious Kingdom and a beautiful crown from the Lord's hand. Wisdom of Solomon 5:16	They shall receive a glorious Kingdom and a beautiful crown from the Lord's hand.

IX

IX	IX
But the merciful goodness of the Lord endureth forever on them that fear Him, and His righteousnsess unto children's children. Psalm 103:17.	The merciful goodness of the Lord endureth forever on them that fear Him, and his righteousness on children's children.

TITLE AND OVERALL FORM

On the first printed score, by J. Walsh in 1743, the title reads, "The Anthem which was Performed in Westminster Abbey for the Funeral of Queen Caroline." Most history books refer to "The Funeral Anthem for Queen Caroline," but more recent editions of the anthem itself employ the text of the opening chorus, "The Ways of Zion Do Mourn." Still other historians make reference to a "Funeral Ode to Queen Caroline" or merely to "Handel's Funeral Anthem."

Handel conceived the Funeral Anthem as a single unit with eleven component parts including choral recitatives, choral "arias," and fugues; a prelude, or sinfonia, was added two years later when he made use of it as the opening section of *Israel in Egypt*. Without solo recitatives and arias to contribute contrasts in mood and texture, he called on his creative powers to overcome these limitations. Only a master composer such as Handel could have solved these problems and still come up with a masterpiece. With nearly a dozen separate movements he has, by employing functional harmony, relating musical forms, and stressing the affinity between text and music, created a unified musical entity divided into two balanced sections with a "solo chorus" in the center. After a mood-creating instrumental opening of fourteen measures, the first section (I-IV) is textually and musically concerned with personal references to the Queen. (See Structural Outline, Table 2.) The texts of the second section (VI-IX) are objective rather than personal in nature; they are related specifically to the traditional English burial service. Movement V stands alone at the center of the anthem, with a general reference to the Queen but also to wise and righteous leaders of all nations.

Referring to the Structural Outline with score in hand,[12] one will observe frequent dominant-tonic relationships between movements. Even of more significance, one notes that the key of G minor dominates the Funeral Anthem, with all movements relating to this tonality. There are three movements that are specifically in the tonic key that serve as major structural points within the work. They are:

1. Opening sinfonia and choruses: "The Ways of Zion Do Mourn" (IIa) and "She Put on Righteousness" (IIb).

[12]Review of this analysis will be facilitated if the reader follows along with a Novello (Watkins Shaw, editor) or a G. Schirmer (William Herrmann, editor) piano-vocal score.

2. Central recitative, "How Are the Mighty Fall'n!" (Va) and chorus, "The Righteous as Shall Be Had in Everlasting Remembrance" (Vb).
3. Concluding benediction: "The Merciful Goodness of the Lord" (IX).

These choruses are the "pillars" on which Handel builds the structure of the Funeral Anthem. From the opening chorus to the central "pillar" (movements II-IV), all pronoun references in the texts are to Queen Caroline:

Movement I: *She* is in bitterness, *her* people sigh, *she* that was great, *princess* of the provinces, *she* put on righteousness, *her* judgment was a robe and a diadem.

Movement II: When the ear heard *her,* then it blessed *her,* and when the eye saw *her,* it gave witness of *her,* *She* delivered the poor.

Movement III: Kindness, meekness and comfort were in *her* tongue, *She* delivered the fatherless, If there was any virtue, if there was any praise, *she* thought on those things.

After movement Vb (VI-IX), textual references are of a general nature and relate to those who have gone to their "reward" with honor and "praise," who have been received in the "glorious kingdom." These texts are as follows:

Movement VI: *Their* bodies are buried in peace, but *their* name liveth evermore.

Movement VII: The people will tell of *their* wisdom and the congregation will show forth *their* praise. *Their* reward also is with the Lord and the care of *them* is with the Most High.

Movement VIII: *They* shall receive a glorious Kingdom.

Movement IX: Benediction—"The merciful goodness of the Lord endureth forever on *them* that fear Him, and His righteousness on children's children."

Table 2. Structural Outline of The Funeral Anthem for Queen Caroline

Movements	I	IIa	IIb	III	IVa	IVb
Biblical Text Sources	—	Lamentations 1:4; 2:10; 1:1 II Samuel 1:19	Job 29:14	Job 29:11	II Samuel 1:19 Lamentations 1:1	Job 29:12 Philippians 4:8
Forms	Prelude: Sinfonia	Chorale Fantasia on *Herr Jesu Christ, du höchstes Gott* (Decius–1610)	Fugue	quasi vocal-chamber-duet form ("choral aria")	Choral Recitative	Chorale Fantasia on *Du Friedefürst, Herr Jesu Christ*
Orchestration	Strings, continuo, organ	Oboes I-II, strings, continuo, organ	Strings continuo, organ	Intro: strings, oboes, continuo, organ	Oboes I-II, strings, continuo, organ	Oboes I-II, strings, continuo, organ
Keys	G minor T–D:	G minor T–D D–T	G minor	E major T–D–SD–T	C minor to G minor I–V	B♭ major T–D–T–V of VI–T
Meters and Tempos	$\frac{4}{4}$ Largo assai	$\frac{4}{4}$ Larghetto e staccato- più mosso	$\frac{4}{4}$ Tempo ordinario	$\frac{4}{4}$ Andante larghetto	$\frac{4}{4}$ Adagio	$\frac{4}{4}$ Andante

Movements	*Va*	*Vb*	*VI*	*VII*	*VIII*	*IX*
Biblical Text Sources	II Samuel 1:19 Lamentations 1:1 (repeat of IIa)	Psalm 112:6 Daniel 12:3	Ecclesiasticus 44:14 (Apocrypha)	Ecclesiasticus 44:15 Wisdom of Solomon 5:15 (Apocrypha)	Wisdom of Solomon 5:16 (Apocrypha)	Psalm 103:17
Forms	Choral recitative	Quasi vocal-chamber-duet form, ("choral aria")	Recitative and Chorale Fantasia on theme from *Ecce quomodo moritur* by Jacob Handl	Choral recitative	Quasi vocal-chamber-duet form ("choral aria")	Benediction. Closing instrumental section
Orchestration	Strings, continuo, organ	Oboes I-II, strings, continuo, organ	Grave: strings Allegro: strings, continuo, organ	Oboes I-II, strings, continuo, organ	Oboes I-II, strings, continuo, organ	Oboes I-II, strings, continuo, organ
Keys	G minor T–D:	G minor T–D D–T	F minor T–D; F major Grave: N of V–V Allegro: F major	D minor D–T V–III–I	A minor T–IV–III–D–T	G minor T–D–T
Meters and Tempos	4/4 Adagio	3/2 Larghetto e staccato	4/4 Grave e piano 2/2 Forte-allegro (repeated)	4/4 Grave Tempo ordinario Adagio	3/4 Larghetto e piano	4/4 Largo

Chrysander, in his complete edition of Handel's works, divided parts
I and II after the choral recitative "How Are the Mighty Fall'n!" (Va);
he began part II with "The Righteous Shall Be Had in Everlasting
Remembrance" (Vb). Observing the number of instances where
dominant-tonic relationships occur, one becomes aware of the importance of continuity at these points. An example of this relationship is
found here in this recitative and chorus. For this reason, as well as the
change in textual focus, part II rightfully begins with "Their Bodies
Are Buried in Peace" (VI). It also seems more reasonable to designate
the "solo chorus" (Vb) as the central "pillar," since the texts that follow
are oriented to the traditional funeral service. The detailed examination of the entire anthem that follows reveals more specifically how
Handel's architectural concepts function in the Funeral Anthem.

MUSICAL ANALYSIS: MOVEMENT II

Architectural concepts, text-music relationships, harmonic tension,
and rhythmic propulsion all contribute to the "flow" of Handel's extended anthem. The opening chorus reveals numerous examples of these
characteristics. After the mood is set by an eighteen-measure sinfonia,
an instrumental introduction to the opening chorus begins with a series
of slow, staccato chords. Continuing on, a plaintive, sustained oboe
line that progresses steadily downward leads into the following chorale
fantasia. The alto section begins a Lutheran hymn familiar to both Queen
Caroline and the composer, set to the text "The Ways of Zion Do
Mourn" (Figure 1). On completion of the first line, two contrapuntal
figures appear in the strings that eventually become associated with the
texts "and she is in bitterness" and "all her people sigh." (Figures
2 and 3.)

Figure 1. Chorale theme: *Herr Jesu Christ, du höchstes Gott;* Handel's
adaptation (Ia)

The   ways   of   Zion   do   mourn
Herr   Jes-   su   Christ,   du   höch -   stes   Gott

Figure 2. Countermelody one

and   she is   in   bit-   ter-   ness

Figure 3. Countermelody two

    all _ _ _ _ _ _   her peo- ple sigh

After stating the chorale melody in each voice part, while a continuous interplay of the countermelodies occurs in accompanying instrumental parts, each voice part in turn presents the first and second counter-melodies. (Observe the close text-music relationship in the setting of each countermelody.) After combining all three themes, Handel brings the section to a brief climax as all voices combine to sing this chorale phrase on sustained half-notes. A descending homophonic statement of "all the people sigh and hang down their heads" follows, then all voices suddenly descend to a unison "D" at the half-cadence, completing the first section of the opening movement. One may compare the setting of the text "All the people sigh" in the final phrase, to the opening chorus of *Israel in Egypt*, where the composer sets the word "sigh" in a similarly affective manner.

Figure 4. Setting of "sigh" in the Funeral Anthem

    sigh,   sigh,   sigh,   sigh,   sigh,   sigh,   sigh,

Figure 5. Affective treatment of "sigh" in the opening chorus of Handel's *Israel in Egypt*

In the second section of the opening chorus (IIb), the text "How are the mighty fall'n!" is repeated verbatim twelve times, three times in four instances.

The striking and contrasting rhythm dramatically expresses personal grief as well as national bereavement at the loss of a monarch. To unify the first movement and drive it to its ultimate conclusion, the composer concludes the section on the dominant of G minor, which leads into the tonic key of the fugue that follows. Although there is some disagreement among musicologists concerning overdotting in Baroque music,[13] the alert conductor will be aware of the fact that the exaggerated dotted rhythms found in the orchestra parts should be sung in similar fashion by the chorus. He will know that many clues to the chorus's singing of rhythms, melodic ornamentation, and dynamics are often discovered in instrumental lines. (See Figure 6.)

Figure 6. Second section: (a) first and second themes in orchestra
(b) first and second themes in chorus

Handel bows to tradition by concluding this chorus with a fugue. The subject is both vigorous and dignified in his setting of the text "She put on righteousness and it clothed her" (IIb). The original organ work

[13]Frederick Neumann, "The Overdotting Syndrome: Anatomy of Delusion," *Musical Quarterly* 67 (July, 1981) 305-347.

by Johann Krieger upon which this fugue is based, was written a step
higher, in A minor. Since the section preceding the fugue concludes
on a dominant chord, the composer is urging the conductor to go directly
(*attacca*) into the fugal section, thus bringing the opening chorus to
climactic yet dignified conclusion.

Figure 7. Fugue subject (1) and counter-subject (2)

(1)

She put on right- eous- ness

(2)

Her judge- ment

was a robe

MUSICAL ANALYSIS: MOVEMENTS III, Vb, AND VIII

Jens Peter Larsen[14] suggests that Handel treats three choruses from
the Funeral Anthem as "choral arias," in place of solo voices. In this
way Handel provides contrasts in texture within a strictly choral form.
Larsen draws a comparison with the Baroque vocal chamber duets of
Steffani that Handel had used as models for twelve duets that he had
composed earlier for Caroline while she was still Duchess of Hannover.
Their lyrical, chamber-like qualities, with appealing melodic lines and
persistent rhythms, offer a complete change of character from the more
serious conventional forms that surround them. These solo choruses
include "When the Ear Heard Her" (III), "The Righteous Shall Be
Had in Everlasting Remembrance" (Vb), and "They Shall Receive a
Glorious Kingdom" (VIII). The chamber duet has a form that consists
of the presentation of melodic material in one solo voice, its repetition
by the second voice, and the subsequent conclusion of the two parts
together. In the four-part choruses Handel follows a similar pattern:

[14]Larsen, 81 and 82.

1. "When the Ear Heard Her" (III)
   a. SA enter with opening themes in the tonic, E flat.
   b. TB sing same music in the dominant, B flat.
   c. SATB together to conclude in the tonic.

Figure 8. (a) Opening theme of III, (b) second theme, (c) third theme

2. "The Righteous Shall Be Had in Everlasting Remembrance" (Vb)
   a. AT enter with opening themes in tonic (G minor).
   b. SB repeat same music in parallel minor of the dominant
      (D minor).
   c. SATB in tonic to the final cadence.

Figure 9. (a) Opening theme of Vb, (b) second theme

last -   -   -   ing   re-

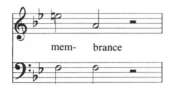

mem-   brance

(b)

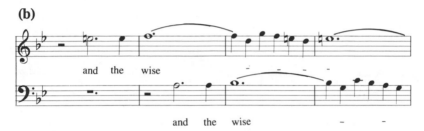

and   the   wise   -   -   -   -

and   the   wise   -   -

-     -   will   shine   as   the   bright-

-          will   shine   as   the   bright-

3. "They shall receive a glorious Kingdom" (VIII)
    a. T and A enter contrapuntally in tonic (A minor) and
       present all melodic material.
    b. B and S follow same pattern in subdominant (D minor).
       Other parts enter but maintain two-part texture until the
       final four measures, which cadence to the relative major of
       the tonic (C major).

c. SA continue in dominant (E minor); TB and SA enter
   separately, maintaining the duet texture.
d. SATB combine and then conclude in the tonic.

Figure 10. (a) Opening theme of VIII, (b) second theme, (c) third theme,
(d) fourth theme

(a)

a. They shall__ re-¬ ceive a glo- rious King,–dom

(b)

A glo- - - - - ri- ous__ King- dom

(c)

they shall re- ceive, they shall re- ceive a glo-

ri- ous - King- dom

(d)

and the beau- ti-ful, beau- ti- ful,

crown_____ from the Lord's hand

MUSICAL ANALYSIS: MOVEMENT IV

The choral recitative "How Are the Mighty Fall'n!" (IVa) refers
back textwise to the opening chorus. This time, however, the words
are associated with a totally different musical treatment. Whereas the
drama of this text emerged in its first setting with a terse, almost sobb-

ing exclamatory rhythm, Handel maintains at this point a sustained, intense, homophonic continuity, expressing deep emotion in the changing harmonies and suspensions. The opening chord leads through diminished sevenths to the parallel major of the tonic; the recitative concludes on the dominant of G minor. "She Delivered the Poor That Cried" (IVb) may be likened to the opening chorus (IIa); as it also may be regarded as a quasi chorale fantasia. In this chorus, for the first and only time in the Funeral Anthem, the soprano section divides into two parts. One can envision a children's choir singing the chorale melody antiphonally with the ATB sections. This second chorale reference is based on a hymn by Decius (1610)—*Du Friedefürst, Herr Jesu Christ*.

Figure 11. (a) Original chorale melody, (b) Handel's text and adaptation in IVb

Figure 12. Repeated opening theme of IVb

Figure 13. Final cadence of the chorale

Figure 14. Contrasting theme that is developed polyphonically

The texts in the final section of this chorus are altered from the original words of the Apostle Paul in Philippians to apply specifically to Queen Caroline. These are the most drastic changes of the Biblical texts within the entire Funeral Anthem. One may speculate that Handel himself may have contributed to these alterations so that he could express, even more explicitly in the music, his own personal feelings toward his deceased monarch. (See "Text Outline and Biblical Sources," Table 1.) At the court she had been his greatest supporter, both as a friend and as a backer of his numerous musical enterprises.

MUSICAL ANALYSIS: MOVEMENT V

A more formal choral recitative, "Their Bodies Are Buried in Peace," opens the traditional burial-service section of the Funeral Anthem. Here, Handel again reverts to the German background that he shared with Queen Caroline as he composes a chorus that quotes from a traditional German Lutheran funeral motet, *Ecce quomodo moritur* by Jacob Handl (1550-1591). In twenty-two measures of sustained homophonic writing, the adagio beginning proceeds from F minor to C major. A sudden change of mood, marked "forte" by the composer, requires a slightly faster, more vigorous tempo to express the text "but their name liveth evermore." The original Handl theme and Handel's adaptation appear in Figure 15.

Figure 15. (a) Phrase from *Ecce quomodo moritur* (b) Handel's adaptation in the Funeral Anthem

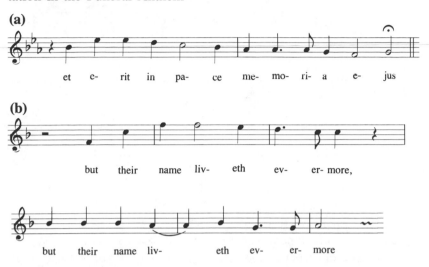

This single phrase of five measures is quoted four times in each repeated section; contrapuntal lines are interpolated between statements. After the first section in F minor the choral recitative appears again, this time in D-flat major, a neopolitan relationship to the dominant of the subdominant. It then proceeds, slightly abbreviated (four measures omitted), to the dominant of the tonic, F Major. A reprise of "But their name liveth evermore" concludes the chorus.

MUSICAL ANALYSIS: MOVEMENT VII

"The People Will Tell of Their Wisdom" opens with a short musical statement of four measures that introduces the second and final fugue. This phrase is in A major, the dominant of the D that follows. The musical setting of "and the congregation will show forth Thy praise" rises to a stirring climax and is followed by a third "choral aria" and a benediction. This quasi-fugue has no development section, but the fugal subject surges through fourteen consecutive entries to a homophonic conclusion that is one of the most exciting climaxes in all of Handel's choruses. The subject appears in Figure 16.

Figure 16. Subject of fugue (VII)

And   the   con- gre- ga-   -   -

-               -   tion , will   shew   forth   their   praise

MUSICAL ANALYSIS: MOVEMENT IX

The benediction, "The Merciful Goodness of the Lord," begins with a stately instrumental largo, an introduction of eight measures, composed in French-overture style. After the choral entry of only two measures, the instrumental accompaniment begins a repeated eighth-note pulse reminiscent of the opening sinfonia; this prevails until the closing eleven measures of an instrumental postlude. The choral setting of the text is traditional and solemn; the tonality is again G minor.

COMMENTS AND RECOMMENDATIONS

This concludes a monumental piece of choral music of approximately fifty minutes in length, which has held the admiration and esteem of scholars and historians for more than two centuries. Without doubt, it is one of Handel's most fervent and sensitive musical expressions. In spite of its association with one of the saddest occurrences in human existence, there are so many emotional moments expressing love, admiration, even joy, that it is surprising that at least excerpts from this masterpiece are not better known and more often performed by choral musicians today.

The three "solo choruses" (III, Vb, and VIII), either separately or as a group, especially should stand on their own as concert pieces. They rightfully deserve to be an important segment of the choral repertory. "The Righteous Shall Be Had in Everlasting Remembrance" should occupy a significant place among church-choir anthems, as it is particularly appropriate for memorial services. The same may be said of "They Shall Receive a Glorious Kingdom," which some will relate, at least textually, to the "In paradisum" from Fauré's *Requiem.* The opening chorus, "The Ways of Zion Do Mourn," preceded by the sinfonia, and concluding with the wonderfully climactic fugue on the text "She put on righteousness," makes an ideal "centerpiece" of approximately fifteen minutes for a concert program. This musical unit contains lyrical, expressive melodic lines, contrasting dramatic rhythms, and eloquent counterpoint; it rises from a slow, ominous beginning to a thrilling climax.

Movement IVa, with its intense, emotional choral recitative, "How Are the Mighty Fall'n!" is also an appealing possibility when combined with the charmingly poignant "She Delivered the Poor That Cried" (IVb). This contrasting musical unit may also take its place on concert programs. It offers intense, eloquent harmonies in the recitative, followed by a quaintness, even a sweetness, in the chorale fantasia. The antiphonal character of the two-part chorale setting of this movement displays some of Handel's most exquisite choral writing. Let me urge more frequent performances of The Funeral Anthem for Queen Caroline. If a full presentation is not possible, rather than letting the work lie dormant because of its length, one may well consider judiciously selected excerpts.

AVAILABLE PERFORMING EDITIONS

At this time two recently published piano-vocal scores of the Funeral Anthem are available; both use the title "The Ways of Zion Do Mourn." One is edited by Watkins Shaw and is published by Novello; the other, by William Herrmann, is published by G. Schirmer. Both editions receive the benefit of modern historical research and an expert knowledge of Baroque performance practices. Unfortunately, at this date, neither publisher has seen fit to provide an accompanying choral-orchestral score; a full score and parts that can be adapted to these editions, however, is available from Edwin F. Kalmus Co., Inc. Hopefully, we may soon look forward to a complete edition published in the *Hallische Händel-Ausgabe*. A second full score with orchestral parts, based on the Chrysander edition of Handel's complete works, vol. 11, is available from Breitkopf & Härtel and Broude Brothers. A nineteenth-century edition of a piano-vocal score, in which three movements have been abbreviated (IV, VII, and IX), is also available through Belwin-Mills Publishers.

A unique edition of the Funeral Anthem appeared in Germany in 1954, edited by Herbert Reich, with the title, *Trauer Hymne*. Part I employs the text of the Latin Requiem, interspersed with German quotes from the traditional funeral service. In addition, it interpolates appropriate chorales between movements in the manner of German Passions. Apparently the object of the edition was to make the work more appealing for general use, and for this reason, all references to Queen Caroline are eliminated. This adaptation is published by Hänssler-Verlag.

BIBLIOGRAPHY

Aspects of Baroque performance practice, including notation, ornamentation, and rhythmic alteration and assimilation are subjects that the enterprising conductor will pursue when preparing a work of Handel for performance. A limited selection of books and articles has been prepared to give a historical perspective and provide a basic knowledge of performance problems that must be solved by the conductor preparing his choir to sing Handel's Funeral Anthem for Queen Caroline.

History and Biography

Burney, Charles. *An Account of Musical Performances in Westminster Abbey.* London: T. Payne and Son, 1785; reprint ed., Amsterdam: F.A.M. Knuf, 1964.

Burney, Charles. *A General History of Music . . . .* London: 1776-89; reprint ed., New York: Harcourt and Brace, 1935.

Deutsch, Otto. *Handel, a Documentary Biography.* New York: W.W. Norton, 1955.

Flower, Newman. *George Frideric Handel, His Personality and His Times.* London: 1923. Revised ed., New York: Scribner's Sons, 1948.

Hawkins, Sir John. *A General History of the Science and Practice of Music.* London: 1776; reprint of the 1853 edition, New York: Dover, 1963.

Hogwood, Christopher. *Handel.* New York: Thames and Hudson, 1984.

Landon, H. C. Robbins. *Handel and His World.* Boston: Little and Brown, 1984.

Lang, Paul Henry. *George Frideric Handel.* New York: W.W. Norton, 1966; reprint ed., 1977.

Larsen, Jens Peter. *Handel's Messiah: Origins, Composition, Sources.* London: Adam and Charles Black, 1957.

Sadie, Stanley. *Handel.* London: John Calder, 1962.

Streatfield, Richard A. *Handel.* London: 1909; reprint ed., New York: Da Capo Press, 1964.

Performance Practice

Arnold, Frank T. *The Art of Accompaniment from a Thorough-Bass as Practiced in the XVIIth and XVIIIth Centuries.* London: Holland Press, 1931; reprint ed., New York: Dover, 1965.

Dart, Thurston. *The Interpretation of Early Music.* New York: Harper and Row, 1964; reprint ed., London: Faber and Faber, 1967.

Donington, Robert. *A Performer's Guide to Baroque Music.* New York: Scribner's Sons, 1973; reprint eds., 1975 and 1978.

Donington, Robert. *Baroque Music: Style and Performance.* New York: W.W. Norton, 1982.

Dolmetsch, Arnold. *The Interpretation of Music of the XVIIth and XVIIIth Centuries Revealed by Contemporary Evidence.* London: Novello, 1915; new ed., New York: H.W. Gray, 1946; reprint ed., St. Clair Shores, MI: Scholarly Press, 1976.

Quantz, Johann Joachim. *Versuch einer Anweisung die Flöte traviersière zu spielen* (1752); Reilly, E.R., trans. *On Playing the Flute.* New York: Free Press, 1966.

Shaw, Watkins. *A Textual and Historical Companion to Handel's Messiah.* London: Novello, 1965.

Periodicals

American Choral Review. New York: American Choral Foundation, 1958-; Research Memorandum, Series, 1959-.

Choral Journal. Lawton, Oklahoma: American Choral Directors Association, 1959-.

Journal of the American Musicological Society. Richmond, Virginia: American Musicological Society, 1948-.

Music and Letters. London: Oxford University Press, 1920-.

The Musical Quarterly. New York: G. Schirmer, 1915-.

Dennis Shrock

Aspects of Performance Practice
During the Classical Era

INTRODUCTION

While concern for performance practices in the music of the Baroque era has been widespread for approximately a decade, such issues as affect the performances of music of the Classical era only recently have received attention. And, while the concern for Baroque music has addressed such practical topics as rhythmic alteration (double dotting or overdotting) and ornamentation, only matters of instrumentation—specifically, the use of original or authentic reproductions of period instruments—have been considered in regard to Classical music. Early instruments demonstrate much about the practices of the time; their timbres and technical attributes provide insight into phenomena such as volume and pitch levels, ensemble balance, and articulation. But the use of early instruments does not necessarily assure appropriate performance practices, and such practices do not depend solely upon the use of early instruments. The conventions of performance are inextricably bound to a proper understanding of notation, and it is the manner in which notation is conceived, and then manifested in sound, that determines the appropriateness of performance practice.

Dennis Shrock is Director of Choral Activities at the University of Oklahoma, director of the Canterbury Choral Society, and choral director for the Oklahoma Symphony. He studied at Westminster Choir College (B. Mus. Ed.), Oberlin Conservatory, and Indiana University (M.M. and D.M. degrees). Before assuming his duties at the University of Oklahoma, he served as head of the undergraduate conducting department at Westminster.

Dr. Shrock is active as an editor of choral works, as a clinician for choral workshops and festivals, as a lecturer in the area of style and repertoire, and as a teacher of conducting technique and rehearsal procedures. He serves on the editorial board of the Choral Journal.

Notation has constituent elements which may be defined and analyzed separately, and which, considered individually, may demonstrate the diversity of representations possible with each element. Sound quality, phrasing and articulation, accentuation, meter and tempo, melodic and rhythmic form, and expression all are characteristics that are determined by particular conventions of notation. The twentieth-century view of these characteristics represents one convention, but only that applicable to the music written during its practice. The eighteenth-century view of the characteristics of notation was in many ways quite different. We know this from numerous primary sources—accounts by composers, performers, teachers, and observers—that give detailed descriptions of the eighteenth-century manner of music in performance.

It is my hope that with the following consideration of these aspects of notation, the modern performer, motivated and supported by actual practices of Classical musicians, may have tangible guidelines for the realization of the aspects of performance intrinsic to the music of the Classical era.

SOUND QUALITY

Although it may be argued that all elements of music in performance contribute to a definable quality of sound, there are certain elements which have a direct influence on timbre and which, I believe, influence it more specifically than others. I begin the discussion of performance practice with the subject of sound quality, even though it is perhaps the most subjective of the elements to be discussed, because it is the element which, considered before the others, can best allow for a proper understanding and execution of the other elements. I have found that the appropriate conception of sound creates a logical and supportive foundation for all elements of musical performance, each assisting the accomplishment of the other, and each consistent with principles of the other.

When one considers its constituent elements, sound quality is not as subjective a factor as one might assume. Amplitude, registration, physical techniques, mechanical construction, pitch levels and fluctuation, and instrumentation all provide details that can be manipulated to produce timbres of sound appropriate to a particular stylistic era. Certain adjectives can even be of considerable aid in describing, hence reproducing a particular sound quality. Türk says that "A beautiful tone must be clear, full, supple, bright, and above all, agreeable; it follows that

it should not be harsh at even the highest degree of loudness . . . ."[1]
Burney praises a voice for being "clear, sweet, and flexible."[2] Quantz
says that "The chief requirements of a good *singer* are that he have
a good, clear, and pure voice. . . ."[3] There is considerable consistency
amongst the writers of the late-eighteenth and early-nineteenth centuries
in their use of adjectives to describe qualities of sound. The terms "pure"
and "sweet" are the most frequently used, and suggest to us not only
an aural image of tone but also of amplitude.

There are many evidences of and no apparent contradictions to the
use of softness, especially in high registers.

. . . Each singing voice, the higher it goes, should be produced increas-
ingly temperately and lightly. . . .[4]

Let him take care . . . that the higher the Notes, the more it is necessary
to touch them with Softness. . . .[5]

Great care must be taken . . . to attack the high tones with the required
sweetness . . . .[6]

---

[1]This study is based on the examination of the primary sources cited, both in their original
forms and in English translation, where one is available. *In each footnote that follows,
the source cited first is the direct source of the quotation.* In the case of a foreign-
language source cited alone or preceding a published English translation, the translation in the text is by myself. Where a translation is cited first, the quotation is taken
from the translation. In order to provide the reader with the opportunity to see the quotations in context, published English-language translations are always cited, even if the
translation given in the text is mine. Daniel Gottlieb Türk, *School of Clavier Playing,*
trans. Raymond Haggh (Lincoln: University of Nebraska Press, 1982) 354;
Klavierschule, oder Anweisung zum Klavierspielen für Lehrer und Lernende (Leipzig
and Halle: 1789; reprint ed., Kassel: Bärenreiter, 1967) 365.
[2]Charles Burney, *A General History of Music from the Earliest Ages to the Present
Period,* 4 vols. (London: 1789) IV, 736; quoted in Carol MacClintock, *Readings in
the History of Music in Performance* (Bloomington: Indiana University Press, 1979) 262.
[3]Johann Joachim Quantz, *On Playing the Flute,* trans. Edward Reilly (London: Faber
& Faber, 1966) 300; *Versuch einer Anweisung die Flöte traversière zu spielen* (Berlin:
1752; reprint ed., Kassel: Bärenreiter, 1974) 281.
[4]Johann Mattheson, *Der vollkommene Capellmeister,* trans. Ernest C. Harris (Ann Ar-
bor: UMI Research Press, 1981) 266; *Der vollkommene Capellmeister* (Hamburg: 1739;
reprint ed., Kassel: 1969) 111.
[5]Pier Francesco Tosi, *Observations on the Florid Song,* trans. Galliard (London: William
Reeves, 1926) 19; *Opinioni de' cantori antichi, e moderni* (Bologna: Forni Editore,
1723; reprint ed., New York: Broude Brothers, 1968) 35.
[6]Giovanni Mancini, *Practical Reflections on the Figurative Art of Singing,* trans. Pietro
Buzzi (Boston: Gorham press, 1912), quoted in Philip A. Duey, *Bel Canto in its Golden
Age* (New York: Da Capo Press, 1980) 116; *Pensieri, e reflessioni pratiche sopra il
canto figurato* (Vienna: 1774).

Even such a late source as Garcia in 1847 says:

> . . . But frequently the charming softness, so pleasing in the high notes,
> is perversely turned into tormenting yells . . . .[7]

It should be noted here that in 1831, the tenor Gilbert-Louis Duprez
shocked the musical world by singing a full-throated, loud high c' (closer
to our high b flat') in Rossini's *Guillaume Tell*. The composer observed:

> I don't like unnatural effects. It strikes my Italian ear as having a stri-
> dent timbre. . . . Nourrit [the tenor whom Rossini liked] had been satisfied
> with a head-tone C, which was what was required.[8]

This mention by Rossini of head voice is not uncommon. There are
many contemporary references to it; called *falsetto, voce di testa,* or
feigned voice, it was in common usage until the mid-nineteenth century.

References to sound timbre are not restricted to descriptions of the
voice. Sources discussing instruments use terms very similar to those
already mentioned. Clearly, there was a decided correlation between
vocal and instrumental sound ideals. Quantz, C.P.E. Bach, Tromlitz,
and Mattheson make frequent mention of this correlation, always to
the effect that the model for instrumental sound should be the singer.
"Our model should be the good singer, whom we should all seek to
imitate."[9] "All musical instruments serve only to imitate the human
voice . . . ."[10]

Today, with the availability of early instruments and their sound repro-
duction on stereo recordings, it is an easy task for the performer to
become not only acquainted, but intimately familiar with the sounds
of eighteenth-century instruments. Upon hearing them, one cannot help
but use the same adjectives used by early writers. Combining then the
actual sounds with the verbal descriptions, the performer should em-
pathically sense the fundamental nature of these sounds and strive to
incorporate them into his own sound production. Neither the singer nor

[7]Manuel Garcia, *Hints on Singing,* trans. Beata Garcia (New York: E. Schuberth &
Co., 1894) 16.
[8]Edmond Michotte, *Richard Wagner's Visit to Rossini and an Evening at Rossini's
In Beau Sejour,* trans. Herbert Weinstock (Chicago: University of Chicago Press, 1968)
97-98.
[9]Johann Georg Tromlitz, *Ausfürlicher und gründlicher Unterricht die Flöte zu spielen*
(Leipzig: 1791), quoted in Eileen Hadidian, "Johann Georg Tromlitz's Flute Treatise:
Evidence of Late 18th c. Performance Practice" (Ph.D. dissertation, Stanford University, 1979) 14.
[10]Mattheson, *Capellmeister,* trans. Harris, 264; 109.

the instrumentalist with a modern instrument can imitate the early sound, but each can adopt a manner compatible with it. Moreover, each can adopt a manner compatible with the other.

It is unfortunate when ensembles make only haphazard efforts to produce stylistic timbres by, for example, combining modern full-bodied strings, winds, and brass with a stylish harpsichord or tracker-action organ, or more frequent and glaring, modern full-bodied vocal sounds with an ensemble of early instruments. Of all the elements of performance practice, I believe that sound quality, as it relates to mutually compatible homogeneous timbres among voices and instruments, is the most important.

A caveat and an opportunity present themselves here. The caveat: decreasing the volume of present sounds to produce softer ones may result in a thin quality no more appropriate than that with which one began. Reduction of volume should not be a process but a result. One should realign the fundamental process of sound production, thereby creating a sound complete in its overtone spectrum. The violinist should not play closer to the bridge, he should play with a pre-Tourte bow, or restring his violin with gut strings, or at the least draw his bow across the string in a manner physically empathic with the experience of using an early bow. The singer should not reduce the space within his present-day vocal apparatus, but should form vowels that resonate with purity instead of richness and should position his muscles to make use of a less pressured production.[11] The opportunity: sounds that are not restricted (not less than they might be) allow the performer freedom and flexibility, not only to produce and execute music with a sense of natural ease, but also to perceive the innate expressive qualities of the music.

Once a particular quality of sound has been established, one must consider its pitch level, which creates boundaries of tessitura, and its property of duration—its relative width and speed of vibration or fluctuation. A standardization of pitch was not common until the very late nineteenth century, and then it was not without variation. Even Verdi complained about the problem.[12] In the latter half of the eighteenth century, pitch could vary from about $a'=360$ Hz to $a'=490$ Hz, though both extremes were probably rare and may have required some transposi-

[11]Mauro Uberti, "Vocal Techniques in Italy in the Second Half of the 16th Century," *Early Music* 9 (October 1981) 486-95.
[12]Guiseppi Verdi, "Letter to Cesarino De Sanctis, January 1, 1871," quoted in Ruth Halle Rowen, *Music Through Sources and Documents* (Englewood Cliffs: Prentice-Hall, 1979) 273.

tion up or down to accommodate various instruments in ensemble or the abilities of various singers. From drawings and specifications of existing unaltered organs, from tuning forks, and from existing wind and brass instruments, one can determine with some degree of dependability the general level of pitch during the time of Mozart and Haydn. An a' in the 1770's was likely to be ca. 415 Hz, while an a' in 1800 was likely to be ca. 420 Hz. A tuning fork used by the maker of Mozart's pianofortes is tuned to 421.6 Hz.[13] This is supposedly the pitch at which Mozart's instruments were tuned.

If we use a'=440 Hz as a point of reference, a'=415 Hz is one-half step lower, or a flat'. Since 421 Hz is quite close to 415 Hz, we may thus assume that in general the music of the Classical Era was performed almost one-half step lower than we are accustomed to today. This half-step distance not only creates a difference in timbre, but causes a difference in the playing technique of certain instruments. Violin strings tuned to a'=415 Hz are not as tight as those tuned to a'=440 Hz, even taking into account the shorter bridge of authentic eighteenth-century instruments. Consequently, a difference in articulation exists: the lower-pitched strings do not respond to sharp attacks or to exceedingly fast tempos.

A wide range of timbres may be created by the various fluctuations possible within the duration of pitch. Normally referred to in the twentieth century as "vibrato," this feature of sound quality was called "tremolo" and considered an ornament in the seventeenth and eighteenth centuries.

> The Tremolo is an ornament . . . which can be applied elegantly on a long note, not only by good instrumentalists but also skilled singers . . . . If we forcefully touch a string or a bell we hear after the stroke a wavelike beat . . . . This trembling reverberation is called tremolo or tremoleto.
>
> One would err if one played every note with tremolo. One should apply it at the end of a piece, or . . . at the end of a passage . . . . Thus one can ornament a final note or other long note.[14]

C.P.E. Bach suggests its similar use on the clavichord: "A long, affettuoso tone is performed with a vibrato. The finger that depresses and

[13]Alexander J. Ellis, *The History of Musical Pitch* (Amsterman: Fritz Knuf, 1968) 26.
[14]Leopold Mozart, *Versuch einer gründlichen Violinschule* (Augsburg: 1756; reprint ed., Frankfurt am Main, 1956) 217-18; *A Treatise on the Fundamental Principles of Violin Playing,* trans. Editha Knocker (London: Oxford University Press, 1948) 203-4.

holds the key is gently shaken.''[15] (This is possible on the clavichord while not on a harpsichord or pianoforte.) Burney comments on hearing a singer: ''In . . . slow movements, whenever he had a long note to express, he . . . produce[d] . . . a cry of sorrow and complaint, such as can only be effected on the clavichord. . . .''[16] Spohr in 1832 is still in agreement: ''In the tremolo the deviation from the perfect intonation of the note should be almost imperceptible to the ear. . . . Avoid its frequent use. . . .''[17] Garcia says, ''What is the tremolo? The trembling of the voice. This intolerable fault ruins every style of singing.''[18]

The simultaneous combination of different timbres, (commonly referred to as instrumentation) is another factor which affects quality of sound. The normal late-seventeenth- and early-eighteenth-century orchestra was comprised of ten to twenty violins, two to six violas, two to eight cellos, two to six basses, winds and trumpets in pairs, and a keyboard instrument.[19] Quantz specifies that with eight violins one needs two violas, two cellos, two basses, and two bassoons; with ten violins only an additional cello; with twelve violins one needs three violas, four cellos, two basses, three bassoons, four oboes, four flutes, and two keyboard instruments.[20] Notice the proportion of winds to strings, even in very large eighteenth-century orchestras. The Dresden Opera orchestra in 1732 had only twenty-five strings, but twelve winds; the Mannheim orchestra in 1756 had thirty-two strings and sixteen brass.[21]

All orchestras had at least one requisite keyboard instrument. Quantz says, ''I assume that the *harpsichord* will be included in all ensembles, whether large or small.''[22] C.P.E. Bach says that ''no piece can be well performed without some form of keyboard accompaniment.''[23] Joseph Haydn is reported to have played a keyboard continuo from the bass

[15]Carl Philipp Emanuel Bach, *Essay on the True Art of Playing Keyboard Instruments*, trans. William Mitchell (New York: W.W. Norton & Co., 1949) 156; *Versuch über die wahre Art das Clavier zu spielen* (Berlin: 1753).
[16]Charles Burney, *The Present State of Music in Germany, the Netherlands, and United Provinces* (London: 1775) 270.
[17]Louis Spohr, *Violinschule* (Vienna: 1832), 20; quoted in Robert Donington, *The Interpretation of Early Music* (London: Faber & Faber, 1963; reprint ed., London: Unwin Brothers, 1975) 234.
[18]Garcia, *Hints*, 18.
[19]*The New Grove Dictionary of Music and Musicians*, s.v. ''Orchestra,'' by Jack Westrup with Neal Zaslaw.
[20]Quantz, *On Playing*, 214; *Versuch*, 185.
[21]Louis Adolphe Coerne, *The Evolution of Modern Orchestration* (New York: MacMillan Co., 1908) 45.
[22]Quantz, *On Playing*, 214; *Versuch*, 185.
[23]C.P.E. Bach, *Essay*, 173.

part in his London Symphonies, 1790–1800.[24]

We must, from the preceding information, assume that the music of the late-eighteenth century was characterized by a distinct quality of sound, somewhat different from that generally produced today. It is my hope that modern performers of the music of the Classicists will consider sound timbre as a constituent aspect of performance practice, and adopt the appropriate softer, lower, less pressured, purer, and more homogeneous characteristics set by the vocal and instrumental constraints of the time.

PHRASING AND ARTICULATION

One of the more apparent and easily controllable factors in the performance of musical notation is duration—the length of time individual notes sound. Relative to their value as represented by printed notational symbols, individual notes may be characterized by a variety of lengths of time, and their combination in linear fashion, therefore, by a variety of degrees and qualities of connection or separation. The duration of individual notes was a factor decided by eighteenth-century performers for various musical reasons. The printed note was not necessarily filled with sound; its intrinsic value was not, as is assumed today, the length it occupied between its surrounding notes—quite the contrary was true. The general conception in the eighteenth century was that the printed note was normally shorter than its printed value.

Phrasing is generally understood to be the practice of combining a group of notes into a musical unit. In this regard, a phrase is customarily meant to include more than two notes, a ''group'' being equivalent to a spoken sentence that contains from several to many words. For purposes of performance practice, however, I will include slurring in the consideration of phrasing, since slurring in the eighteenth century was very much a characteristic of phrasing. Slur marks, it must be understood, existed for two purposes: one, to join notes together in a legato fashion, and two, to indicate syllabification in vocal music. The former use of the slur has come to be associated exclusively with instrumental music, though there are notable instances of this ''phrasing'' slur in eighteenth-century vocal music. See, for example, the ''Laudate pueri'' from Mozart's *Vesperae solennes de Confessore, K. V.* 339, or any of approximately two-dozen occurrences in Haydn's *Missa in*

---

[24]*The New Grove Dictionary of Music and Musicians,* s.v. ''Continuo,'' by Peter Williams.

Angustiis, Hob. XXII: 11 (as samples: the soprano part of the "Kyrie," measures 64 and 65, 74 and 75, 77 and 78, 125 and 126, and 141 and 142). This usage of the slur in the vocal music is clearly articulative— joining together some notes while separating others—leading one to assume that the eighteenth-century meaning of the slur was the same whether it was used as an actual phrasing mark or one of syllabification. It is interesting that all instances of vocal slurring conform to patterns of normal accentuation, and support the assumption that notes without or between slurs are generally separated one from another.

Articulation is generally understood to be the quality of attack of individual sounds; the term thus refers to the degree of force which characterizes the inception of individual tones. Articulation, then, obviously incorporates volume and factors of mechanical or physical production (such as diction), but it includes duration as well, for terms such as "staccato" and "legato" are articulation terms.

During the Classical era, the clarity of phrasing (the evident separation between one musical idea and another or between one slur and another) was, I believe, more obvious than it generally is rendered today. This is due partly to the amount of space and the obviousness of that space recommended in the various primary sources, and also due to the soft quality of the ends of slurs. Also, the limitations of the early instruments, which were in large part responsible for the soft timbre generally in favor during the time, suggest a regular practice of beginning sounds more softly than they would become throughout their durations. Leopold Mozart, in his *Violinschule,* says that "every tone, even the strongest attack, has a small if barely audible softness at the beginning of the stroke."[25] Tartini concurs:

> To draw a beautiful tone from the instrument, place the bow on the strings gently at first and then increase the pressure. If the full pressure is applied immediately, a harsh, scraping sound will result.[26]

This general nature of soft articulation is carried further and specified regarding other instruments and the voice in discussions of *messa di voce.* Though specifically an ornament, *messa di voce,* the practice of making a crescendo followed by a diminuendo on a single note, had such widespread usage and influence it served as a general characteristic of articulation.

---

[25]Leopold Mozart, *Versuch,* 102; *Treatise,* 97.
[26]Guiseppe Tartini, "Letter to Signora Maddalena Lombardini, 1760," trans. Charles Burney (London: 1771; reprint ed., London: 1913) 11; quoted in Donington, *Interpretation,* 538.

Geminiani says, "In playing all long Notes the Sound should be begun soft, and gradually swelled till the Middle, and from thence gradually softened till the End."[27] Quantz, speaking to flautists, says:

> If you must hold a long note for either a whole or a half bar, which the Italians call *messa di voce,* you must first tip it gently with the tongue, scarcely exhaling; then you begin pianissimo, allow the strength of the tone to swell to the middle of the note, and from there diminish it to the end of the note in the same fashion. . . .[28]

Mancini, speaking to singers, says:

> Messa di voce describes that action which . . . gives to each long note a gradation, putting in it at the first a little voice, and then with proportion reinforcing it to the very strongest, finally taking it back with the same gradation as used in swelling.[29]

C.P.E. Bach, speaking to keyboard accompanists, says:

> When the principal part has a long held note which according to the rules of good performance, should commence pianissimo, grow by degrees to a fortissimo, and return similarly to a pianissimo, the accompanist must follow with the greatest exactness.[30]

Notice that the recommendations are consistent for the application of *messa di voce* on all long notes, something that suggests a pervasive practice. Quantz even recommends its usage on short notes: "Yet each note, whether it is a quarter note, eighth note, or sixteenth note, must have its own Piano and Forte, to the extent that the time permits."[31]

The intended usage of *messa di voce,* and I believe the implication in the primary sources, is for soloists. No specific mention is made of its use in ensembles. This does not mean that it was absent from ensembles; a practice so extensive could hardly, I am sure, have been absent from this mode of performance. Besides, the germination of the articulation/ornament is from the philosophy of timbre related to the mechanics of the instruments. My assumption is that a modicum of *messa*

[27]Francesco Geminiani, *The Art of Playing on the Violin* (London: 1751), ed. David Boydon (London: Oxford University Press, n.d.) 2.
[28]Quantz, *On Playing,* 165; *Versuch,* 140.
[29]Mancini, *Pensieri,* 76; *Practical Reflections on Figured Singing* (Vienna: 1774), trans. Edward Foreman, *Masterworks on Singing,* vol. 7 (Champaign: Pro Musica Press, 1967) 44.
[30]C.P.E. Bach, *Essay,* 371.
[31]Quantz, *Versuch,* 140; *On Playing,* 166.

di voce was practiced by performers in ensembles as a consistent quality for all notes of length; soloists merely practiced it to a much greater extent.

Still another aspect of the soft sound character idealized by the Classicists is expressed in instructions referring to the ends of phrases and slurs. Türk says that "the end of the phrase is rendered more noticeably by gently lifting the finger from the key . . . ."[32] Tromlitz says that "slurring is responsible for the fact that the second note is often very unclear and at times inaudible . . . ."[33] Leopold Mozart further clarifies: "The first of two slurred notes should be stressed . . . by playing it louder; . . . the second note should be joined to it softly. . . ."[34] This integration of dynamic expression into slurring is notably absent from most present-day performances. By maintaining a flow of amplitude which expresses long phrases and phrase groups, the modern performer loses a clarity of detail and an intended aspect of eighteenth-century music.

Clarity of phrases was important to the Classicists. Garcia, as late as 1846, says in specific reference to the slur, "Where notes are united in groups,

the last note of the group must be quitted as soon as intonated."[35] Rousseau says that one should make perceptible

> the separation of the phrases in such a manner that one feels in their inflection as well as in their cadences the beginning, fall, and greater or lesser connections just as one feels all of these with the help of punctuation in speech.[36]

Quantz advises that "the end of what goes before, and the start of what follows, should be well separated. . . ."[37]

This aspect of separation needs to be considered along with what was assumed to be a normal detachment of individual notes. The Classical

---

[32]Türk, *Klavierschule*, 341; *School*, 330.
[33]Tromlitz, "Flute Treatise," 23.
[34]Leopold Mozart, *Versuch*, 135; *Treatise*, 123-24.
[35]Garcia, *Hints*, 31.
[36]Jean-Jacques Rousseau, *Dictionnaire de musique* (Paris: 1768; reprint ed., New York: Johnson Reprint Corp., 1969) 370-71; quoted in Hermann Keller, *Phrasing and Articulation* (New York: W.W. Norton & Co., 1965) 19.
[37]Quantz, *Versuch*, 104-5; *On Playing*, 122.

musician considered the usual flow of rhythm to be much less legato than the twentieth-century musician does. The most obvious and consistent practice of this was evident in conventions of keyboard performance, and was called *normal touch.* Marpurg says that

> in contrast to legato and staccato is the ordinary style of playing in which the finger is lifted from the key just before the following note is played. This ordinary style, being always taken for granted, is never marked . . . . Playing in the ordinary manner . . . means that the notes are held for slightly less than their full value . . . . If certain notes should be held for their full value, *ten,* or *tenuto* is written above them . . . .[38]

Türk is in concert with this when he says that "For tones which are to be played in customary fashion · · · the finger is lifted a little earlier from the key than is required by the duration of the note."[39] Dom Bedos de Celles speaks generally:

> All the notes, in execution, whether ornamented or not, are partly in *hold* and partly in *silence;* which means that they all have a certain length of *sound* and a certain length of *silence,* which united make the whole value of the note.[40]

C.P.E. Bach goes further by saying that "Tones which are neither detached, connected, nor fully held are sounded for half their value . . . ."[41] This seemed to Türk to be too defined and extreme. He wrote, in direct reference to the C.P.E. Bach statement:

> Taken in general, this kind of playing does not seem to me to be the best. For 1) the character of a composition necessitates a variety of restrictions in this respect; 2) the distinction between the tone which is actually detached and that which is to be played in the customary manner is practically abolished; and 3) the execution would probably become too . . . [choppy] if every note not slurred was held for only half of its value . . . .[42]

[38]Friedrich Wilhelm Marpurg, *Anleitung zum Clavierspielen* (Berlin: 1765; reprint ed., New York: Broude Brothers, 1969) 28-29; quoted in Elizabeth Loretta Hays, "F.W. Marpurg's *Anleitung zum Clavierspielen (Berlin: 1755) and Principes du Claveçin (Berlin: 1756): Translation and Commentary,* vols. 1 and 2 (Ph.D. dissertation, Stanford University, 1977) VII, 9-10.
[39]Türk, *School,* p. 345; *Klavierschule,* 356.
[40]Dom Bedos de Celles, *L'art du facteur d'orgues* (Paris: 1766-78) 18; quoted in Arnold Dolmetsch, *The Interpretation of the Music of the Seventeenth and Eighteenth Centuries* (London: Oxford University Press, 1946) 282.
[41]C.P.E. Bach, *Essay,* 157.
[42]Türk, *School,* 345-46; *Klavierschule,* 356.

All writers agree, however, that "If the composer wants to have notes articulated as a unit, he must put a slur over them."[43] In general, however, it seems that, without markings to the contrary, the durational value of the notation is less than it appears. Czerny, writing in 1842 when the articulation had become more legato, said that

> Beethoven . . . insisted on legato technique, which was one of the unforgettable features of his playing; at that time all other pianists considered that kind of legato unattainable, since the *hammered, detached* staccato technique of Mozart's time was still *fashionable.*"[44]

> A clear . . . style [was] more inclined to *staccato* than to *legato.* . . .The pedal [was] hardly ever used and never necessary."[45]

This *normal touch* was not limited to keyboard performance: Tromlitz refers to a similar concept in flute playing, and likewise Leopold Mozart with regard to the violin. Clearly then, some discernable quality of separation characterized the performance of instrumental music in general—that is, as already noted by Tromlitz, unless notes were connected by slurs. "In [slurred passages] the fingers should remain on the keys for the entire value of the notes in order to avoid even the slightest separation between them."[46]

Styles of musical expression had a bearing on articulation and many, like Tartini, advise a more connected or legato articulation for expressive reasons:

> In performance it is important to distinguish between cantabile and allegro music. In cantabile passages the transition from one note to the next must be made so . . . no interval of silence is perceptible between them; in allegro passages, on the other hand, the notes should be somewhat detached.[47]

C.P.E. Bach says the same: "In general, the briskness of allegros is expressed by detached notes and the tenderness of adagios by broad, slurred notes . . . even when . . . not so marked."[48]

[43]Tromlitz, "Flute Treatise," 18.

[44]Carl Czerny, "Recollections from My Life," (M: 1842), *Musical Quarterly* 42 (July 1956) 307.

[45]Carl Czerny, *Pianoforte Schule* (London: 1839), quoted in Fritz Rothschild, "Mozart's Pianoforte Music," *The Score*, no. 9 (September 1954) 4.

[46]Türk, *Klavierschule*, 355; *School*, 344.

[47]Guiseppi Tartini, *Traité des agréments de la musique* (Paris: 1771), trans. Cuthbert Girdlestone (Celle und New York: Hermann Moeck, 1961) 55.

[48]C.P.E. Bach, *Essay*, 149.

Specific references to qualities of articulation for vocalists, other than the *messa di voce*, are mostly in the manner of admonitions not to break a phrase in the middle of a word and not to use the tongue or chin to aid in fast passage-work. Petri says not to aspirate the sound of an "h" in order to produce each sound in fast passage-work, but does admit that

> when in rapid and running passages the short notes proceed uninterruptedly for so long a time that it would be impossible to execute them all with a single breath, then one can at times leave out one or two short notes and feign short rests.[49]

This sort of recommendation occurs in the nineteenth century also.

It is difficult to discern the exact physical means by which fast passage-work was to be accomplished. In the Baroque era, *passaggi,* such as were used for ornamentation, and melismas, such as are found in the music of J.S. Bach and Handel, were apparently produced by movements in the throat. Mersenne says that "ornaments are the most difficult of all things to do in singing, because it is necessary only to beat the air of the throat without the aid of the tongue . . . ."[50] Many writers refer to the throat, and none to the chest or stomach for articulation until the late eighteenth century; and then the practice is qualified as seen in the following statement by Quantz.

> A singer who articulates all fast passage-work from the chest can hardly produce it as quickly as one who produces it in the throat, although the former method, because of its distinctness, is always superior to the latter, particularly in large places.[51]

In another place, however, he says, "every note of passage-work . . . for the voice must be performed distinctly and stressed by a gentle breath of air from the chest. . . ."[52]

Though it is difficult to determine exactly what is meant by "the throat" and "the chest," I believe that the basic articulation used by the vocalists in the Classical era was, in keeping with the general soft timbre of the time, light. Moreover, I believe that the articulation of vocal and instrumental performers was compatible in technical produc-

---

[49]Johann Samuel Petri, *Anleitung zur practischen Musik, vor Neuangehende Sänger und Instrumentspieler* (Lauben: 1767) 192; quoted in Philip A. Duey, *Bel Canto in its Golden Age* (New York: De Capo Press, 1980) 82.
[50]Marin Mersenne, *Harmonie universelle* (Paris: 1635); quoted in MacClintock, *Readings,* 171.
[51]Quantz, *On Playing,* 287; *Versuch,* 266.
[52]Ibid, *On Playing,* 124; *Versuch,* 45.

tion and aural effect. Each of the aspects of both phrasing and articulation as presented in primary sources reinforces and clarifies the other; the application of one is helpful to the application of the other, so that soft attacks and releases, *messa di voce,* slurring, *normal touch,* and expressive caesuras all combine in a unified and musically logical manner of execution.

ACCENTUATION

In the entry titled "Performing Practice" in *The New Grove Dictionary of Music and Musicians,* it is stated "that there is no 'lost tradition' separating the modern performer from the music of Haydn, Mozart and their successors comparable with that which separates him from Machaut, or even from Monteverdi."[53] Though the statement is clearly relative—comparing traditions of earlier to more-recent times—it is misleading because it implies that present-day performers are in the same realm of tradition as Mozart and Haydn, tradition being defined in further sentences as contact with the repertoire and the instruments of the time. Tradition in connection with the meaning of notation is not mentioned. It is assumed, as is often the case today, that the conception of notation in the music after 1750 is relatively the same as it is today.

Such is not the case. Accentuation, the rendering of sounds with greater or lesser emphasis, is a lost tradition. The word "accentuation" has even become obscure—unfamiliar to most contemporary performers. Throughout the eighteenth and nineteenth centuries, however, the word was in prevalent use and its meaning clearly understood.

> In Common Time, remember well by Heart,
> The first and third is the accented part;
> And if your music Tripla-Time should be,
> Your Accent is the first of ev'ry three.[54]

In every musical measure, each note received a stress relative to its metric placement. On one level (that described by Tans'ur in the preceding quotation), a heirarchy of stress was determined by the beats;

---

[53]*The New Grove Dictionary of Music and Musicians,* s.v. "Performing Practice," by Howard Mayer Brown and James W. McKinnon.

[54]William Tans'ur, *A Musical Grammar and Dictionary: or a General Introduction to the Whole of Music* (London: c. 1819) 27-28; quoted in George Houle, "The Musical Measure as Discussed by Theorists from 1650 to 1800" (Ph.D. dissertation, Stanford University, 1960) 265.

on another level, the design was governed by the notes within the beats; on yet another level, it was the phrase, or articulation markings, word declamation, and subjectively expressive factors. Each of these situations or reasons gave shape to music so that no two successive notes had the same force of weight. The following quotations from a variety of primary sources will address the common considerations affecting accentuation, from the most obvious and regular emphasis of beats and notes within beats, to the most subtle and varied emphasis of notes affected by certain musical circumstances.

> When in a succession of several tones of apparently the same duration, some of these are given more emphasis than others in a certain mantained (uniform) order, there then arises through these accents the sensation we call meter . . . .

> Every measure has good and bad parts. This means although all quarter notes are equal according to their outer value or duration, . . . there is more emphasis on one . . . than upon another.[55]

> Generally the accent . . . or the stress of tone falls on the ruling or strong beats [which] are as follows: In every bar, the first note of the first quarter, the first note of the half-bar or third quarter in ⁴⁄₄ time; the first note of the first and fourth quarters in ⁶⁄₄ and ⁶⁄₈ time; [etc.].[56]

> Of the different beats of a measure, there are some more prominent, more marked than the others, though of equal duration: The *beat* that is more marked is called *strong beat*: that which is marked less is called *weak beat*. The strong beats are the first in two-beat measures, the first and third in three- and four-beat measures. The second beat is always weak in all measures, and it is the same with the fourth in the four-beat measure.[57]

[55]Türk, *Klavierschule*, 88, 91; *School*, 88, 90.
[56]Leopold Mozart, *Versuch*, 257; *Treatise*, 219-20.
[57]Rousseau, *Dictionnaire;* quoted in George Houle, "The Musical Measure," 259.

Beat divisions are also not regarded as having the same internal value, for in duple figures the first, third, fifth, and seventh, and in triple figures the first, fourth, seventh, and tenth members are strong or accented, the others weak or transitory. The same is true for smaller note values.[58]

If any one of them [the beats] is divided, the first note of every division also is accented a little.[59]

If, however, these notes [beats] are divided into smaller values, such as quarter notes in Alla breve time, for example, the first note of the second time-unit receives more emphasis and the quarter notes themselves behave like time-units . . . .

If the bar is divided into still smaller values such as eighth notes, each of these will have a different degree of emphasis . . . .

How to play these notes with respect to their different weight and to the accents placed on them will easily be understood from what has been said about duple time . . . . In fast movements, or in time signatures where the number of notes can be divided by three, such as $\frac{12}{8}$ or $\frac{6}{4}$ and in all similar cases, the first note of three is invariably emphasized, and the emphasis on the other time-units depends on whether they are even or uneven . . . .[60]

---

[58]Türk, *School*, 91; *Klavierschule*, 91.
[59]Augustus Frederic Christopher Kollmann, *An Essay on Musical Harmony* (London: 1796) 73; quoted in George Houle, "The Musical Measure," 260.
[60]Johann Georg Sulzer, *Allgemeine Theorie der schönen Künste* (Leipzig: 1771-74) 498-99.

As necessary as it is to place an emphasis on the first tone of a section or phrase member, it is also important to keep the following limitation in mind: only the first tone that falls on a strong beat must be so stressed. The beginning tone of every period and the like must be given an even more marked emphasis than an ordinary strong beat. Strictly speaking, these beginning tones are themselves stressed to a larger or smaller part of the whole, that is, after a full cadence, the beginning tone (of the following section) must be more strongly marked than after a half cadence, or merely after a phrase division, etc. . . .

One must observe a slight stress (hardly noticeable) on the first note under a slur. In example (g) this light stress . . . is on the notes marked: + , even though they are weak notes; in example (h) it is on F-sharp, D, B, etc. The notation in (k) indicates that all notes are slurred but with a gentle stress on the first, third, fifth and seventh notes.[61]

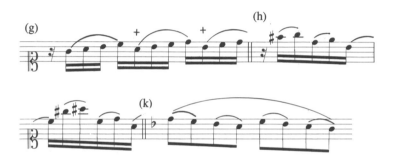

Much was written in the eighteenth and nineteenth centuries about accentuation. Indeed, no other subject of performance practice was discussed more frequently or thoroughly. Dr. Donald Trott, in a study titled "Patterns of Accentuation in the Classical Style as Supported by Primary Sources and as Illustrated in the Late Masses of Joseph Haydn," has collected writings on the subject by thirty-six authors.[62] Each provides consistent support for the theories of the others, thereby demonstrating apparently widespread and basically uniform practice. Differences of thought occur only as to the relative audible presence or emphasis of the stresses. Holden says that though "there is a certain emphasis or

[61]Türk, *Klavierschule,* 336-37, 355; *School,* 325-26, 344.
[62]Donald Trott, "Patterns of Accentuation in the Classical Style as Supported by Primary Sources and as Illustrated in the Late Masses of Franz Joseph Haydn" (DMA document, University of Oklahoma, 1984).

accent laid on the beginning of every measure, . . . there is no occasion to make [it] always stronger, or louder than the rest . . . ."[63] And Kirnberger says:

> If one hears a succession of equal pulses that are repeated . . . experience teaches us that we . . . divide them metrically in our minds . . . in such a way that we put an accent on the first pulse of each group or imagine hearing it stronger than the others.[64]

Holden and Kirnberger are alone in this particular viewpoint. Not one of the other thirty-four authors questions the actual existence of emphasis. One author, Koch, speaks about its exaggerated practice:

> Don't misunderstand this expression "weight" or "emphasis" and believe that I would apply the word to that bad kind of string playing which gives a very strong emphasis with the bow in spite of the fact that the notes themselves contain the actual division of beats (implied by emphasis), and plays the other notes, lacking this inner accent, so lightly that the consequent performance proceeds by a kind of hobble.[65]

From the mid eighteenth century to the very early nineteenth century, one can see a trend away from regularity and sameness in the degrees of emphasis, to variety and actual difference. None of the early- or mid-eighteenth-century authors speaks of one strong beat being more emphasized than another (though they sometimes imply complex gradations by relating musical accentuation to oratory). Leopold Mozart is the first to say that strong beats are louder than strong notes within the beats. After him, most of the others state it also. Kirnberger says that "of the accented beats [in quadruple meter], the first is in turn stressed more than the third . . . ."[66] Hereafter, this was to become standard practice. Sulzer speaks of an occasional displacement of accent:

> When speaking of the triple meter, . . . it must be noted that the second beat can also be . . . long, [stressed], but only in the case when the caesura

[63]John Holden, *An Essay towards a Rational System of Music* (Glasgow: 1770) 32-33; quoted in George Houle, "The Musical Measure," 186.

[64]Johann P. Kirnberger, *The Art of Strict Musical Composition*, trans. David Beach and Jurgen Thym (New Haven: Yale University Press, 1982) 383; *Die Kunst des reinen Satzes in der Musik*, 2 parts (Berlin & Königsberg, 1774-79), part 2, 105.

[65]Heinrich Christoph Koch, *Versuch einer Anleitung zur Composition*, 3 vols. (Leipzig: 1782-93), vol. 2, p. 280 (footnote); quoted in George Houle, "The Musical Measure," 254.

[66]Kirnberger, *Composition*, 392.

falls on the first beat, as here.

Mur - re   nicht, Lie - ber   Christ:

But if the tempo is fast or if the beat consists of tripled divisions, . . . then the triple always has the first quality, which is to say — ∪ ∪ .[67]

Türk adds to this

> those which fall on a strong beat or on an important part of the measure, the beginning tones of sections . . . and phrase members, . . . appoggiaturas, . . . dissonances, . . . and syncopation.[68]

And Burney suggests an emphasis to the third beat in triple time:

> Musicians have long agreed [that] . . . in triple time, . . . the *first* note and the *last* are accented, the *second* unaccented. . . . If the *third* note in triple time is accented in serious music, it is always less forcibly marked than the first.[69]

Callcott agrees: "The Measures of Triple Time consist of three parts; the first *strong,* the two others *weak*: although the last part is rather *strong* in comparison of the Middle part."[70]

None of the authors states or even implies that any level of accentuation (of the beat, within the beat, of articulation markings, or of phrases) minimizes or replaces any other level. They simply acknowledge an increasing number of factors and a variety of gradations of emphasis, each new consideration of accentuation being added to the existing list of factors. It was not until the second half of the nineteenth century that regular emphasis of the beat became undesirable. Richard Wagner, speaking of a performance of the Overture to Weber's *Der Freischutz*

[67]Sulzer, *Allgemeine,* 499.
[68]Türk, *Klavierschule,* 336; *School,* 325-326.
[69]Charles Burney, Music Articles in the *Cyclopedia: or Universal Dictionary of Arts, Sciences and Literature,* ed. A. Rees, 45 vols. (London: 1819), vol. 1: *Accent;* quoted in George Houle, "The Musical Measure," 259-60.
[70]John Wall Callcott, *A Musical Grammar* (London: 1806) 41; quoted in George Houle, "The Musical Measure," 246.

in 1864, gives a very clear illustration.[71]

"I arranged with the excellent executants that they were to play
this theme:

legato, and with an equable piano, i.e., without the customary
commonplace accentuation and *not as follows:*

Though Wagner's intent to alleviate metrical accentuation in this passage
is clear, one should not assume that the practice was dead; indeed, its
continued existence is shown by the fact that Wagner had to work against
it. In 1876, Wagner engaged Heinrich Porges to give detailed witness
to the first production of the *Ring* operas. Wagner writes to Porges as
early as 1872,

> I have you in mind for a task which will be of the greatest importance
> to the future of my enterprise. I want you to follow all my rehearsals
> very closely . . . and to note down everything I say, even the smallest
> details, about the interpretation and performance of our work, so that
> a tradition goes down in writing.[72]

Porges detailed all facets of notation, with frequent mention of regular,
acceptable, and desirable metric accentuation.

For twentieth-century performers, so accustomed to equal reitera-
tion of notes or to gradations of emphasis only with regard to phrase
growths, it seems a sacrifice to impart stress to every downbeat, to the
beginning of every slur, or to the first note of groups of notes within
beats. Accentuation at the expense of structural phrasing is, I believe,
not called for. Neither is the reverse: the sacrifice of accentuation for
the sake of phrases. Accentuation, being an integral facet of the entire
subject of composition, provides the music with logic and expressive
nuance.

[71]Richard Wagner, *On Conducting, A Treatise on Style in the Execution of Classical
Music,* trans. Edward Dannreuther (London: William Reeves, 1919) 54.
[72]Heinrich Porges, *Wagner Rehearsing the Ring, An Eye-Witness Account of the Stage
Rehearsals of the First Bayreuth Festival,* trans. Robert Jacobs (London: Cambridge
University Press, 1983) vii.

METER AND TEMPO

Though composers and theorists of the late eighteenth and early nineteenth centuries attempted to indicate tempo with some degree of mathematical precision, and although many of these writers commented upon the importance of performing in a proper tempo, the overwhelming majority of their information conveys an unequivocal practice of tempo variance and fluctuation. Proper tempo was neither a fixed nor a steady rate of speed. It was movement which best expressed the supposed character of a work, section of a work, phrase, or even motif, and in this regard, to the musicians of the time, tempo was flexible and highly expressive.

Given guidelines for the basis upon which relative tempos were determined, followed by an array of musical or technical factors that influenced fluctuation of that speed, I believe the modern performer should be able to gain insight into the musical philosophies and practices of the time. Quantz says that:

> The means I find most serviceable as a guide to establish the tempo . . . . is the pulse beat of the hand of a healthy person.
>
> In regular common [four-four] time:
> *Allegro assai,* one pulse beat for each half note;
> *Allegretto,* one pulse beat for each quarter note;
> *Adagio cantabile,* one pulse beat for each eighth note;
> *Adagio assai,* two pulse beats for each eighth note.
>
> In Alla breve time:
> *Allegro,* one pulse beat for each whole note;
> *Allegretto,* one pulse beat for each half note;
> *Adagio cantabile,* one pulse beat for each quarter note;
> *Adagio assai,* two pulse beats for each quarter note.[73]

Türk, replying directly to Quantz's recommendations, says:

> Even though this manner of measuring has shortcomings, . . . I am still very much inclined to teach beginners to observe it, as it will at least teach them that allegro assai should be played approximately twice as fast as allegretto, etc. . . . .
>
> Compositions in alla breve . . . should be played twice as fast [as compositions in common time] . . . .[74]

[73]Quantz, *Versuch,* 261, 264; *On Playing,* 283, 285-86.
[74]Türk, *Klavierschule,* 111-12; *School,* 108.

Wolf agrees with this proportional valuation. "As to the tempo of our present *Allegretto,* its half note is equivalent to a quarter note of an *Andante.*"[75] Quantz and Marpurg specify a figure of eighty beats per minute for the pulse rate of which they speak, and they use this figure, with its half and double multiples, to give recommended speeds for various tempo terms. Their charts include also M.M. 60 and M.M. 120 as moderately slow and fast tempos respectively. They clearly specify that alla-breve time is twice as fast as common time.

Applied practically, I believe this means that the tempo terms at the beginnings of Mozart's "Ave verum corpus", the "Tuba mirum" portion of the *Requiem,* and the "Overture" of Haydn's *Creation,* apply to the half note (their meters all being alla breve), not the quarter note. The *Largo, Adagio,* or *Andante* terms refer to the speed of the half note, indicating a faster tempo than that which we hear in most modern performances.

Many factors, however, mitigate general recommendations and suggest gradations of tempo not so strictly proportional as the charts indicate. These factors, I believe, are not contradictory to the charts and the general recommendations, or to each other, but are affirmations of the shadings for which the pulse beat is a basis or foundation.

> The skilled player . . . can find the right tempo from the note values, figures, passages and the like. The pace of an allegro with thirty-second notes must not be as fast as that of an allegro containing only eighth notes.[76]

> As to tempo . . . you must judge the requirements of each piece by the individual context. The key and meter throw some light on the subject. A slow piece in two-four or six-eight time is played a little more quickly, and one in Alla breve or three-two time is played more slowly than one in Common or three-four time. . . . The tempo must be set in accordance with the most difficult passage-work. If there are only eighth notes in three-four time, only sixteenth notes in three-eight time, or only eighth notes in six-eight and twelve-eight time, the fast tempo is indicated. But if there are sixteenth notes or eighth-note triplets in three-four time, thirty-second notes or sixteenth-note triplets in three-eight time, or sixteenth notes in six-eight and twelve-eight time, a moderate tempo is indicated . . . .[77]

> The pace of a composition . . . is based on its general content as well

[75]Ernst Wilhelm Wolf, *Musikalischer Unterricht* (Dresden: 1788) 28.
[76]Türk, *Klavierschule,* 111; *School,* 107.
[77]Quantz, *Versuch,* 262-63; *On Playing,* 285-86.

as on the fastest notes and passages contained in it. Passages in the major mode which are repeated in the minor may be taken somewhat more slowly in this repetition, because of the expression.[78]

Every passion and every sentiment—in its intrinsic effect as well as in the words by which it is expressed—has its faster or slower . . . tempo.[79]

The more searching the harmony, the less rapid the tempo, so that the mind has the time to grasp the progression of dissonances and the rapid changes in the modulation. . . .[80]

Special words are written at the start of each piece which are supposed to give its character, such as *Allegro* (lively), *Adagio* (slow) and so forth. But both slow and fast have their gradations, and . . . [tempo] must be inferred from the music itself.[81]

[Tempos] of the same name, as Adagio or Allegro, are swifter in triple than in common time. . . .[82]

An allegro for the church or in ecclesiastical cantatas . . . must be given a far more moderate tempo than an allegro for the theater or in the so-called chamber styles . . . .[83]

The above quotations address themselves to the subject of tempo rate, or to the establishment of a particular speed. The following quotations address themselves to the subject of tempo fluctuation, or alteration within an already established speed.

I do not claim that one should measure off a whole piece according to the pulse beat, for that would be absurd . . . .[84]

It is difficult to specify all the places where quickening and hesitating can take place; nevertheless, I shall seek to make at least some of them known. . . . The tempo is taken gradually slower for tones before certain fermatas, . . . toward the end of a composition (or part of a composition) which is marked diminuendo, . . .[and] for tender . . . or melancholy passages concentrated in one point. Certain thoughts which are repeated in a more intensified manner (generally higher) require the tempo to be increased to some extent. Sometimes when gentle feelings are

[78]C.P.E. Bach, *Essay,* 151, 161.
[79]Kirnberger, *Composition,* 376.
[80]Rousseau, *Dictionnaire,* 210-11; quoted in Leonard Ratner, *Classic Music Expression, Form and Style* (New York: Schirmer Books, 1980) 200.
[81]Leopold Mozart, *Versuch,* 30; *Treatise,* 33.
[82]James Grassineau, *A Musical Dictionary* (London: 1740; reprint ed., New York: Broude Brothers, 1966) 3.
[83]Türk, *Klavierschule,* 111-12; *School,* 107.
[84]Quantz, *Versuch,* 261-62; *On Playing,* 284.

interrupted by a lively passage, the latter can be played somewhat more rapidly. A hastening of tempo may also take place in a passage where a vehement effect is unexpectedly to be aroused.[85]

[Certain sequential passages] can be effectively performed by gradually and gently accelerating, and immediately thereafter retarding.[86]

It is not pretended here that the barrs [sic] . . . should have a constant measure; for the unite [sic] or crotchet [quarter note] may be taken swifter or slower according to the humor. . . .[87]

If it seems that the tempo should be either faster or slower, . . . and that a change is necessary, the change must not be made impetuously and suddenly, but gradually . . . . If a composition is to be performed effectively, it must be played not only in the proper tempo but also in the same tempo from beginning to end, not sometimes fast, sometimes slow.[88]

This final statement by Quantz, in light of the others made by him, does not mean that the internal tempo of a piece must be strict, but that like characters or passages of music are to be performed in like tempos. Quantz clarifies by saying that "to end slower or faster than one began is incorrect . . . ."[89] And C.P.E. Bach concurs:

In affettuoso playing, the performer must avoid frequent and excessive ritards, which tend to make the tempo drag. . . . Every effort must be made despite the beauty of detail to keep the tempo at the end of a piece exactly the same as it was at the beginning.[90]

Tempo rubato was an important form of tempo fluctuation in the seventeenth and eighteenth centuries. It was understood in three ways: first and mainly as a metric nonalignment, the bass line and tempo of a composition remaining steady while the upper line or lines moved in quicker or slower tempo so as not to coincide with the bass; second, as having inverted, which is to say displaced, accents within the measure, this entailing the accentuation of weak beats (see ACCENTUATION); third, as the late Romantic composers understood it, the accelerating and retarding of a portion of the entire texture of a musical compositon. Türk says:

[85]Türk, *Klavierschule*, 371-72; *School*, 360.
[86]C.P.E. Bach, *Essay*, 161.
[87]Roger North, *Musicall Grammarian* (London: 1725), quoted in John Wilson, ed., *Roger North on Music* (London: Novello & Co., 1959) 99.
[88]Quantz, *Versuch*, 256-57; *On Playing*, 279-80.
[89]Ibid., *Versuch*, 256; *On Playing*, 279.
[90]C.P.E. Bach, *Essay*, 161.

The so-called *Tempo rubato* or *robato* (really *stolen* time) I consider the ultimate means available to the performer for expressing his taste and insight. . . . Commonly it is understood as a shortening or lengthening of notes, or the displacement of them. There is something taken (stolen) from the duration of a note and thus another note is given that much more, as in the following examples . . . .''[91]

C.P.E. Bach describes it as ''When the execution is such that one hand seems to play against the bar and the other strictly with it . . . .''[92] W.A. Mozart says:

The fact that I always maintain the beat accurately amazes everyone. They simply cannot understand the idea that the left hand goes on as usual during tempo rubato in an Adagio. They imagine that the left hand always follows along.[93]

Many other writers of the time discussed this concept:

When the Bass goes an exactly regular Pace, the other Part retards or anticipates in a singular Manner. . . .[94]

[Tempo rubato] refers to the procedure in which a solo singer or the performer of a Concerto changes two adjacent notes of the melody . . . .[95]

[Tempo rubato] is a detraction of part of the time from one note, and restoring it by increasing the length of another, or vice versa; so that whilst a singer is . . . singing ad libitum, the orchestra, which accompanies him, keeps the time firmly and regularly.[96]

[91]Türk, *Klavierschule*, 374; *School*, 363.
[92]C.P.E. Bach, *Essay*, 161.
[93]Wolfgang Amadeus Mozart, ''Letter to his father, 1777,'' quoted in Ruth Halle Rowen, *Music Through Sources and Documents* (Englewood Cliffs: Prentice-Hall, 1979) 228.
[94]Tosi, *Observations*, 156; *Opinioni*, 115-16.
[95]Heinrich Christoph Koch, *Musikalisches Lexikon* (Frankfurt am Main: 1802) 1502-3.
[96]Domenico Corri, *The Singer's Preceptor*, (London: 1810; reprint ed., *The Porpora Tradition*, ed. Edward Foreman (Champaign; Pro Musica Press, 1968) 6.

A displacement of values (in melody) which increases the duration of some notes at the expense of others. . . . To render the tempo rubato effective the accompaniment must be kept strictly in time.[97]

It should be understood that matters of *tempo rubato* and other expressive liberties were generally directed towards solo performers. Indeed, the quotations offered here are from primers on the flute, keyboard instruments, and the singing voice (as well as dictionaries). Türk, before all of his comments regarding tempo fluctuation, says, "I am assuming . . . that the means which I am about to describe will only be used when one is playing alone or with a very attentive accompanist."[98] I do not believe, however, that this means that ensembles should perform without any variation of tempo. An aspect of musical expression so important for a performer alone could hardly have been absent for performers in ensemble. Ensembles should also feel the freedom to perform with a modicum of tempo fluctuation, subtle and slight.

MELODIC AND RHYTHMIC FORM

Thus far, our study of performance practices has dealt with pitch as it relates to levels and timbres, and duration as it relates to values of individual notes. The conventions of the late eighteenth and early nineteenth centuries had, in addition, means of altering perceived pitches and rhythms. This alteration was more in the manner of a change of the notation than a perception of it. The performer perceived that the value of a quarter note, for instance, was less than it appeared. He did not perceive the value to be long. But the performer perceived that the proportional value of a sixteenth note following a dotted eighth note (♪. ♪) was as it appeared—3:1. He then altered that value to suit his expressive desires. The perception of duration, or the "normal" manner of treatment was incorporated into the change. (i.e., The dotted quarter note would have been separated from the sixteenth note, no matter how long or short each was.) Consequently, the forms that the pitches or rhythms could assume here are considered under a category different from SOUND QUALITY and PHRASING AND ARTICULATION.

[97]Garcia, *Hints,* 62.
[98]Türk, *School,* 360; *Klavierschule,* 371.

Melodic Form

The term "melodic form" refers specifically to ornamentation. No other manner of pitch alteration seems to have been in practice during the Classical era. Many thorough studies have been devoted to ornamentation, and the subject in its complexity requires more space than is appropriate here, so I will not attempt to discuss the practice in its entire scope. I refer the reader to the Neumann and Dannreuther volumes, which are currently in circulation.[99] The Neumann book covers certain types of ornaments from the beginning of the seventeenth century only until approximately 1780. The Dannreuther book is a collection of quotations from primary sources of the seventeenth to the mid nineteenth centuries.

I shall discuss what I feel is a particularly notable misconception about late-eighteenth- and very-early-nineteenth-century ornamentation—to wit: the appoggiatura. C.P.E. Bach, in his *Versuch,* provides a comprehensive and detailed representation of the types of ornamentation in use during his time. He says:

> All embellishments notated in small notes pertain to the following tone. Therefore, while the preceding tone is never shortened, the following tone loses as much of its length as the small notes taken from it.
>
> Appoggiaturas are among the most essential embellishments.
>
> The usual rule of duration . . . is that they take from a following tone of duple length one-half of its value and two-thirds from one of triple length. In addition the examples of Figure 74 and their executions should be carefully studied.
>
> Appoggiaturas which depart from this rule of duration should be written as large notes.[100]

[97]Garcia, *Hints,* 62.
[98]Türk, *School,* 360; *Klavierschule,* 371.
[99]Frederick Neumann, *Ornamentation in Baroque and Post-Baroque Music* (Princeton: Princeton University Press, 1983) and Edward Dannreuther, *Musical Ornamentation* (London, 1893-95; reprint ed., New York: Kalmus, n.d).
[100]C.P.E. Bach, *Essay,* 84, 87, 90.

Figure 74

Bach does specify, however, variable appoggiaturas—those both longer and shorter than the common rule. Unfortunately, he does not indicate in what musical situations they might be preferable.

Quantz discusses two types of appoggiatura, the *accented* and the *passing*.

> *Accented appoggiaturas* . . . are held for half the value of the following principal note [unless] the note to be ornamented by the appoggiatura is dotted . . . [and therefore] divisible into three parts. The appoggiatura receives two of these parts, but the note itself only one part. Therefore the notes in Fig. 13 are played as illustrated in Fig. 14.

Fig. 13   **Fig. 14**

Passing appoggiaturas occur when several notes of the same value descend in leaps of thirds (see Fig. 5). When performed they are expressed as shown in Fig. 6.

Fig. 5   Fig 6

It is not enough to be able to play the different types of appogiaturas with their proper values when they are marked. You must also know how to add them at the appropriate places when they are not indicated. To learn this, observe the following rule: if a long note follows one or more short ones on the downbeat or upbeat, and remains in a constant harmony, an appoggiatura may be placed before the long note.[101]

Leopold Mozart is in agreement and uses the symbol $\texttt{♪}$ for short, passing appoggiaturas. Türk also agrees, though he does not use the $\texttt{♪}$. Both Mozart and Türk, however, indicate the short appoggiaturas by sixteenth or thirty-second notes. Eighth and quarter notes are used in the examples of long or accented appoggiaturas, which are those still most predominantly used. Türk says:

To appoggiaturas which must only be played short or even shorter than the common rule requires, belong the following: (1) Those which would cause noticeable mistakes in the harmony if they were to receive the note values due them. . . . (2) Those which for various reasons would be too hard and unpleasant if they were given the customary duration.[102]

Geminiani says of the common, accented appoggiatura, that it "is supposed to express Love, Affection, Pleasure, etc. It should be made pretty long, giving it more than half the Length or Time of the Note it belongs to . . . ."[103] A fascinating example of the long appogiatura is given by Joseph Haydn:

The style of singing a recitative, for example,

Quae   me -   ta -   more - pho   - sis

[101]Quantz, *Versuch*, 78-79; *On Playing*, 93-96.
[102]Türk, *Klavierschule*, 228-28; *School*, 219-20.
[103]Geminiani, *Violin*, 7.

must be as follows,

and not,   Quae me - ta -   more - pho   - sis

Quae me - ta - more - pho   - sis

Otherwise the note before the last, the penultimate g¹, would be completely suppressed. And this style is applicable to all other similar cases. [104]

From the above quotes, one should assume that the long appoggiatura—that receiving at least half the value of the note it precedes—was the more common, and the one applied most frequently. The appoggiatura of short duration, taken from the time value of the note it precedes *or* follows, was the exception to the basic rule. I would suggest that the rhythmic value of the note following the appoggiatura, along with the expressive nature of the music, should guide the performer in this choice. The appoggiatura before a half or longer note in a slow tempo (especially if the music is serious), or before notes of equal duration (i.e. ♪♩♩ or ♩ ♩♩) in a fast tempo should be long. The short appoggiatura should be applied when indicated either by ♪ or sixteenth or thirty-second notes in light-hearted music, or in situations where the long appoggiatura clearly produces an adverse effect.

Rhythmic Form

The term "rhythmic form" refers to the shape some notated combinations take that differs from their appearance. Categories of this include: *quantitas intrinseca,* double dotting or overdotting, textural conformity, and recitative.

Quantitas Intrinseca

Quantitas intrinseca can be translated easily as "intrinsic quantity." It refers to the length many notes receive because of their importance—their placement on accented (see ACCENTUATION) parts of the measure. Consequently, the intrinsic or inherent durations of some notes are longer than might ordinarily be the case, or than might be notated. "The different lengths of notes apparently equal, according to their time or value, is called *Quantitas Temporalis Intrinseca,* or the inner duration."[105]

[104]Franz Joseph Haydn, "Letter accompanying the manuscript of his *Applausus Cantata,* 1768," quoted in Ruth Halle Brown, *Music Through Sources and Documents* (Englewood Cliffs: Prentice-Hall, 1979) 225.
[105]Wolfgang Caspar Printz, *Phrynis Mitilenaeus, oder Satyrischer Componist* (Dresden: 1696) 18; quoted in George Houle, "The Musical Measure," 177.

Such duration coincides exactly with the strong or ''good'' beats described in reference to accentuation.

> If the subdivisions of notes are duple, all odd numbered notes 1, 3, 5,
> 7, etc. are considered long and all even numbered notes 2, 4, 6, 8, etc.
> are short.

> If the subdivisions . . . are three in number, the first is long and the
> second and third are short.

> When the first part is silent, the second is long and the third is short.[106]

> There are in every type of meter ''good'' and ''bad'' beats. That which
> is termed ''good'' is longer intrinsically . . . . A beat which is termed
> ''bad'' is shorter intrinsically . . . .[107]

> Of two successive notes of equal appearance and time-value, . . .
> one will always be long and the other short according to their inner value.
> [108]

The actual length of the notes under consideration is questionable. Muffat, representing a late-seventeenth-century view, says that certain notes
within beats in quick tempos are ''altered in the French style, by adding the value of a dot to the odd numbered notes.''[109] It seems, however,
that the lengthening was not so strict during the eighteenth century.

> Whenever possible, principal notes must always be emphasized more
> than passing notes. In addition to this rule, the shortest note values in
> every piece of *moderate tempo,* and even *adagio,* must be played uneven-
> ly although they look alike; so that the attacking notes of every figure,
> namely, the first, third, fifth, and seventh, are held somewhat longer
> than the passing, namely, the second, fourth, sixth, or eighth. But this
> lengthening should not amount to a dot. For example, if the eight
> sixteenth-notes under (k), (m), and (n) below are played slowly with
> the same value, they will not sound as pleasing as if the first and third
> of four are heard a little longer, and with a stronger tone, than the second
> and fourth.

[106]Ibid.; 178.
[107]Marpurg, *Anleitung,* 18; trans. Hays, V 9.
[108]Johann Adam Hiller, *Anweisung zum musikalisch-richtigen Gesänge* (Leipzig: 1774)
47; quoted in Fritz Rothschild, *Musical Performance in the Times of Mozart and
Beethoven* (London: Adam & Charles Black, 1961) 16.
[109]Georg Muffat, *Florilegium secundum* (Passau: 1698), quoted in George Houle, ''The
Musical Measure,'' 212.

Excepted from this rule, however, is first, quick passage-work in a very fast tempo in which time does not permit unequal execution, and in which length and strength must therefore be applied only to the first of every four notes. Also excepted is all quick passage-work for the voice, unless it is slurred. Since every note of this kind of passage-work for the voice must be performed distinctly and stressed by a gentle breath of air, . . . there can be no inequality in them. Further excepted are the notes above which strokes or dots are found [staccato].[110]

[The accented beat of a slur] is not only played somewhat louder, but it is also sustained rather longer, while the second is slurred onto it quite smoothly and quietly and somewhat late.[111]

We know from experience that of two successive notes of equal nature, . . . for example two crochets [quarter notes], one is audibly slightly longer than the other.[112]

The comments about *quantitas intrinseca* decline in the late eighteenth century. Türk, who treats many matters of rhythm in great detail, makes no direct recommendation for lengthening good notes affected by accentuation; he only refers to "inwardly long" notes. No writer after Wolf in 1788 even mentions it. My assumption, therefore, is that while the practice of emphasis in accentuation continued into the nineteenth century, the practice of lengthening declined. Moreover, I believe that none of the note values in the music of the Classical era, except those which are dotted, were lengthened beyond their printed value, but were merely lengthened beyond what might have been their normal articulated value. A pattern of four quarter notes as seen in (a) below might have been rendered as in (b). In light of all the information regarding articulation and accentuation, this seems logical: length of some degree is compatible with emphasis.

[110]Quantz, *Versuch*, 105-6; *On Playing*, 123-24.
[111]Leopold Mozart, *Versuch*, 135; *Treatise*, 123-24.
[112]Friedrich Wilhelm Marpurg, *Kritische Briefe* (1759-63), letter 13, "Von den Verschiedenen Taktarten" (September 15, 1759), 99; quoted in Fritz Rothschild, *Musical Performance*, 16.

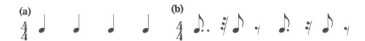

Overdotting

The convention of extending the value of a dotted note is best termed "overdotting" rather than "double dotting," for the precise value of the extension is sometimes more or less than half again the value of the dot. Overdotting has been for many years now an acknowledged aspect of performance practice in music of the Baroque period. Modern performers have not, however, acknowledged the practice in the music of Mozart, Haydn, and other Classicists. The following advice from the late eighteenth century attests to its continuance:

> In dotted eighth, sixteenth, and thirty-second notes, you depart from the general rule [a *dot* standing over a note has half the value of the note it follows], because of the animation that these notes must express. It is important to observe that the notes after the dots in (c) and (d) must be played just as short as those in (e), whether the tempo is slow or fast.

> As a result, the dotted notes in (c) receive almost the time of a full quarter-note . . . . With regard to the length of the dot and the shortness of the first note, . . . where the dot stands after every second note, . . . the notes d' and c' in (a) must be just as short as those in (b), whether the tempo is slow or fast. [113]

> Short notes which follow dotted ones are always shorter in execution than their length. Dots after long notes or after short ones in slow tempos. . . . are all held. However, in rapid tempos, prolonged successions of dots are performed as rests . . . .[114]

---

[113]Quantz, *Versuch*, 58-59; *On Playing*, 67-68.
[114]Leopold Mozart, *Versuch*, 39; *Treatise*, 41.

(a)   (b)

The Short notes which follow dotted ones are always shorter in execution than their notated length.[115]

Dotted notes as in (a) are played as in (b), . . . the dot treated as a rest, and the last note taken shorter than its strict value.[116]

(a)   (b)

Textural Conformity

Another aspect of rhythmic form might be called "textural conformity," one rhythmic configuration—usually a dotted figure as discussed above—to another, prevailing configuration—usually a triplet grouping. "The first two notes of a triplet are always played against the first of the duplet, even if the first of the two binary notes is dotted."[117]

With the advent of an increased use of triplets in common or four-four time, as well as in two-four and three-four, many pieces have appeared which might be more conveniently written in twelve-eight, nine-eight, or six-eight. The performance of other lengths against those notes is shown in Figure 117. [118]

Figure 117

[115]C.P.E. Bach, *Essay*, 157.
[116]Johann Carl Friedrich Rellstab, *Anleitung für Clavierspieler* (Berlin: 1790) 12; quoted in Robert Donington, *The Interpretation of Early Music* (London: Faber & Faber, 1963; reprint ed. London: Unwin Brothers, 1975) 445.
[117]Marpurg, *Anleitung*, 24; trans. Hays, V 25.
[118]C.P.E. Bach, *Essay*, 160.

A different practice is presented by Quantz:

> . . . You must not strike the short note after the dot with the third note
> of the triplet, but after it. . . . If you were to play all the dotted notes
> found beneath the triplets in accordance with their ordinary value, the
> expression would be very lame and insipid, rather than brilliant and ma-
> jestic.[119]

The musical example here appears exactly as it does in the Quantz
Versuch—the sixteenth notes are aligned under the third note of the triplet
figures. Because of this, one might assume that Quantz's reference to
the "ordinary value" of dotted notes means that they were generally
considered as triple valuations. His recommendation then to "strike the
short note after the dot with the third note of the triplet" would seem
to suggest performing the dotted-eighth/sixteenth figure as written. One
might assume, however, that Quantz was literal in his reference to "the
ordinary" or printed value of dotted notes. If so, he would be recommending that the value of the dotted eighth note be longer than written
(perhaps 5/6 of the triplet duration). It is this latter case I find to be
most logical since information concerning *quantitas intrinseca* and overdotting give such consistent advice for extending the value of many dotted
notes beyond their printed value. Indeed, if one combines the advice
given by treatise writers of the time concerning the variable duration
of printed note values (see PHRASING and ARTICULATION), the
flexible treatment of printed rhythmic values through tempo fluctuation (see METER and TEMPO), the alterable length of rhythmic notation in association with metric accentuation (*quantitas intrinseca*), and
the liberties of all these factors idealized by expressive performance
(see EXPRESSION), one cannot but realize that the treatment of dotted rhythmic notes and triplet values against duple ones were also
variable—not necessarily to be performed other than as the rhythm was
printed, and not necessarily shorter *or* longer—merely variable. The
modern performer is free to alter rhythmic figurations to suit his expressive desires. It seems to me that tempo and articulation should be

[119]Quantz, *On Playing,* 68; *Versuch,* 59.

a practical guide: very fast tempos in a normal manner of articulation lend themselves to the Bach practice, while the Quantz is suited to very slow tempos with emphatic articulation.

Recitative

Recitative (secco) has always been considered as a declamatory style, and as such, flexible in tempo. It is more, however; it is flexible in rhythm. The performer is free to alter rhythms to suit purposes of oratorical expression. Actually, the performer's alteration of printed rhythms in recitative is obligatory.

> One does not measure the recitative while singing. Meter, which is in character in the airs, spoils the declamation of recitative. . . . The composer, in notating the recitative with fixed meter, is only attempting to establish a relationship between the basso continuo and the voice part, to indicate only approximately how one must determine the length of syllables and cadences.[120]

> In an Italian *recitative* the singer does not always adhere to the tempo, and has the freedom to express what he is to execute quickly or slowly, as he considers best, and as the words require.[121]

> Some recitatives, in which the bass and perhaps other instruments express a definite theme or a continuous motion which does not participate in the singer's pauses, must be performed strictly in time for the sake of good order. Others are declaimed now slowly, now rapidly according to the content, regardless of the meter, even though their notations be barred.[122]

> [Even though recitative] is noted in true [metered] time, the performer is at liberty to alter the Bars, or Measure, according as his subject requires. . . . [123]

> In addition to free fantasies, cadenzas, *fermatas* and the like, those passages marked *recitativo* must be played more according to feeling than to meter.[124]

---

[120]Rousseau, *Dictionnaire,* 399; quoted in Ruth Halle Rowen, *"Music Through Sources and Documents,"* 197-98.
[121]Quantz, *On Playing,* 292; *Versuch,* 272.
[122]C.P.E. Bach, *Essay,* 421.
[123]John Hoyle, *Dictionarium musica* (London: 1770; reprint ed., New York: Broude Brothers, 1976) 79-80.
[124]Türk, *Klavierschule,* 370; *School,* 359

The duration of the notes that accompany *secco recitative* and the rhythmic placement of cadential chords are determined by the performer and not by the metric notation. Concerning duration:

> In *accompanied recitative* . . . one should write the word *Sostenuto* on all the instrumental parts, especially the bass, which, without this would play only dry and detached strokes on each change of note, as in ordinary recitative.[125]

> In recitatives with sustained accompanying instruments, the organ holds only the bass, the chords being quitted soon after they are struck.

> Even if the score expresses tied white notes, the sharply detached execution is retained.[126]

Note that both references are to accompanied recitatives. C.P.E. Bach's instruction, "The organ holds only the bass," is not meant to be applied, as is sometimes thought, to *secco recitative*. It is only meant to reinforce the intention that no keyboard chords are held, even on the organ, during accompanied recitative. Concerning rhythmic placement of cadential chords, there is recommendation that in operatic or theatrical recitatives of a nature that would warrant fast delivery, the chords ought to be simultaneous with the singing voice.

> In general the bass in all cadences of theatrical recitatives, whether accompanied with violins or plain, must begin its two notes, usually forming a descending leap of a fifth, during the last syllable; these notes must be performed in a lively manner, and must not be too slow.[127]

> When the declamation is rapid, the chords must be ready instantly . . . . These fiery recitatives often occur in operas where the orchestra has a wide range with basses playing *divisi,* while the singer declaims upstage, far removed from his accompaniment. Such being the case, the first harpsichordist, when there are two, does not wait the termination of the singer's cadences, but strikes on the final syllable the chord which should rightly be played later.[128]

This practice seems to be in keeping with earlier eighteenth-century recommendations.

However, in sacred recitatives, the chords ought to be sounded after the voice part has finished singing.

---

[125]Rousseau, *Dictionnaire,* 403-4; quoted in Ruth Halle Rowen, *Music Through Sources and Documents,* 198.
[126]C.P.E. Bach, *Essay,* 422.
[127]Quantz, *On Playing,* 292; *Versuch,* 272.
[128]C.P.E. Bach, *Essay,* 421-22.

> In the accompanied Recitatives, notice that the accompaniment should not enter until after the singer has finished singing the text completely, even though the score often shows the contrary. . . . One must be careful to allow the last syllable of the Recitative to be heard completely and then the accompaniment must come in promptly on the downbeat.[129]

In keeping with many of the previously discussed conventions of performance practice, it seems that the nature and expressive content of the music are the determining factors as to the amount or type of ornamentation or rhythmic alteration. No one solution is appropriate for all works in all situations.

EXPRESSION

The music of the Classical era is not devoid of extra-musical characteristics so often solely associated with Romanticism. Indeed, many of the same characteristics that give Romantic music its quality of aestheticism, and many of the same mannerisms in performance that are considered innate to Romantic music, are also to be seen and utilized in the music of the late eighteenth and very early nineteenth centuries. References to passions and character, and to gradations of volume and tempo impossible to notate, suggest performances one could characterize by no better word than "expressive."

> The performer . . . must spare no pains to discover and deliver correctly the passion that the composer has sought to express. Everything depends upon a [performance] by good players who know how to apply the passion . . . in its proper place, [and know] how to make the greatest possible distinction in the characters. The player has not only to follow closely every marking and direction, and play the work as is written, . . . he has to enter into the passion that is to be expressed.[130]

> Good execution must be *expressive,* and *appropriate to each passion that one encounters* . . . The performer of a piece must seek to enter into the principal and like passions that he is to express. And since in the majority of pieces passions alternate, the performer must know how to judge each passion and constantly make his rendering conform to it. Only then will he do justice to the intentions of the composer, and to the ideas he had in mind while composing. . . . Musical execution may be compared to the delivery of an orator. The orator and the musician have,

---

[129]Haydn, "Letter," 223.
[130]Leopold Mozart, *Versuch,* 252; *Treatise,* 215.

in common, the same aim . . . namely, to make themselves masters of
the hearts of their listeners, to arouse or calm their passions, and to
transport them from one sensation to another.[131]

The application of various degrees of volume represents the most extensive and, I believe, notable of the specific recommendations regarding expresison. I say "notable," because modern performers are in
general quite reticent to employ shadings of loud and soft in music of
the late eighteenth century.

Good expression ought . . . to be *diversified.* Light and shade must continually be kept up. For truly, you will never be affecting if you perform all notes at the same strength or the same weakness; if you perform, so to speak, always in the same color, and do not know how to
bring out and hold back the sound at the proper time. Thus, it is necessary
to introduce a continual interchange of loud and soft.[132]

Of piano and forte. They are both extremely necessary to express the
Intention of the Melody; and as all good Musick should be composed
in Imitation of a Discourse, these two Ornaments are designed to produce the same Effects that an Orator does by raising and falling his
Voice.[133]

Even with the most painstaking markings, it is not possible to specify
every degree of loudness and softness of tone. The many words we have
for this purpose are by far not sufficient to indicate all possible gradations. The player must himself feel and learn to judge what degree of
loudness and softness of tone is required by the character of the music
to be expressed in any given instance.[134]

It is not possible to describe the contexts appropriate to the forte or piano
because for every case covered by even the best rule there will be an
exception.[135]

For perfect precision with respect to forte and piano it is not enough
to make ritornellos loud and to play softly from the point where the voice
begins, . . . one [needs] the finer shadings of the loud and soft.[136]

All who have heard [C.P.E.] Bach playing the clavichord must have been

[131]Quantz, *Versuch,* 100, 107; *On Playing,* 119, 124-25.
[132]Ibid., *Versuch,* 107; *On Playing,* 124.
[133]Geminiani, *Violin,* 7.
[134]Türk, *Klavierschule,* 348; *School,* 338.
[135]C.P.E. Bach, *Essay,* 163.
[136]Johann Friedrich Reichardt, *Briefe eines aufmerksamen Reisenden* (Frankfurt und
Leipzig: 1774), quoted in Oliver Strunk, *Source Readings in Music History* (New York:
W.W. Norton & Co., 1950), 702.

struck by the continual refinement of shadow and light which gives character to his performance.[137]

The signs *f* and *p*, signifying the strong and the weak, do not suffice. Often they are supplied only to prevent gross errors. If they were really to be sufficient, it would be necessary to write them below every note.[138]

Otherwise, there are factors in addition to volume that are varied to give expression to musical performance.

If in an allegro the principal theme frequently occurs, it must always be clearly differentiated in its execution from the auxiliary themes. Whether majestic or flattering, gay or bold, the principal theme can always be made apparent to the ear in a unique manner by the liveliness or moderation of the movements of the tongue, chest, and lips, and also by the Piano and Forte. Generally, the alteration of Piano and Fortes does benefit to repetitions.[139]

Variation of reprises is essential today. Every performer is expected to do it. [In addition] where passages are languishing and sad, the performer must languish and grow sad. When it is lively and gay, the performer must likewise put himself into that mood. It must be realized from the many passions which music depicts that the skilled musician has need of special talents and the ability to use them judiciously.[140]

The player . . . must not only pay the closest attention to the legatos which are written out and indicated, but since in many compositions nothing is indicated at all, he must know how to apply legato and staccato himself in a tasteful manner and in proper places.

The player must be guided by the passion. Sometimes a note requires a rather lively attack, at other times a moderate one, and at still other times one that is hardly perceptible.[141]

Heavy and light execution also contribute a great deal to the expression of the prevailing character. However, it is just as difficult to specify in each instance exactly the necessary heavy or light execution for individual passages or tones as it is to indicate every degree of loudness or softness exactly.

Compositions of an exalted, serious, solemn, pathetic, and similar

[137]Carl Friedrich Cramer, *Magazin der Musik* (Hamburg: 1783-86), 1217; quoted in Robert Donington, *The Interpretation of Early Music*, 490.
[138]Sulzer, *Allgemeine*, quoted in Frederick Dorian, *The History of Music in Performance* (New York: W.W. Norton & Co., 1942), 167.
[139]Quantz, *Versuch*, 115; *On Playing*, 133.
[140]C.P.E. Bach, *Essay*, 152.
[141]Mozart, *Versuch*, 259, 261; *Treatise*, 220, 222.

character must be given a heavy execution . . . . A somewhat lighter and decidedly softer execution is required by compositions of a pleasant, gentle, agreeable character. . . .

Whether a heavy or light execution is to be chosen may also depend upon the tempo. A presto must be played more lightly than an allegro, and this in turn more lightly than an andante, etc.

Meter has a very decided influence on heavy and light execution, or certainly should have. . . . The larger the values of the main beats of a measure, the heavier the execution. Therefore, a composition in three-two time, for example, is played more heavily than it would be if it were in three-four or even three-eight time.

The final and indispensable requisite for good performance . . . is without doubt a personal and genuine feeling for all the emotions and passions which may be expressed in music.[142]

These statements concerning the necessity and variety of expression in musical performance ought to encourage the modern performer to seek to discover more than technical aspects of the music of the late eighteenth and very early nineteenth centuries. One should study the music with an understanding that decisions regarding its technical aspects may have been motivated by expressive reasons. And, one should also be able to detect an innate rationale for and unification of the technical and expressive, each giving support and logic to the other. One should not, however, assume that any quality or quantity of expression is valid. Variety does not give license to the disregard of limits nor to exaggeration; definable qualities and parameters exist. It is the combination of all the factors of performance practice—sound quality, articulation and phrasing, accentuation, meter and tempo, and melodic and rhythmic form—which in their appropriate applications will guide the intrinsic expression.

Finally, all these must be governed by that undefinable quality of taste, which is

The faculty of giving to expression the amount of force, fire, and life proportionate to the intensity of the impression. Practically, the word "style" would be better; it is nothing else but the proper and adequate use of the elements of force, emphasis, accents, nuances, and tempo, according to the structure of a piece or phrase.[143]

[142]Türk, *Klavierschule*, 353, 360; *School*, 342, 348-49.
[143]Charles Avison, *An Essay On Musical Expression*, (London: 1752; reprint ed., New York: Broude Brothers, 1967) 10.

G. Roberts Kolb

The Vocal Quartets of Brahms
(ops. 31, 64, and 92)
A Textual Encounter[1]

Brahms wrote sixty quartets for solo voices and piano (or two pianos).
Of these, eighty percent are either *Liebeslieder* or *Zigeunerlieder*. The
remainder, however, are more heterogeneous. Bound by neither the
common elements of waltz time nor Gypsy folk elements, they express
a variety of different images and emotions. It is with this latter group
that we will be concerned here.

Specifically, we shall look at three *opera* (31, 64, and 92) that contain ten of these twelve quartets, the remaining two having been published
with four *Zigeunerlieder* in op. 112. As we consider briefly each quartet
in turn, our starting point will be the text. One can begin elsewhere,
of course, by centering one's analysis on harmonic, formal, or motivic

---

[1]The quartets discussed in this article are contained in volume 20 of the Brahms *Sämt-
liche Werke*. The German texts to the quartets are given as shown in *Opühls Brahms
Texte*, (revised edition) (Ebenhausen bei München: Langewiesche-Brandt, 1983).
Translations are by the present author.

*G. Roberts Kolb is a graduate of Occidental College, where he sang and
studied under Howard Swan and managed the Occidental College Glee Clubs.
He holds a master's degree in Choral Conducting from California State University, Fullerton and a D.M.A. in Choral Music from the University of Illinois.
He received the ACDA Julius Herford Dissertation Award for the best choral-
music dissertation of 1984. Dr. Kolb has taught at Smith College, where he
conducted the Smith choirs and glee club, and he is currently Associate Professor of Music and Director of Choral Activities at Hamilton College in Clin-
ton, New York.*

elements. To do so is common, and these elements are certainly important. They are not, however, equally important in all the quartets, and as we look to see how Brahms responded to his chosen texts, we will find that the principal expressive device is sometimes the formal structure, sometimes the harmonic writing, sometimes pictorialism, and often a combination of these and other elements. Thus the traditional analytical tools will not be ignored, but will be applied discriminately.

Drei Quartette, op. 31 (1864)

1. "Wechsellied zum Tanze" (Goethe)

Die Gleichgültigen

Komm mit, o Schöne, komm mit mir
  zum Tanze;
Tanzen gehöret zum festlichen Tag.
Bist du mein Schatz nicht, so kannst
  du es werden,
Wirst du es nimmer, so tanzen wir
  doch.
Komm mit, o Schöne, komm mit mir
  zum Tanze;
Tanzen gehret zum festlichen Tag.

The Indifferent Ones

Come with, o beautiful one, come with
  me to the dance;
Dancing is part of a festive day.
If you are not my sweetheart, you can
  become so,
If you never become so, then let's
  dance anyway.
Come with, o lovely one, come with me
  to the dance;
Dancing is part of a festive day.

Die Zärtlichen

Ohne dich, Liebste, was wären die
  Feste?
Ohne dich, Süße, was wäre der
  Tanz?
Wärst du mein Schatz nicht, so
  möcht' ich nicht tanzen,
Bleibst du es immer, ist Leben ein
  Fest.
Ohne dich, Liebste, was wären die
  Feste?
Ohne dich, Süße was wäre der
  Tanz?

The Tender Ones

Without you, dearest love, what would
  holidays be?
Without you, sweet one, what would
  the dance be?
If you were not my sweetheart, I would
  not want to dance.
If you remain so always, life is a
  holiday.
Without you, dearest love, what would
  holidays be?
Without you, sweet one, what would
  the dance be?

Die Gleichgültigen	*The Indifferent Ones*
Laß sie nur lieben, und laß du uns tanzen!	Let them merely love, and let us dance!
Schmachtende Liebe vermeidet den Tanz.	Languishing love avoids the dance.
Schlingen wir fröhlich den drehenden Reihen,	We weave joyously the twisting round dances,
Schleichen die andern zum dämmernden Wald.	The others steal to the darkening woods.
Laß sie nur lieben, und laß du uns tanzen!	Let them merely love, and let us dance!
Schmachtende Liebe vermeidet den Tanz.	Languishing love avoids the dance.

Die Zärtlichen	*The Tender Ones*
Laß sie sich drehen, und laß du uns wandeln!	Let them turn, and let us wander!
Wandeln der Liebe ist himmlischer Tanz.	Love's wandering is a heavenly dance.
Amor, der nahe, der höret sie spotten.	Cupid, who draws near, who hears them mocking,
Rächet sich einmal, und rächet sich bald.	Takes revenge once and for all, and takes revenge soon.
La sie sich drehen, und la du uns wandeln!	Let them turn, and let us wander!
Wandeln der Liebe is himmlischer Tanz.	Love's wandering is a heavenly dance.

Goethe's poem portrays two contrasting couples, one "indifferent" and one "tender." This contrast becomes the basis of Brahms's setting, as alto and bass are given the role of *die Gleichgültigen*, soprano and tenor *die Zärtlichen*. "The indifferent ones" sing first, as in the poem, and Brahms has portrayed their indifference in several ways. They are introduced by eight measures for the piano—the same eight measures that accompany the voices in Example 1. The minor key and the almost ostinato rhythm of each measure lend a certain aloofness and objectivity to the dance. This aloofness is enhanced as the singers, rather than singing together, sing in a rhythmic canon a measure apart. Finally, Brahms has written melodies with virtually no conjunct motion, again suggesting detachment.

Example 1 "Wechsellied zum Tanze" (mm. 9-16)

Example 2 "Wechsellied zum Tanze" (mm. 33-40)

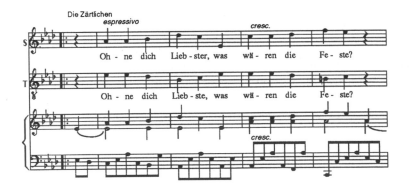

"The tender ones" are portrayed by reversing the "indifferent" devices (Ex. 2). The minor key becomes major, the marked ostinato rhythm yields to smoothly flowing eighth notes, the singers now sing together, and the melodies are usually conjunct. Furthermore, Brahms has added the marking *espressivo*, confirming what is already inherent in the music.

This scheme of differentiation results in four verses, of which the odd numbered are musically identical, as are the even numbered. Having set all four of Goethe's verses, however, Brahms was not yet finished. After verse four comes something of a textual coda, in which Brahms combined the last two lines of each of the couples, a dramatic device that was not available to Goethe because of the limitations of his medium, but one that is certainly in keeping with the spirit of the poem. At the beginning of this section (Ex. 3), the conjunct/disjunct and major/minor contrasts between the couples are preserved. The sense of two simultaneous conversations is achieved through a clever musical device: if the soprano/tenor measures were omitted, the bass, alto, and piano would proceed naturally, as if nothing at all were missing.

The last verse of Goethe's poem ends with the prediction that Cupid will have his revenge on *die Gleichgültigen*; that they too, after all their mocking, will fall in love and become "tender ones." Given this, it may be significant that one of the "indifferent" devices is missing in Example 3, as alto and bass sing together for the first time, taking the first step towards the realization of that prediction. By the end of the piece, although they continue to sing "indifferent" words, *die Gleichgültigen* sing them in harmony with *die Zärtlichen* in major mode, and in conjunct motion. In Brahms's setting, at least, love triumphs!

Example 3 "Wechsellied zum Tanze" (mm. 109-117)

2. "Neckereien" (Moravian)

Fürwahr, mein Liebchen, ich will nun frein,	Truly, my dearest, I would woo now;
Ich führ als Weibchen dich bei mir ein.	I'll lead you home with me as my bride.
Mein wirst du, o Liebchen, fürwahr du wirst mein,	You'll be mine, o dearest, truly you'll be mine—
Und wolltest dus auch nicht sein.	Whether you want to or not!
"So werd ich ein Täubchen von weißer Gestalt,	"Then I'll become a dove, white in form;
Ich will schon entfliehen, ich flieg in den Wald,	I'll fly right away, I'll fly into the forest;
Mag dennoch nicht Deine, mag dennoch nicht dein,	For I don't want to be yours, I don't want to be yours,
Nicht eine Stunde sein."	Not even for an hour."
Ich hab wohl ein Flintchen, das trifft gar bald,	I have a flintlock that finds its mark quite quickly,
Ich schieß mir das Täubchen herunter im Wald.	I'll shoot down the dove in the wood.
Mein wirst du, o Liebchen, fürwahr du wirst mein,	You'll be mine, o dearest, truly you'll be mine—
Und wolltest dus auch nicht sein.	Whether you want to or not!
"So werd ich ein Fischchen, ein goldener Fisch,	"Then I'll become a fish, a golden fish,
Ich will schon entspringen ins Wasser frisch;	I'll leap into the fresh water;
Mag dennoch nicht Deine, mag dennoch nicht dein,	For I don't want to be yours, I don't want to be yours,
Nicht eine Stunde sein."	Not even for an hour."
Ich hab wohl ein Netzchen, das fischt gar gut,	I have a fine net that fishes very well;
Ich fang mir den goldenen Fisch in der Flut;	I'll catch the golden fish in the stream;
Mein wirst du, o Liebchen, fürwahr du wirst mein,	You'll be mine, o dearest, truly you'll be mine—
Und wolltest dus auch nicht sein.	Whether you want to or not!
"So werd ich ein Häschen voll Schnelligkeit,	"Then I'll become a hare full of speed
Und lauf in die Felder, die Felder breit,	And run across the meadows, the broad meadows;
Mag dennoch nicht Deine, mag dennoch nicht dein,	For I don't want to be yours, I don't want to be yours,
Auch nicht eine Stunde sein."	Not even for an hour."
Ich hab wohl ein Hündchen, gar pfiffig und fein,	I have a fine hound, so sly and swift,
Das fängt mir das Häschen im Felde schon ein;	That will seize the hare in the meadow for me;
Mein wirst du, o Liebchen, fürwahr du wirst mein,	You'll be mine, o dearest, truly you'll be mine—
Und wolltest dus auch nicht sein.	Whether you want to or not.

Like the first poem in this opus, "Neckereien" involves two characterizations; here, however, the two individuals are engaged directly in dialogue. In the first verse, the young man announces his intention to court his beloved and to make her his bride. This provides a foundation for the six verses that follow, as the girl tells how she will escape him and the lad answers, asserting how he will foil her escape. Quite naturally, the girl's verses are sung by soprano and alto, the boy's by tenor and bass.

Brahms again used musical ideas or themes to enhance the expression of the text, but here they are associated with ideas or sentiments rather than with individual characters. The first such theme—let us call it A—is shown in Example 4. This theme, including both subject and countersubject, becomes associated with the assertion in the last two lines of each male verse that the girl will indeed be won.

Example 4 "Neckereien" (mm. 1-8, tenor and bass only)

The musical ideas in Examples 5 and 6, which we shall call B and C respectively, are combined with A to create verses two through five. B is used for the teasing repartee at the beginning of each verse, while C is used for the concluding refrain of the female verses ("I don't want to be yours, even for an hour"), just as A, as indicated above, ends the male verses.

Example 5 "Neckereien" (mm. 16b-20, soprano and alto only)

So werd__ ich ein Täub - chen von wei - ßer Ge - stalt, ich
So werd ich ein Täub - chen von wei - ßer Ge - stalt, ich

will____ schon ent-flie - hen, ich flieg____ in den Wald;
will schon ent-flie - hen, ich flieg in den Wald;

Example 6 "Neckereien" (mm. 21-24a, soprano and alto only)

den-noch nicht Dei -ne, mag den-noch nicht dein, nicht ei- ne Stun - de sein.
den-noch nicht Dei -ne, mag den-noch nicht dein, nicht ei- ne Stun - de sein.

Each "stimulus-response" unit of the dialogue is set off by piano interludes of two measures in length, which occur between verses one
and two and again between verses three and four, while the paired verses
(two/three and four/five) overlap by a beat.

Having established a predictable pattern, however, Brahms departed
from it radically in the last two verses—a departure that provides both
musical and dramatic climaxes and gives us an insight into Brahms's
own opinion of the eventual outcome of the dialogue. The separateness
of the two parties to the dialogue is abrogated through an overlapping
of the verses: the women sing the first half of verse six even as the
men are singing the last half of verse five. Similarly, the last half of
six and the first half of seven are sung simultaneously. The men then
finish verse seven alone (A), with a slight motivic extension on the word
fürwahr. All four voices join together for a final flourish on their respective last lines of text, and a two-measure coda for the piano, drawn
from the earlier interludes, finishes the piece.

One new musical idea occurs in the setting of these final two stanzas. B is replaced by new material for the first part of each verse. It

was necessary to construct a new theme that could be sung simultaneously with A, and Brahms has responded to the image of the "hare full of speed" with a new triplet rhythm that intensifies the excitement of the chase as the poem—and the song—nears its end. Finally, it is certainly not accidental that the last lines of verse six are sung, not to the accustomed C, but to A. Thus, while the words continue to deny any interest in being the lad's sweetheart, the music, which has always been associated with "you will be my sweetheart," suggests otherwise. And so again, as in "Wechsellied zum Tanze," Brahms seems to be indicating, albeit subtly, that love will be victorious.

3. "Der Gang zum Liebchen" (Bohemian, Wenzig)

Es glänzt der Mond nieder,	The moon shines down;
Ich sollte doch wieder	I should go again
Zu meinem Liebchen,	To my dearest;
Wie mag es ihr gehn?	How might she be?
Ach weh, sie verzaget	Alas, she despairs
Und klaget, und klaget,	And laments and laments,
Daß sie mich nimmer	That she will never
Im Leben wird seh'n.	See me in this lifetime.
Es ging der Mond unter,	The moon went down;
Ich eilte doch munter,	I hastened briskly,
Und eilte, daß keiner	And hastened so that no one
Mein Liebchen entführt.	Might carry off my beloved.
Ihr Täubchen, o girret,	You little doves, o coo,
Ihr Lüftchen, o schwirret,	You gentle breezes, o whistle,
Daß keiner mein Liebchen,	So that no one might
mein Liebchen entführt.	Carry off my beloved.

This poem is radically different from the other two in opus 31. There is no dialogue, there are no characterizations, and the mood that was light and carefree in the earlier numbers is here lyrical, pensive, and sad.

The setting is strophic, with a coda. The texture of the vocal lines is largely homophonic, as the soprano melody is supported by the other voices. The eight-measure introduction for piano, which also serves as an interlude between the two verses, anticipates the soprano melody in its opening measures. This melody is accompanied by a rising pattern of conjunct and repeated pitches, in parallel tenths, that suggests the path of the moon as it gently rises and makes its way across the sky (Ex. 7).

Example 7 "Der Gang zum Liebchen" (mm. 1-8)

In Brahms's setting, each verse comprises five textual phrases, as the last line of each strophe of the poem is repeated. The first two phrases move from the tonic (E flat) to the dominant. Phrase three begins with a momentary modal shift to B-flat minor—a poignant expression of despair—and then moves back to the tonic in preparation for phrase four, which is set to virtually the same music as the first phrase. The difference is a significant one, however, for the music of the first phrase includes regular low E flats in the piano, which act as an intermittant tonic pedal. When the music returns with the fourth phrase, this has become a B flat, or dominant pedal. The repetition of the last line of text (phrase five) centers upon the subdominant before returning to the tonic.

At the end of the second strophe, the second ending provides an extension of V[7], avoids a resolution in the voices, and returns again to the music of the opening/interlude, this time extending to new melodic heights as it moves to the subdominant before returning, with the voices repeating *mein Liebchen entführt*, to the tonic.

"Der Gang zum Liebchen," then, is simple in form and relatively simple harmonically. The harmonic effect is enriched by considerable use of appoggiaturas and suspensions, but its simplicity remains, as it supports the soprano melody without overshadowing it.

Quartette op. 64 (1874)

1. "An die Heimat" (Sternau)

Heimat!	Homeland!
Wunderbar tönendes Wort!	Wonderful sounding word!
Wie auf befiederten Schwingen	As on feathered wings
Ziehst du mein Herz zu dir fort.	You draw my heart to you.
Jubelnd, als müßt ich den Gruß	Rejoicing, as I must bring the greeting
Jeglicher Seele dir bringen,	Of every soul to you,
Trag ich zu dir meinen Fuß,	I carry my footstep to you,
Freundliche Heimat!	Friendly homeland!
Heimat!	Homeland!
Bei dem sanft klingenden Ton	The gentle sound of that word
Wecken mich alte Gesänge,	Awakens in me the old songs
Die in der Ferne mich flohn;	That escape me in the distance;
Rufen mir freudenvoll zu	[The songs] Call me joyfully to
Heimatlich lockende Klänge:	The sounds that entice me homeward:
Du nur allein bist die Ruh,	"You alone are rest,
Schützende Heimat!	Sheltering homeland!"
Heimat!	Homeland!
Gib mir den Frieden zurück,	Restore to me the peace
den ich im Weiten verloren,	That I lost abroad;
Gib mir dein blühendes Glück!	Give me your blossoming happiness!
Unter den Bäumen am Bach,	Under the trees by the brook,
Wo ich vor Zeiten geboren,	Where I was born in time past,
Gib mir ein schützendes Dach,	Give me a sheltering roof,
Liebende Heimat!	Loving homeland!

Each of the three verses of this poem speaks of a different aspect of the enticement of the homeland or of the poet's response to it. Brahms eschews any sort of strophic setting, responding instead to each verse as a separate entity. Musical unity is achieved through an extended setting of the last two words of each verse (*freundliche Heimat, schützende Heimat*, and *liebende Heimat*). These words are repeated so as to encompass a thirteen-measure section; the music is in the tonic (G) and is identical for all three phrases. Example 8 shows the end of the first strophe, the first of the three occurrences.

Example 8 "An die Heimat" (mm. 36-48)

The last measure of each of these ". . . Heimat" sections overlaps with the first measure of a second unifying device, a four-measure modulatory phrase that is derived from the arpeggiated piano introduction (Ex. 9) and establishes a different tonal center for each of the three verses.

Example 9 "An die Heimat" (mm. 1-4)

These unifying devices bind together three dissimilar verse settings. The first strophe sings of flying home, rejoicing; musically, this finds expression in pseudo-canonic, "flying" triplet melodies (Ex. 10). With the last line of the first strophe ("I carry my footstep to you"), Brahms anticipates the quieter, reflective mood of the second strophe. The piano is marked *calmato*, and the vocal lines suggest sighing as they move toward both the homeland and the home key. The principal melodic idea (sung first by the soprano and then by the tenor, who passes it on to the alto) pauses for a moment under the anticipated weight of a burden at the word *trag* ("carry"), but the homeward footsteps are no burden at all, and the line rises effortlessly by half-steps before leaping joyously, first by fourth (soprano) and then by fifth (alto), with that discovery.

The second strophe speaks of the old songs, with their softly ringing tones. The songs are simple, at least when heard through the curtain of memory, and the musical setting is largely homophonic and unaccompanied (Ex. 11).

Example 10 "An die Heimat" (mm. 13-16, 22-24)

Example 11 "An die Heimat" (mm. 52-56)

The third strophe seeks a haven of peace and happiness "under the trees by the brook." This *Sehnsucht* is expressed in a long-breathed phrase (derived from the *trag ich zu dir* phrase that closed the first strophe) that is sung first by the tenor and then later by the alto and soprano in intensifying juxtaposition. Meanwhile, the brook, as the symbolic representation of the object of that yearning, runs gently throughout, twisting and turning, in the piano (Ex. 12).

The quartet comes to a close after the final ". . . Heimat" section with an eleven-measure coda over a tonic pedal, while the voices continue singing *liebende Heimat*, at first in a brief double canon and then in longer chords that move to a final tonicization of G.

Example 12 "An die Heimat" (mm. 85-89)

2. "Der Abend" (Schiller)

Senke, strahlender Gott—	Sink, radiant God—
die Fluren dürsten	the fields thirst
Nach erquickendem Tau,	For refreshing dew,
der Mensch verschmachtet,	the man languishes,
Matter ziehen die Rosse—,	Exhausted pull the horses—
Senke den Wagen hinab!	Lower sinks the chariot!
Siehe, wer aus des Meers	Behold, who out of the sea's
krystallner Woge	crystalline wave
Lieblich lächelnd dir winkt!	Entices you with a lovely smile!
Erkennt Dein Herz sie?	Does your heart recognize her?
Rascher fliegen die Rosse,	Swifter fly the horses,
Thetys, die Göttliche, winkt.	Thetys, the divine, beckons.

Schnell vom Wagen herab
    in ihre Arme
Springt der Führer,
    den Zaum ergreift Kupido,
Stille halten die Rosse,
Trinken die kühlende Flut.
	Rapidly from the chariot down
	    into her arms
	Springs the driver;
	    Cupid seizes the bridle;
	Still hold the horses,
	To drink of the refreshing stream.

An dem Himmel herauf
    mit leisen Schritten
Kommt die duftende Nacht;
    ihr folgt die süße
Liebe. Ruhet und liebet!
Phoebus, der liebende, ruht.
	Upward to heaven
	    with gentle steps
	Comes the scented night;
	    after it follows sweet
	Love. Rest and love!
	Phoebus, the loving one, sleeps.

The musical form of this song could be described as ABB'A', with key areas of G minor, B flat, B flat, and G respectively. But such formal considerations must be regarded as secondary in importance to the word painting that abounds in this setting.

The first stanza is a musical picture of exhaustion. The repetitive beginning of the phrases (Ex. 13) suggests stumbling and weariness. Even the harmony is too weary to change at the same time in both hands of the keyboard (Ex. 14).

Example 13 "Der Abend" (mm. 5-10)

The sinking of the chariot (the sun) in the last line of the stanza is musically depicted through an elongation of the phrase, with a "winding down" of the contrapuntal lines.

Example 14 "Der Abend" (mm. 13-18, piano only)

In the second stanza, Thetys beckons, the adrenalin flows a bit, and the horses fly faster. The mode changes from minor to major, and the keyboard rhythm picks up considerably, changing from a pattern of two quarter notes followed by a quarter rest to continuously running eighth notes. The vocal phrases seem longer and carry more energy, freed as they are from the false starts of the first verse. At the third line ("faster fly the horses"), the rhythm of the piano increases again, this time from eighth notes to eighth-note triplets.

The impetus of this new excitement carries us without pause into the third stanza, which the women begin as the men finish the second. The music here is the same as was sung by the men at the beginning of the second verse, but the piano continues to increase the excitement, now with eighth notes in the bass against eighth-note triplets in the treble. All this activity comes to a virtual standstill at line three ("still hold the horses"): the piano reverts abruptly to the rhythm of the first stanza, and all motion ceases in the voices. Brahms did not hesitate to depart from the ABB'A' formal structure where the expression of the text demanded it.

The fourth stanza begins like the first, although now in the parallel major. Of special interest in this stanza is Brahms's treatment of the first word in the third line, for it belongs grammatically to the final phrase of the second line. A comparison of this passage (Ex. 15) with the corresponding passage in the first stanza (Ex. 16) reveals how Brahms has added chromatic passing tones and appoggiaturas in order to wed the two phrases together, so that the textual continuity is preserved and the listener does not realize until the second measure of line three that the *Liebe* measure is musically a part of a new line.

Example 15 "Der Abend" (mm. 85-91)

Example 16 "Der Abend" (mm. 13-18)

The song ends with a "restful" elongation of the last line of the poem, as the text is repeated in continuously falling lines.

3. "Fragen" (Turkish, Daumer)

Ich sprach zum Herzen:	[1]	"Mein liebes Herz, was ist dir?"
Es sprach:	[2]	"Ich bin verliebt, das ist mir."
Ich sprach:	[3]	"Wie ist dir denn zu Mut?"
Es sprach:	[4]	"Ich brenn in Höllenglut."
Ich sprach:	[5]	"Erquicket dich kein Schlummer?"
Es sprach:	[6]	"Den litte Qual und Kummer?"
Ich sprach:	[7]	"Gelingt kein Widerstand?"
Es sprach:	[8]	"Wie doch bei solchem Brand?"
Ich sprach:	[9]	"Ich hoffe, Zeit wirds wenden."
Es sprach:	[10]	"Es wirds der Tod nur enden."
Ich sprach:	[11]	"Was gäbst du, sie zu sehn?"
Es sparch:	[12]	"Mich, dich, Welt, Himmelshöhn."
Ich sprach:	[13]	"Du redest ohne Sinn,"
Es sprach:	[14]	"Weil ich in Liebe bin."
Ich sprach:	[15]	"Du mußt vernünftig sein."
Es sprach:	[16]	"Das heißt, so kalt wie Stein."
Ich sprach:	[17]	"Du wirst zu Grunde gehen!"
Es sprach:	[18]	"Ach, möcht es bald geschehen!"

I said to my heart:	[1]	"My beloved heart, what troubles you?"
It said:	[2]	"I am in love, that's what troubles me."
I said:	[3]	"How do you feel then?"
It said:	[4]	"I burn in hell-fire."
I said:	[5]	"Doesn't slumber relieve you?"
It said:	[6]	"The endured torment and grief?"
I said:	[7]	"Does no resistance succeed?"
It said:	[8]	"How, with such a bond?"
I said:	[9]	"I hope time will change things."
It said:	[10]	"Only death will end it."
I said:	[11]	"What would you give to see her?"
It said:	[12]	"Myself, you, the world, the heavens."
I said:	[13]	"You speak without sense—"
It said:	[14]	"Because I am in love."
I said:	[15]	"You must be rational!"
It said:	[16]	"You mean as cold as stone."
I said:	[17]	"You will go to your grave!"
It said:	[18]	"Ah, may it soon come to pass!"

Like nos. 1 and 2 of opus 31, this poem is a dialogue—in this instance a conversation between the mind and heart of a man in love. Here, however, the dialogue does not shift from verse to verse, but from line to line. The odd-numbered lines, the rational "questions," are sung homophonically by soprano, alto, and bass; the even-numbered lines, the impassioned "responses," are given to the tenor.

After three measures of piano introduction, which establish a nervous, insistent rhythm that continues with few interruptions throughout much of the quartet, the first eight lines of the poem are set without a break, without a moment of silence in the vocal texture. Text repetition is frequent, as words or phrases seem to be repeated as necessary to fill in Brahms's musical ideas. This is limited, however, to a partial repetition of a line, or, at most, a single complete repetition—until lines seven and eight, each of which is repeated three times, making four statements in all. This device of multiple textual repetitions appears throughout the quartet as a means of creating interior climaxes. With lines seven and eight we come to the end of one ''idea-group,'' in which each question posed by the ''rational being'' has been concerned with the well-being of the heart. These first eight lines are set apart, then, by the repetition of the last lines and a brief piano interlude. This interlude, however, lasts less than a measure, for the next ''idea-group'' (a brief respite from the insistent questioning of the first couplets) consists of only two lines, as if Brahms were unwilling to give such a small segment too much independence. These lines, each of which is sung twice, begin in the same key and conclude with a wonderful modulation from A through its parallel minor to F (Ex. 17).

Following lines nine and ten, the interlude is longer (two measures) and confirms the new tonal center. The ensuing section in F comprises the next group, lines eleven through fourteen, the first two of which are sung only once, while the last two are stated five times. During this section, the driving, insistent rhythm of the piano is absent.

Example 17 ''Fragen'' (mm. 38-42)

There follows a modulatory interlude that returns us to the dominant as the driving keyboard rhythm returns. Since the last group—the last four lines of the poem—represents the climax of the entire song, we are not surprised to discover in its setting a somewhat grander scale. The first two lines are set not once, but twice, with a three-measure extension in the repetition of line sixteen, which serves harmonically to return us to the tonic for the final couplet. These lines are sung only four times (as compared with five times for lines thirteen and fourteen), but a combination of interior word repetitions and longer note values results in the actual time allotted to the two lines being nearly twice that of any other couplet. Thus the elongation device remains consistent, both for each individual section and for the work taken as a whole.

Quartette, opus 92 (1884)

1. "O schöne Nacht" (Daumer)

O schöne Nacht!	O lovely night!
Am Himmel märchenhaft	In heaven, like a fairytale,
Erglänzt der Mond in seiner	Shines the moon in all its splendor;
ganzen Pracht;	
Um ihn der kleinen Sterne liebliche	Around it the little stars are lovely
Genossenschaft.	Company.
Es schimmert hell der Tau	The dew shimmers brightly
Am grünen Halm; mit Macht	On the green blade; With might
Im Fliederbusche schlägt	The nightingale sings
die Nachtigall;	in the lilac bush;
Der Knabe schleicht zu seiner	The youth steals softly to his
Liebsten sacht—	Love—
O schöne Nacht!	O lovely night!

The text offers five images of a "lovely night": the moon, the stars, the shimmering dew, the nightingale, and the youth stealing softly to his beloved. The first four constitute a "nature group"; the last involves the poet (or the singer) more directly. Brahms utilizes this natural division by assigning each of the first four images to solo lines: bass, tenor, alto, and soprano, respectively. The fifth he gives to all.

The piece begins with a four-measure keyboard introduction in which is heard a syncopated motif that will play a major role in the piano accompaniment throughout the song. This leads into a four-part, gently undulating setting of the words *o schöne Nacht!* (Ex. 18).

Example 18 "O schöne Nacht" (mm. 4-8, voices only)

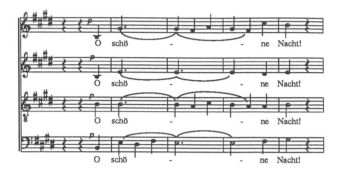

After a four-measure keyboard interlude, the bass sings of the moon in a long and gently arched phrase. Then follows the tenor, whose faster notes and repetitive melody suggest the many *kleine Sterne* that surround the moon. This leads into an altered repetition of the *o schöne Nacht* phrase of Example 18. When the alto proceeds to sing of the dew to the same music as the bass did after the first *o schöne Nacht,* we suspect some sort of modified strophic form. But no, this is denied by the soprano, who sings excitedly of the nightingale, while the piano provides pictorial trills.

A descending arpeggio leads into the last line of text, which is sung first by the men and then by the men and women together in a rhythmic canon a measure apart. All parts finally come together at the word *sacht,* and the word is set in such a way as to convey an image of the youth moving stealthily and carefully through the night, perhaps even on tiptoe (Ex. 19).

The quartet concludes with a third statement of *o schöne Nacht,* but now extended and repeated so as to provide a section large enough to balance the rest of the work.

Example 19 "O schöne Nacht" (mm. 58-61)

2. "Spätherbst" (Allmers)

Der graue Nebel tropft so still	The gray mist drips so still
Herab auf Feld und Wald und Heide,	Upon field and forest and heather,
Als ob der Himmel weinen will	As if the sky would weep
In übergroßem Leide.	In overwhelming sorrow.
Die Blumen wollen nicht mehr blühn,	The flowers want to bloom no more,
Die Vöglein schweigen in den Hainen,	The birds are silent in the grove,
Es starb sogar das letzte Grün;	Even the last green has died,
Da mag er auch wohl weinen.	While it desires also to weep.

Brahms has set these two verses in a modified strophic form. On the simplest level, the texture is that of an independent soprano melody supported in accompanimental fashion by the other three voices and the piano. But the accompanimental elements are made up of several layers, each of which is expressive of a different aspect of the poem.

After the left hand of the piano tolls the opening of the song, it commences with a triplet rhythm that will continue inexorably throughout the quartet, fragmenting only at the end of each strophe, as if to underscore the inescapable presence of death. Above this, throughout the first verse, the ostinato rhythmic pattern of the right hand of the piano pictorializes the dripping of the mist (*der graue Nebel*). Meanwhile, the lower three voices have begun in a dull homophony that captures the grayness of a world filled only with silence and death (Ex. 20).

Over this complex, layered accompaniment, the soprano melody is simple yet impassioned. The most prominent characteristic of the melody is a triplet melisma that occurs at the end of all lines but the third in each verse. This figure seems to grow almost improvisationally out of the singer's need to lament in *übergroßem Leide*. These melismatic figures are imitated by the accompanying voices (Ex. 20), so that the vocal texture is permeated by this weeping motif.

Example 20 "Spätherbst" (mm. 1-8)

The melodic line of the second stanza is unchanged. Modifications do occur, however, in both the piano and accompanying vocal parts. The image of the dripping mist is not found in the second strophe of the poem, and thus the "dripping" motif is abandoned in the right hand of the piano part. It is replaced by sustained chords: the resulting fuller sound adds a bit of intensity, a sense of greater involvement, after the detached character of the mist motif. The vocal parts are virtually the same, but for an occasional exchange of parts for brief periods and the addition of passing tones and appoggiaturas that also contribute to a higher intensity for this second verse.

A repetition of the last three words provides the opportunity for a brief cadential extension that shifts without warning to the parallel major (Ex. 21, m. 28). A new idea is introduced here, as the soprano lament ends with a new sighing motif (dotted eighth and sixteenth) that is imitated by the alto and tenor as the ostinato triplet rhythm in the left hand of the piano disintegrates for the last time.

3. "Abendlied" (Hebbel)

Friedlich bekämpfen	Peacefully struggle
Nacht sich und Tag.	Night and day.
Wie das zu dämpfen	How to quench it,
Wie das zu lösen vermag!	How to resolve it!
Der mich bedrückte,	You who oppressed me,
Schläfst du schon, Schmerz?	Do you sleep already, pain?
Was mich beglückte,	What made me happy,
Sage, was war's doch, mein Herz?	Speak—what was it, my heart?
Freude wie Kummer,	Joy, like sorrow,
Fühl ich, zerran,	I feel melt away;
Aber den Schlummer	But slumber
Führten sie leise heran.	Carried them gently on.
Und im Entschweben,	And in the soaring away,
Immer empor,	Ever upwards,
Kommt mir das Leben	The entirety of life seems to me
Ganz, wie ein Schlummerlied vor.	just like a lullaby.

In this song we discover yet again that elements of structure take second place to elements of textual/musical expression. Brahms began stanzas one and three with the same music, but after four measures each moves in a different direction, following the lead of the text. Aside from the unity of key (the quartet begins and ends in F) and the reappearance of the two-measure piano introduction as an interlude between stanzas one and two, there are virtually no other structural pinions. Rather,

Example 21 "Spätherbst" (mm. 25-33)

the work can almost be called through-composed, as each verse seems to call forth its own setting.

Thus, in stanza two, as the poet begins to forget his pains and his joys with the advent of night (or death), the tessitura and texture change dramatically. The soprano is tacet for the first two lines, but the textures remains four-part, as the piano assumes the role of the fourth melodic voice, a contrabass (Ex. 22). The opening of this verse is a contrapuntal development of the soprano phrase at the beginning of the work (Ex. 23). We are apparently moving toward a cadence on A (the

Example 22 "Abendlied" (mm. 15-23)

mediant key), but this is denied by the sudden outcry of the soprano
(''What was it that made me happy?'') (Ex. 22), which is also related
motivically to the opening phrase of the work. After touching briefly
on the tonic, the harmony moves to a diminished seventh on V, which
eventually resolves only to V^7 in the voices, the ultimate resolution to
the tonic not coming until the piano interlude before stanza three. The
resulting feeling of incompleteness, of irresolution, coincides with the
textual idea of searching for the lost pain and happiness, but being unable
to find them.

Example 23 ''Abendlied'' (mm. 3-6, soprano only)

As mentioned above, stanza three begins like stanza one. After four
measures, where the first stanza moved somewhat abruptly to A, the
third stanza remains in F but shifts to the minor mode. The last line
is extended so as to pictorially express the text (''carries them gently
on'').

Stanzas three and four are linked musically without a break—a treatment suggested by the continuation of an idea from the one into the
other and signaled by the use of *und* as the first word in the last stanza.
The second line of verse four is treated madrigalistically by the soprano
with a quickly rising line on ''ever upwards.'' The last two lines are
treated in a more extended fashion and are repeated in their entirety.
The setting here is characterized by the continual presence of non-
harmonic tones that lend a somewhat impressionistic flavor—one that
suggests the death-blurred vision through which ''the entirety of life
seems . . . just like a lullaby.''

4. ''Warum?'' (Goethe)

Warum doch erschallen himmelwärts die Lieder?	Why do the songs resound heavenwards?
Zögen gerne nieder Sterne, die droben blinken und wallen,	They gladly pull down the stars, which winkle and undulate on high;
Zögen sich Lunas lieblich Umarmen,	They draw down the moon's lovely embrace;
Zögen die warmen, wonnigen Tage, seliger Götter, gern uns herab!	They draw the warm, delightful days of the blessed gods gladly to us!

Brahms chose an unbalanced setting for this text. He divided the text into two major sections, the first of which includes only the first line—the question that generates the remainder of the text. To this first line he then allotted twenty-two measures in common time; the balance he set in thirty-three measures of 6/8.

The key is B flat, but the piece begins with a V⁷ of B flat and moves quickly to a surprising G-flat chord, at which point the soprano begins a series of imitative entries (Ex. 24), one for each voice, which modulate from G flat to B to C and then to F, whereupon repetitions of *himmelwärts* and *die Lieder* again establish V⁷ of B flat, only to deny it yet again, with the cadence this time on D. With the change of meter at the second line of text, however, this D becomes the third of a B-flat chord, which appears finally as a tonic for the first time in the quartet.

Example 24 "Warum?" (mm. 3-5a, soprano only)

At this point, the rigid contours of the opening question are replaced by a lilting, graceful, gentle, *grazioso* motion (Ex. 25) that will characterize the entire second section.

Example 25 "Warum?" (mm. 23-25)

Example 26 "Warum?" (mm. 45-55)

There is little or no imagery here: the main interest is harmonic. Line two moves from I to V. Line three begins on I once again, but soon modulates to G flat, where we remain for several measures, as line three concludes with a full I-IV-V-I cadence in G flat. A one-measure piano interlude then returns the tonality to B flat by way of an augmented sixth-chord, and line four begins in B flat, just as did lines two and three. The harmonic departure of this line is to D, the mediant and balancing tonality to G flat. We return via a circle of fifths (A-D-G) to ii of B flat, whereupon the last phrase of the text is canonically extended to provide a convincing cadence on B flat (Ex. 26).

It is difficult to generalize about the vocal quartets. We have seen that for some the principal interest is found in the harmonic activity. Others are intriguing for the cleverness with which Brahms has manipulated structural elements to enhance the drama of the poem. Still others charm us with their pictorial devices—devices that are expressive of specific words and phrases as well as of general emotional moods. At least one has yielded rudimentary motivic development. If any generalization is to be made, it must be that the quartets are a repository of a surprising variety of musical ideas and expressions, and that these musical ideas can be seen, in greater or lesser degree, as a result of Brahms's own response to his chosen texts.

Robert Shaw

The Texts of
Britten's *War Requiem*[1]

It may be that the greatest originality and "sheerest" genius of Benjamin Britten's *War Requiem* lie in his infusion of Wilfred Owen's World War I poetry into the Latin Mass for the Dead.

The Requiem Mass, quite apart from its religious significance, is a remarkable poetic and dramatic accomplishment. Its central poem is

---

[1]This article has been adapted for print by the author and editor from letters to Mr. Shaw's choruses in Cleveland and Atlanta and a spoken text delivered to performers of the work, most recently in 1982. Quotations of both Latin and English texts from the *War Requiem* are as given in the full score (Boosey and Hawkes HPS 742); these sometimes differ slightly from versions published elsewhere. The poems of Wilfred Owen are published in several editions, the most accessible of which is C. Day Lewis, ed., *The Collected Poems of Wilfred Owen* (London: Chatto and Windus), 1964. The most recent and by far the most comprehensive edition is John Stallworthy, ed., *Wilfred Owen: the Complete Poems and Fragments,* 2 vols. (New York: W.W. Norton), 1984. The poems of Wilfred Owen (©1963, Chatto and Windus, Ltd.) are quoted by the kind permission of New Directions Publishing Corporation. (Ed.)

A native Californian, Robert Shaw came to music by way of philosophy, English literature, and religion, his majors at Pomona College. Fred Waring heard a concert he conducted with the college's Glee Club and invited him to organize the Fred Waring Glee Club. Soon he was also preparing choruses for Arturo Toscanini and the NBC Symphony Orchestra. In New York he founded the Collegiate Chorale and later the Robert Shaw Chorale. Mr. Shaw served as Music Director of the San Diego Symphony and then joined the conducting staff of the Cleveland Orchestra under George Szell. In 1966 he became the Music Director of the Atlanta Symphony Orchestra.

Mr. Shaw's honors include seven Grammy Awards and honarary degrees and awards from over thirty U.S. colleges, universities, and foundations. He was awarded the first Guggenheim Fellowship ever presented to a conductor.

the *Dies irae*, attributed to Thomas of Celano in the thirteenth century, which describes, with extravagant imagery but incisive poetic economy, the "Final Judgement" of Christian tradition. And the poetry of Wilfred Owen, while tragically limited in total output, is vast in its human concern, and without an equal among the "war poets" of this century for invention and individuality.

However, given even these two great texts, it is Britten's own literary sensibilities and dramatic vision that structure and inspire the *War Requiem*. No composer of our time has been more sensitive to values of language. Certainly no English composer has set so many distinguished English texts, lyric or narrative, ranging over six or more centuries.

Wilfred Owen was killed in action just seven days before the armistice in November of 1918—upon his return to the front-line trenches after being wounded and hospitalized; and Britten dedicated his score to the memory of four close friends killed in action in the Second World War, a quarter of a century later. But they shared a passionate conviction: that war in their time was an intolerable outrage and a violation not only of human goodness, but of Christianity itself.

Britten's plan was simple, but remarkably effective. He gave to an adult mixed chorus and soprano soloist, accompanied by a full symphony orchestra, the complete and traditional Latin text of the Requiem Mass. At four points in the Mass these adult voices are joined by the voices of boys, singing from a distance (or another area) texts peculiarly appropriate to the innocence of children.

But at nine eloquent moments—philosophically critical and profoundly disturbing—Britten interrupts the sequence of the Mass to let Owen's poetry shine through in its native, living language, as commentary—or even contradiction. These words are given to a tenor and a baritone, accompanied by a chamber orchestra, and by the end of the work we realize that they also represent an English and a German soldier, and both are dead.

1. Early in the Requiem the choir sings "Unto thee all flesh shall come."
   —The English soldier then interrupts the Latin text:
   "What passing-bells for these who die as cattle?"

2. At the beginning of the *Dies irae* the brasses announce, with wondrous fanfare, the "Day of Judgement."
   —The German soldier responds wistfully, "Bugles sang
   . . . and bugles answered. . . . Voices of boys were by
   the river-side." But "sleep mothered them."

3. With the "Rex tremendae" the choir laments its misery and fear of standing at last before the "King of awful majesty."
    —But the soldiers brag and boast together, with patently false courage: "Out there, we've walked quite friendly up to Death. . . ."

4. With the "Recordare" and the "Confutatis" the chorus pleads that they be not numbered among the "accursed."
    —And Owen's poetry addresses the awesome cannon of World War I:
    ". . . May God curse thee, and cut thee from our soul!"

5. At the "Lacrymosa" the Latin prayer asks that on the day of resurrection "This newly departed soul be spared."
    —And the English soldier turns toward his comrade, just now killed: "Move him into the sun— . . . if anything might rouse him now / The kind old sun will know."

6. With the *Offertorium* the choir recalls the glorious promises of Jehovah to Abraham.
    —The soldiers then join in a bitter, contradictory retelling of Abraham's sacrifice of Isaac, in which Abraham ignored Jehovah's command and "slew his son,—and half the seed of Europe, one by one."

7. With the *Sanctus* the orchestra and chorus join in grand fanfares and shouts of "Hosanna in the highest!"
    —And at this holiest of moments the composer and poet resign themselves to an inconsolable denial of the Christian ecclesiastical assurances of immortality: "when I do ask white Age he saith not so. . . . It is death."

8. At the *Agnus Dei* the choir chants softly its triple litany: "O Lamb of God . . . . grant us peace."
    —The tenor alternates with the choir, recalling a crucifix beside a French farm road, where the Lamb of God has had a leg shot off—a victim of scribes and priests who condone wars.

9. Finally, in the *Libera me,* as the chorus for the last and most terrifying time pictures the Judgement Day and falls back trembling and silent, the two soldiers meet. The allegory—the metaphor—is a trench, a tunnel, a dugout. The reality is the grave (or Hell):
    "I am the enemy you killed, my friend. . . . Let us sleep now. . . ."

There seems to be general agreement that the *War Requiem* is the profoundest work Britten . . . produced . . . . It was received as a work of vast scope, in which the composer, by giving it all the technical resources and emotional power at this command, so transcends the personal that he seems to comprehend the sufferings, to transfigure the grief, and to honour the potential goodness of humankind.[2]

The blazing sincerity of feeling on the part of both Britten and World War I poet Wilfred Owen, whose poetry forms a counterpoint to the Latin Requiem Mass text, is still overpowering. . . . Purely as a document of compassion and protest, this remains a major artistic statement.
                                                Robert Finn, *Cleveland Plain Dealer*[3]

[The *War Requiem* is] almost certainly Britten's most profound work . . . though grandiose in size, deeply reflective and penetrating in expressiveness. . . . The impact is emotional, not cerebral. . . . one of his most original works in actual combination of sounds . . . a sublime achievement.
                                                Harriett Johnson, *New York Post*

If among all works of art there is a more eloquent expression of loathing for war than the *War Requiem,* I don't know about it.
                                                George W. Kimball, *Rochester Times Union*

The most convincing musical sermon yet written on the repulsive futility of human sacrifice.
                                                Stephen Hammer, *Rochester Daily Record*

So, of the major works of music created since World War II, it is doubtful if any has made so profound, immediate, and universal an impression. Audiences have wept, critics in most instances have surrendered to its impact, and the work has been found on the news and editorial pages as well as among the music reviews.

It has not found unequivocal favor among avant-garde composers or like-minded critics. It has been accused of being ''eclectic''—a pastejob of past composers' creativity, of being ''contrived'' and ''formalized,'' both as to musical content and calculated effect.

Such evaluation is understandable. A great deal of the choral writing

---

[2]William Plomer's liner notes to Britten's own recording of the *War Requiem*, London A4255. Reprinted by permission of Decca Records, London.
[3]This and the following quotations from newspapers were probably taken from reviews of Mr. Shaw's performances of the *War Requiem*. It was not possible to locate their precise sources. (Ed.)

shows enormously the influence of the Verdi *Messa da Requiem*. Except for the *Lux aeterna*, which Britten saves for a giant coda, the *War Requiem* borrows Verdi's basic textual and formal groupings for its six main movements. In some instances his writing amounts almost to a personal paraphrase:

1. The opening *Requiem aeternam* begins with the pianissimo unison chanting of the chorus.

2. The *Dies irae* has the fanfares which Verdi borrowed from Berlioz and almost identical splashes of choral/brass rhetoric in a disturbing and animated tempo.

3. The "Lacrymosa" recalls inevitably, by tempo and by texture, the slow, plaintive lyricism of Verdi.

4. "Quam olim Abrahae" is in both cases a brisk fugato.

5. For each, the *Agnus Dei* presents a slow, simple, hymn-like, unison tune.

6. The *Libera me* is similarly polyphonic and dramatic, recalling with fanfares the *Dies irae* and enclosing a soaring soprano solo.

But Britten never tried, so far as I know, to create an absolutely novel and solitary musical language. If the Cages and Stockhausens are true prophets of a new musical order, then Britten, indeed, may be hopelessly lapped and doomed to be forgotten.

It is worth noting in passing, however, that Bach was not a significant musical innovator—nor Haydn, nor Mozart, nor indeed almost anyone until the strange psycho-social compulsions of our century. On this subject, Stravinsky writes in his *Poetics of Music:*

It just so happens that our contemporary epoch offers us the example of a musical culture that is day by day losing the sense of continuity and the taste for a common language.

Individual caprice and intellectual anarchy, which tend to control the world in which we live, isolate the artist from his fellow-artists and condemn him to appear as a monster in the eyes of the public; a monster of originality, inventor of his own language, of his own vocabulary, and of the apparatus of his art. The use of already employed materials and of established forms is usually forbidden him. So he comes to the point of speaking an idiom without relation to the world that listens to him. His art becomes truly unique, in the sense that it is incommunicable and

shut off on every side. The erratic block is no longer a curiosity that
is an exception; it is the sole model offered neophytes for emulation.
. . . Times have changed since the day when Bach, Handel and Vivaldi
quite evidently spoke the same language which their disciples repeated
after them, each one unwittingly transforming this language according
to his own personality. The day when Haydn, Mozart, and Cimarosa
echoed each other in works that served their successors as models, successors such as Rossini, who was fond of repeating in so touching a way
that Mozart had been the delight of his youth, the desperation of his
maturity, and the consolation of his old age.[4]

I asked Morton Gould some years ago about avant-garde concert life
in New York: pianists immobile before a keyboard for six minutes of
composed silence, cellists hanging from balconies in mini-bikinis, one
hundred metronomes set at different speeds and simultaneously
released—the last to run down determining the length of the composition. "Robert," he said, "a lot of it goes a little way." Elizabeth Sprague
Coolidge, asked why she had put on the series of avant-garde concerts
in Washington's art galleries replied, "Young man, I may be deaf, but
I'm not blind!"

So, the *War Requiem* is somewhere between Palestrina and Stravinsky (and not far from Bartók) in musical language; and within only two
decades it has become less difficult for most of us to hear and perform.
The point, however, is its extraordinary emotional impact. It has passion.

It was written for the consecration of the rebuilt Cathedral of St.
Michael in Coventry in the Spring of 1962. It has thus reached its twenty-
fifth anniversary, and Owen's texts their sixty-fifth anniversary, in what
begins to emerge as nearly an entire century of uninterrupted war.

The Requiem Mass, of course, is a social as well as a religious
phenomenon. The company of believers gathers together to consider
and to celebrate the fact of death—which is also to say the "facts of
life." Here we face the ultimate questions of existence and eternity.
In a sense, there are no others. Anyone who has held the hand of a
dying friend has been lost in the no man's land of IS and IS NOT. *(Birth
is its own mystery—and a biological/religious/socio-logical/political/legal
conundrum and controversy as well. At what moment does the*

[4]Igor Stravinsky, *Poetics of Music* (Cambridge, MA: Harvard University Press, 1947)
73-74.

embryo—or incipient animal—become a "living soul?")

Moreover, behind the elaborate and codified petition for the preservation ("salvation") of the human soul, the Requiem Mass is a somewhat grim—though mostly unspoken—celebration of survival.

William Plomer, contemporary British poet and librettist-collaborator with Britten, in his introduction to Britten's own recording, writes:

> Owen was only 25, but his poems were profound, and are profoundly disturbing. They made no appeal to the accepted opinions of his time about poetry or war. They were not about what soldiers gloriously did but what they had unforgivably been made to do to others and to suffer themselves. Owen did not accept what he called "the old Lie" that it was necessarily glorious or even fitting to die for one's own or any other country, or that a country was necessarily or perhaps ever justified in making the kind of war he knew. As he saw and experienced it, war appeared as a hellish outrage on a huge scale against humanity, and a violation of Christianity. He shared the destiny of millions on both sides, but he had the sensibility to see what war now really meant, and the power to explain it.
>
> "I am not concerned with poetry. My subject is War, and the pity of War. The Poetry is in the pity."
>
> Into his poetry went the pity, not of a detached outsider or a sentimentalist, nor simply that of a humane officer for his men whose lives he cannot save and to whom he cannot hold out hope, but the pity of an imaginative man for fellow-sufferers unable to speak for themselves to later generations.[5]

Owen's own words, from his letters:

> I suppose I can endure cold and fatigue and the face-to-face death as well as another; but extra for me there is the universal pervasion of *Ugliness*. Hideous landscapes, vile noises, foul language, and nothing but foul, even from one's own mouth (for all are devil ridden)— everything unnatural, broken, blasted; the distortion of the dead, whose unburiable bodies sit outside the dug-outs all day, all night—the most execrable sights on earth. In poetry we call them the most glorious. But to sit with them all day, all night . . . and a week later to come back and find them still sitting there, in motionless groups, THAT is what saps the "soldierly spirit."[6]
>
> Your letter reached me at the exact moment it was most needed—

[5]Plomer, liner notes.
[6]Harold Owen and John Bell, eds., *Wilfred Owen: Collected Letters* (London: Oxford University Press), 1967, 431-2. Letter 482 to Susan Owen (Wilfred's mother) 4 February 1917.

when we had come far enough out of the line to feel the misery of billets [rest and recreation]; and I had been seized with writer's cramp after making out my casualty reports. . . . The Battalion had a sheer time last week. I can find no better epithet: because I cannot say I suffered anything; having let my brain grow dull: That is to say my nerves are in perfect order.

It is a strange truth: that your *Counter-Attack* [a new poem by his friend and inspiration, Siegfried Sassoon] frightened me much more than the real one: though the boy by my side, shot through the head, lay on top of me, soaking my shoulder, for half an hour.

Catalogue? Photograph? Can you photograph the crimson-hot iron as it cools from the smelting? That is what Jones' blood looked like, and felt like. My senses are charred.

I shall feel again as soon as I dare, but now I must not. I don't take the cigarette out of my mouth when I write Deceased over their letters.[7]

Plomer's notes continue:

It is now clear that Owen was the outstanding English poet of the First World War, and, because the Second World War was a continuation of it, of that too. War has been the central horror of European history in this century; and Owen, mourning young lives tormented and treated as expendable, was to speak as directly to mourners in 1945 as to those of 1918; furthermore, since the fear of war is now universal, his elegies speak to us directly. They are a warning.

To nobody grieving for the deaths of friends in the War which broke out again more than twenty years after his death did Owen speak more directly than to Britten, who has dedicated the *War Requiem* to the memory of four of its victims. Perhaps no composer has shown so remarkable a response to poetry, and no English composer has been more responsive to English poetry. And since there is no motif more predominant and recurrent in Britten's works than that of innocence outraged and ruined, what could be more natural than that Britten, deeply moved by Owen's poetry, should be no less moved by the fate of the man who wrote it, his youth, his promise, his passionate tenderness, his rare talent cut off by the senseless violence of war? Being so moved, Britten's impulse was to set Owen's most memorable poems for singing. It was a sure instinct that prevented him from setting them separately, or as a sequence. Certainly they have a kind of monumental nobility that enables them to stand alone, but he saw, as nobody else could have seen, that they could stand beside the scared liturgy of the Mass for the Dead, and, musically, be combined with it.

[7]Ibid., 581. Letter 664 to Siegfried Sassoon on 10 October 1918.

Let us now turn to Britten's libretto, and examine that combination. I will call your attention to those lines which triggered Britten's selection of Owen's verses and tell you those things which occur to me concerning their conjunction.

I. *Requiem aeternam*

Chorus

Requiem aeternam dona eis Domine,	Grant them eternal rest, O Lord:
et lux perpetua luceat eis.	and let everlasting light shine on them.

Note the poetic value in having the noun and verb share the same linguistic root: "lux - luceat" vs. "light - shine" (Latin/Romance vs. English/German).

Boys' choir

Te decet hymnus, Deus in Sion;	To thee, O God, praise is meet in Sion,
et tibi reddetur votum	and unto thee shall the vow be performed
in Jerusalem;	in Jerusalem.
exaudi orationem meam,	Hearken unto my prayer:
ad te omnis caro veniet.	unto thee shall all flesh come.

Note that it is the undisturbed purity of innocent boys that allows them to sing this hymn.

Tenor solo

What passing-bells for these who die as cattle?
    Only the monstrous anger of the guns.
    Only the stuttering rifles' rapid rattle
Can patter out their hasty orisons.
No mockeries for them from prayers or bells,
    Nor any voice of mourning save the choirs,—
The shrill, demented choirs of wailing shells;
    And bugles calling for them from sad shires.

What candles may be held to speed them all?
    Not in the hands of boys, but in their eyes
Shall shine the holy glimmers of good-byes.
    The pallor of girls' brows shall be their pall;
Their flowers the tenderness of silent minds,
And each slow dusk a drawing-down of blinds.

On the one hand: " . . . Hearken unto my prayer: unto thee *shall all flesh come.*" On the other: "What passing-bells for these *who die as cattle?*"

In addition to the myriad, disturbing, fragmentary associations that surround this juxtaposition—"cattle-bells," "man-made flesh," "man-made meat," "butcher-boys," "boys butchered"—in addition to these connotations, here, within the first few minutes of this extended work, is squarely placed its rather total argument, titled (by Owen) "Anthem for Doomed Youth."

Let me call your attention to the verbal elements of assonance, alliteration, and the like—those matters of speech which exalt meaning with mystery and music.

Lines three and four bring us not only the alliteration of "*rifles*" *r*apid *r*attle," but, even more importantly, the inner onomatopoetic alliteration of "stu*tt*ering, ra*tt*le, pa*tt*er."

Lines five and six set forth "no *m*ockeries for *th*em" or "*v*oice of *m*ourning." Obviously, we have the "m" alliterations, though they are reversed. Perhaps more significantly, we have a "v" sound poised against a voiced "th" sound. Both of these are voiced consonants and both are made at the forward wall of mouth and teeth. The effect in consonants is similar to Owen's "half-rhymes:" "sun - sown," "once - France," etc. Repeat a few times, "*m*ockeries for *th*em;" "*v*oice of *m*ournin*g*." Concentrate upon the alliteration, the half- or false-alliterations, and the reverse orders. These seem to me to be moments wherein music and mystery enter.

Line twelve brings us a beautiful play upon robbing "pallor" to provide a "pall."

Consider the last few words of lines thirteen and fourteen: "te*n*der*n*ess of sile*n*t mi*n*ds;" "drawi*n*g dow*n* of bli*n*ds." Note the parallelism of "n" sounds: seven "n" sounds in eight words. These certainly contribute enormously to the poem's wistful, saddened diminuendo.

Chorus

Kyrie eleison,	Lord, have mercy upon us,
Christe eleison,	Christ, have mercy upon us,
Kyrie eleison.	Lord, have mercy upon us.

II. *Dies irae*

Chorus

Dies irae, dies illa,	The Day of Wrath, that day
Solvet saeclum in favilla,	shall dissolve the world in ashes,
Teste David cum Sibylla.	as witnesseth David and the Sibyl.
Quantus tremor est futurus,	What trembling there shall be
Quando Judex est venturus,	when the Judge shall come
Cuncta stricte discussurus!	who shall thresh out all thoroughly!

Tuba mirum spargens sonum	The trumpet, scattering a wondrous sound
Per sepulchra regionum	through the tombs of all lands,
Coget omnes ante thronum.	shall drive all unto the Throne.
Mors stupebit et natura,	Death and Nature shall be astounded
Cum resurget creatura,	when the creature shall rise again
Judicanti responsura.	to answer to the Judge.

Baritone solo:

Bugles sang, saddening the evening air,
And bugles answered, sorrowful to hear.

Voices of boys were by the river-side.
Sleep mothered them; and left the twilight sad.
The shadow of the morrow weighed on men.

Voices of old despondency resigned,
Bowed by the shadow of the morrow, slept.

"Bugles sang. . . ." It is, of course, a "natural" to couple the "tuba mirum," the "wondrous trumpet," with "bugles sang." But, by the extraordinary collaboration of Britten and Owen, in one moment we have the "tuba mirum" calling, even "driving" all unto the Throne; and, immediately following, bugles are calling, are "singing," but *only bugles answer*, "sorrowful to hear." The voices of boys who once were by the riverside can never again respond.

During the first several readings I found this poem a bit obscure. I could not place the boys "by the riverside" in their time. *When* were they by the riverside, and what time is it now?

The poem is incomplete—probably about half of its intended duration—and some of the subsequent lines, even though incomplete, dispel some of the obscurity. Lines nine and ten read:

[Blank] that dying tone
Of receding voices that will not return.[8]

Almost certainly the poet is recalling the voices of his and others' youth, voices of friends now "mothered" by the "sleep" of death—"receding voices that will not return." "The voices of old despondency" are those which remain, "bowed by the shadow of the morrow," who are able to sleep only the sleep of fatigue and resignation, knowing that sooner rather than later the more final sleep will also "mother" them (including Owen himself).

Again, note the beautiful rhymes, "air - hear," "side - sad." Recall,

[8]Lewis, 128; Stallworthy, 487. Stallworthy has "drying" for Lewis's "dying."

also, the sensitive contrast between the "wondrous trumpet" of the *Dies irae* which wakes the dead, and this sad song, answered only by further sorrow.

Soprano solo and chorus:

Liber scriptus proferetur,	A written book shall be brought forth
In quo totum continetur,	in which shall be contained all for
Unde mundus judicetur.	which the world shall be judged.
Judex ergo cum sedebit,	And therefore when the Judge shall sit,
Quidquid latet, apparebit:	whatsoever is hidden shall be manifest,
Nil inultum remanebit.	and naught shall remain unavenged.
Quid sum miser tunc dicturus?	What shall I say in my misery?
Quem patronum rogaturus,	Whom shall I ask to be my advocate,
Cum vix justus sit securus?	when scarcely the righteous may be without fear?
Rex tremendae majestatis,	King of awful majesty,
Qui salvandos salvas gratis,	who freely savest the redeemed;
Salva me, fons pietatis.	save me, O fount of mercy.

Tenor and baritone solos

Out there, we've walked quite friendly up to Death;
    Sat down and eaten with him, cool and bland,—
Pardoned his spilling mess-tins in our hand.
We've sniffed the green thick odour of his breath,—
Our eyes wept, but our courage didn't writhe.
He's spat at us with bullets and he's coughed
    Shrapnel. We chorussed when he sang aloft;
We whistled while he shaved us with his scythe.

Oh, Death was never enemy of ours!
    We laughed at him, we leagued with him, old chum.
No soldier's paid to kick against his powers.
    We laughed, knowing that better men would come,
And greater wars; when each proud fighter brags
He wars on Death—for Life; not men—for flags.

The essence of this poem and its placement obviously is its bravado—satirical, cynical, and sorrowful. In a Hallmark world, cynicism is not highly rated. But we need to remember that it is not the *lack* of sensitivity which makes a cynic, but sensitivity's constancy and vulnerability.

Lin Yutang wrote in 1935 in *My Country and My People* (perhaps with insufficient prescience of the pathology of "europeanization"):

To learn tolerance, one needs a little sorrow and a little cynicism of the
Taoist type. True cynics are often the kindest of people, for they see

the hollowness of life, and from the realization of that hollowness is generated a kind of cosmic pity.

Pacifism, too, is a matter of high human understanding. If man could learn to be a little more cynical, he would also be less inclined toward warfare. That is perhaps why all intelligent men are cowards. The Chinese are the world's worst fighters because they are an intelligent race, backed and nurtured by Taoist cynicism and the Confucian emphasis on harmony as the ideal of life. . . .

An average Chinese child knows what the European gray-haired statesmen do not know, that by fighting one gets killed or maimed, whether it be an individual or nation.[9]

It is entirely possible, of course, that the West by now has sufficiently "oriented" the East in the virtues and devices of killing to provide its own destruction.

Back to Hell-fellow, wail-met: note in lines four, five, and six the terms borrowed from the first-hand experience with poison gas: "the green thick odour of his breath," "sniffed," "wept," "spat," "coughed"— but none of them is used in context of gas.

Compare, for examples, the latter half of Owen's poem entitled "Dulce et decorum est:"

Gas! Gas! Quick, boys! An ecstasy of fumbling,
Fitting the clumsy helmets just in time,
But someone still was yelling out and stumbling
And floundering like a man in fire or lime.
As under a green sea, I saw him drowning.
In all my dreams before my helpless sight
He plunges at me, guttering, choking, drowning.

If in some smothering dreams, you too could pace
Behind the wagon that we flung him in,
And watch the white eyes writhing in his face,
His hanging face, like a devil's sick of sin;
If you could hear, at every jolt, the blood
Come gargling from the froth-corrupted lungs,
Bitter as the cud
Of vile, incurable sores on innocent tongues,—
My friend, you would not tell with such high zest
To children ardent for some desperate glory,
The old Lie: Dulce et decorum est
Pro patria mori.[10]

[9]Lin Yutang, *My Country and My People* (Edina, MN: Halcyon House, 1937) 59.
[10]Stallworthy, 140; Lewis, 55.

I recast and translate:

> My friend, you would not tell in such high mood
> To youth, susceptible to your effrontery,
> The old Lie: sweet it is and very good
> To die for country.

The most pathetic thing of all in "Out there. . . ." is the line "but our courage didn't writhe": paralysis, choking, and spasm are omnipresent, except in our will—or so we brag.

"We whistled while he shaved us with his scythe"—a bitter turn of metaphor, and certainly an intended pun ("close shave" courtesy of the "Grim Reaper").

"We laughed at him, we leagued with him"—a nice parallelism between "laughed" and "leagued," but the line reads more richly if you can point up the disparate "at" and "with" without losing forward motion.

"No soldier's paid to kick against his powers"—of course not; soldiers are paid to greet him, "old chum"; soldiers are paid to die.

Chorus

Recordare Jesu pie,	Remember, merciful Jesu,
Quod sum causa tuae viae:	that I am the cause of thy journey,
Ne me perdas illa die.	lest thou lose me in that day.
Quaerens me, sedisti lassus:	Seeking me didst thou sit weary:
Redemisti crucem passus:	thou didst redeem me, suffering the cross:
Tantus labor non sit cassus.	let not such labor be frustrated.

[Verse omitted]

Ingemisco, tamquam reus:	I groan as one guilty;
Culpa rubet vultus meus:	my face flushes at my sin.
Supplicanti parce Deus.	Spare, O God, me, thy suppliant.
Qui Mariam absolvisti,	Thou who did'st absolve Mary,
Et latronem exaudisti,	and did'st hear the thief's prayer,
Mihi quoque spem dedisti.	hast given hope to me also.
Inter oves locum praesta,	Give me place among thy sheep
Et ab haedis me sequestra,	and put me apart from the goats,
Statuens in parte dextra.	setting me on the right hand.
Confutatis maledictis,	When the damned are confounded
Flammis acribus addictis,	and assigned to sharp flames,
Voca me cum benedictis.	call thou me with the blessed.
Oro supplex et acclinis,	I pray, kneeling in supplication,
Cor contritum quasi cinis	a heart contrite as ashes,
Gere curam mei finis.	take thou mine end into thy care.

Baritone solo

Be slowly lifted up, thou long black arm,
Great gun towering toward Heaven, about to curse;

Reach at that arrogance which needs thy harm,
And beat it down before its sins grow worse;

But when thy spell be cast complete and whole,
May God curse thee, and cut thee from our soul!

Britten extracted the lines above from a longer poem:

*Be slowly lifted up, thou long black arm,
*Great gun towering toward Heaven, about to curse;
Sway steep against them, and for years rehearse
Huge imprecations like a blasting charm!
*Reach at that arrogance which needs thy harm,
*And beat it down before its sins grow worse;
Spend our resentment, cannon, yea, disburse
Our gold in shapes of flame, our breaths in storm.

Yet, for men's sakes whom thy vast malison
Must wither innocent of enmity,
Be not withdrawn, dark arm, thy spoilure done,
Safe to the bosom of our prosperity.
*But when thy spell be cast complete and whole,
*May God curse thee, and cut thee from our soul![11]

The chief relationship between the Latin and Owen here is Britten's sensibility to the imagery of "cursing." Obviously, it is the center of Owen's poem: "Great gun . . . about to curse!" Though for the moment you appear necessary, once your malignancy is accomplished, God damn you and cut you from our soul!

The association with the Latin is made clearer by a better translation of "Confutatis maledictis." "Male-diction" = "ill to speak"—to curse. Therefore the line means "When the *accursed* are confounded and assigned to sharp flames. . . ."

Notice, also, the parallel imagery between the Latin "Flammis acribus"—"sharp flames"—and Owen's "shapes of flame" in line eight.

I find lines nine and ten provocative for two reasons: first, the use of the word "malison." We are well acquainted with the word "benison," from the Latin "bene," meaning "well ("bene-diction" = "to say well"); therefore, a blessing. The suffix "son" is both Middle English and Old French in different spellings. It might well come from

[11]Sonnet ("On Seeing a Piece of Our Heavy Artillery Brought into Action"). Stallworthy, 151; Lewis, 85.

roots which give us words like *sound* and *sonor*. If so, then as "benison" is a blessing, "malison" is a cursing.

The second interest for me in these lines is that this "blasting," "storming," "flaming," and "cursing" must ultimately "wither" (burn) the enmity out of all men, spoiler and spoiled alike.

This is the only one of Owen's poems—to my knowledge—which might imply a partisan "right or wrong" to his war. In the main his subject, as he states over and over again, is "war and the pity of war, the poetry is in the pity." It is *all* wrong. There is *no* right.

But in this poem, in lines five and six, he says to the "great gun . . . about to curse," "Reach at that arrogance which needs thy harm, and beat it down before its sins grow worse. . . ." Taken in its entire context, one can only assume, I think, that the "arrogance" which he had in mind, for the moment, at least, was Prussian. It could be a partisan line.

I am not really sure of this. Lines seven and eight are so utterly satirical, and lines thirteen and fourteen so impassioned, that it is possible that he may have been totally satirical throughout; that is, he feeds us a crumb of political expediency, leads us to the brink of a justification for war, only so that it may crumble beneath the weight of *our own* arrogance. The great irony is that Britten gives the entire poem to the baritone soloist who, in the great final "Strange Meeting," turns out to be the *German* soldier!

Soprano and chorus (return to the opening of the *Dies irae*)

Dies irae, dies illa,	The Day of Wrath, that day
Solvet saeclum in favilla,	shall dissolve the world in ashes,
Teste David cum Sibylla.	as witnesseth David and the Sibyl.
Quantus tremor est futurus,	What trembling there shall be
Quando Judex est venturus,	when the Judge shall come
Cuncta stricte discussurus!	who shall thresh out all thoroughly!
Lacrimosa dies illa,	Lamentable is that day
Qua resurget ex favilla,	on which guilty man shall arise
Judicandus homo reus,	from the ashes to be judged.
Huic ergo parce Deus.	Spare then this one, O God.

Tenor solo

Move him into the sun—
Gently its touch awoke him once,
At home, whispering of fields unsown.
Always it woke him, even in France,
Until this morning and this snow.
If anything might rouse him now
The kind old sun will know.

Think how it wakes the seeds,—
Woke, once, the clays of a cold star.
Are limbs, so dear-achieved, are sides,
Full nerved—still warm—too hard to stir?
Was it for this the clay grew tall?
—O what made fatuous sunbeams toil
To break earth's sleep at all?

"Move him into the sun. . . . " Surely is one of the most beautiful and touching of Owen's lyrics.

Immediately preceding the poem are the final couplets of the *Dies irae* (notable also because the entire *Dies irae*, with the exception of these concluding four lines, has been in three-line verses; the two couplets bring a severity and finality to the whole poem). "Lacrimosa dies illa. . . ."—"lamentable is the *day* on which guilty *man shall rise* from the ashes. . . . Spare then *this one,* O God."

Owen's poem links with the *Missa pro defunctis* at two points. The first point is that resurrection—a reawakening—is the common theme. On the one hand "man shall *rise*"; on the other, "If anything might *rouse* him now. . . . Was it for this the clay grew tall? . . . To break earth's sleep. . . ?"

The second point is that the Latin says very specifically, "Spare then *this* one," and similarly, the poet also takes as his point of departure a very specific occurance, this here-now boy, just-now dead.

How poignant, how wistful is the poet's equation of sunlight with life, and how succinctly documented by evolutionary recall in the second stanza. (I am trying for the moment to remember my "beginnings of life" lessons. Was it that the "star" finally cooled enough to support life, or was it that the sun "woke, once, the clays of a cold star?") Whatever the evolutionary sequence, it was certainly not for a moment such as this that the "clay grew tall," that mud became man.

-O what made fatuous sunbeams toil
To break earth's sleep at all?

Note the wonderful rhymes:

Sun - sown, once - France;
snow - now - know;
Seeds - sides, star - stir;
tall - toil - all.

Chorus

Pie Jesu Domine,	Merciful Lord Jesu:
Dona eis requiem. Amen.	give them peace. Amen.

III. *Offertorium*

Boys' choir

Domine Jesu Christe, Rex gloriae,	O Lord Jesus Christ, King of Glory,
libera animas omnium fidelium	deliver the souls of all the faithful
defunctorum de poenis inferni,	departed from the pains of hell
et de profundo lacu:	and from the depths of the pit:
libera eas de ore leonis,	deliver them from the lion's mouth,
ne absorbeat eas tartarus,	that hell devour them not,
ne cadant in obscurum.	that they fall not into darkness.

Chorus

Sed signifer sanctus Michael	But let the standard-bearer Saint Michael
repraesentet eas in lucem sanctam:	bring them into the holy light:
quam olim Abrahae promisisti,	which, of old, Thou didst promise
et semini ejus.	unto Abraham and his seed.

Baritone and tenor solos

So Abram rose, and clave the wood, and went,
And took the fire with him, and a knife.
And as they soujourned both of them together,
Isaac the first-born spake and said, My father,
Behold the preparations, fire and iron,
But where the lamb for this burnt-offering?
Then Abram bound the youth with belts and straps,
And builded parapets and trenches there,
And stretchèd forth the knife to slay his son.
When lo! an angel called him out of heaven,
Saying, Lay not thy hand upon the lad,
Neither do anything to him. Behold,
A ram, caught in a thicket by its horns;
Offer the Ram of Pride instead of him.
But the old man would not so, and slew his son,—
And half the seed of Europe, one by one.

And then it goes on:

Boys' choir

Hostias et preces tibi	We offer unto Thee, O Lord,
Domine laudis offerimus:	sacrifices of prayer and praise:
tu suscipe pro animabus illis,	do Thou receive them for the souls of those
quarum hodie memoriam facimus:	whose memory we this day recall:
fac eas, Domine,	make them, O Lord,
de morte transire ad vitam.	to pass from death unto life.

Chorus

Quam olim Abrahae promisisti,	Which of old Thou didst promise,
et semini ejus.	unto Abraham and his seed.

This, of course, is the most "natural" of all the linkings: "Which of old Thou did'st promise to Abraham and his seed" to "So Abram rose. . . ." and disposed of his own as well as "half the seed of Europe, one by one." But even this is not the entire linking; for it is immediately followed by "Hostias et preces tibi. . . .": "*we offer* unto Thee *sacrifices* with prayer."

The first is a natural verbal and narrative association, contrived between liturgy and poet by the composer. The second is a linking which somehow includes all of us as participants even in that earlier sacrifice. We are also involved in "offerings, sacrifices, and prayers"; and whether our participation be as performer or worshipper, we are up to our ears in something.

Britten makes doubly sure that we understand. After the parable of "The Old Men and the Young" (Owen's title for "So Abram rose. . . . ") and after the "Hostias" (sung in our behalf by more "innocent" voices), after, in point of fact, the parable which has been completely turned upside down from its original Biblical telling, we are once again allotted the music for "Quam olim Abrahae" (note well!) completely upside down—melody inverted, dynamics reversed!

Involvement and responsibility are the prices of understanding. To make sure we see Abram's guilt as our own, Owen even has Abram building "parapets and trenches," the basic symbol of World War I warfare: for narrative purposes, to catch Isaac's blood; but for Owen's purposes, whole dugouts full. Pick a war from I to X.

IV. *Sanctus*

Soprano solo and chorus

Sanctus, sanctus, sanctus	Holy, holy, holy
Dominus Deus Sabaoth.	Lord God of Sabaoth.
Pleni sunt coeli	Heaven and earth are full
et terra gloria tua.	of thy glory.
Hosanna in excelsis.	Hosanna in the highest.
Benedictus qui venit	Blessed is he that cometh
in nomine Domini.	in the name of the Lord.
Hosanna in excelsis.	Hosanna in the highest.

Baritone solo

After the blast of lightning from the East,
The flourish of loud clouds, the Chariot Throne;
After the drums of Time have rolled and ceased,
And by the bronze west long retreat is blown,

Shall life renew these bodies? Of a truth
All death will He annul, all tears assuage?—
Fill the void veins of Life again with youth,
And wash, with an immortal water, Age?

When I do ask white Age he saith not so:
"My head hangs weighed with snow."
And when I hearken to the Earth, she saith:
"My fiery heart shrinks, aching. It is death.
Mine ancient scars shall not be glorified,
Nor my titanic tears, the sea, be dried."

This is the most dense and grave of the poems in the *War Requiem*. Alongside the lyric fluency of "Move him into the sun. . . ." it is lumpy and knotted. Alongside "Out there. . . ." and "So Abram rose. . . ." it has not even the laughter of cynicism or satire. After its matted, unrubbed honesty, the next poem, "One ever hangs. . . ," sounds like Lenten doggerel. Its apparent link is the visual ecstasy of "Sanctus, sanctus, sanctus," the sublime eruption of heavenly light, with "the blast of lightning from the East." I say "apparent" because, though Britten has taken the *Sanctus* and "Benedictus" very seriously musically and developed them at some length with flashes of brilliance and shadows of tenderness, what has happened textually is that he has linked the *Sanctus* imagery to the first line of Owen's poem in order to introduce the most uncompromising, unpalatable (to Christian traditionalism) and hope-forsaken sermon on Life and Death.

This is a brave despair to raise in the holiest moment of Christian liturgy. And the lines betray this weight. The poem rather lurches along. Neither in word nor rhythm is it fluent. Almost all the lines are loaded with thick nouns and granitic verbs. Out of one hundred fourteen words, ninety-four are words of one syllable. This in itself need not yield gnarled density if the poet were content to *waste* a few of them (as in "One ever hangs. . . .").

Certainly in terms of argument this poem would find its essential environment (in the *Missa pro defunctis*) at a point of inconsolable denial of one of the "resurrection" references. That in the *Dies irae*, however, was beautifully handled by "Move him gently. . . ." Moreover, it was too early for this *summation*. And, "Heaven" knows, once one has begun the "In paradisum," it is *much* too late. Were one to consider putting this poem as epilogue—one could not have written the Mass at all. Actually, the ''Hostias'' offers the most direct confrontation: ''Make them, o Lord, to pass from death unto life'' with ''It is death!'' And Britten has Owen say it just as soon after that as he can.

It had to be said, if Owen was to be a part of the *War Requiem*; and ''I am the enemy you killed, my friend. . . .'' had to be saved to the last. Perhaps there is some significance in saying ''It is death'' at this holiest and most mystical moment. Certainly there is no equivocation. Neither Age nor Earth, ''snow'' nor ''fiery heart'' credits immortality. ''Some say the world will end with fire, some with ice.'' (Robert Frost) For Owen, too, either ''would suffice.''

V. *Agnus Dei*

Tenor solo

One ever hangs where shelled roads part.
　In this war He too lost a limb
But His disciples hide apart;
　And now the Soldiers bear with Him.

Chorus

Agnus Dei, qui tollis peccata mundi, 　　Lamb of God, who takest away the sins
dona eis requiem. 　　　　　　　　　　　of the world, grant them rest.

　　　Near Golgotha strolls many a priest,
　　　　And in their faces there is pride
　　That they were flesh-marked by the Beast
　　　　By whom the gentle Christ's denied.

Agnus Dei, qui tollis peccata mundi, 　　Lamb of God, who takest away the sins
dona eis requiem. 　　　　　　　　　　　of the world, grant them rest.

　　　The scribes on all the people shove
　　　　And bawl allegiance to the state,
　　But they who love the greater love
　　　　Lay down their life; they do not hate.

Agnus Dei, qui tollis peccata mundi, 　　Lamb of God, who takest away the sins
dona eis requiem sempiternam. 　　　　　of the world, grant them rest eternal.

Dona nobis pacem.

　This is a logical, ''occasional'' choice for linkage with the *Agnus Dei*. It appears to have been written for an actual roadside crucifix near Ancre. (''At a Calvary Near Ancre'' is the title in his book of published poems.) Undoubtedly the Jesus-figure on the cross had lost a leg in action. The metaphor sounds as though the poem came quickly: the priests and the scribes, the church and the state—ever enemies of the Lamb of God; peace, to be found only in self-sacrifice.

A letter from Owen to his mother from the hospital on the Somme (before his convalescence in England and final return to the front) comments further on Christianity and war:

> Already I have comprehended a light which never will filter into the dogma of any national church: namely, that one of Christ's essential commands was: Passivity at any price! Suffer dishonour and disgrace; but never resort to arms. . . . be killed; but do not kill. It may be a chimerical and an ignominious principle, but there it is. It can only be ignored: and I think pulpit professionals are ignoring it very skilfully and successfully indeed. . . . And am I not myself a conscientious objector with a very seared conscience? . . . Christ is literally in no man's land. There men often hear His voice: Greater love hath no man than this, that a man lay down his life for a friend.
>   Is it spoken in English only and French?
>   I do not believe so. Thus you see how pure Christianity will not fit in with pure patriotism. [12]

I find this more concentrated, intense, and moving than the verses which Britten selected; but the others make their point, and a natural three-part form as well—and (strangely—because they are not Owen's finest lines) perhaps the most tear-provoking moment in the entire work.

VI. *Libera me* (final movement)

Soprano solo and chorus

Libera me, Domine, de morte aeterna,	Deliver me, O Lord, from death eternal
in die illa tremenda:	in that fearful day:
Quando coeli movendi sunt	When the heavens and the earth shall
et terra:	be shaken:
Dum veneris judicare	When Thou shalt come to judge
saeculum per ignem.	the world by fire.
Tremens factus sum ego, et timeo,	I am in fear and trembling
dum discussio venerit,	till the sifting be upon us,
atque ventura ira.	and the wrath to come.
Quando coeli movendi sunt	When the heavens and the earth shall
et terra.	be shaken.
Dies illa, dies irae,	O that day, that day of wrath,
calamitatis et miseriae,	of calamity and misery,
dies magna et amara valde.	a great day and exceeding bitter.
Libera me, Domine. . . .	Deliver me, O Lord. . . .

---

[12]*Collected Letters*, 461. Letter 512 to Susan Owen, [16?] May 1917.

Tenor solo

It seemed that out of battle I escaped
Down some profound dull tunnel, long since scooped
Through granites which titanic wars had groined.
Yet also there encumbered sleepers groaned,
Too fast in thought or death to be bestirred.
Then, as I probed them, one sprang up, and stared
With piteous recognition in fixed eyes,
Lifting distressful hands as if to bless.

And no guns thumped, or down the flues made moan.
"Strange friend," I said, "here is no cause to mourn."

Baritone solo

"None," said the other, "save the undone years,
The hopelessness. Whatever hope is yours,
Was my life also; I went hunting wild
After the wildest beauty in the world.

For by my glee might many men have laughed,
And of my weeping something had been left,
Which must die now. I mean the truth untold,
The pity of war, the pity war distilled.
Now men will go content with what we spoiled.
Or, discontent, boil bloody, and be spilled.
They will be swift with swiftness of the tigress,
None will break ranks, though nations trek from progress.
Miss we the march of this retreating world
Into vain citadels that are not walled.
Then, when much blood had clogged their chariot-wheels
I would go up and wash them from sweet wells,
Even from wells we sunk too deep for war,
Even the sweetest wells that ever were.

I am the enemy you killed, my friend.
I knew you in this dark; for so you frowned
Yesterday through me as you jabbed and killed.
I parried; but my hands were loath and cold."

Tenor and baritone soloists (together)

"Let us sleep now. . . ."

Boys' choir, chorus, and soprano solo (together)

In paradisum deducant te Angeli:	In paradise may the angels lead thee;
in tuo adventu	at thy coming
suscipiant te Martyres,	may the martyrs receive thee,
et perducant te	and bring thee
in civitatem sanctam Jerusalem.	into the holy city, Jerusalem.
Chorus Angelorum te suscipiat,	May the choir of Angels receive thee,
et cum Lazaro quondam paupere	and with Lazarus, once poor,
aeternam habeas requiem.	mayest thou have eternal rest.

Requiem aeternam dona eis, Domine;	Rest eternal grant unto them, O Lord:
et lux perpetua luceat eis.	and let light eternal shine upon them.
Requiescant in pace. Amen.	May they rest in peace. Amen.

"Strange Meeting" is Owen's title for this poem. Unfinished, it is the most haunted and haunting of his war poetry. It is written in ink with corrections in pencil; there is no date, but it is surmised to have been written in the last few months of his life.[13]

First, look again at the uniquely sensitive rhymes. They make a poem in themselves:

'scaped - scooped
groined - groaned
'stirred - stared
eyes - bless
moan - mourn

years - yours
wild - world
laughed - left
'told - 'tilled
spoiled - spilled
tigress - progress
world - walled
wheels - wells
war - were
friend - frowned
killed - cold

Second, it is interesting to note that Britten has edited the poem in one significant passage. (Eleven lines of Owen's poem are omitted in Britten's setting—two or three of them, I feel, of real value; and two lines are added from a series of couplets which closely parallel this poem and may have been sketches towards its final form.) But, as regards the "significant" omission: between lines eight and nine of the *War Requiem* text, Owen had written:

And by his smile, I knew that sullen hall,
By his dead smile I knew we stood in Hell.
With a thousand pains that vision's face was grained;
Yet no blood reached there from the upper ground.

[13]See Stallworthy, 306-310 for complete text of the poem with all layers of corrections, changes, and additions.

Now, certainly the last of these lines joins nicely to "And no guns thumped, or down the flues made moan"; but the presence of the first two of them would do gross injury to the final moments of the *War Requiem* (as, I think also, they harm Owen's poem). The necessary dramatic point is to maintain the obscurity, the mystery, and the place of this "strange meeting" until the final "I am the enemy you killed, my friend." One must not know until this moment that *both* are dead. Or if one surmises it, he must not be told.

Here is Britten's great sense of poetry and drama helping the Owen to complete his "unfinished" work, with an eraser.

Bernard Rogers—in a class at Juilliard,—when asked "How do you compose?" responded, "I start with a blank piece of paper and an eraser—when I've erased everything unnecessary, I have a piece of music."[14]

Of interest to me are the following discarded readings:

Line 1:   "It seemed to me that from my dugout I escaped"
             (How greatly that sheds light on lines two, three, four, and five: so much more based now in experience, than imagination.)

Line 12:   "The unachieved" (for "hopelessness")

Line 18:   "The pity of war, the one thing war distilled."
                (for: "The pity of war, the pity war distilled")

Line 29:   "I was a German conscript, and your friend."
             Or "am the German whom you killed, my friend."
             (for: "I am the enemy you killed, my friend.")

Compare a few parallel lines from the groups of couplets:

Lines 19-22:
             "Be we not swift with swiftness of the tigress.
             Let us break ranks, and we will trek from progress.

             Let us forgo men's minds that are brutes' natures.
             Let us not sup the blood which some say nurtures."

Lines 27-28:
             (for: "Even the sweetest wells that ever were." These are not in "Strange Meeting"; Britten added them from the couplets. They might have been followed or preceded by:)

[14]As told to a class the author attended.

"For now we sink from men as pitchers falling,
But men shall raise us up to be their filling."

"Finally," remarks Blunden,

widely as the setting and substance of "Strange Meeting" are felt and
apprehended, it is peculiarly a poem of the Western Front; it is a dream
only a stage further on than the actuality of the tunnelled dug-outs with
their muffled security, their smoky dimness, their rows of soldiers pain-
fully sleeping, their officers and sergeants and corporals attempting to
awaken those for duty, and the sense presently of "going up" the ugly
stairway to do someone in the uglier mud above a good turn. Out of
those and similar materials Owen's transforming spirit has readily created
his wonderful phantasma.[15]

What is the final poetic and dramatic result of Britten's "fabrication?"
Certainly, in the first place, we have an extraordinary humanizing and
contemporizing of an ancient and remote liturgy of remembrance. The
wars of this century are our wars; Owen's death and his pity at the death
of others are remote neither from our memories nor our premonitions.
And so the ancient words are fused with the immediacy of today—and
tomorrow.

Second, and conversely, Owen's words gain a catholicity, and a dignity
of historical association. His "pity" becomes somewhat grander by the
setting of his parable of Abram and Isaac in a centuries-old matrix.

But what of the final philosophic confrontation?:

Shall life renew these bodies? Of a truth
All death will He annul, all tears assuage?

I suppose most of us will call it as we've learned it. Certainly for
Owen, Age and Earth answered a resounding "No!"

It is interesting, it seems to me, to note that in terms of text alone
(setting aside, for the moment, the accretions of tradition), the Missa
is entirely a *petition:* "Make them, O Lord, to pass from death unto
life. . . ," "Deliver me, O Lord, from death eternal. . . ," "In paradise
may the angels lead thee. . . ," "Let eternal light shine on them. May
they rest in peace." Some, undoubtedly, could recite this in full confidence that it already had been assured. With others, even of similar

[15]Edmund Blunden, ed., *The Poems of Wilfred Owen* (London: Chatto and Windus,
1931) 128.

religious tradition, it might be murmured "bowed and kneeling" with "heart contrite as ashes," and uncertain—not quite sure.

For still others it must suffice that after all, there is still in man's being—an unearthly being—a mystery into which none of the statistical forms of man's intelligence can carry him. That it involves a life beyond the present, most men have hoped and few gainsaid.

For me, it is wonder enough that Owen's words and Britten's vision are a part of the life-force in the man-thing. Whether any one of us "makes it" in a hereafter I find unimportant alongside the presence of humanity such as this.

Index

accentuation, 289
  in the Classical era, 295–301
agogic stress, 160, 162
Alpin, John, 109n
American Choral Directors Association, 93
Andrews, H.K., 158
appoggiatura, 308
arranging, choral, 67–73
Arcadelt, Jacques, 128
arsis, 165
articulation, 21, 29, 31, 286
  in the Classical era, 288–95
  intensity of, 30
Attaingnant, Pierre, 145, 150

Bach, Carl Philipp Emanuel, 284, 286, 287, 292, 293, 304n, 305, 308, 315n, 317, 318n, 320n, 321n
Bach, Johann Sebastian, 23
  Art of the Fugue, 229, 241
  cantatas, 19, 22
  Christ lag in Todesbanden, 68
  Mass in B Minor, 53
  motets, 20, 234n
  Passions, 20
balance, 21, 30
bar lines, 161–62
Barnard, John, 104n
Baroque, 24
Bartók, Béla, vocal arrangements, 68
basso-continuo realization, 21
Beethoven, Ludwig van, 58
  Symphony No. 3 (*Eroica*), 24
Benedictine monks (Solesmes), 161
Bernhard, Christoph, 219, 223
Besseler, Heinrich, 162
Brahms, Johannes
  motets, tempo relationships, 20, 22
  German Requiem, 15, 57
  vocal arrangements, 68

Brahms, Johannes (cont.)
  vocal quartets
  "Abend, Der" (op. 64, no. 2), 339–42
  "Abendlied" (op. 92, no. 3), 349–52
  "An die Heimat" (op. 64, no. 1), 334–39
  "Fragen" (op. 64, no. 1), 343–45
  "Gang zum Liebchen, Der" (op. 31, no. 3), 332–33
  "Neckereien" (op. 31, no. 2), 329–32
  "O schöne Nacht" (op. 92, no. 1), 345–47
  "Spätherbst" (op. 92, no. 2), 347–49
  "Warum?" (op. 92, no. 4), 352–55
  "Wechsellied zum Tanze" (op. 31, no. 1), 324–28
Breig, Werner, 222
Britten, Benjamin,
  vocal arrangements, 68
  War Requiem, 19, 357–83
Brodde, Otto, 224
Brown, David, 96, 97, 107
Bruckner, Anton, 57
Brumel, Jachcs, 129
Burney, Charles, 283, 287, 300
Buszin, Walter, 235, 244
Byrd, William, 94, 95

cadence
  hemiola, 165
  structure of, 31
Cavazoni, Girolamo, 131, 133, 150
chant, Gregorian, 161
chori spezzati, 221
College Music Society, 93
Collins, Walter, 93, 99

concerto grosso, 240–54
conducting, choral, 15, 18, 35, 40
    communication of, 18, 23, 25, 26,
        33
    energy, 33
    expressive conducting, 26
    gestures, 27, 38
    inspiration, 18, 23, 32
    orientation, musicological vs.
        voice-teacher, 39–40
    process of, 15–33
    rejuvenation of, 18, 32
    spirituality of, 15
    technique of, 16, 24, 33
continuo, 287
creative experience
    limitation, 61–64
    order, 64–65
    perception, artistic, 53–57
    technique, 57–61
Cummings, William, 68
curricula, choral, 16
Czerny, Carl, 293

Decker, Harold, 18
Dedekind, Constantin Christian, 219
direction, linear, 24, 28, 29, 30, 31
duration, unity of, 28. *See also* musi-
    cal elements
Dürr, Alfred, 235, 239n, 248, 251n
Dürr, Walther, and Gerstenberg,
    Walter, "Rhythm," 154–55
dynamics, 21, 29, 31
    intensity of, 30

ear, 16, 18, 23–24
    auditory perception, 24
    ear/voice relationship, 29
education, 19, 20, 22, 23, 33, 41–44
Ehmann, Wilhelm, 242n, 247, 249,
    252, 253
elements, musical, 24, 28, 32
energy, 15
ensemble, unity of, 28, 31
expression, in the Classical era, 319–
    22
eye music, 202

falsetto, 284
Fellowes, Edmund, 94, 97
Ferabosco, Domenico, 128, 129, 132,
    133, 149, 150
Festa, Costanzo, 143

Finck, Heinrich, 159
Fogliano, Jacobo, 128

Gabrieli, Giovanni, 221, 229
Garcia, Manuel, 284, 287, 291, 307n
Gebhard, H., 236
Geier, Martin, 218, 220
Geminiani, Francesco, 290, 310, 320n
genres, choral, 18–20
    cantata, 15
    masses, 15, 69
    motets, 15, 69
    requiem, 15
Gibbons, Orlando, 94
Grassineau, James, 304n
Gudewill, Kurt, 228

Handel, George Frideric
    Funeral Anthem for Queen
        Caroline,
        adaptations, later, 259–61
        Biblical sources, 258–61
        Burney, Charles, contemporary
            comments, 256
        chorus, use of (Larsen), 257–
            58
        editions, subsequent, 258, 262,
            266, 277–78
        musical analysis of, 266–76
        performing forces in
            Westminster Abbey, 257
        structural outline of, 262–63
        use in other works, by Handel,
            256–58, 267, 277
        Willes, Edward (author of
            text), 258
    Messiah, 22, 56
    oratorios, 20
    and Queen Caroline, friendship
        with, 255–56, 262, 274
Handl, Jacob, *Ecce quo modo
    moritur*, 274–75
harmony, 29
Harnoncourt, Nikolaus, 247–48, 253
Haydn, Franz Joseph, 286, 287, 310,
    319
    Creation, 303
    masses, 20
    Missa in Angustiis, 288–89
head voice, 284
Herz, Gerhard, 251
Hindemith, Paul, *Einfall*, 53, 56
Hughes, Dom Anselm, 97, 102, 104

improvisation, 21
instrumentation, 21
    in the Classical era, 287
integration, musical, 94–96, 109
intensity, 20, 24, 28, 30–32
International Federation of Choral
    Music, 93

Jeppesen, Knud, 157
Johann Georg II, Elector, 219, 220
Josquin des Près, 141, 145
    *Missa l'homme armé super voces
        musicales*, 180–81
    motets, 19

Kennedy Scott, Charles, 156
Kirnberger, Johann P., 299, 304n
Kodály, Zoltán, 16
    vocal arrangements, 68

Larsen, Jens Peter, 257–58, 262, 269
Lasso, Orlando di, 69, 130, 139, 140,
    141, 143, 145, 149
Liber usualis, 161
Ligeti, György, *Lux aeterna*, 15
Luther, Martin, 229

Mancini, Giovanni, 290
Marpurg, Friedrich Wilhelm, 290,
    292, 303, 312n, 313n, 315n
Maschera, Florentino, 132, 133
Mattheson, Johann, 219, 283n
McKelvy, James, "varia-bar sys-
    tem," 162
melody, 29
Mendelssohn, Felix, *Festgesang*, 68
mensural music, 155
Mensurstrich, 162
mental-aural image, 16–17, 18, 20,
    23, 25, 27, 32
Mersenne, Marin, 294
messa di voce, 289–91
meter
    in the Classical era, 302–7
    duple, 25
    triple, 25
Monte, Philippe de, 141
Monteverdi, Claudio
    madrigals, 19
    sacred works, 20
    Scherzi musicali, 21
Monteverdi, Giulio Cesare, 21
Morales, Cristóbal de, 143

Morley, Thomas, 94
Moser, Hans Joachim, 221
Mozart, Leopold, 286n, 289, 291,
    296n, 299, 304n, 310, 313n,
    314n, 319n, 321n
Mozart, Wolfgang Amadeus, 240–
    41, 286, 306
    C-Minor Mass, 19
    Requiem, tempo of, 303
    Vesperae solennes de Confessore,
        K.V. 339, 288
musica ficta, 21
musical elements, 20–21
Musicalisches Gesangbuch, 229
musicianship, 16, 37

Nanino, Giovanni Maria, 131–33, 150
Neumann, Werner, 235, 244, 246
Noble, Jeremy, 98, 103, 105, 113,
    115–16, 119
notation
    contemporary systems of, 22
    mensural, 173–82
note groupings (binary and ternary),
    156

ornamentation, 21, 308
Owen, Wilfred, 357–83
    "At a Calvary Near Ancre," 376–
        78
    "Dulce et decorum est," 369–70
    "Old Man and the Young, The,"
        374–75
    Sonnet ("On Seeing a Piece of
        Our Heavy Artillery
        Brought into Action"), 371
    "Strange Meeting," 379–82

Palestrina, Giovanni Pierluigi, 139
    masses, 22
performance, 27, 33, 35–47
    criteria, 36
    keyboard, *normal touch*, 292
    stage etiquette, 45
    style, 39
performance practice, 16, 22–23
    musica ficta, 21
    tactus, 24
phrasing, 29, 31
    Baroque, 16
    in the Classical era, 288–95
    slurring, 288
    intensity of, 30

phrasing (cont.)
  macro, 16
  See also performance practice; ex-
      pressive components
pitch, 20, 21, 24, 28
  unifying, 29
plainsong, 155–56
polyphony, Renaissance era, 155–66
Poulenc, Francis,
  chansons, 20
prima prattica, 21
proportion
  sesquialtera, 179, 181, 184–85,
      192–93, 195–214
  sextupla, 192–96, 203–14
  tripla, 179–81, 184–85, 192–93,
      195–214
pulse, 24, 25, 31
Purcell, Henry, anthems, 20

Quantz, Johann Joachim, 283, 284,
      287, 291, 294, 302, 303,
      304n, 305, 309, 313n, 314n,
      317n, 318n, 320n, 321n,
Quitscheiber, Georg, *De canendi
      elegentia, octodecim praecep-
      ta studosis necessaria*, 183n

Ramin, Günther, 247
reconstruction, 98–101
Regnart, Jacob, 131, 139, 140–42
rehearsals, 20
  choral, 24, 26–32
  energy of, 19
  goals of, 64
  methods, 27
  orchestral, 16
  procedures of, 16–17, 18
  score preparation, 23
Reiners, Klaus, 247
Renaissance era, 24, 153–66
  homophony, 159–60, 162
  music editions, 161–62
  performing conventions, 160–61
  rhythmic patterns, 154–66
    conducting, 164–66
    teaching, 164–66
  tactus, 167–216
  tempo, 167–216
repertoire, choral, 15, 18–19, 39
  conductor's choice of, 27–28
  Renaissance, 20

repertoire, choral (cont.)
  selection of, 67
  standard, 43
Reulx, Anselmo, 128, 129, 132, 133,
      150
rhythm, 29
  definition of, 154
  ensemble, 28
  microrhythms, 157–66
    patterns of, 162–64
rhythmic form
  double dotting (overdotting), 311,
      314–15
  macrorhythm, 157
  quanititas intrinseca, 311–13
  recitative, 311, 317–19
  textural conformity, 311, 315–17
Richafort, Jean, 145
Richter, Friedrich, 234
Rifkin, Joshua, 220
Rilling, Helmuth, 18, 247
Rore, Cipriano de, 129, 132–33, 150
Rossini, Gioacchino, 284
Rousseau, Jean-Jacques, 291, 296n,
      304n, 317n, 318n
rubato, 29, 31
  intensity of, 30–31
  See also expressive components
Ruffo, Vincenzo, 139

Sachs, Curt, 156
Schein, Johann Hermann, "Nun lob
      mein Seel," 168
Schering, Arnold, 235
Schubert, Franz, 58
  Lieder, 19
  Ständchen, 68
Schuman, William, *Prelude for
      Voices*, 68
Schütz, Heinrich
  Becker Psalter, 229
  Catalogus, 219
  Geistliche Chormusic, motets, 20
  International Heinrich Schütz Fes-
      tival, 218
  Italian Madrigals, 223
  Opus ultimum, 217–32
    "German Magnificat," 217, 218,
        219, 221, 224, 228
    Guben, discovery of
        manuscripts, 220
    "London manuscript," 221
    "Psalm 100," 217, 218, 224, 228

Schütz, Heinrich (cont.)
    Psalm 119, 217, 218, 224
    Psalmen Davids, 229
    Schwanengesang, 220, 223, 227
score,
    form of, 23
    structural analysis of, 20, 23
    study of, 16–17, 20–21, 27, 59
seconda prattica, 21
Shaw, Robert, 18, 246
Sicher, Fridolin, 145
Singbewegung, 230
Solesmes monks, 161
sonority, 30
sound quality, 282–88
Spitta, Friedrich, 220
Spitta, Heinrich, 221
Spitta, Philipp, 220
Spohr, Louis, 287
Sterbemotetten, 241–42
Steude, Wolfram, 217, 222
Stevens, Denis, 95, 97, 162
Stravinsky, Igor, 61
    choral-orchestral works, 20
    contemporary music, writings on, 361
    Symphonie de Psaumes, 15
structure, 25, 28, 30, 33
    analysis of score, 16–17, 20–21
    clarity of, 30
    components of, 20–21, 29
    and form, 23
style, 33
    performance practice, 22
Sulzer, Johann Georg, 297, 299, 321n
Swan, Howard, 15
syncopation, 156, 160

tactus, 24, 155, 166, 167–216
Tartini, Guiseppe, 289, 293
temperament, 21
tempo, 21, 25, 31
    in the Classical era, 302–7

tempo (cont.)
    and *tactus*, 167–216
    tempo rubato, 305
Terry, Charles Sanford, 237, 239
text, musical
    prima prattica, 21
    seconda prattica, 21
text setting, 95
texture, 29
thesis, 165
Thomas, Kurt, 247
timbre, 20, 21, 24, 28
    unity of, 29
    vocal, 30
Tomkins, Thomas, 94
Tosi, Pier Francesco, 283, 306n
Tromlitz, Johann Georg, 284, 291, 293
tuning, 21
Türk, Daniel Gottlieb, 282, 283n,
    291, 292, 296n, 297n, 300,
    302, 303n, 304n, 305n, 307n,
    310, 313n, 317n, 320n, 322n

Verdi, Giuseppe, 285
    Messa da Requiem, 361
vibrato, 286
vocal groups
    King's Singers, 69
    Robert Shaw Chorale, 69
    Robert Wagner Chorale, 69
voice, 15

Wagner, Richard, 300
Weelkes, Thomas, 93–126
    "O Lord, Grant the King a Long
        Life ," 104, 110, 113, 118
    self-quotation, 96
    services, 93–96
Wert, Giaches de, 141
Willaert, Adrian, 68, 130, 145–46,
    148, 150
Winterfeld, Carl von, 229
Wullner, Franz, 241
Wulstan, David, 99